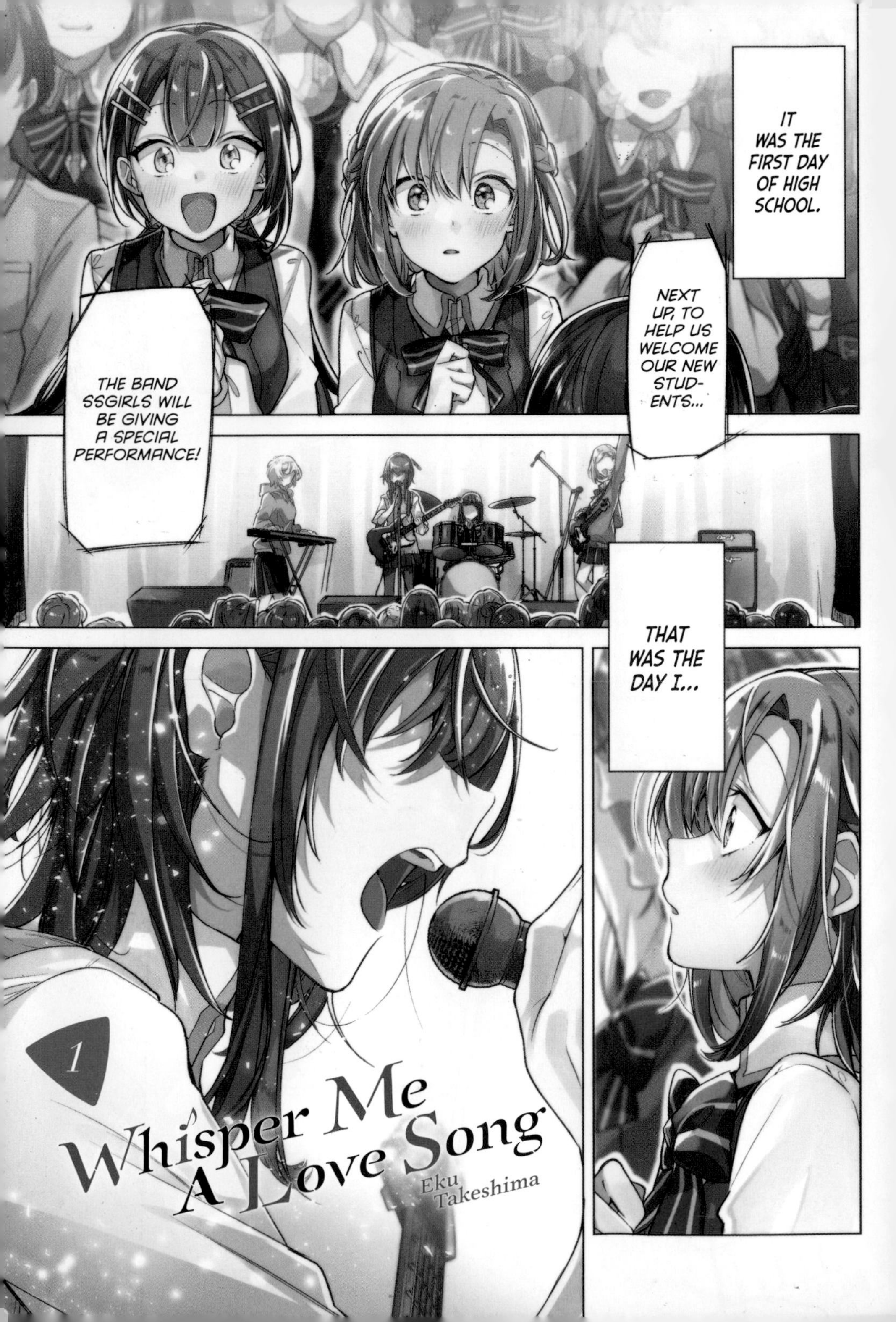
IT WAS THE FIRST DAY OF HIGH SCHOOL.
NEXT UP, TO HELP US WELCOME OUR NEW STUDENTS...
THE BAND SSGIRLS WILL BE GIVING A SPECIAL PERFORMANCE!
THAT WAS THE DAY I...
1
Whisper Me A Love Song
Eku Takeshima

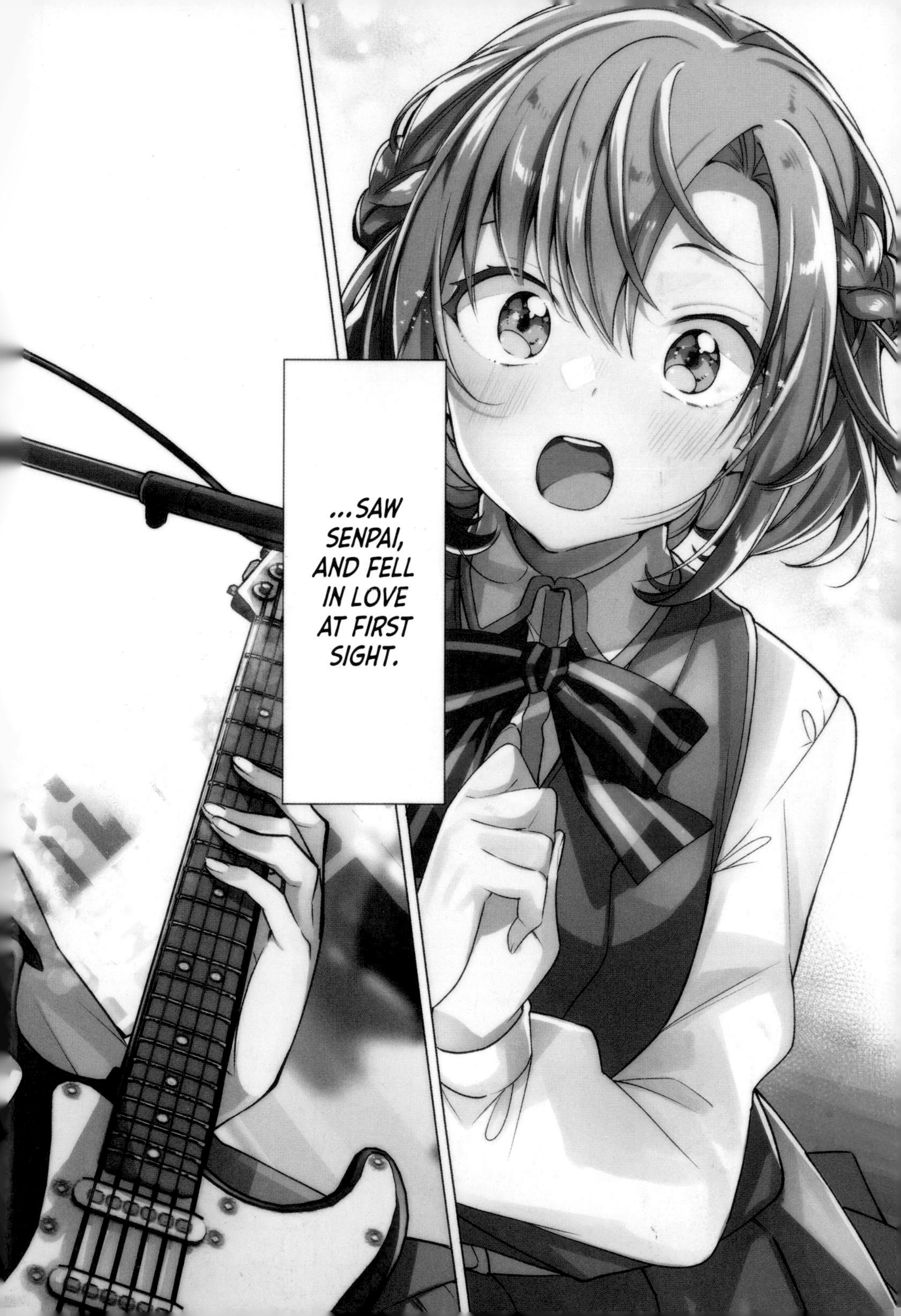
...SAW SENPAI, AND FELL IN LOVE AT FIRST SIGHT.

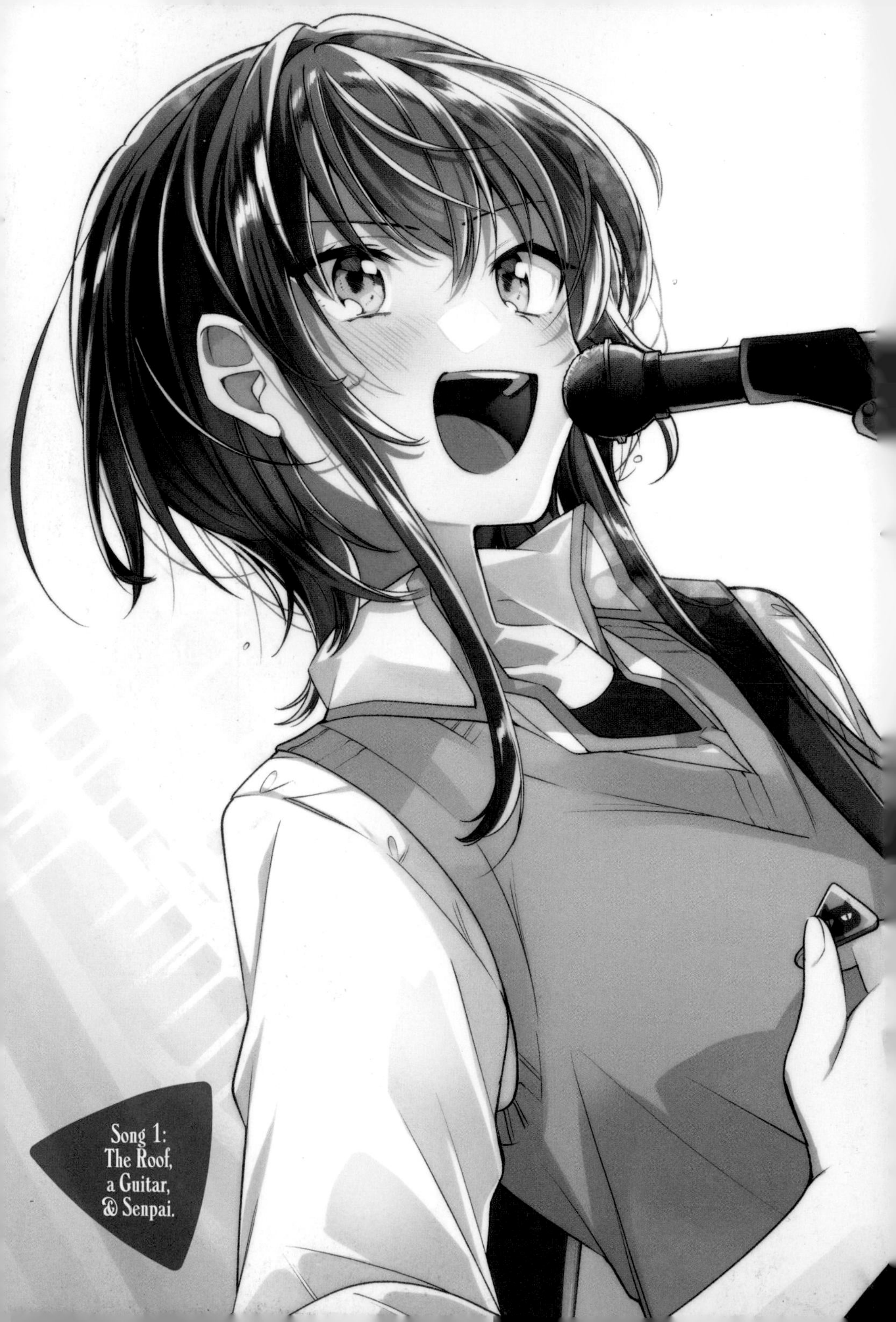
Song 1:
The Roof,
a Guitar,
& Senpai.

contents

Song 1   The Roof, a Guitar, & Senpai.   1

Song 2   First Love, Cherry Blossoms, & Kouhai.   37

Song 3   Their Time Together After Class.   75

Song 4   A Classroom on a Rainy Day.   101

Song 5   Love, a Date, and Then...   127

          Bonus Comics   160

          Afterword   166

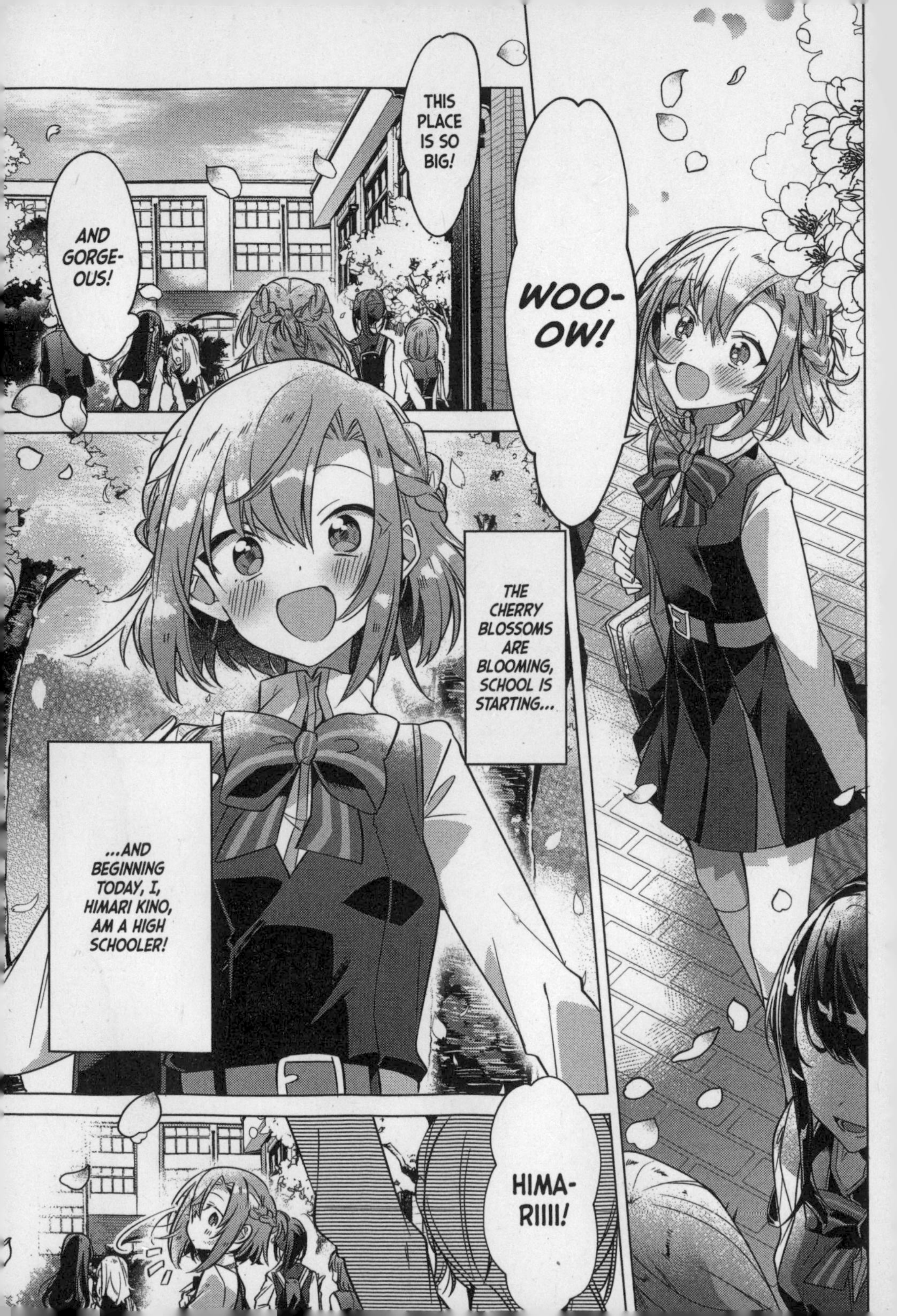
WOO-OW!
THIS PLACE IS SO BIG!
AND GORGE-OUS!
THE CHERRY BLOSSOMS ARE BLOOMING, SCHOOL IS STARTING...
...AND BEGINNING TODAY, I, HIMARI KINO, AM A HIGH SCHOOLER!
HIMA-RIIII!

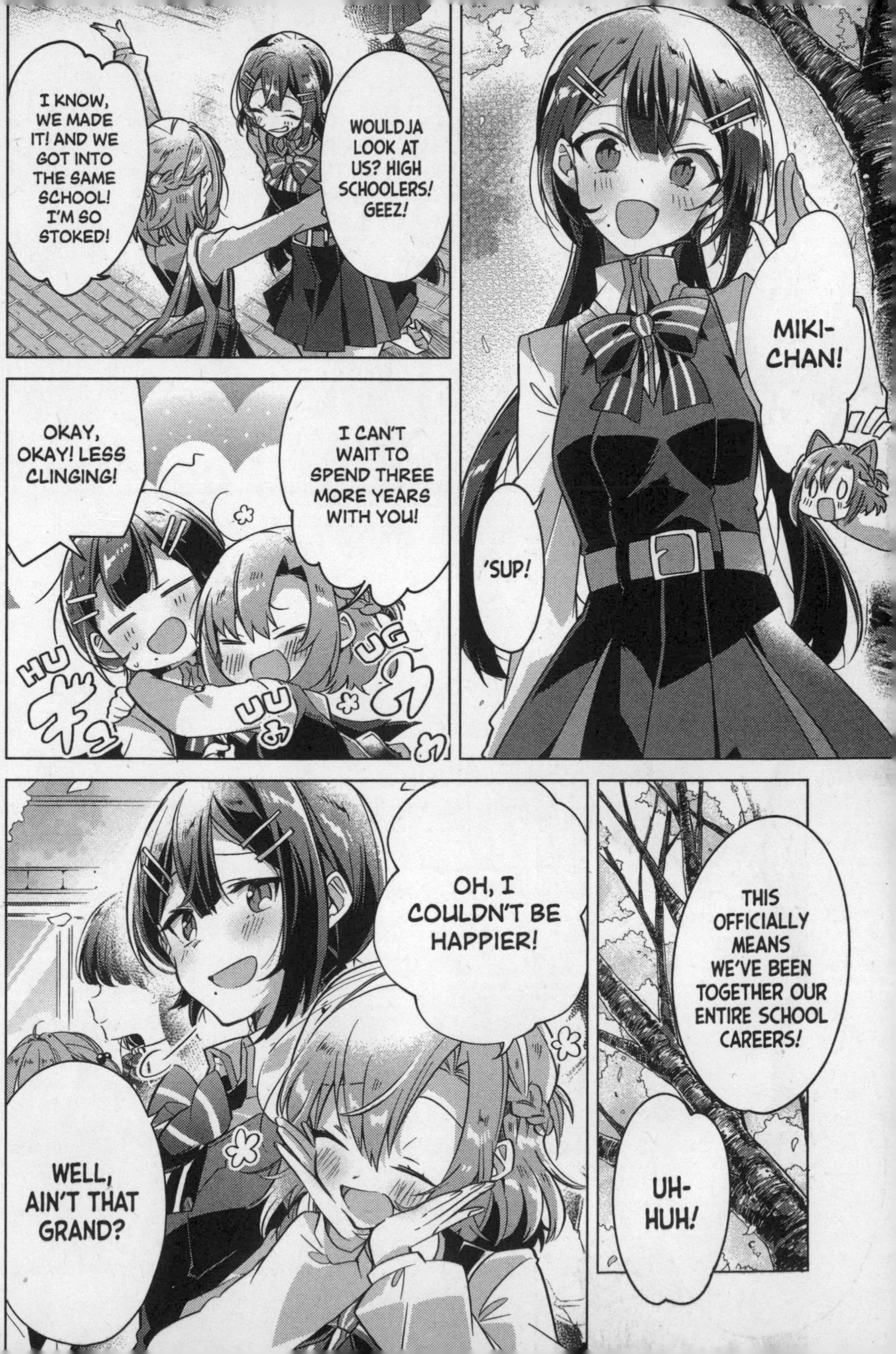
MIKI-CHAN!
'SUP!
WOULDJA LOOK AT US? HIGH SCHOOLERS! GEEZ!
I KNOW, WE MADE IT! AND WE GOT INTO THE SAME SCHOOL! I'M SO STOKED!
I CAN'T WAIT TO SPEND THREE MORE YEARS WITH YOU!
OKAY, OKAY! LESS CLINGING!
THIS OFFICIALLY MEANS WE'VE BEEN TOGETHER OUR ENTIRE SCHOOL CAREERS!
UH-HUH!
OH, I COULDN'T BE HAPPIER!
WELL, AIN'T THAT GRAND?

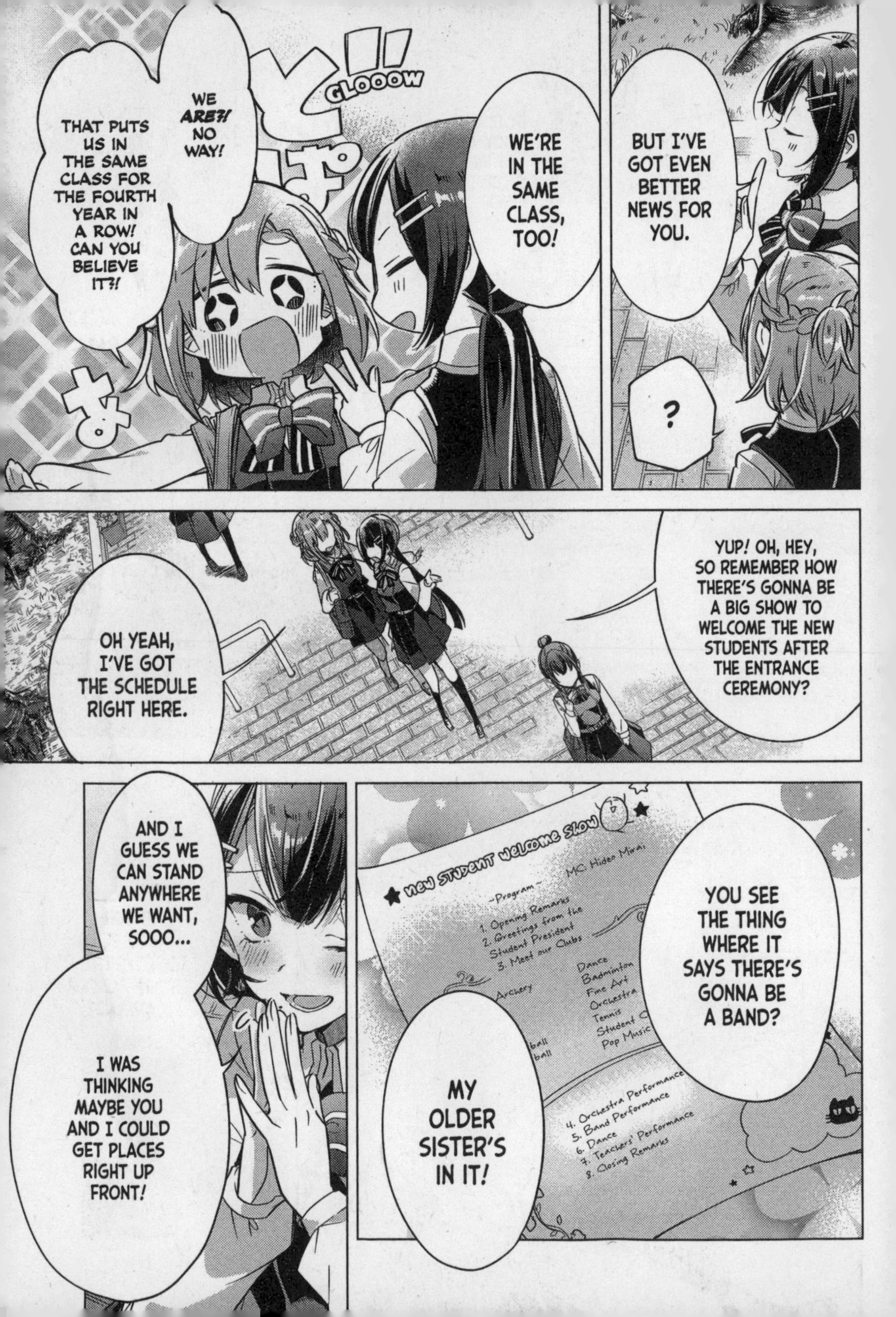
BUT I'VE GOT EVEN BETTER NEWS FOR YOU.
?
WE'RE IN THE SAME CLASS, TOO!
GLOOOW
WE ARE?! NO WAY!
THAT PUTS US IN THE SAME CLASS FOR THE FOURTH YEAR IN A ROW! CAN YOU BELIEVE IT?!
YUP! OH, HEY, SO REMEMBER HOW THERE'S GONNA BE A BIG SHOW TO WELCOME THE NEW STUDENTS AFTER THE ENTRANCE CEREMONY?
OH YEAH, I'VE GOT THE SCHEDULE RIGHT HERE.
New Student Welcome Show
MC: Hideo Mirai
~Program~
1. Opening Remarks
2. Greetings from the Student President
3. Meet our Clubs
Archery
Dance
Badminton
Fine Art
Orchestra
Tennis
Pop Music
4. Orchestra Performance
5. Band Performance
6. Dance
7. Teachers' Performance
8. Closing Remarks
YOU SEE THE THING WHERE IT SAYS THERE'S GONNA BE A BAND?
MY OLDER SISTER'S IN IT!
AND I GUESS WE CAN STAND ANYWHERE WE WANT, SOOO...
I WAS THINKING MAYBE YOU AND I COULD GET PLACES RIGHT UP FRONT!

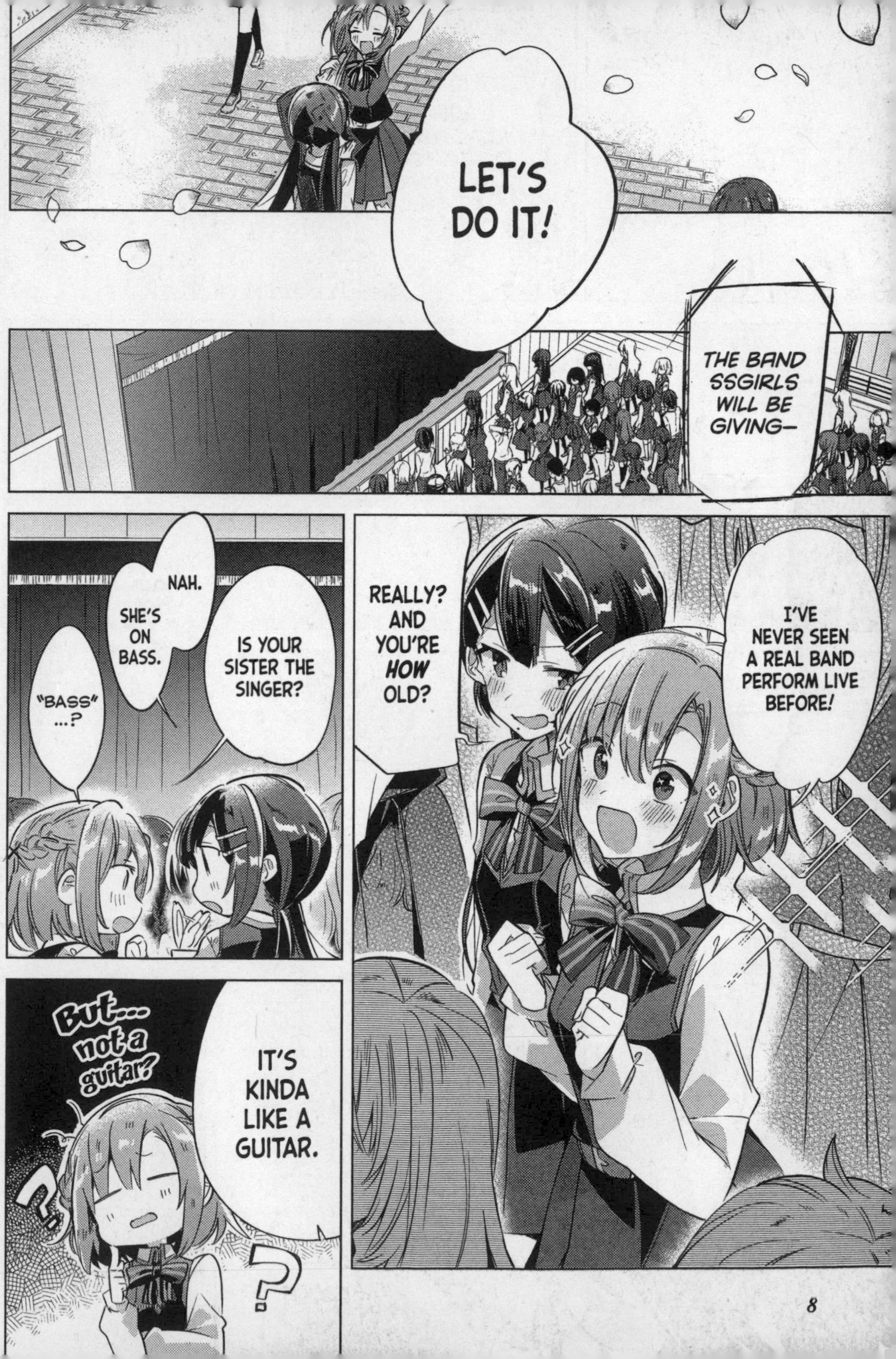
LET'S DO IT!
THE BAND SSGIRLS WILL BE GIVING—
I'VE NEVER SEEN A REAL BAND PERFORM LIVE BEFORE!
REALLY? AND YOU'RE *HOW* OLD?
IS YOUR SISTER THE SINGER?
NAH. SHE'S ON BASS.
"BASS" ...?
IT'S KINDA LIKE A GUITAR.
But... not a guitar?

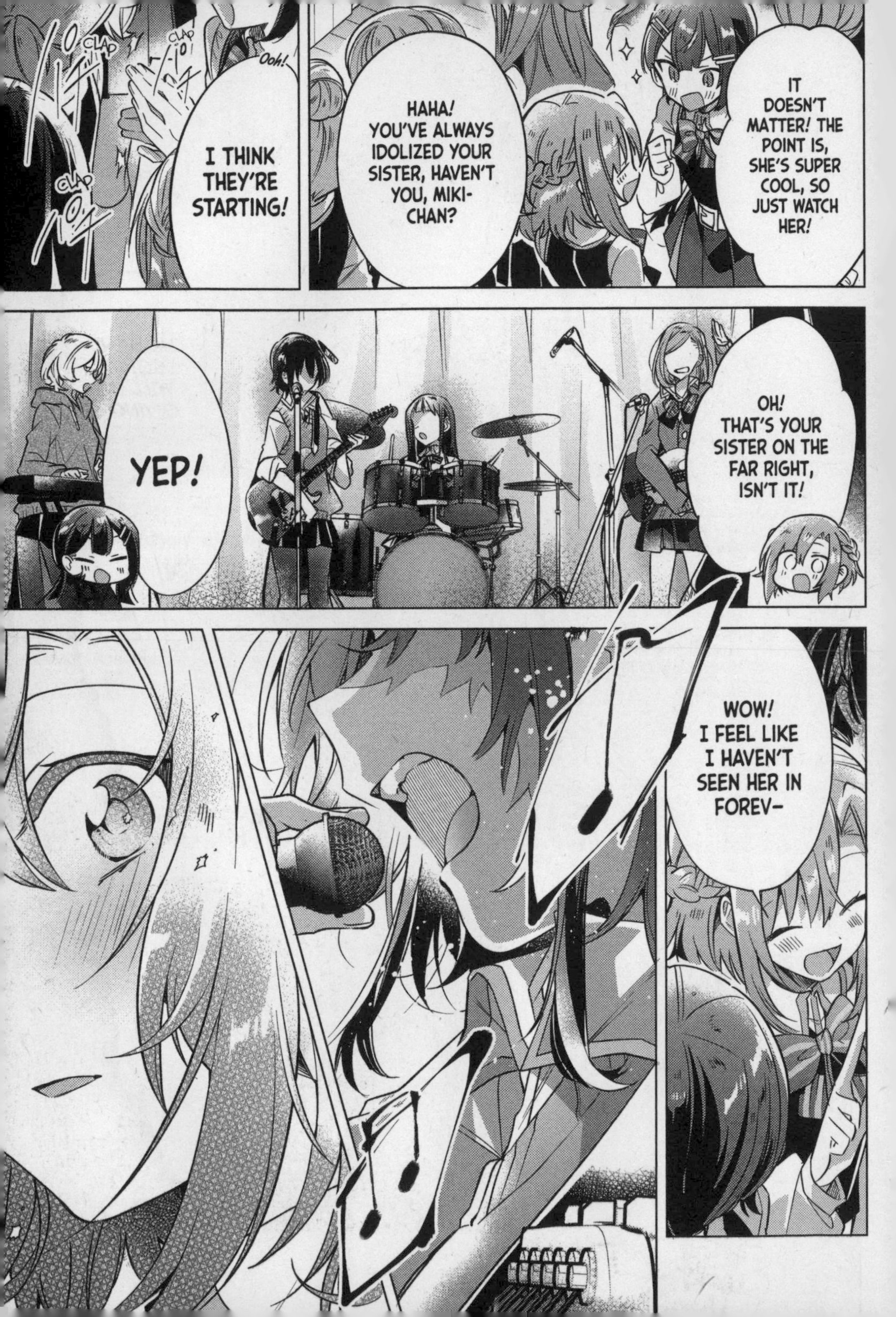
HAHA! YOU'VE ALWAYS IDOLIZED YOUR SISTER, HAVEN'T YOU, MIKI-CHAN?
IT DOESN'T MATTER! THE POINT IS, SHE'S SUPER COOL, SO JUST WATCH HER!
Ooh!
I THINK THEY'RE STARTING!
CLAP
CLAP
CLAP
OH! THAT'S YOUR SISTER ON THE FAR RIGHT, ISN'T IT!
YEP!
WOW! I FEEL LIKE I HAVEN'T SEEN HER IN FOREV–

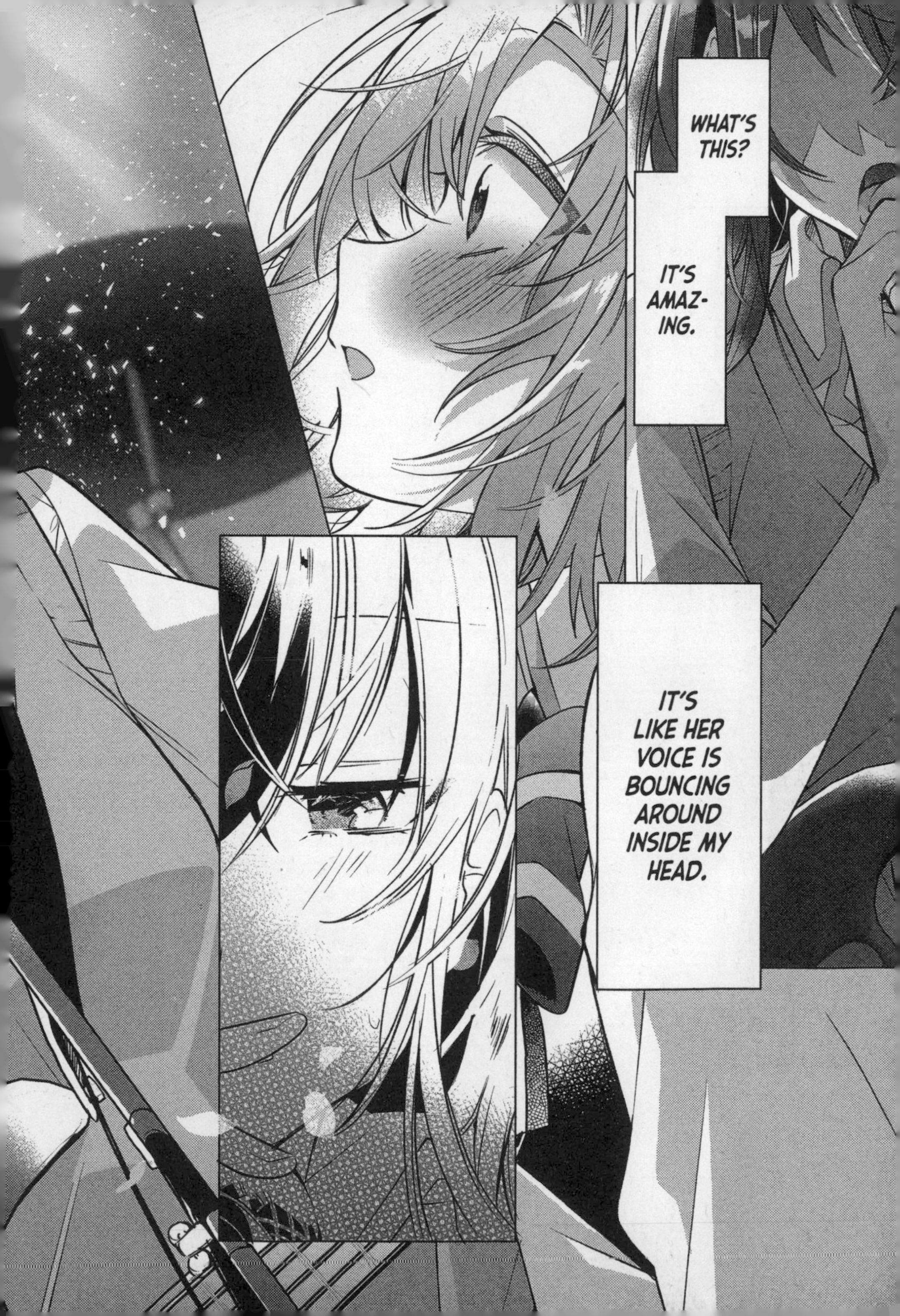
WHAT'S THIS?
IT'S AMAZ-ING.
IT'S LIKE HER VOICE IS BOUNCING AROUND INSIDE MY HEAD.

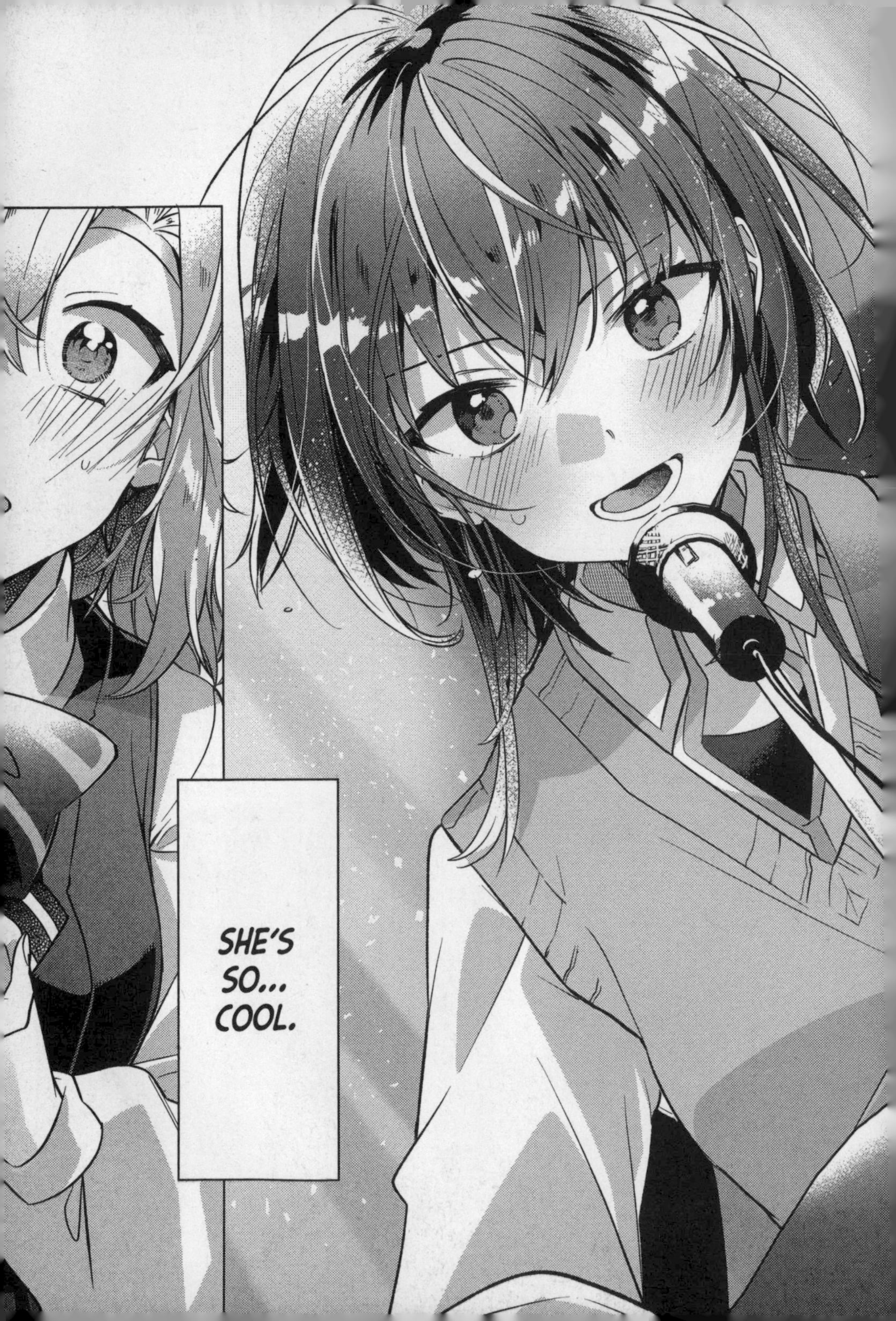
SHE'S SO... COOL.

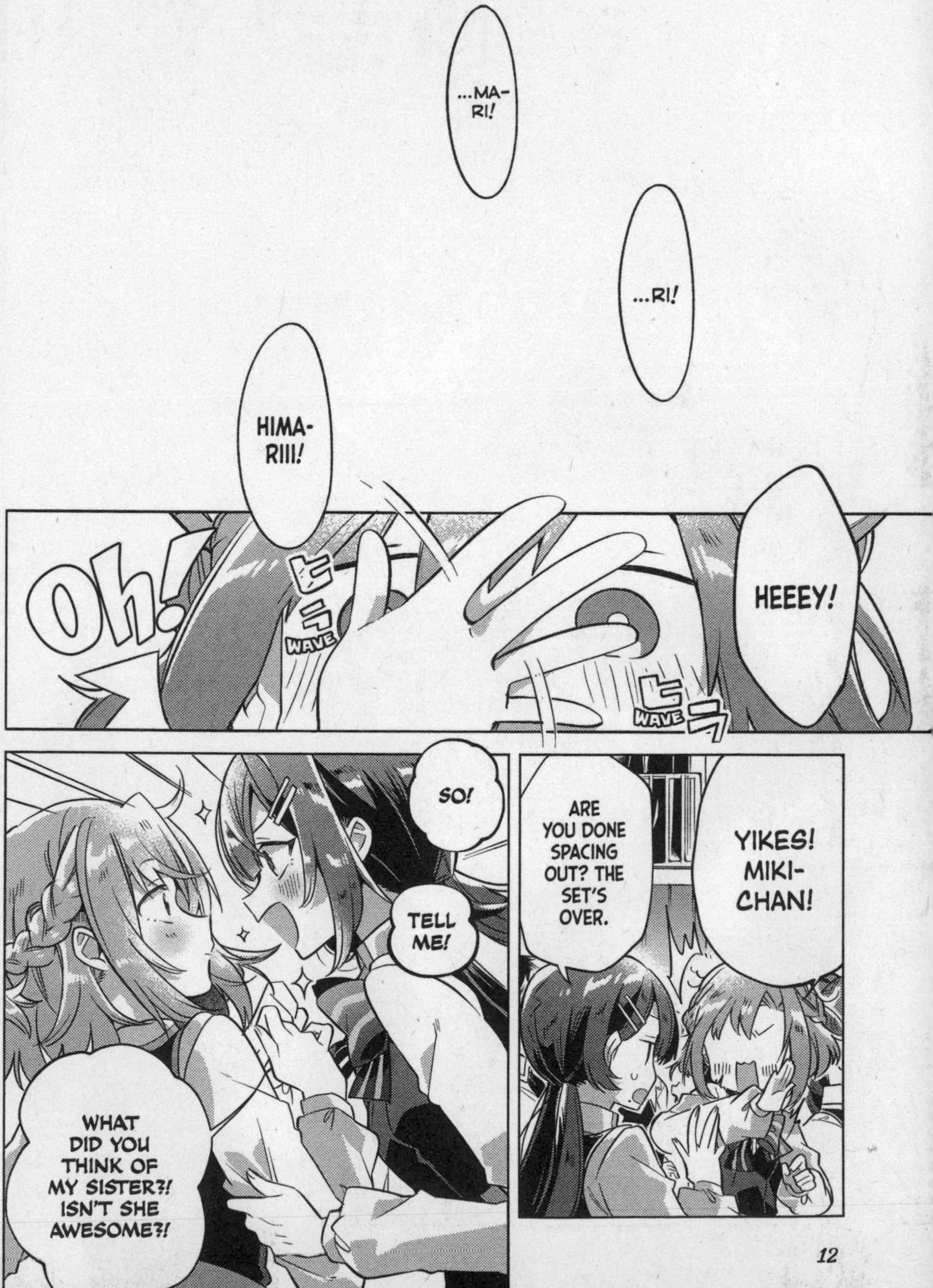
...MA-RI!
...RI!
HIMA-RIII!
HEEEY!
ヒラ WAVE
Oh!
ヒラ WAVE
YIKES! MIKI-CHAN!
ARE YOU DONE SPACING OUT? THE SET'S OVER.
SO!
TELL ME!
WHAT DID YOU THINK OF MY SISTER?! ISN'T SHE AWESOME?!

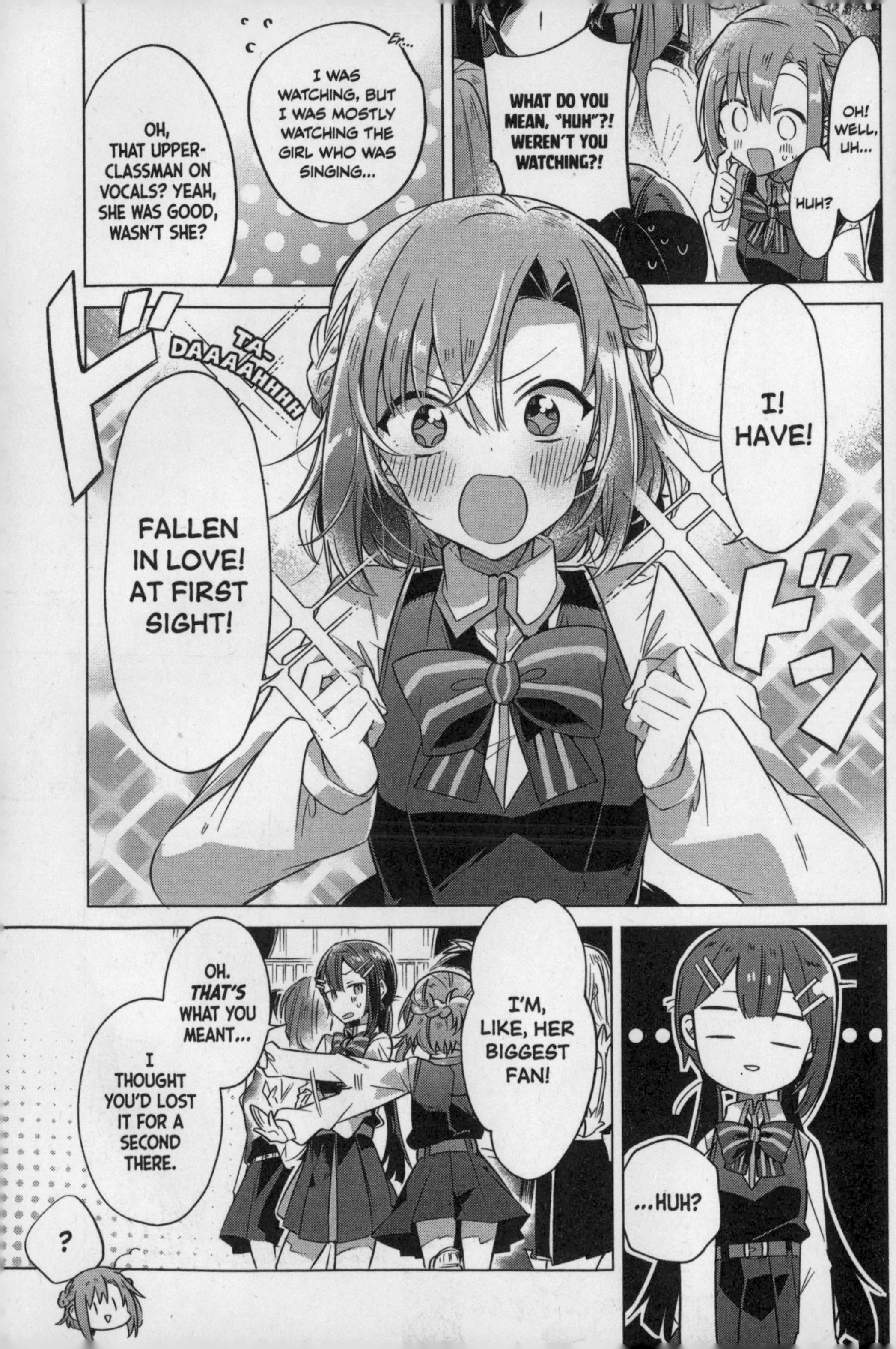
OH! WELL, UH...
HUH?
WHAT DO YOU MEAN, "HUH"?! WEREN'T YOU WATCHING?!
Er...
I WAS WATCHING, BUT I WAS MOSTLY WATCHING THE GIRL WHO WAS SINGING...
OH, THAT UPPER-CLASSMAN ON VOCALS? YEAH, SHE WAS GOOD, WASN'T SHE?
I! HAVE!
TA-DAAAAAHHHH
FALLEN IN LOVE! AT FIRST SIGHT!
...
...HUH?
I'M, LIKE, HER BIGGEST FAN!
OH. THAT'S WHAT YOU MEANT...
I THOUGHT YOU'D LOST IT FOR A SECOND THERE.
?

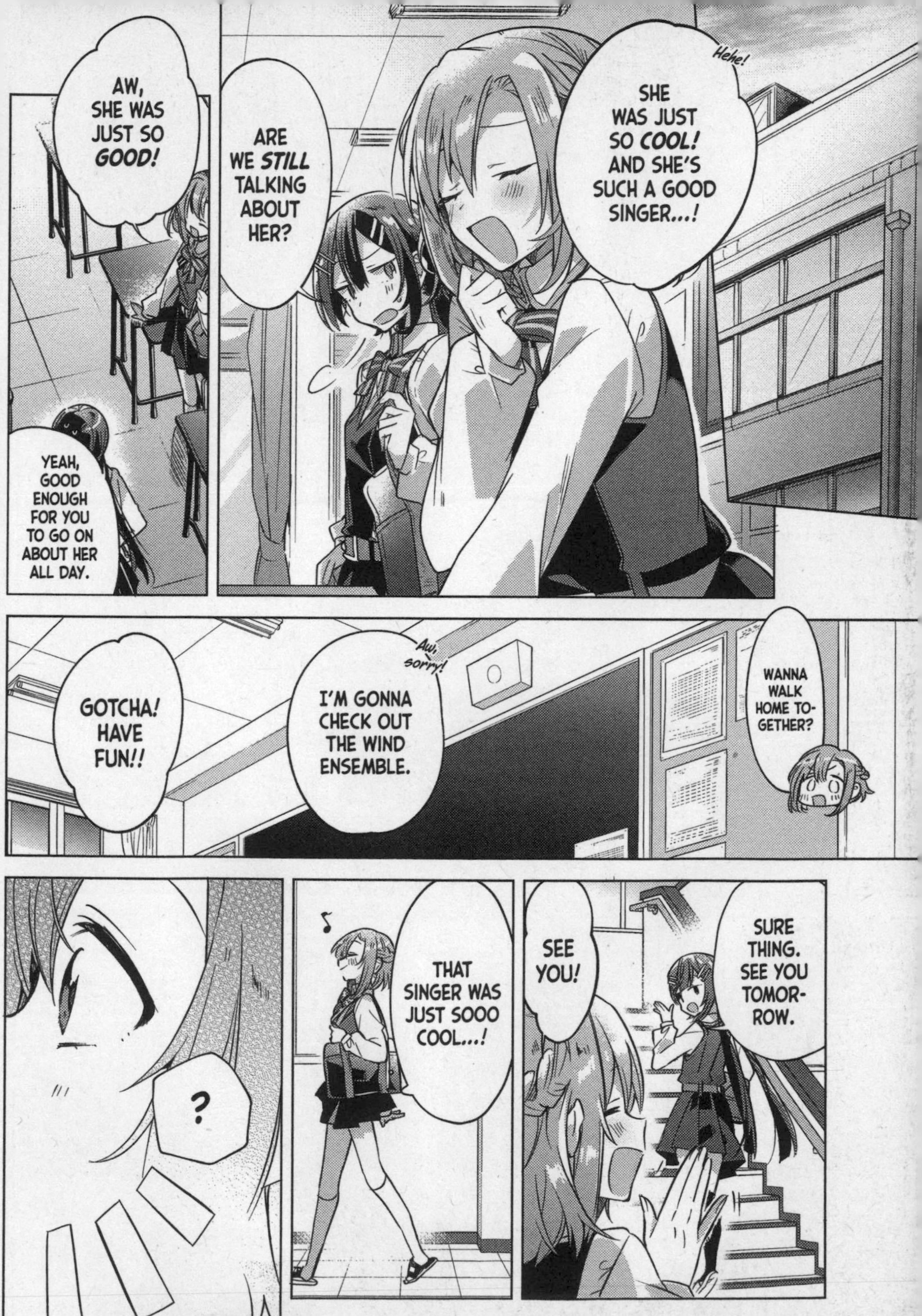
Hehe!
SHE WAS JUST SO *COOL!* AND SHE'S SUCH A GOOD SINGER...!
ARE WE *STILL* TALKING ABOUT HER?
AW, SHE WAS JUST SO *GOOD!*
YEAH, GOOD ENOUGH FOR YOU TO GO ON ABOUT HER ALL DAY.
WANNA WALK HOME TO-GETHER?
Aw, sorry!
I'M GONNA CHECK OUT THE WIND ENSEMBLE.
GOTCHA! HAVE FUN!!
SURE THING. SEE YOU TOMOR-ROW.
SEE YOU!
THAT SINGER WAS JUST SOOO COOL...!
?

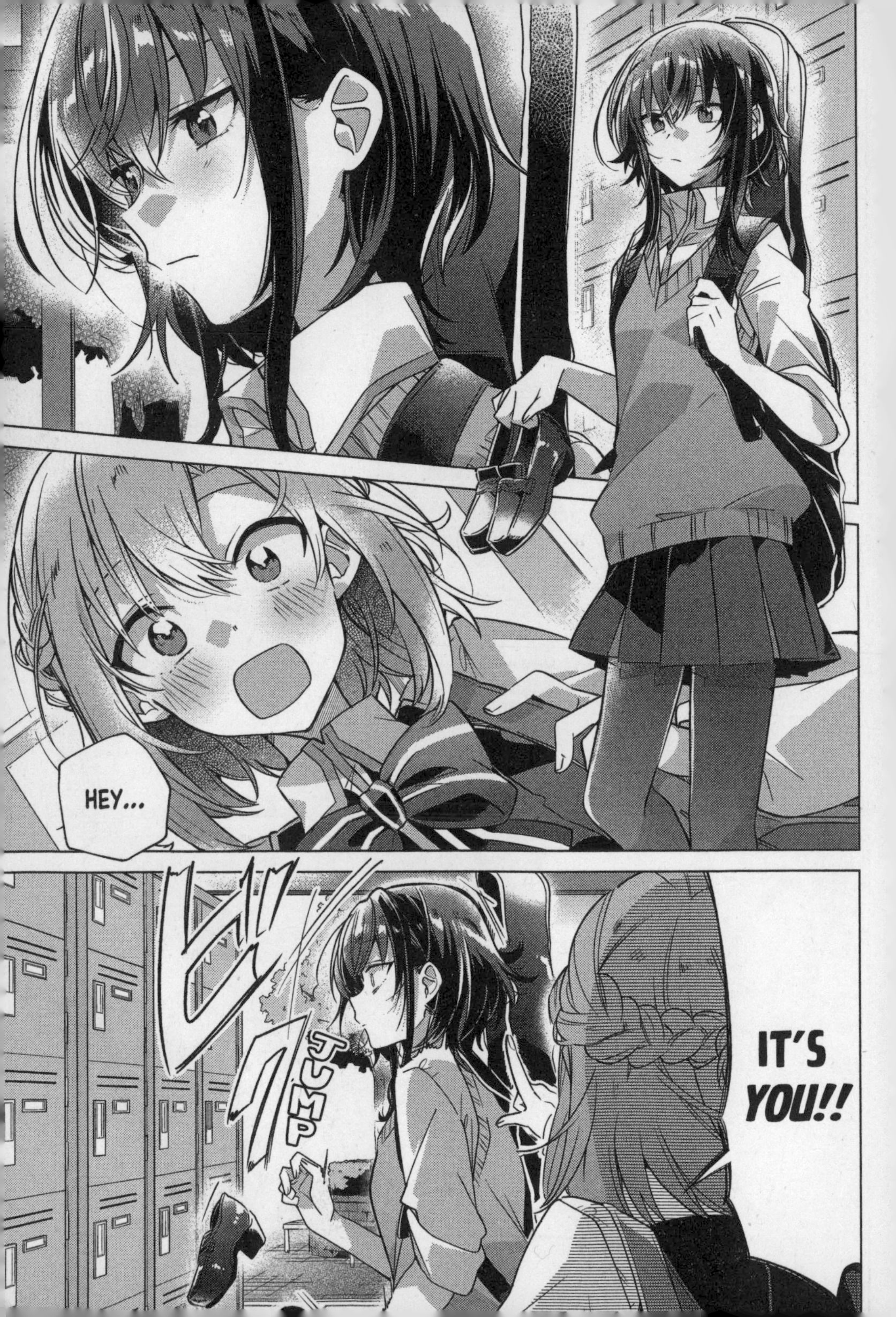
HEY...
JUMP
IT'S YOU!!

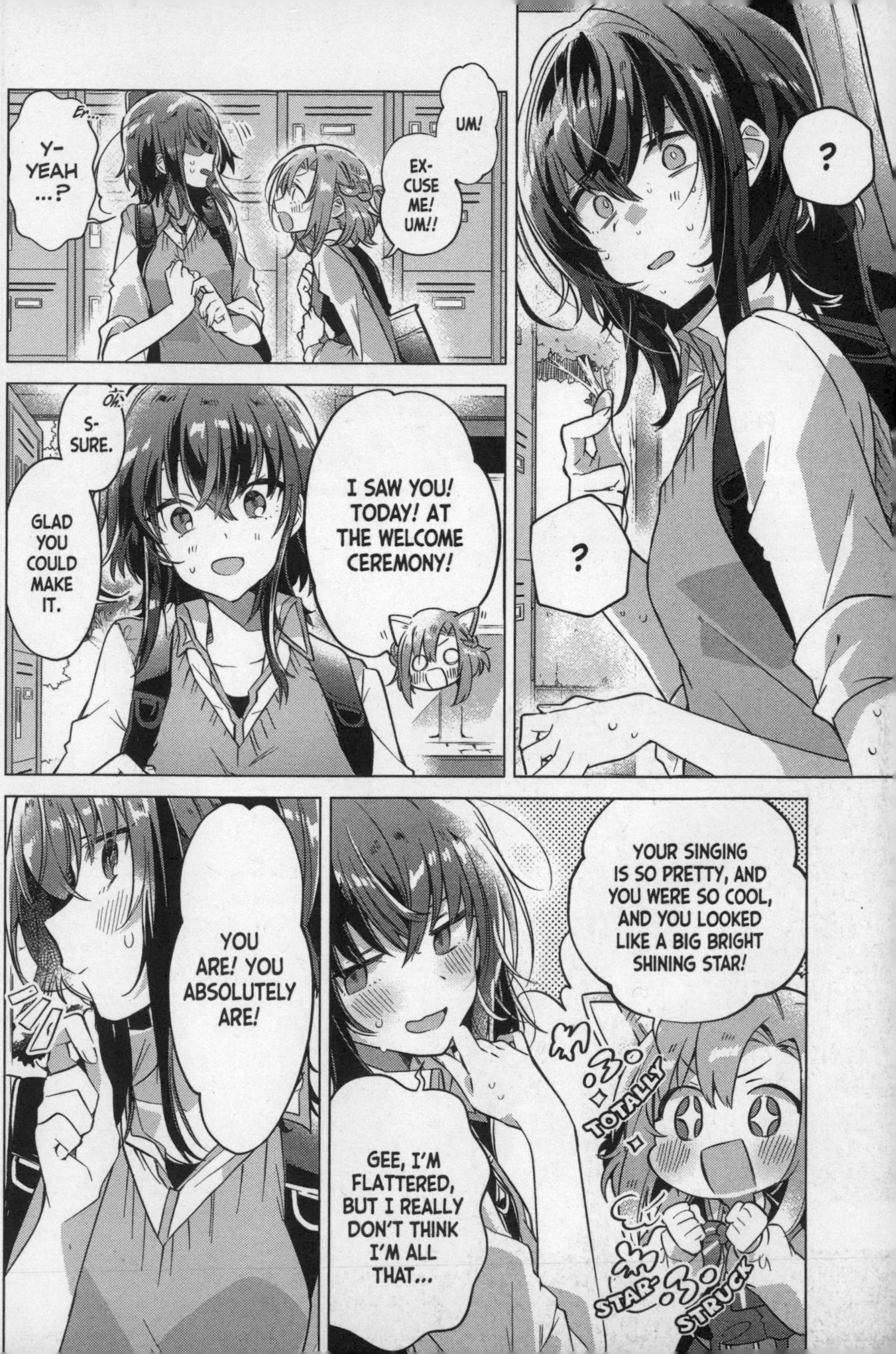
?
?
UM!
EX-CUSE ME! UM!!
Er...
Y-YEAH ...?
I SAW YOU! TODAY! AT THE WELCOME CEREMONY!
Oh.
S-SURE.
GLAD YOU COULD MAKE IT.
YOUR SINGING IS SO PRETTY, AND YOU WERE SO COOL, AND YOU LOOKED LIKE A BIG BRIGHT SHINING STAR!
TOTALLY STAR-STRUCK
GEE, I'M FLATTERED, BUT I REALLY DON'T THINK I'M ALL THAT...
YOU ARE! YOU ABSOLUTELY ARE!

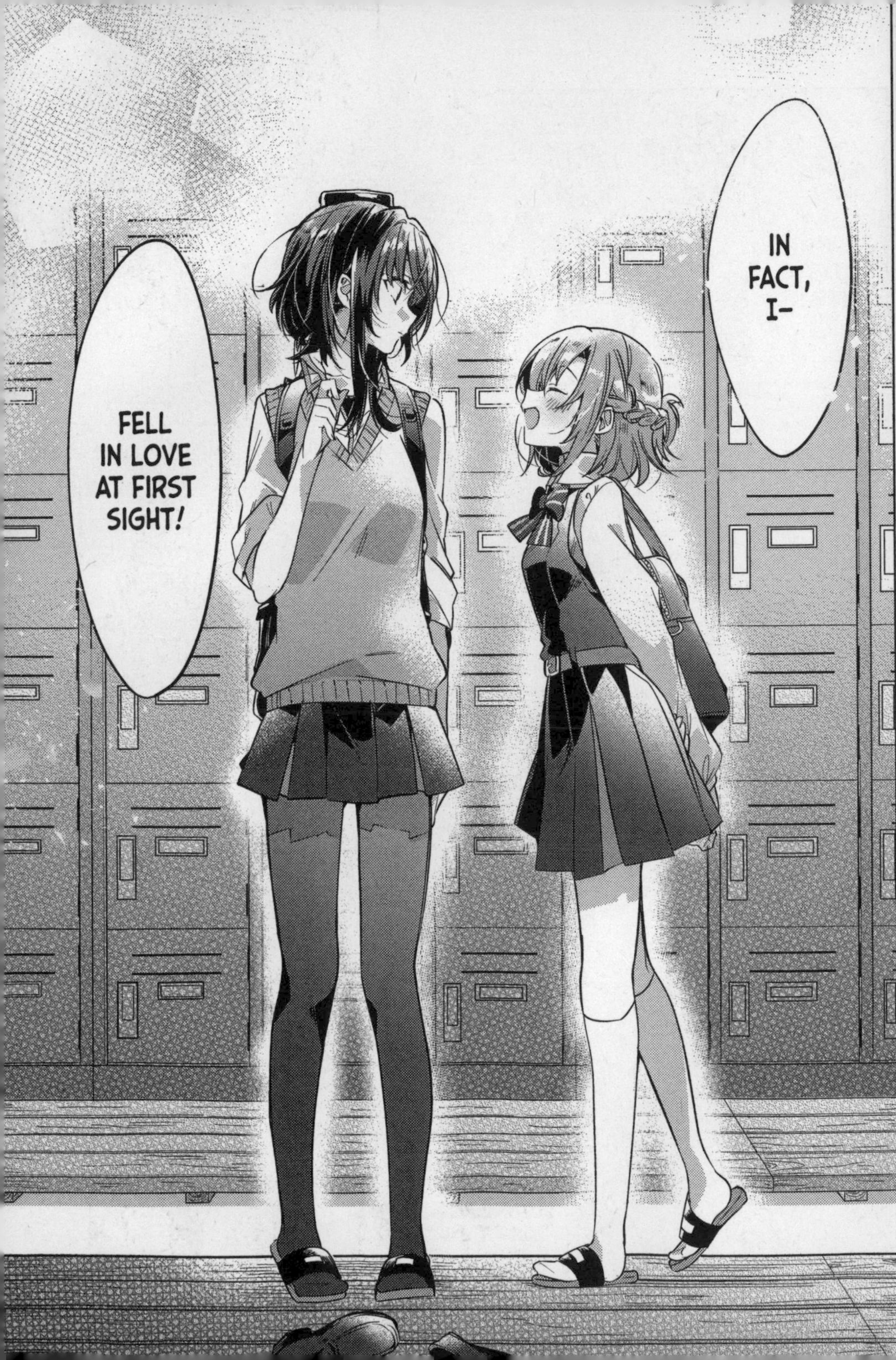
IN FACT, I–
FELL IN LOVE AT FIRST SIGHT!

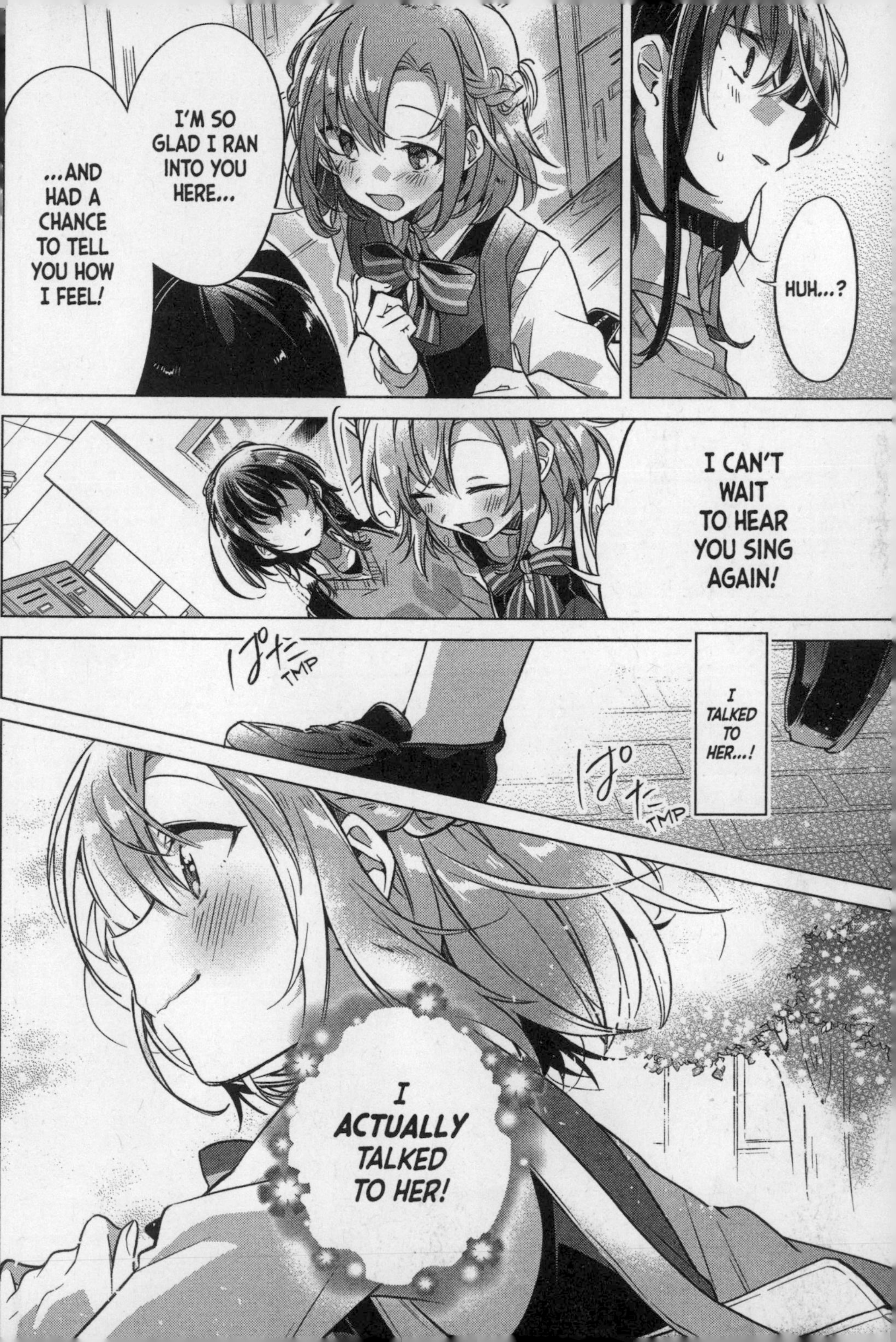
HUH...?
I'M SO GLAD I RAN INTO YOU HERE...
...AND HAD A CHANCE TO TELL YOU HOW I FEEL!
I CAN'T WAIT TO HEAR YOU SING AGAIN!
I TALKED TO HER...!
ぱた TMP
ぱた TMP
I ACTUALLY TALKED TO HER!

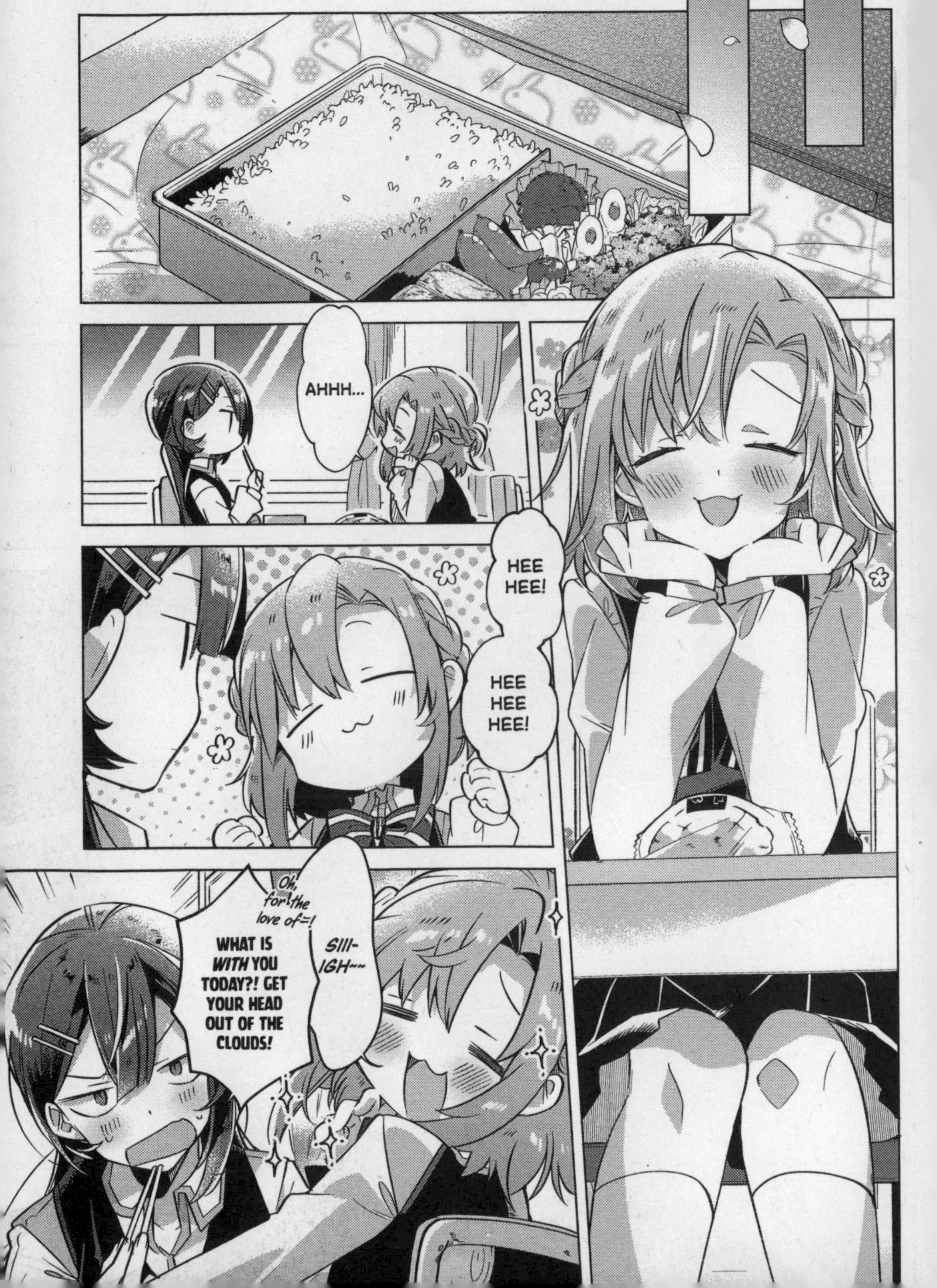
AHHH...
HEE HEE!
HEE HEE HEE!
SIIII-IGH~~
Oh, for the love of=!
WHAT IS *WITH* YOU TODAY?! GET YOUR HEAD OUT OF THE CLOUDS!

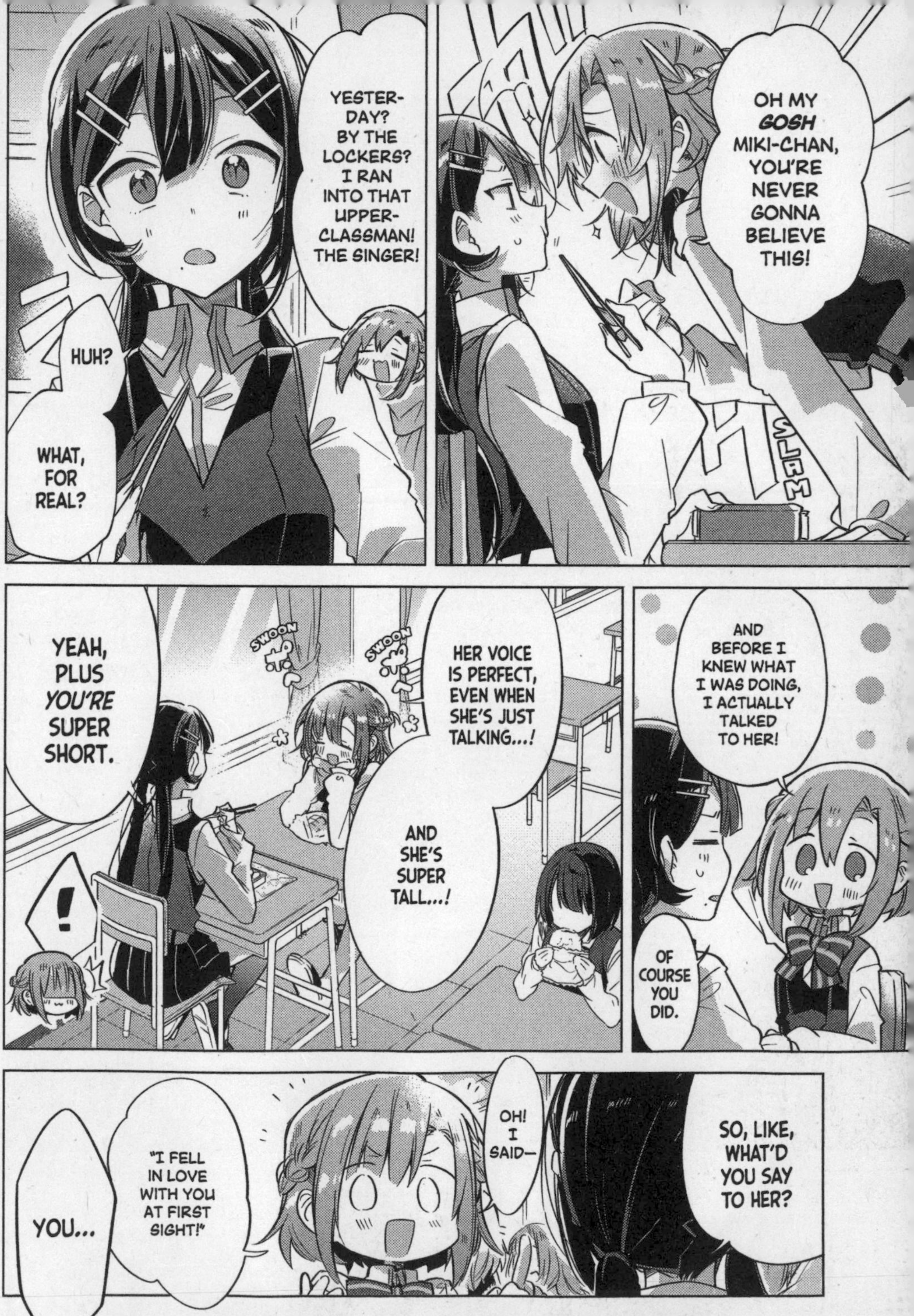
OH MY *GOSH* MIKI-CHAN, YOU'RE NEVER GONNA BELIEVE THIS!
SLAM
YESTER-DAY? BY THE LOCKERS? I RAN INTO THAT UPPER-CLASSMAN! THE SINGER!
HUH?
WHAT, FOR REAL?
AND BEFORE I KNEW WHAT I WAS DOING, I ACTUALLY TALKED TO HER!
OF COURSE YOU DID.
HER VOICE IS PERFECT, EVEN WHEN SHE'S JUST TALKING...!
SWOON
SWOON
AND SHE'S SUPER TALL...!
YEAH, PLUS *YOU'RE* SUPER SHORT.
!
SO, LIKE, WHAT'D YOU SAY TO HER?
OH! I SAID—
"I FELL IN LOVE WITH YOU AT FIRST SIGHT!"
YOU...

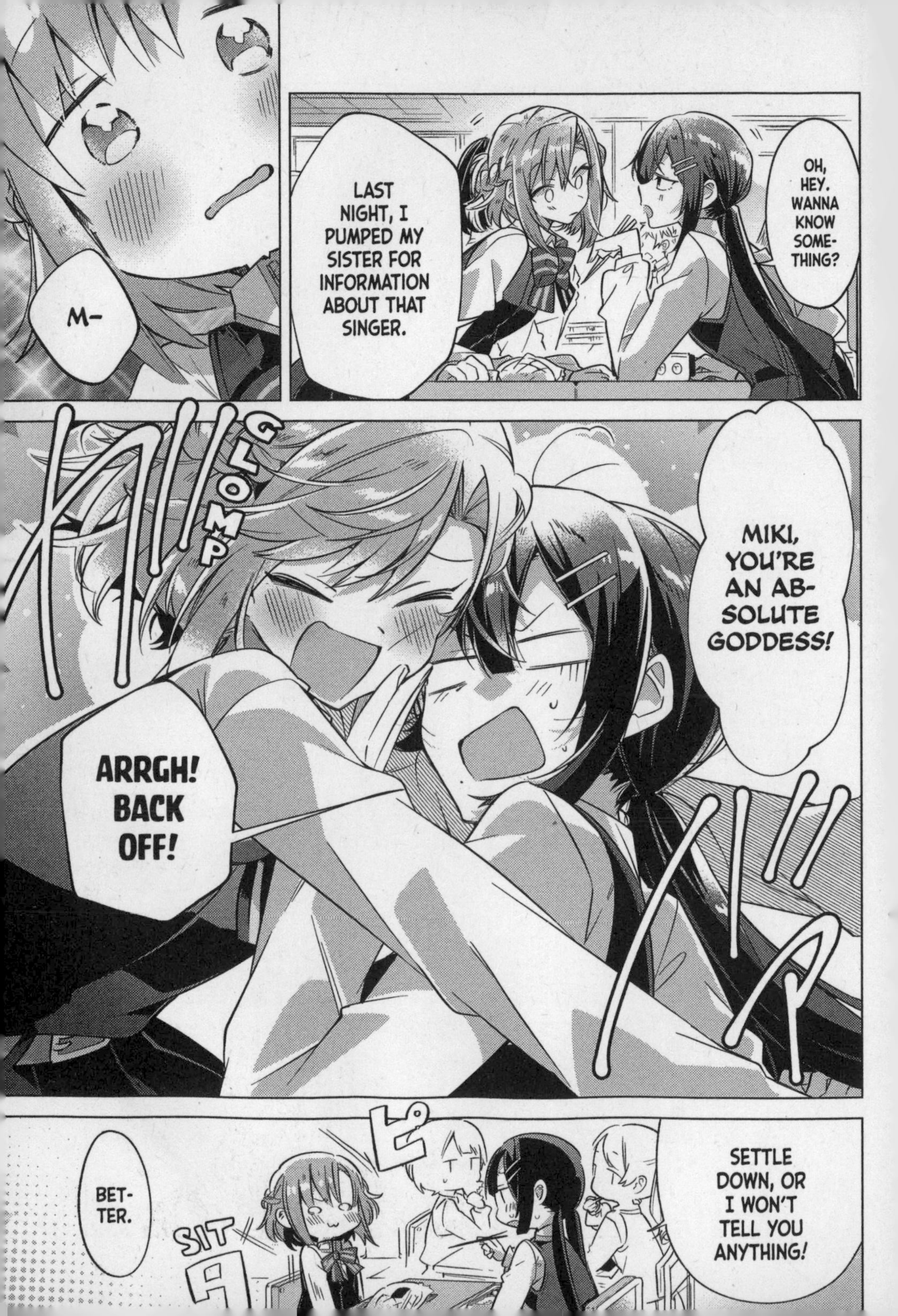
OH, HEY. WANNA KNOW SOME-THING?
LAST NIGHT, I PUMPED MY SISTER FOR INFORMATION ABOUT THAT SINGER.
M–
MIKI, YOU'RE AN AB-SOLUTE GODDESS!
GLOMP
ARRGH! BACK OFF!
SETTLE DOWN, OR I WON'T TELL YOU ANYTHING!
SIT
BET-TER.

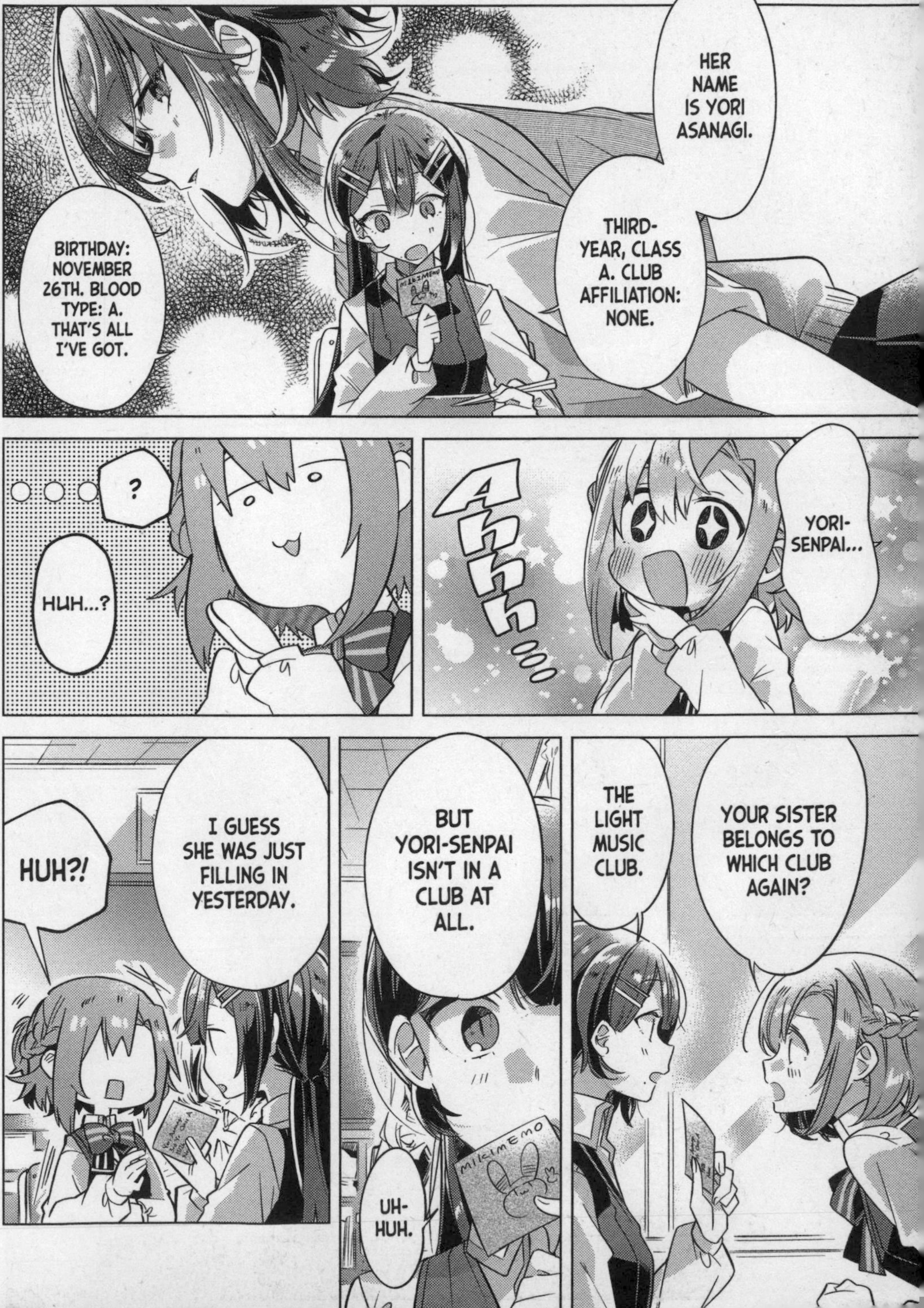
HER NAME IS YORI ASANAGI.
THIRD-YEAR, CLASS A. CLUB AFFILIATION: NONE.
BIRTHDAY: NOVEMBER 26TH. BLOOD TYPE: A. THAT'S ALL I'VE GOT.
YORI-SENPAI...
Ahhhh
...?
HUH...?
YOUR SISTER BELONGS TO WHICH CLUB AGAIN?
THE LIGHT MUSIC CLUB.
BUT YORI-SENPAI ISN'T IN A CLUB AT ALL.
UH-HUH.
I GUESS SHE WAS JUST FILLING IN YESTERDAY.
HUH?!

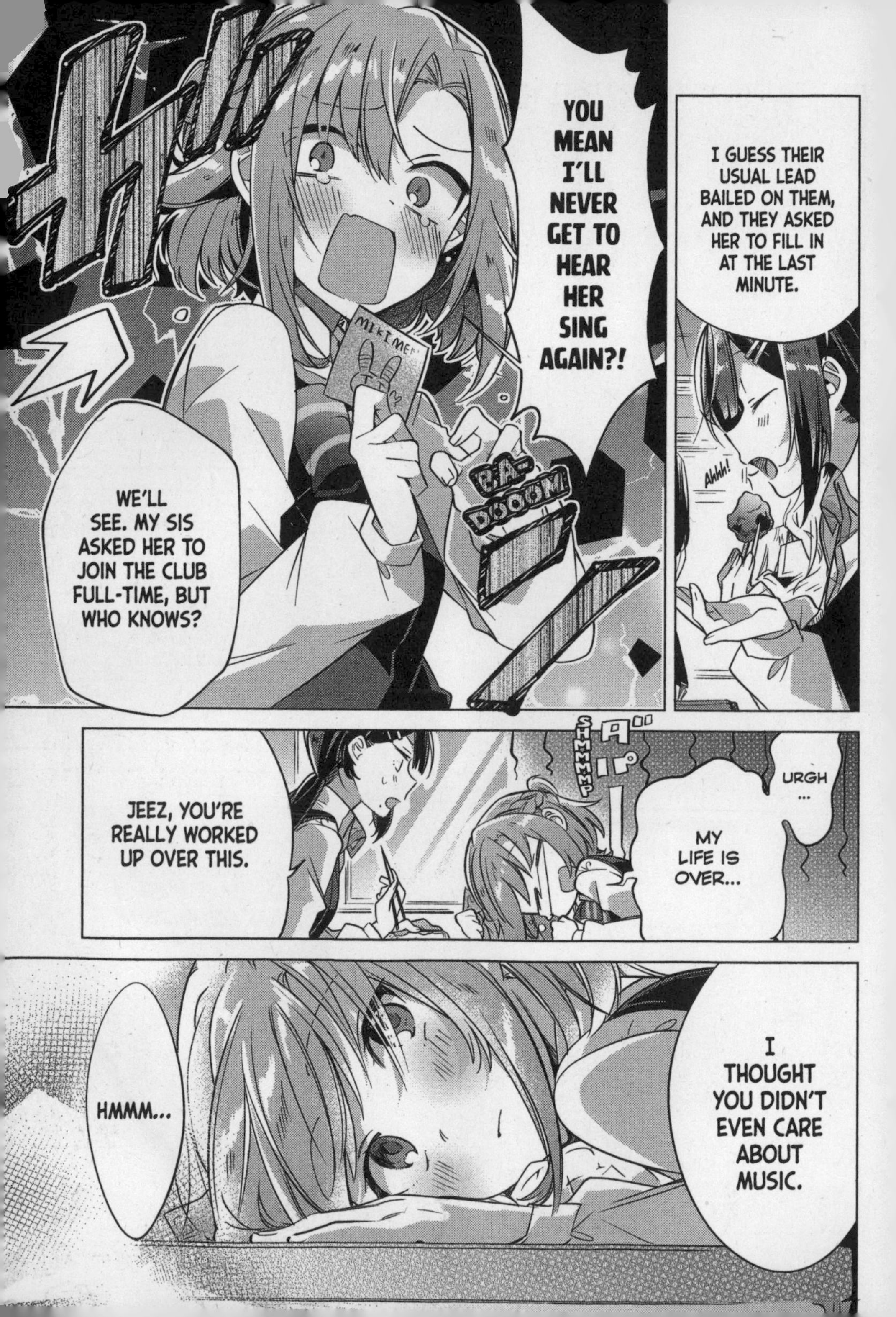
I GUESS THEIR USUAL LEAD BAILED ON THEM, AND THEY ASKED HER TO FILL IN AT THE LAST MINUTE.
Ahhh!
YOU MEAN I'LL NEVER GET TO HEAR HER SING AGAIN?!
BA-DOOOM!
WE'LL SEE. MY SIS ASKED HER TO JOIN THE CLUB FULL-TIME, BUT WHO KNOWS?
URGH ...
MY LIFE IS OVER...
SHMMMMP
JEEZ, YOU'RE REALLY WORKED UP OVER THIS.
I THOUGHT YOU DIDN'T EVEN CARE ABOUT MUSIC.
HMMM...

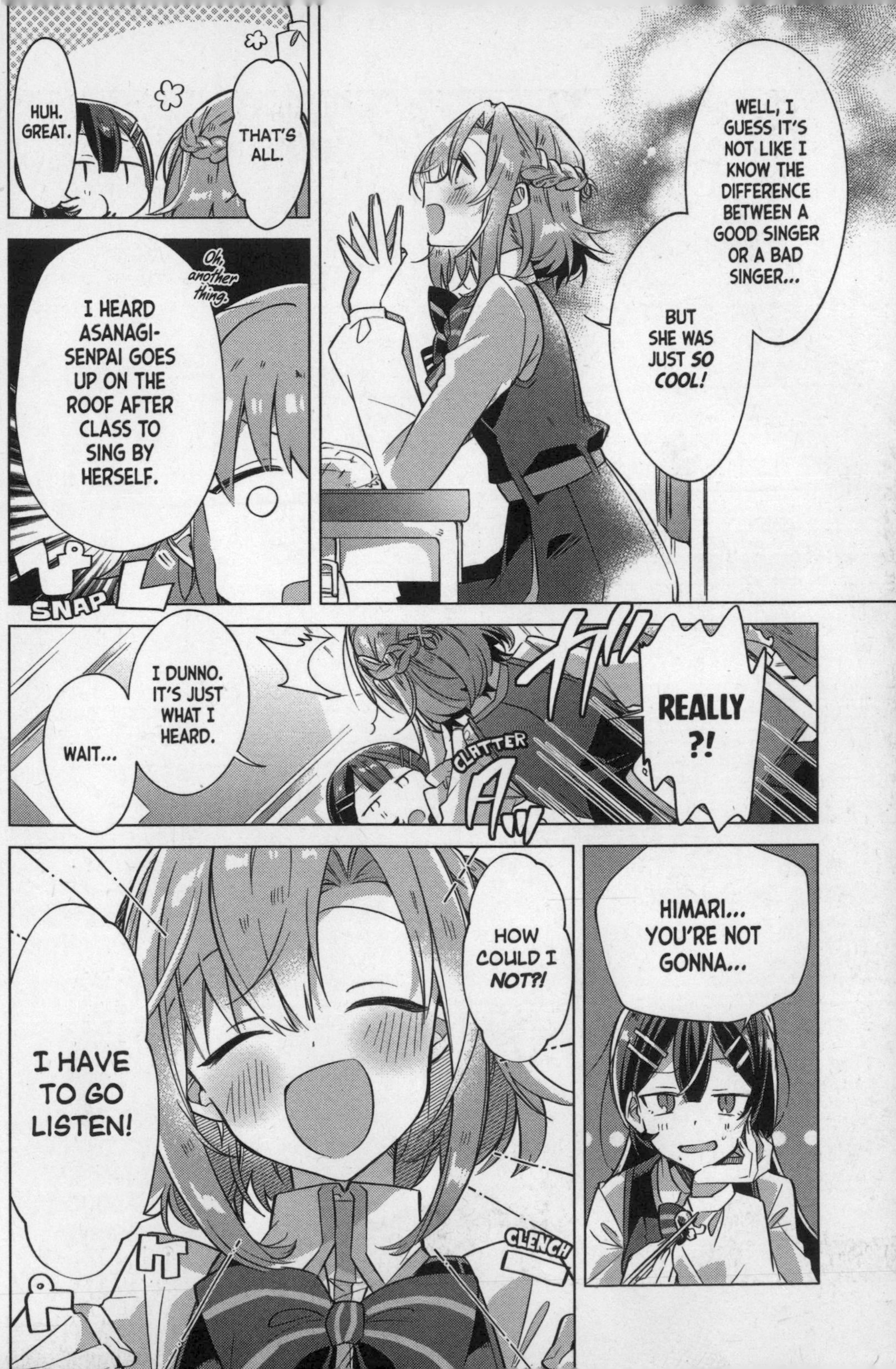
WELL, I GUESS IT'S NOT LIKE I KNOW THE DIFFERENCE BETWEEN A GOOD SINGER OR A BAD SINGER...
BUT SHE WAS JUST SO COOL!
THAT'S ALL.
HUH. GREAT.
Oh, another thing.
I HEARD ASANAGI-SENPAI GOES UP ON THE ROOF AFTER CLASS TO SING BY HERSELF.
SNAP
REALLY ?!
CLATTER
I DUNNO. IT'S JUST WHAT I HEARD.
WAIT...
HIMARI... YOU'RE NOT GONNA...
HOW COULD I NOT?!
I HAVE TO GO LISTEN!
CLENCH

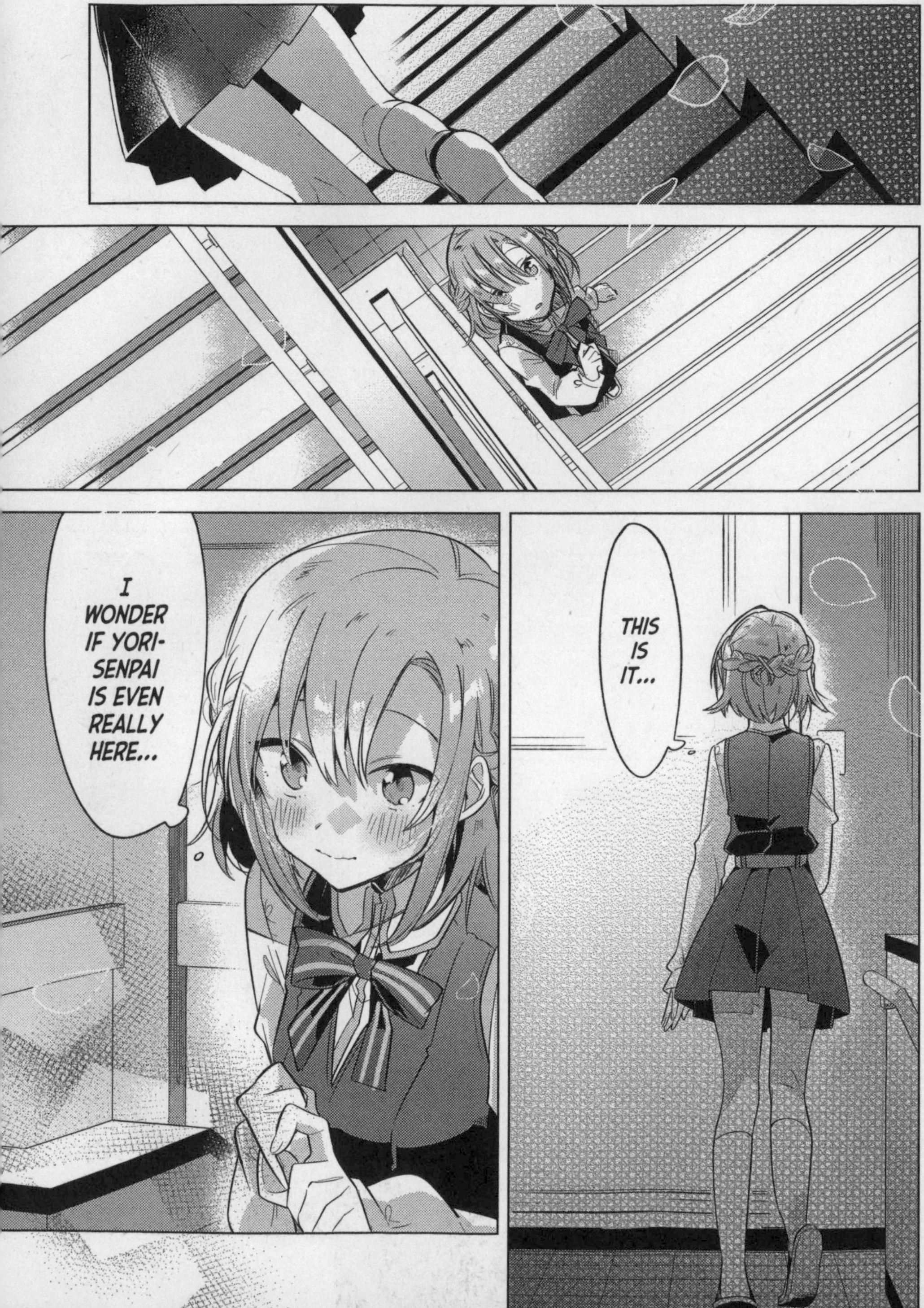
THIS IS IT...
I WONDER IF YORI-SENPAI IS EVEN REALLY HERE...

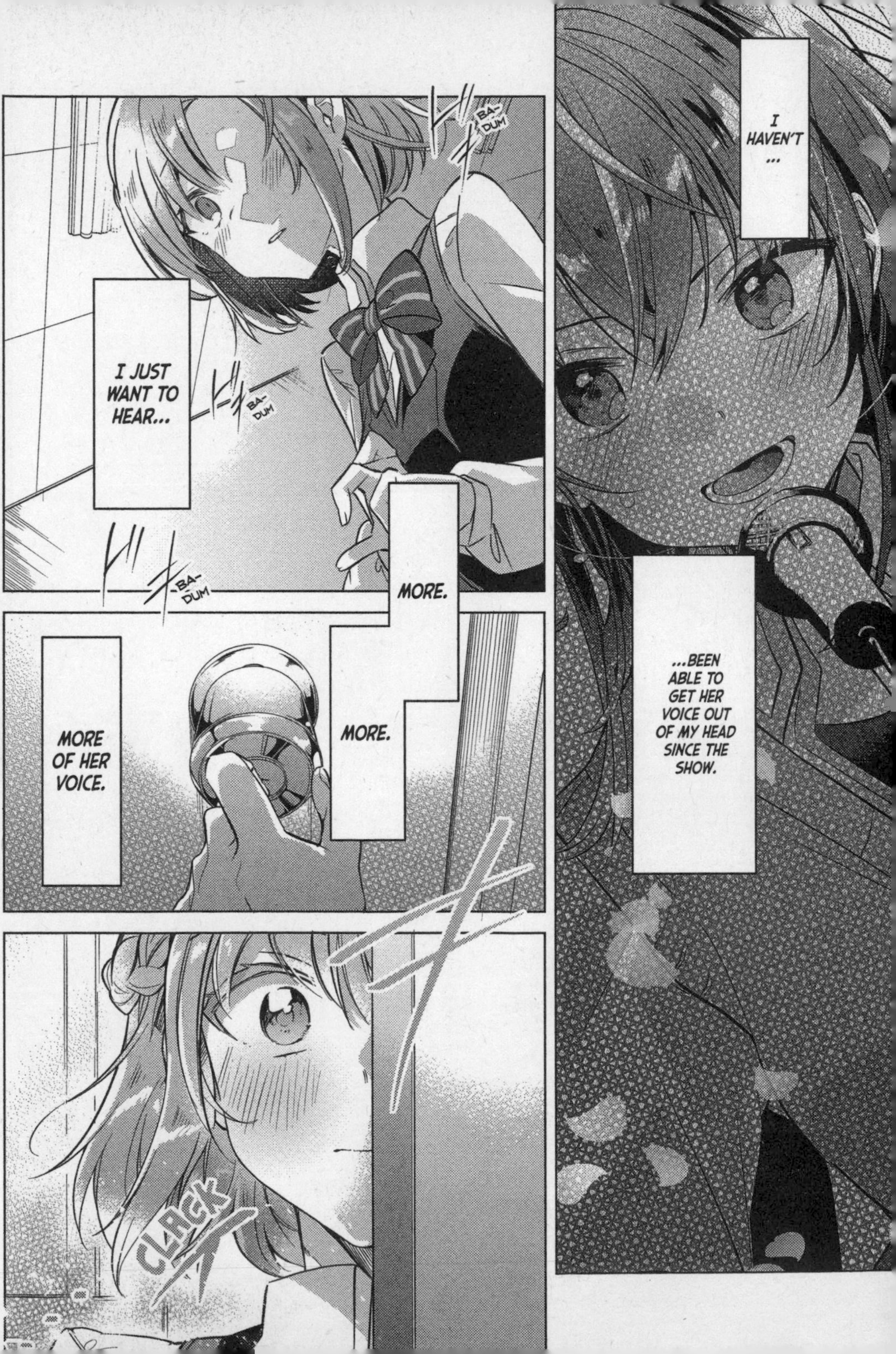
I HAVEN'T ...
...BEEN ABLE TO GET HER VOICE OUT OF MY HEAD SINCE THE SHOW.
BA-DUM
I JUST WANT TO HEAR...
BA-DUM
BA-DUM
MORE.
MORE.
MORE OF HER VOICE.
CLACK

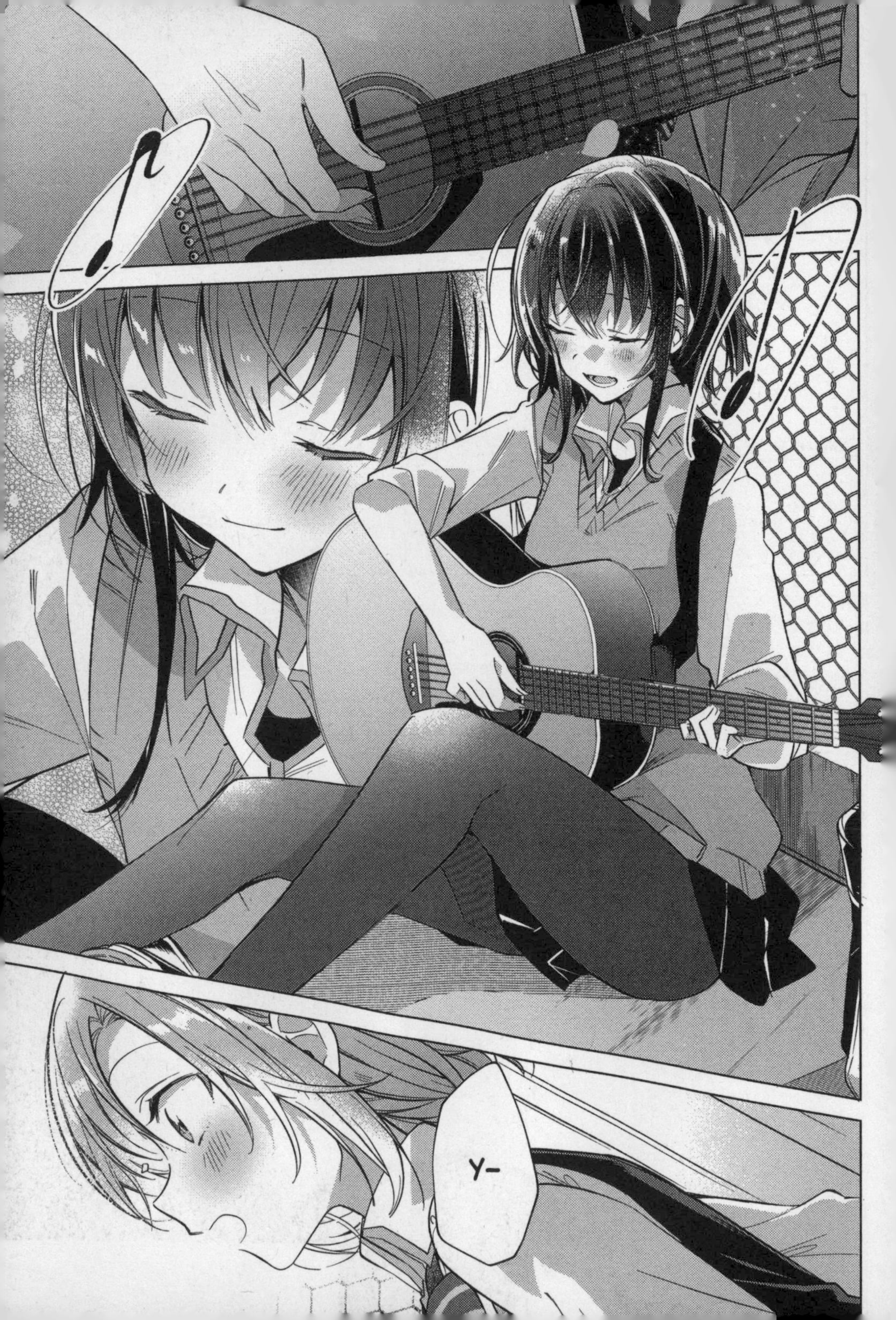
Y-

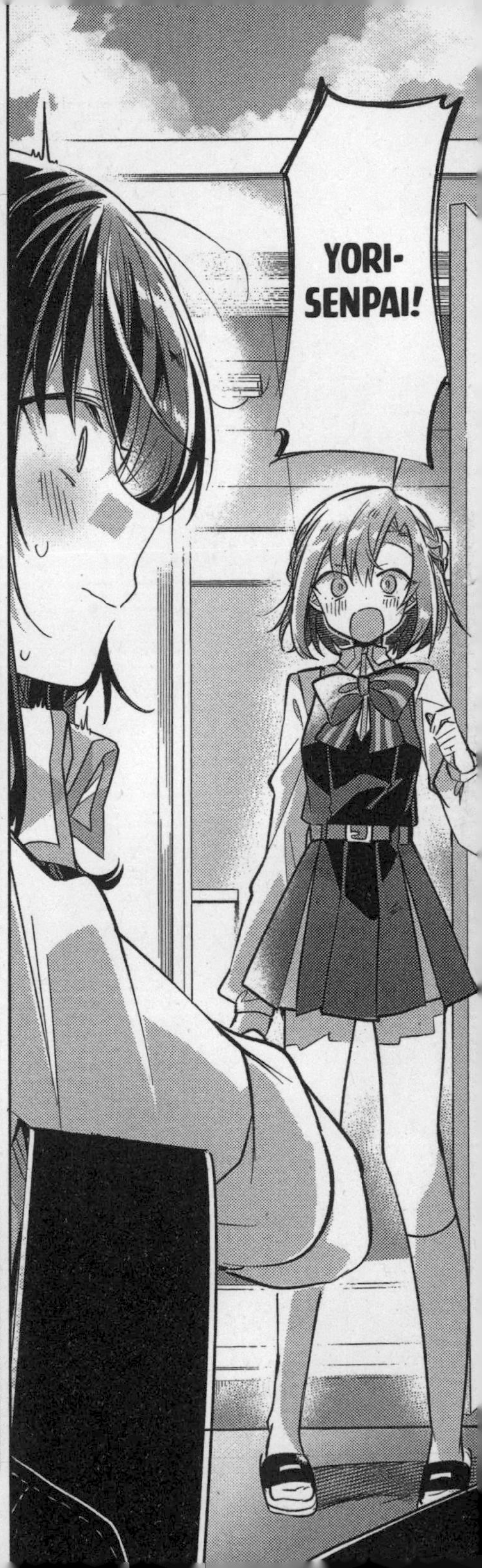
YORI-SENPAI!

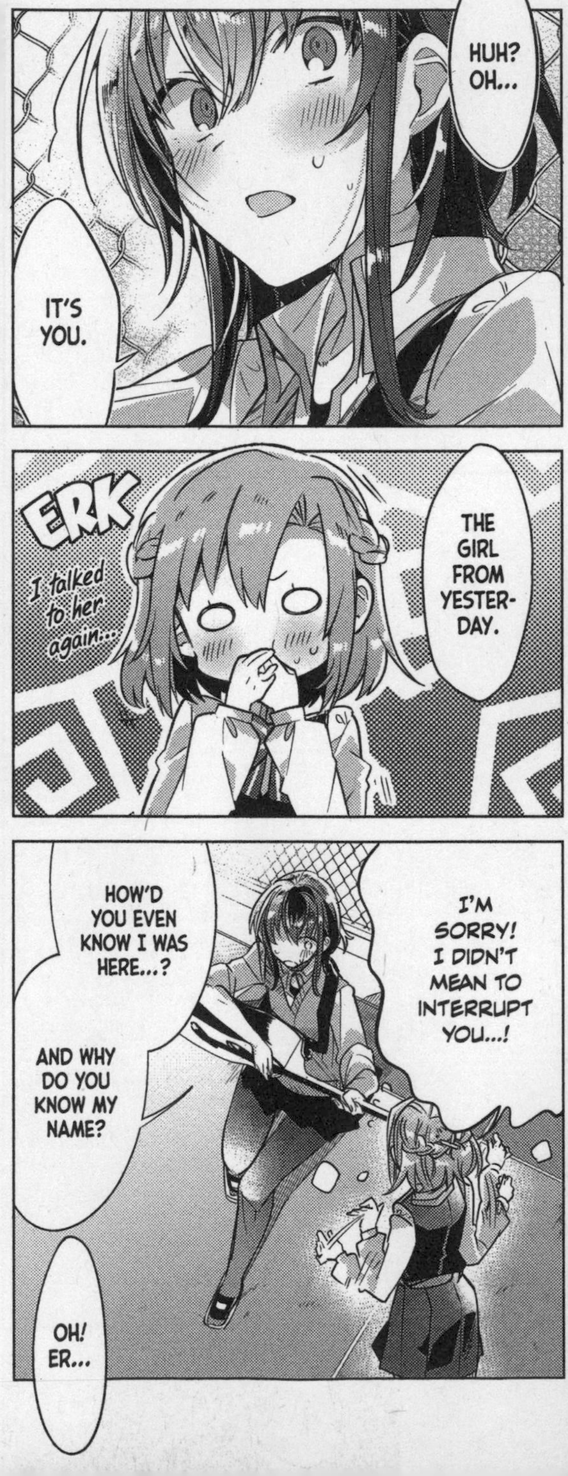
HUH? OH...
IT'S YOU.
THE GIRL FROM YESTER-DAY.
ERK
I talked to her again...
I'M SORRY! I DIDN'T MEAN TO INTERRUPT YOU...!
HOW'D YOU EVEN KNOW I WAS HERE...?
AND WHY DO YOU KNOW MY NAME?
OH! ER...

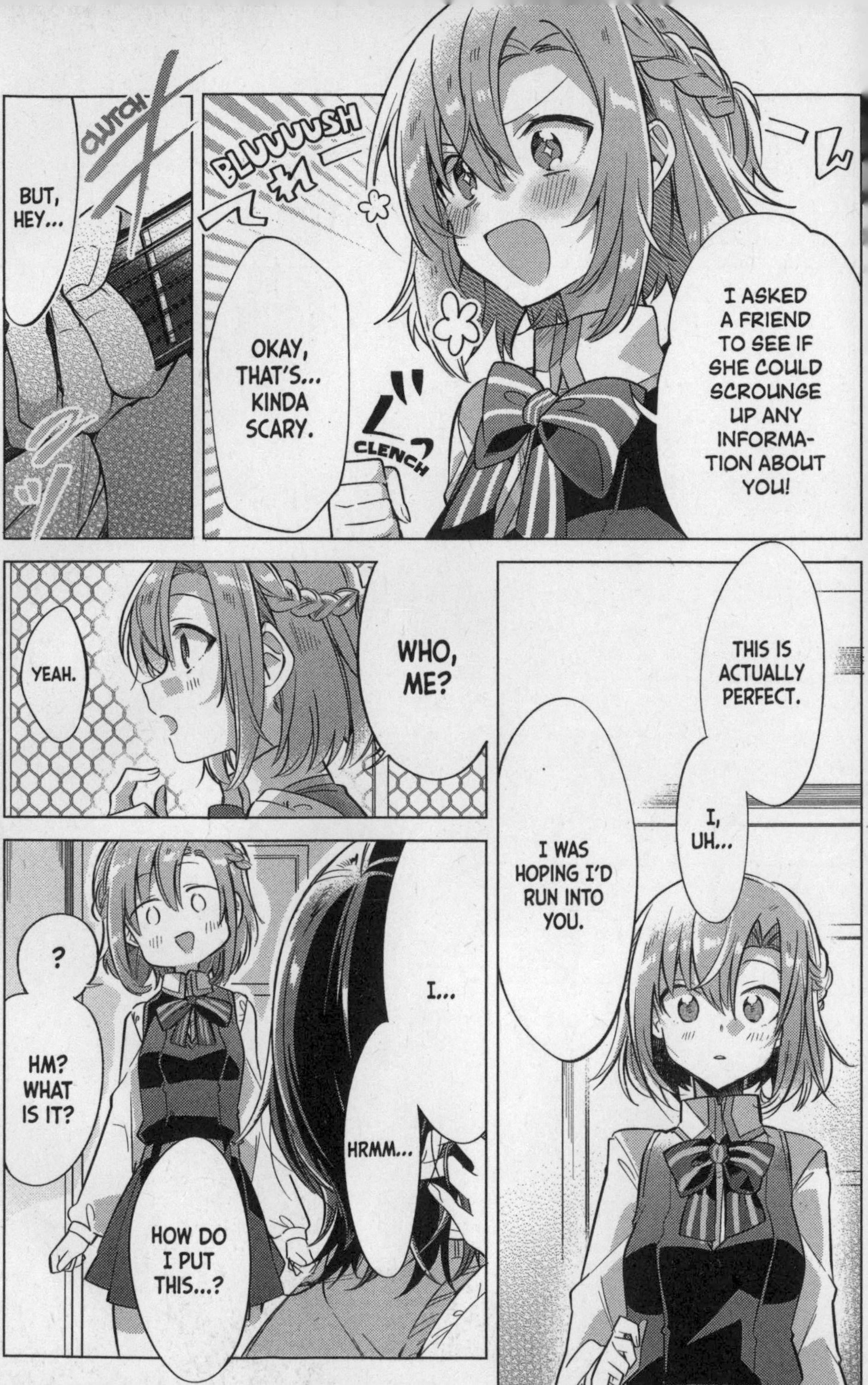
I ASKED A FRIEND TO SEE IF SHE COULD SCROUNGE UP ANY INFORMATION ABOUT YOU!
BLUUUUSH
CLENCH
OKAY, THAT'S... KINDA SCARY.
CLUTCH
BUT, HEY...
THIS IS ACTUALLY PERFECT.
I, UH...
I WAS HOPING I'D RUN INTO YOU.
WHO, ME?
YEAH.
I...
HRMM...
HOW DO I PUT THIS...?
?
HM? WHAT IS IT?

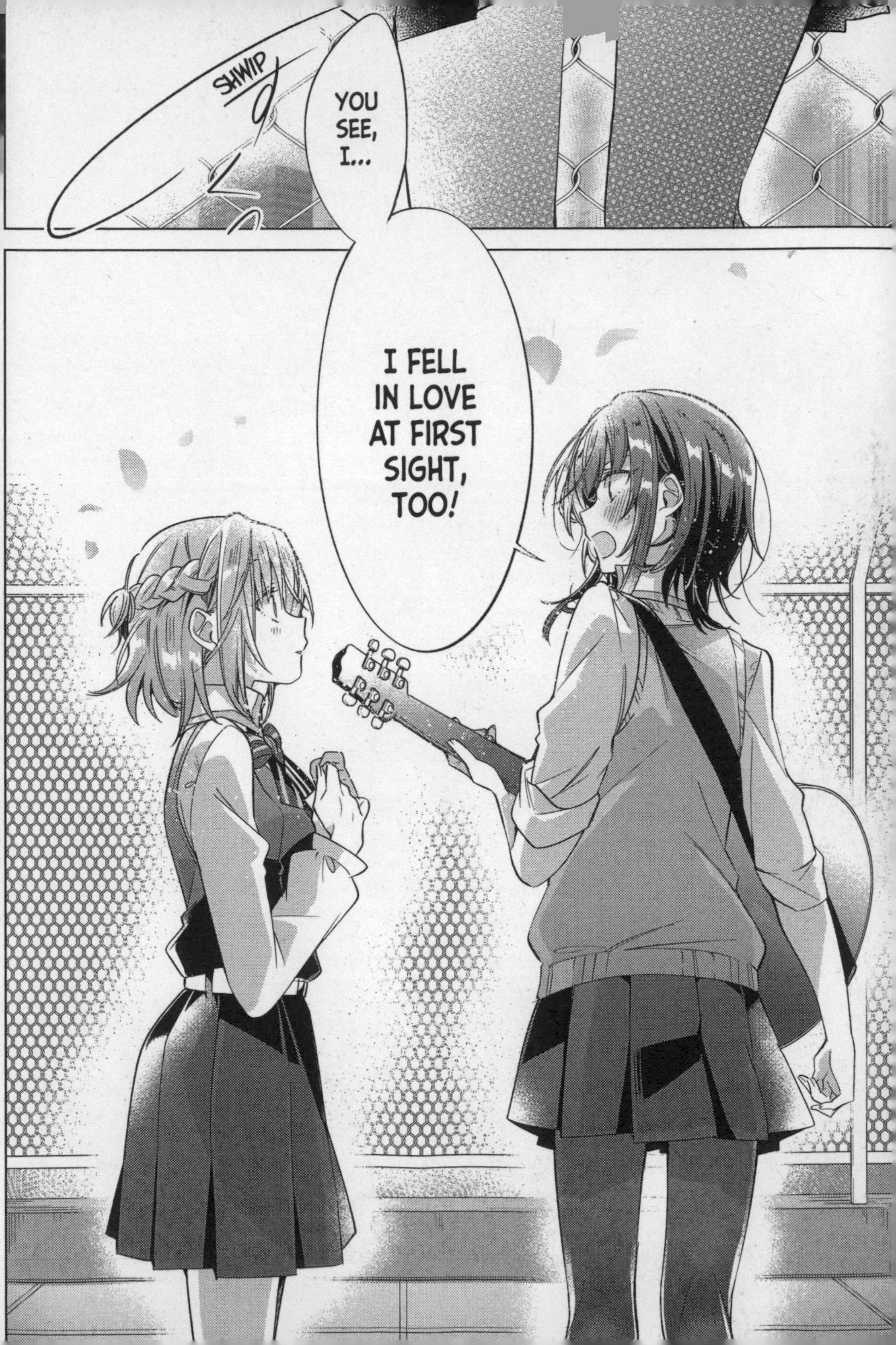
YOU SEE, I...
SHWIP
I FELL IN LOVE AT FIRST SIGHT, TOO!

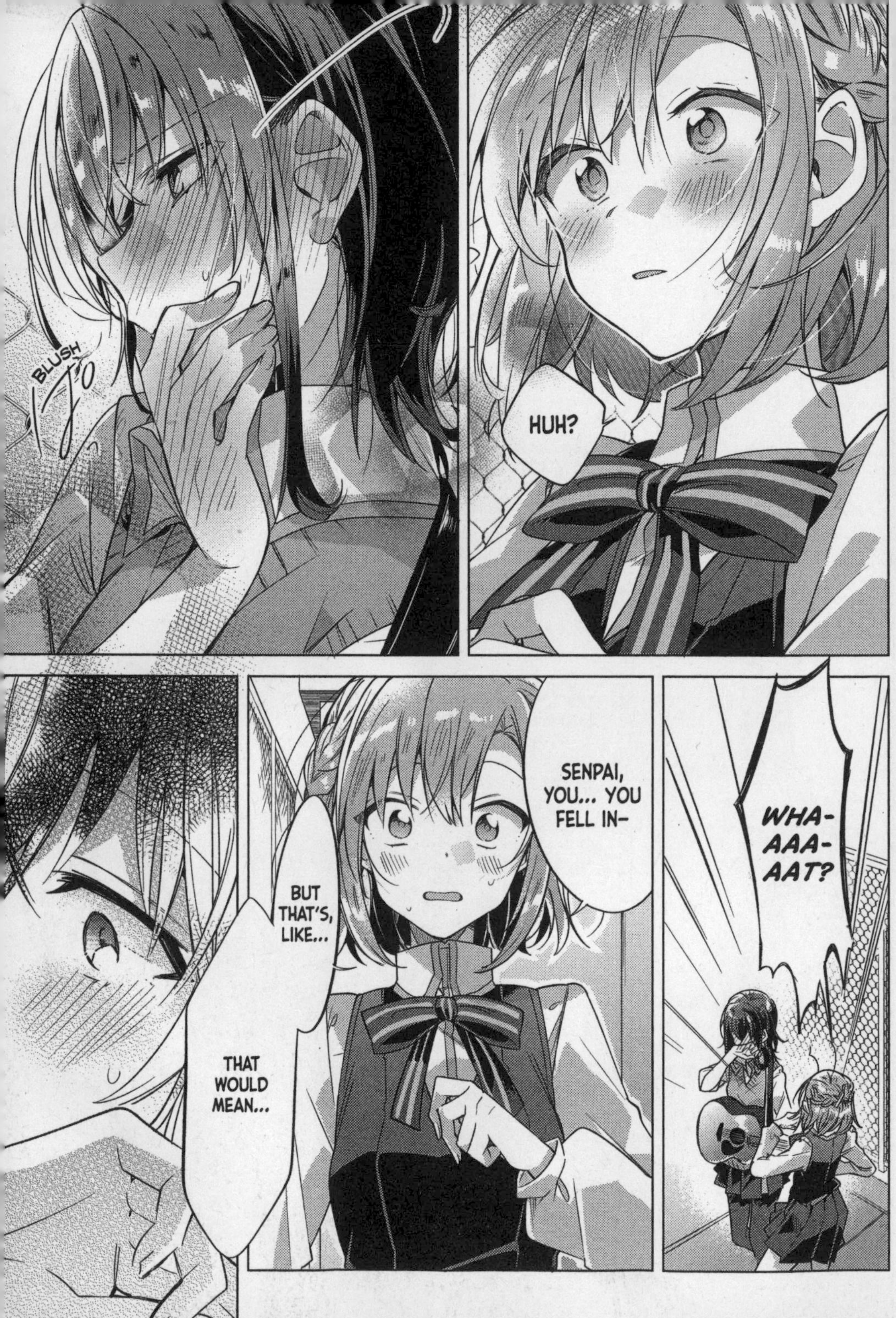
HUH?
BLUSH
WHA-AAA-AAT?
SENPAI, YOU... YOU FELL IN–
BUT THAT'S, LIKE...
THAT WOULD MEAN...

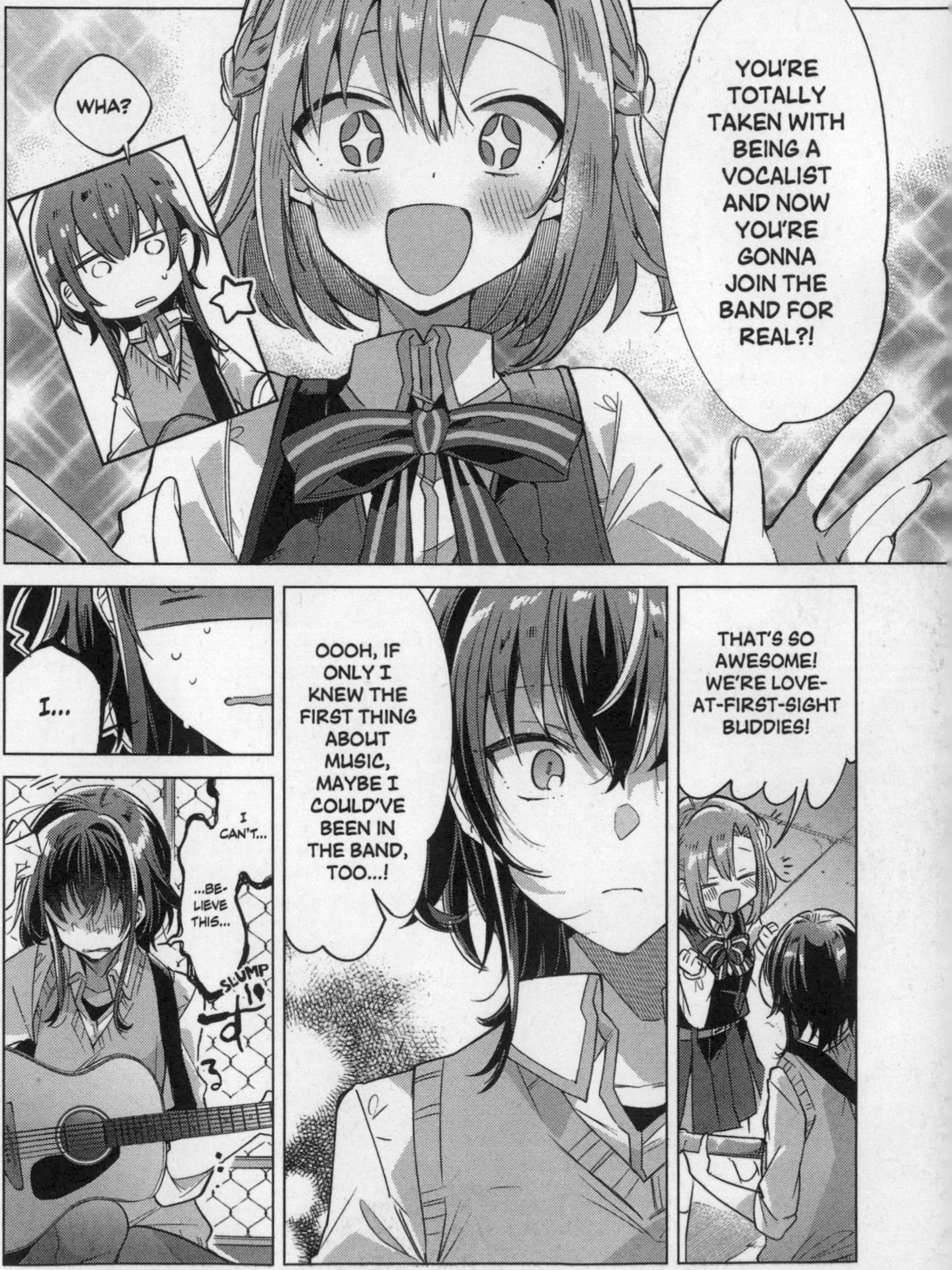
YOU'RE TOTALLY TAKEN WITH BEING A VOCALIST AND NOW YOU'RE GONNA JOIN THE BAND FOR REAL?!
WHA?
THAT'S SO AWESOME! WE'RE LOVE-AT-FIRST-SIGHT BUDDIES!
OOOH, IF ONLY I KNEW THE FIRST THING ABOUT MUSIC, MAYBE I COULD'VE BEEN IN THE BAND, TOO...!
I...
I CAN'T...
...BE-LIEVE THIS...
SLUMP

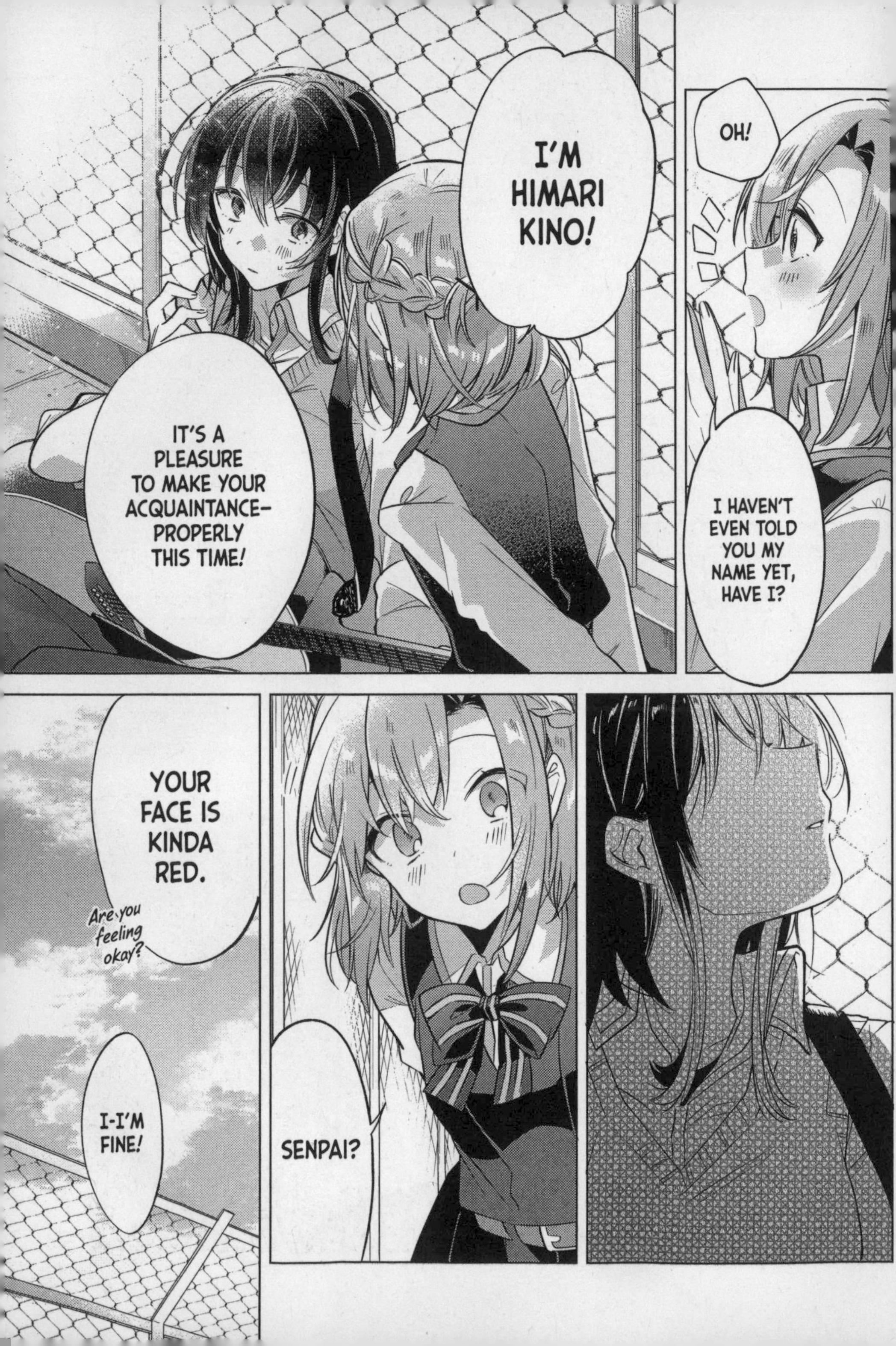
OH!
I HAVEN'T EVEN TOLD YOU MY NAME YET, HAVE I?
I'M HIMARI KINO!
IT'S A PLEASURE TO MAKE YOUR ACQUAINTANCE—PROPERLY THIS TIME!
SENPAI?
YOUR FACE IS KINDA RED.
Are you feeling okay?
I-I'M FINE!

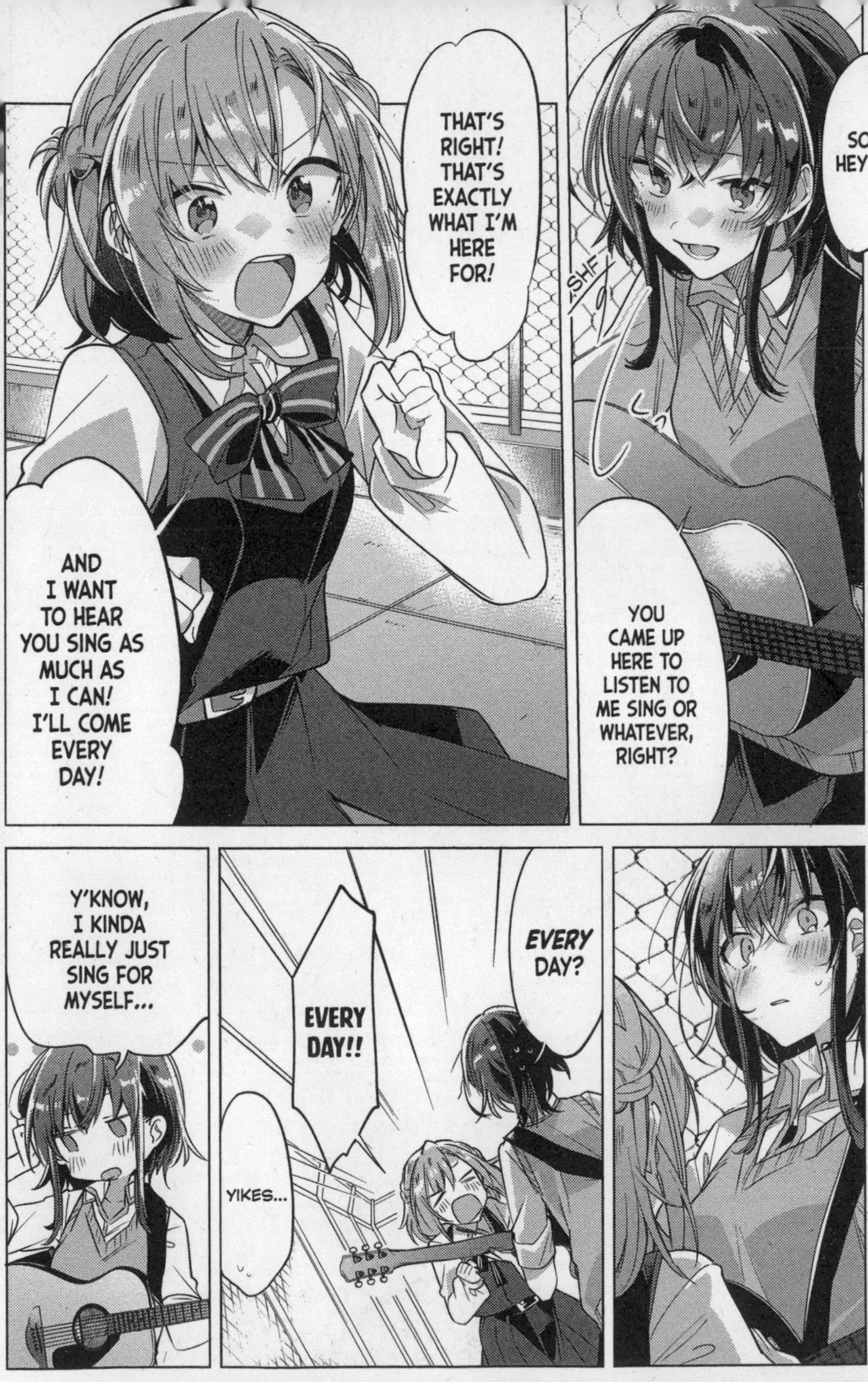
SO, HEY...
SHF
YOU CAME UP HERE TO LISTEN TO ME SING OR WHATEVER, RIGHT?
THAT'S RIGHT! THAT'S EXACTLY WHAT I'M HERE FOR!
AND I WANT TO HEAR YOU SING AS MUCH AS I CAN! I'LL COME EVERY DAY!
EVERY DAY?
EVERY DAY!!
YIKES...
Y'KNOW, I KINDA REALLY JUST SING FOR MYSELF...

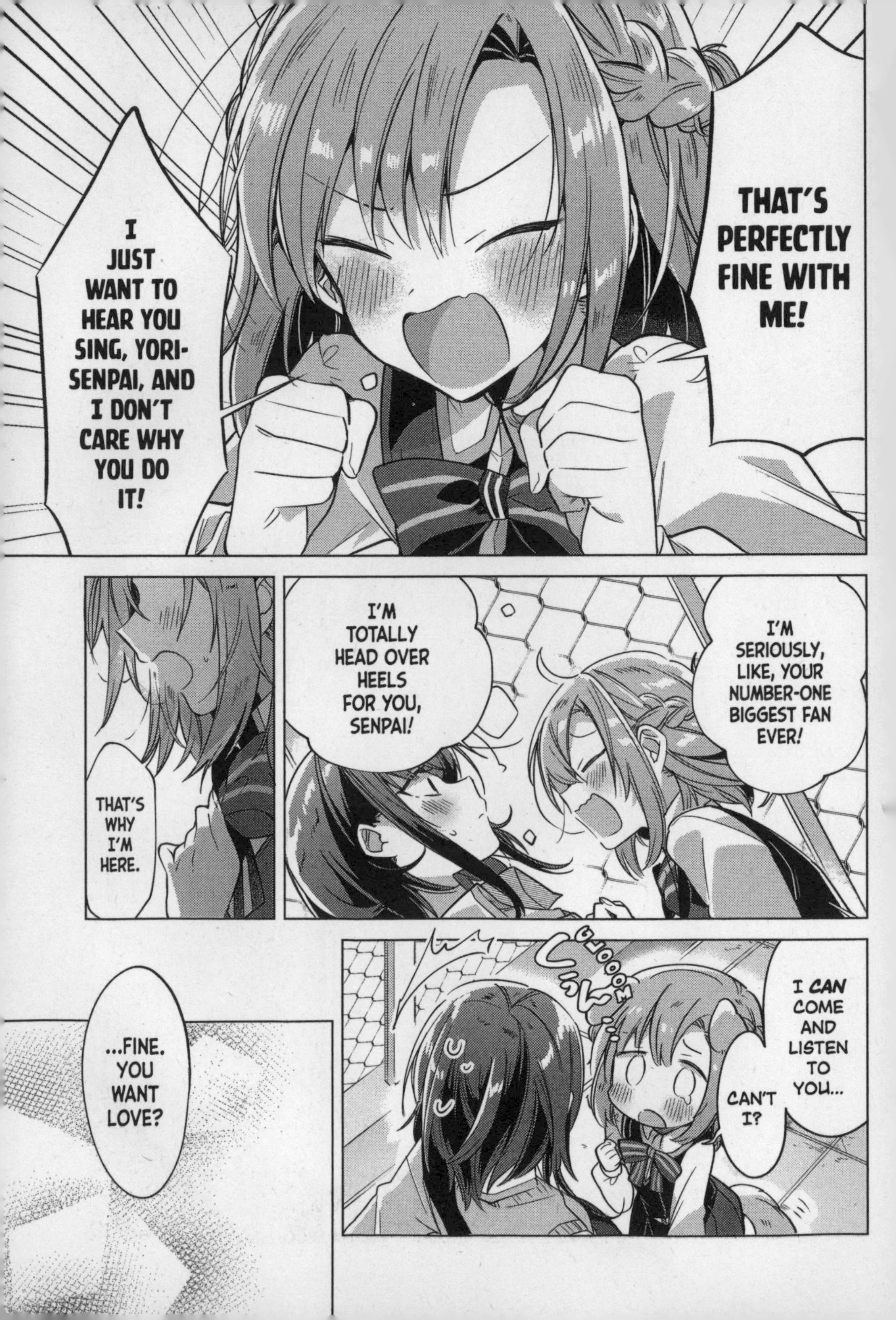
THAT'S PERFECTLY FINE WITH ME!
I JUST WANT TO HEAR YOU SING, YORI-SENPAI, AND I DON'T CARE WHY YOU DO IT!
I'M SERIOUSLY, LIKE, YOUR NUMBER-ONE BIGGEST FAN EVER!
I'M TOTALLY HEAD OVER HEELS FOR YOU, SENPAI!
THAT'S WHY I'M HERE.
I CAN COME AND LISTEN TO YOU...
CAN'T I?
...FINE. YOU WANT LOVE?

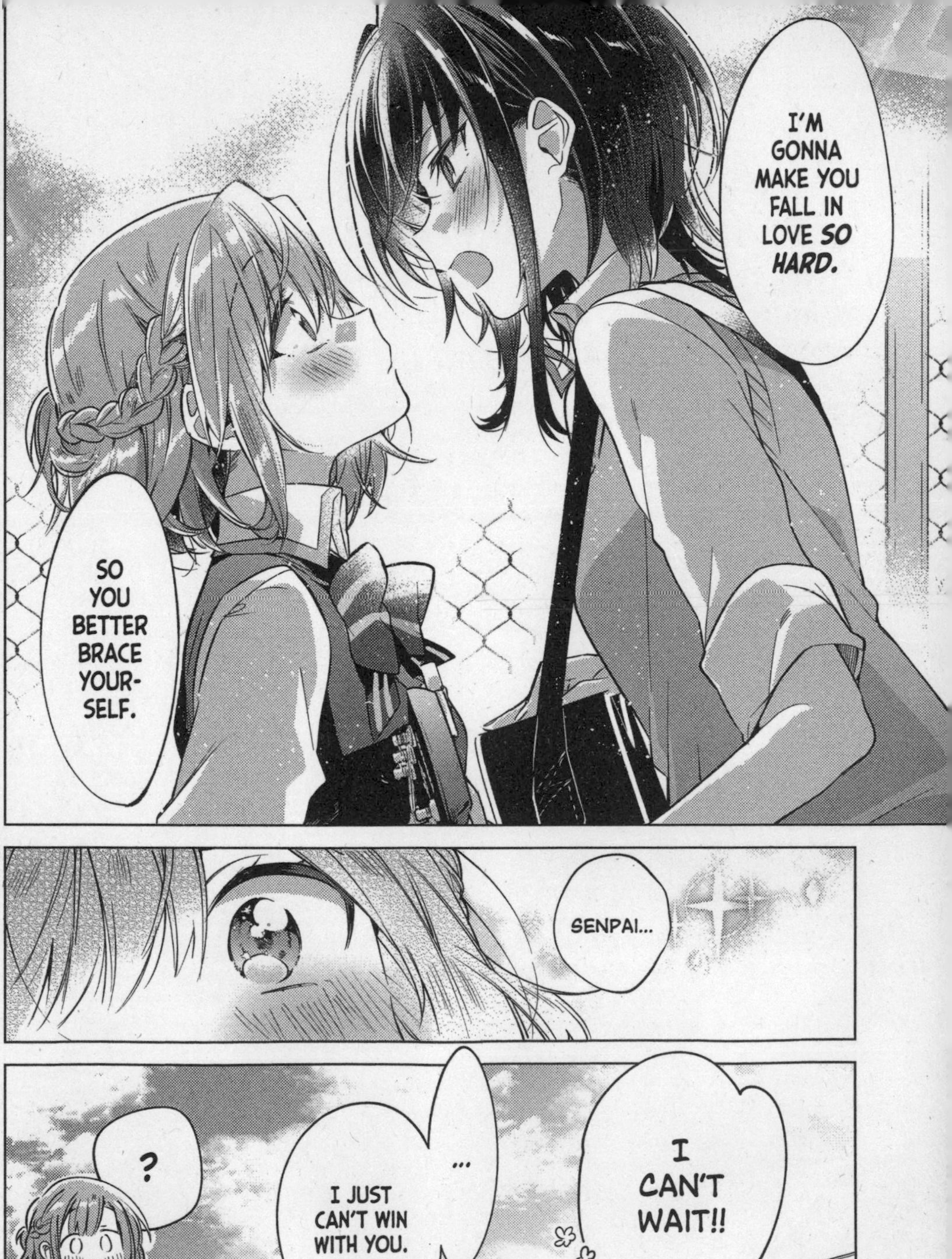
I'M GONNA MAKE YOU FALL IN LOVE SO HARD.
SO YOU BETTER BRACE YOUR-SELF.
SENPAI...
I CAN'T WAIT!!
...
I JUST CAN'T WIN WITH YOU.
?

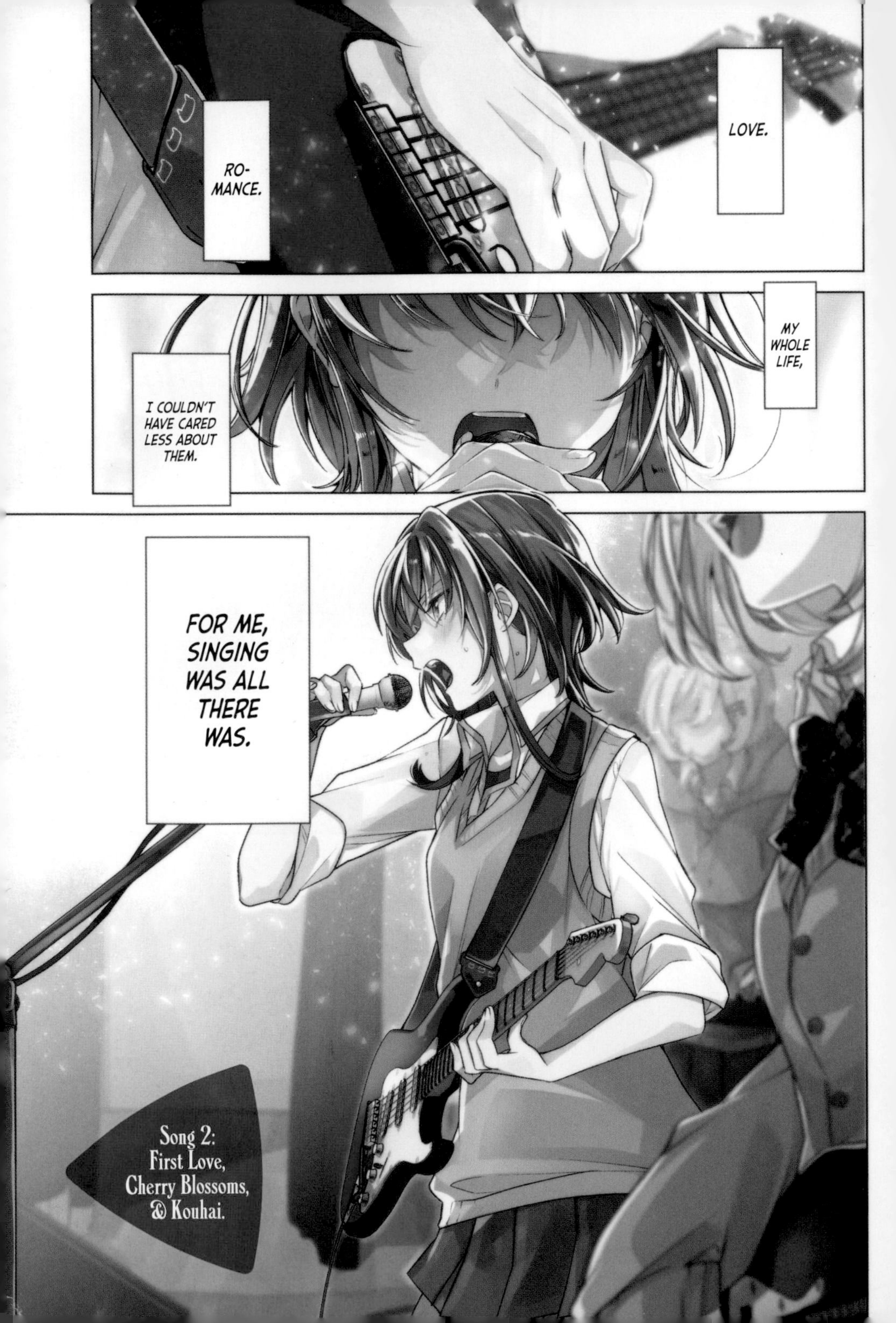
LOVE.
RO-MANCE.
MY WHOLE LIFE,
I COULDN'T HAVE CARED LESS ABOUT THEM.
FOR ME, SINGING WAS ALL THERE WAS.
Song 2: First Love, Cherry Blossoms, & Kouhai.

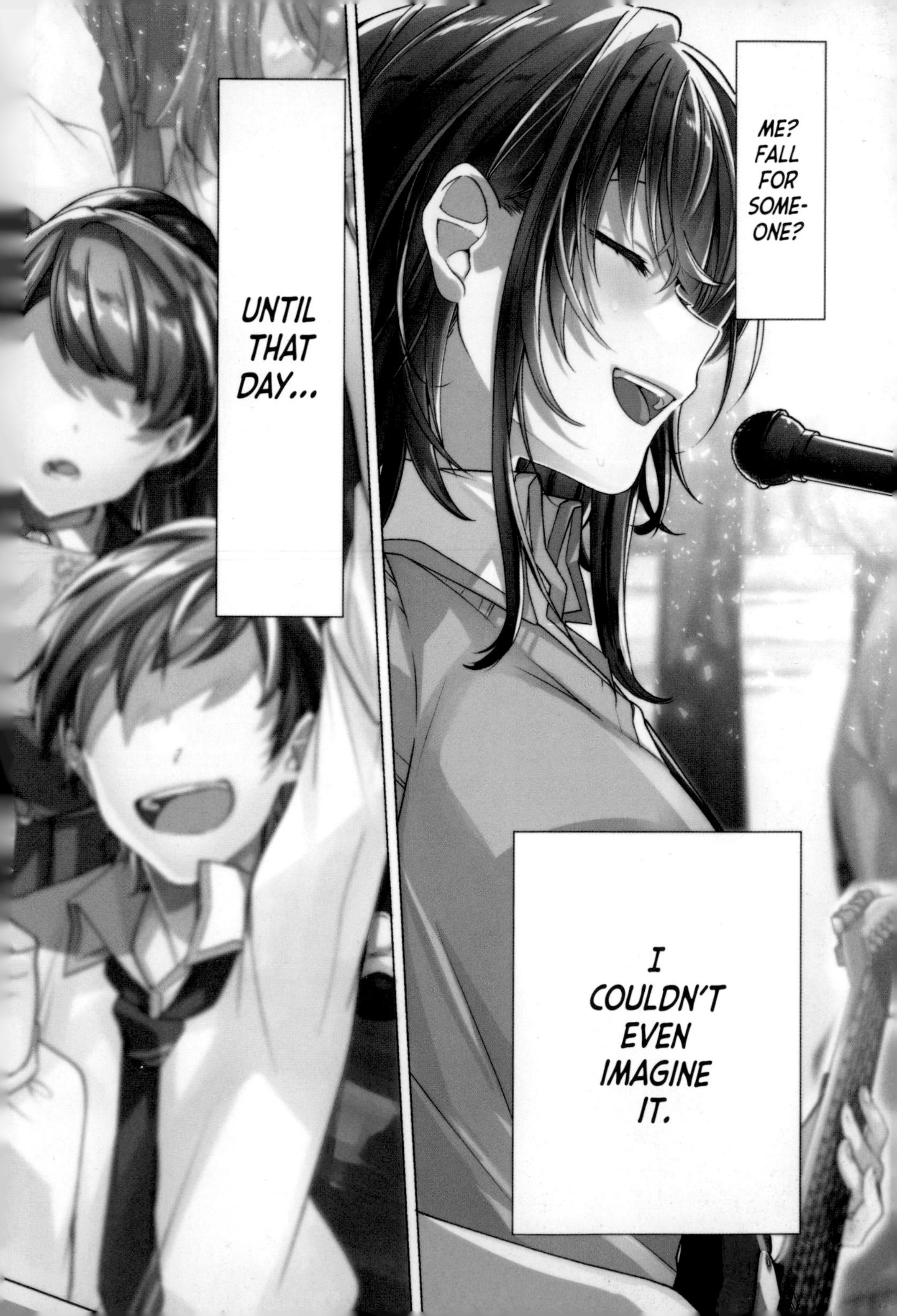
ME? FALL FOR SOME-ONE?
I COULDN'T EVEN IMAGINE IT.
UNTIL THAT DAY...

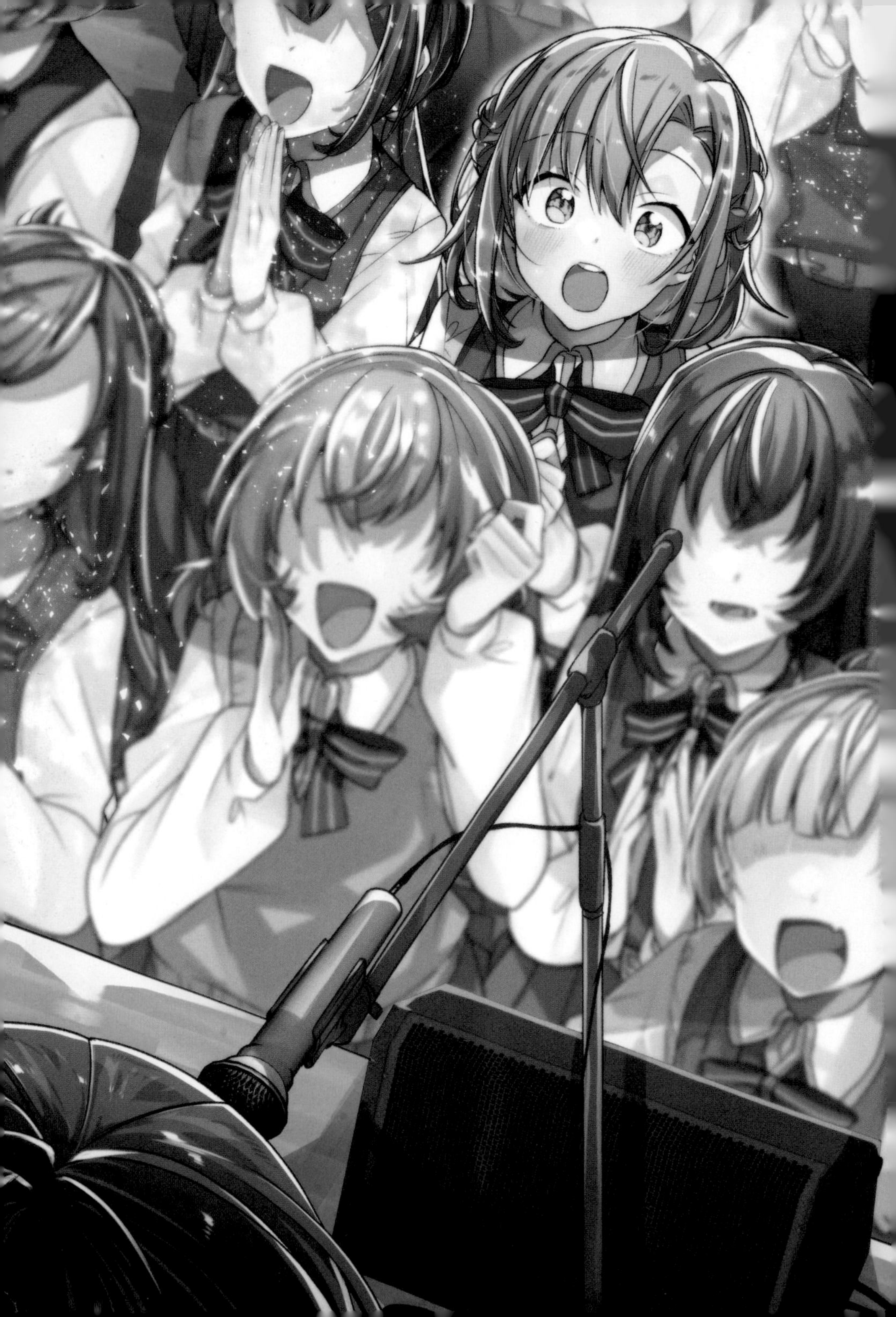

Whisper Me A Love Song

Eku Takeshima

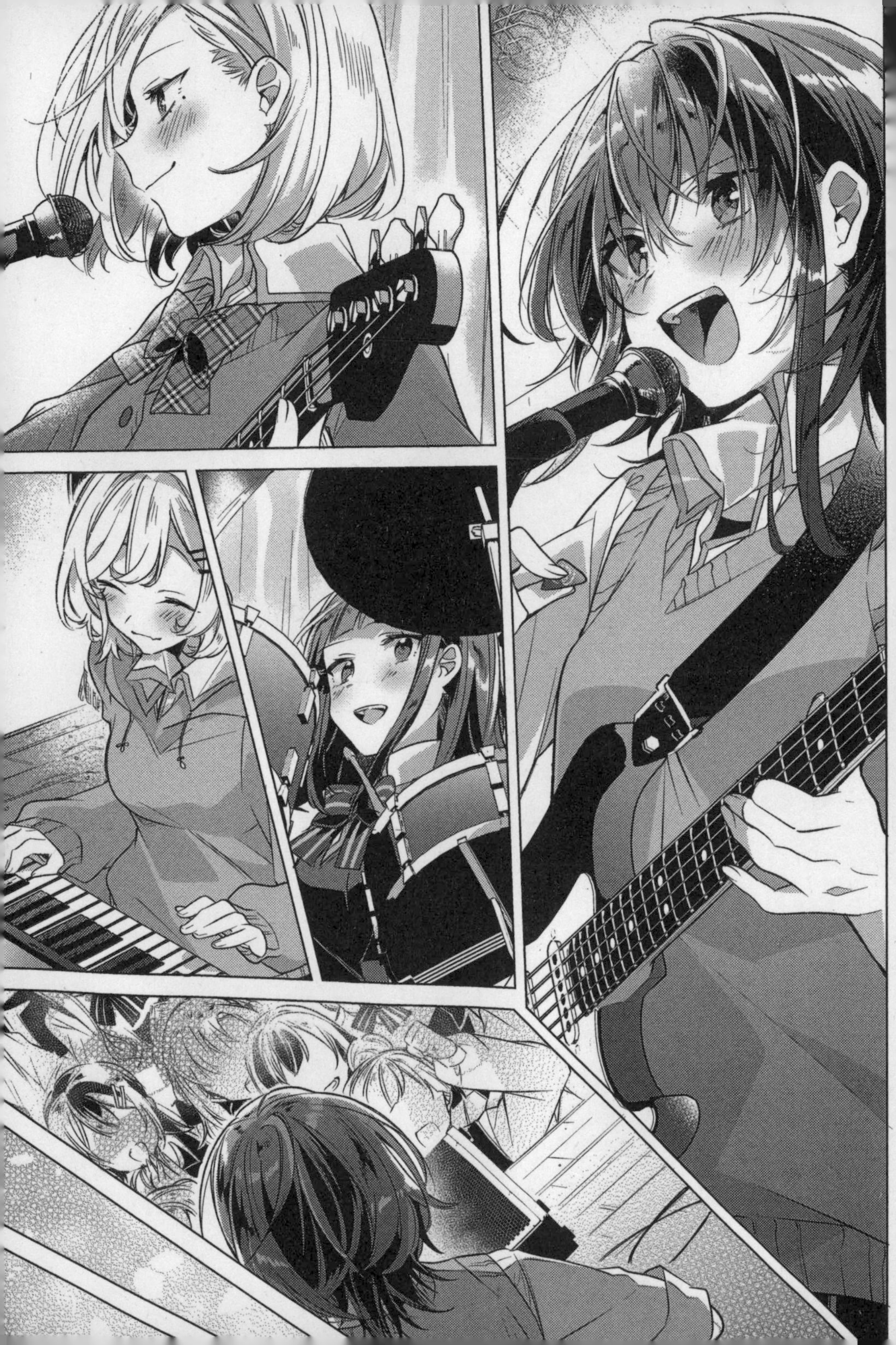

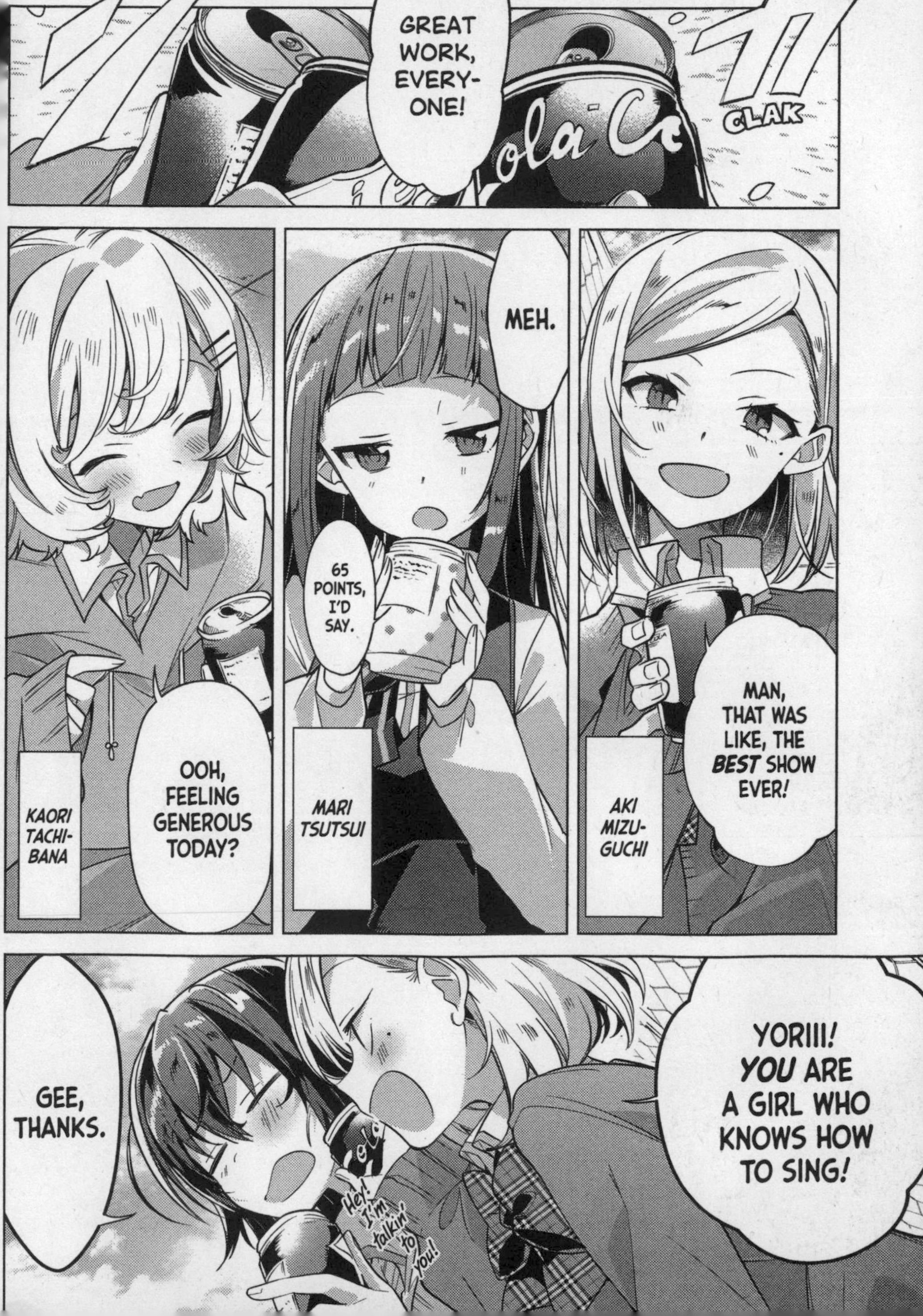
GREAT WORK, EVERYONE!
CLAK
MAN, THAT WAS LIKE, THE *BEST* SHOW EVER!
AKI MIZUGUCHI
MEH.
65 POINTS, I'D SAY.
MARI TSUTSUI
OOH, FEELING GENEROUS TODAY?
KAORI TACHIBANA
YORIII! *YOU* ARE A GIRL WHO KNOWS HOW TO SING!
Hey! I'm talkin' to you!
GEE, THANKS.

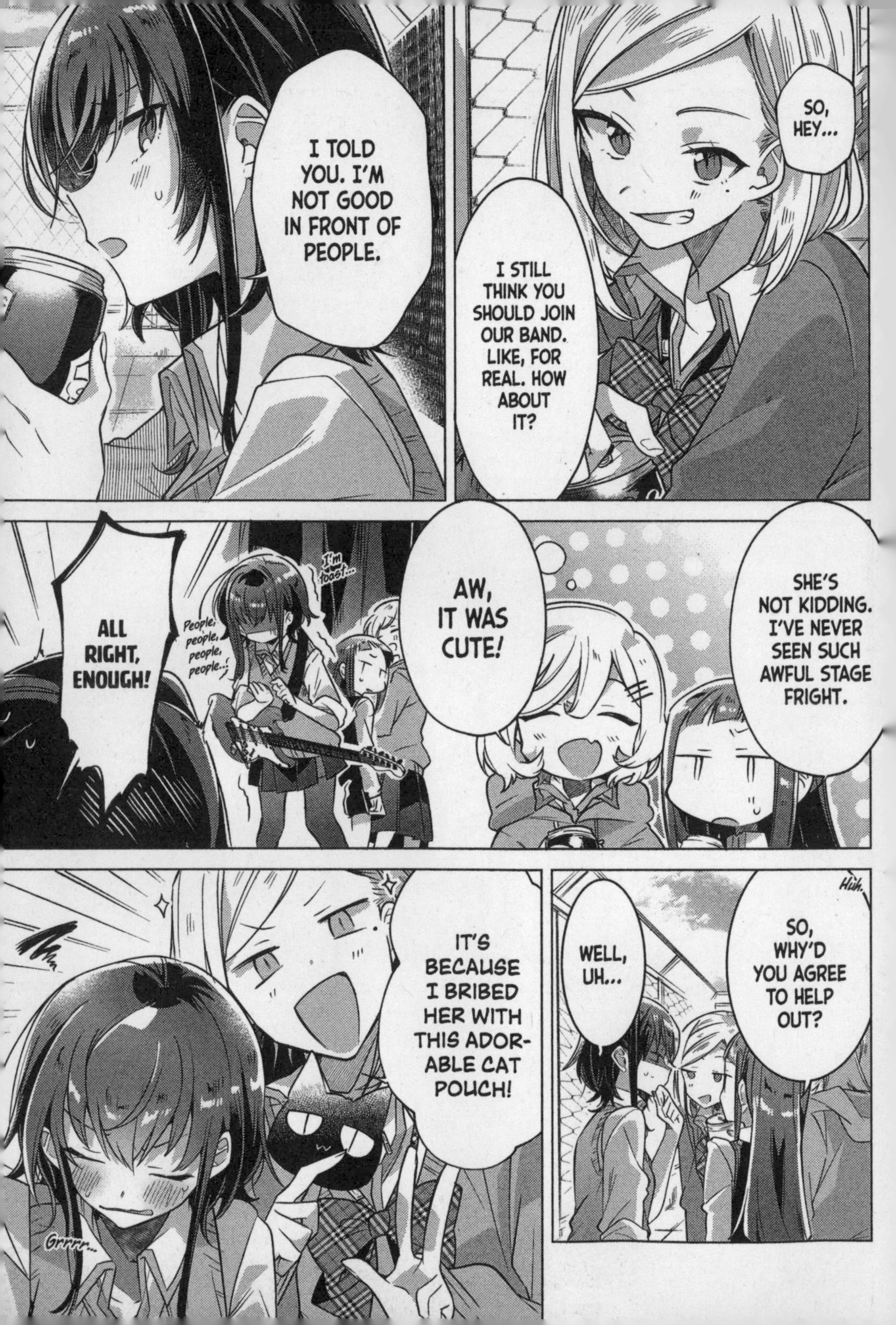

SO, HEY...
I STILL THINK YOU SHOULD JOIN OUR BAND. LIKE, FOR REAL. HOW ABOUT IT?
I TOLD YOU. I'M NOT GOOD IN FRONT OF PEOPLE.
SHE'S NOT KIDDING. I'VE NEVER SEEN SUCH AWFUL STAGE FRIGHT.
AW, IT WAS CUTE!
I'm toast...
People, people, people, people...!
ALL RIGHT, ENOUGH!
Huh.
SO, WHY'D YOU AGREE TO HELP OUT?
WELL, UH...
IT'S BECAUSE I BRIBED HER WITH THIS ADORABLE CAT POUCH!
Grrrr...

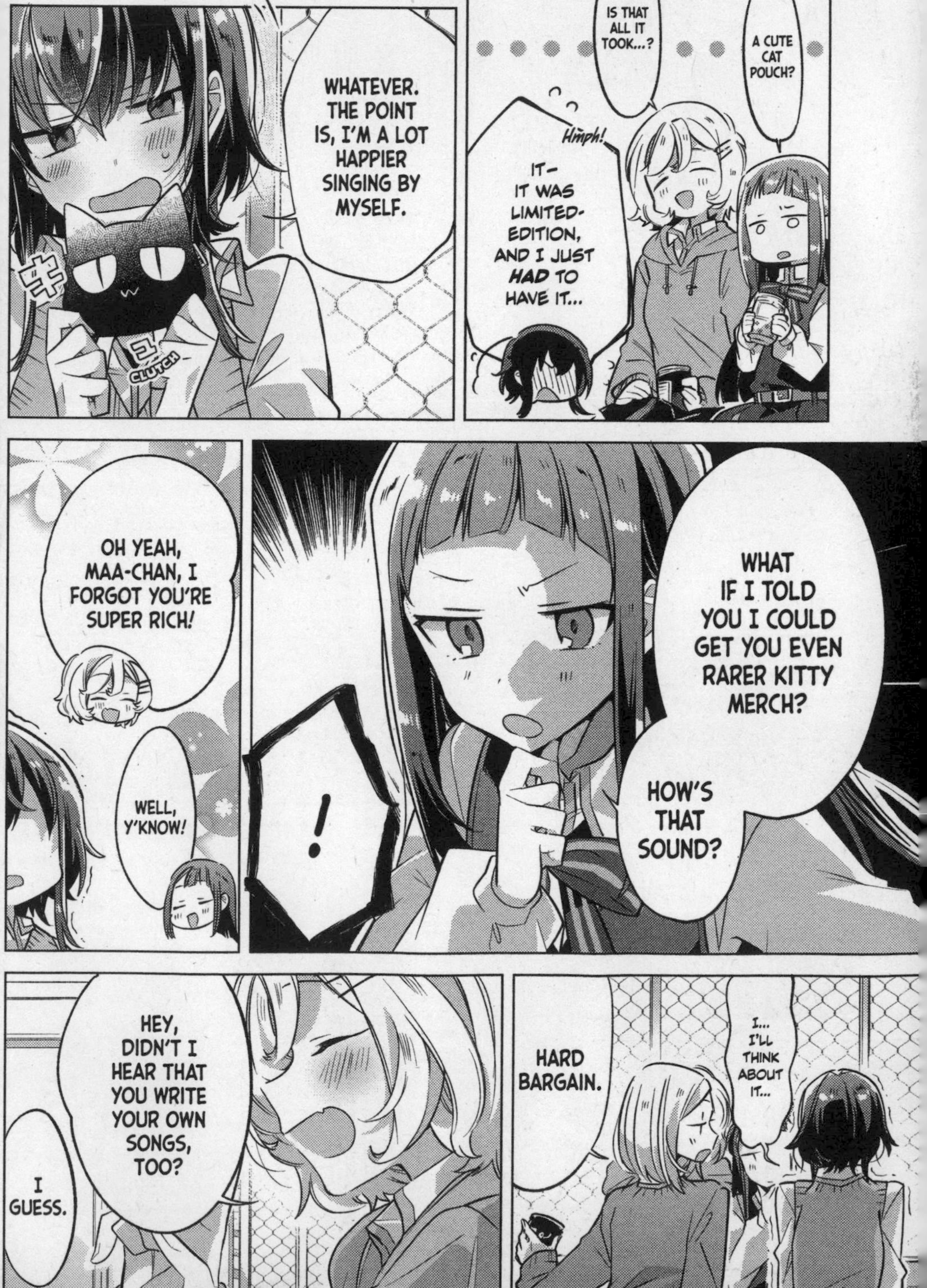
A CUTE CAT POUCH?
IS THAT ALL IT TOOK...?
Hmph!
IT— IT WAS LIMITED-EDITION, AND I JUST HAD TO HAVE IT...
WHATEVER. THE POINT IS, I'M A LOT HAPPIER SINGING BY MYSELF.
CLUTCH
WHAT IF I TOLD YOU I COULD GET YOU EVEN RARER KITTY MERCH?
HOW'S THAT SOUND?
!
OH YEAH, MAA-CHAN, I FORGOT YOU'RE SUPER RICH!
WELL, Y'KNOW!
I... I'LL THINK ABOUT IT...
HARD BARGAIN.
HEY, DIDN'T I HEAR THAT YOU WRITE YOUR OWN SONGS, TOO?
I GUESS.

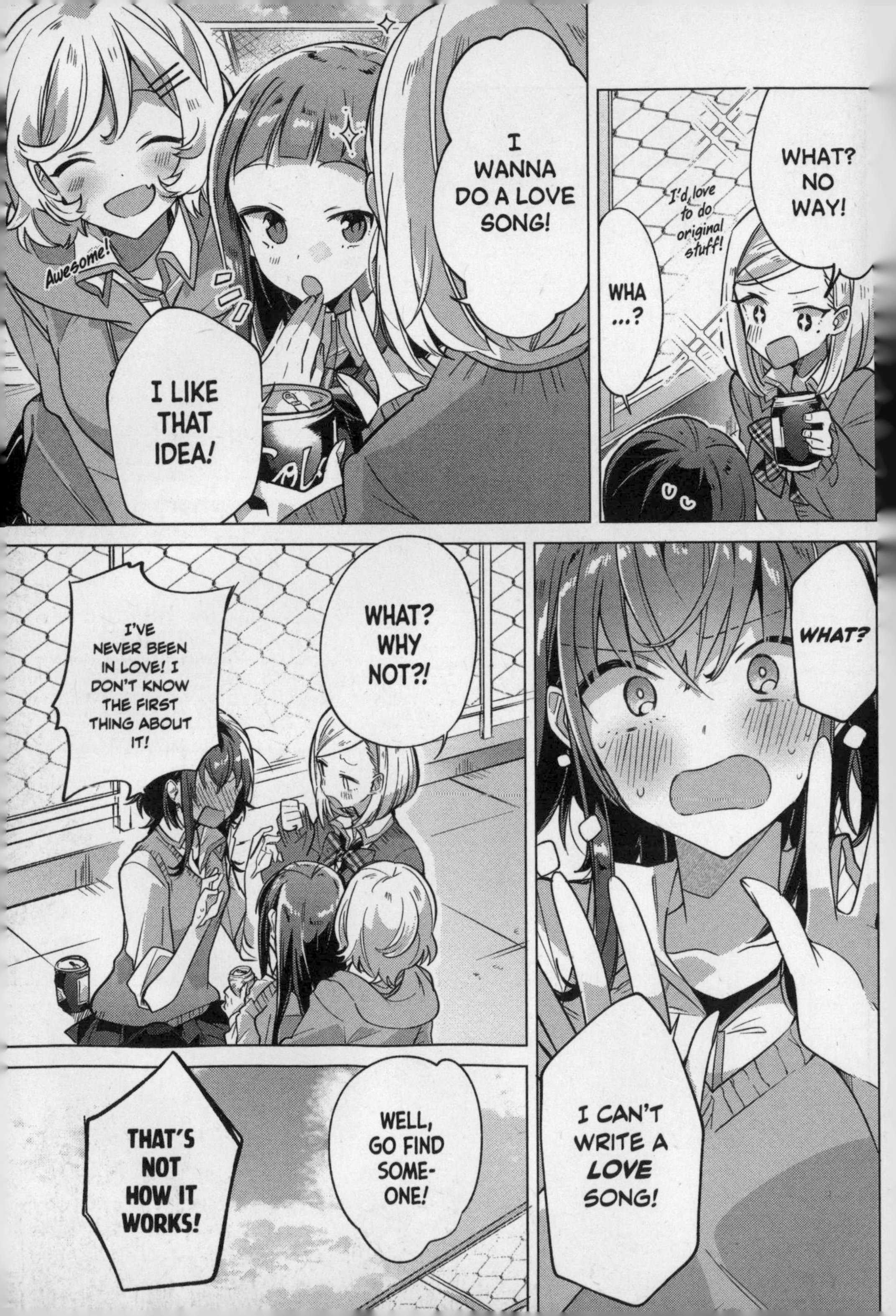
WHAT? NO WAY!
I'd love to do original stuff!
WHA ...?
I WANNA DO A LOVE SONG!
Awesome!
I LIKE THAT IDEA!
WHAT?
I CAN'T WRITE A *LOVE* SONG!
WHAT? WHY NOT?!
I'VE NEVER BEEN IN LOVE! I DON'T KNOW THE FIRST THING ABOUT IT!
WELL, GO FIND SOME-ONE!
THAT'S NOT HOW IT WORKS!

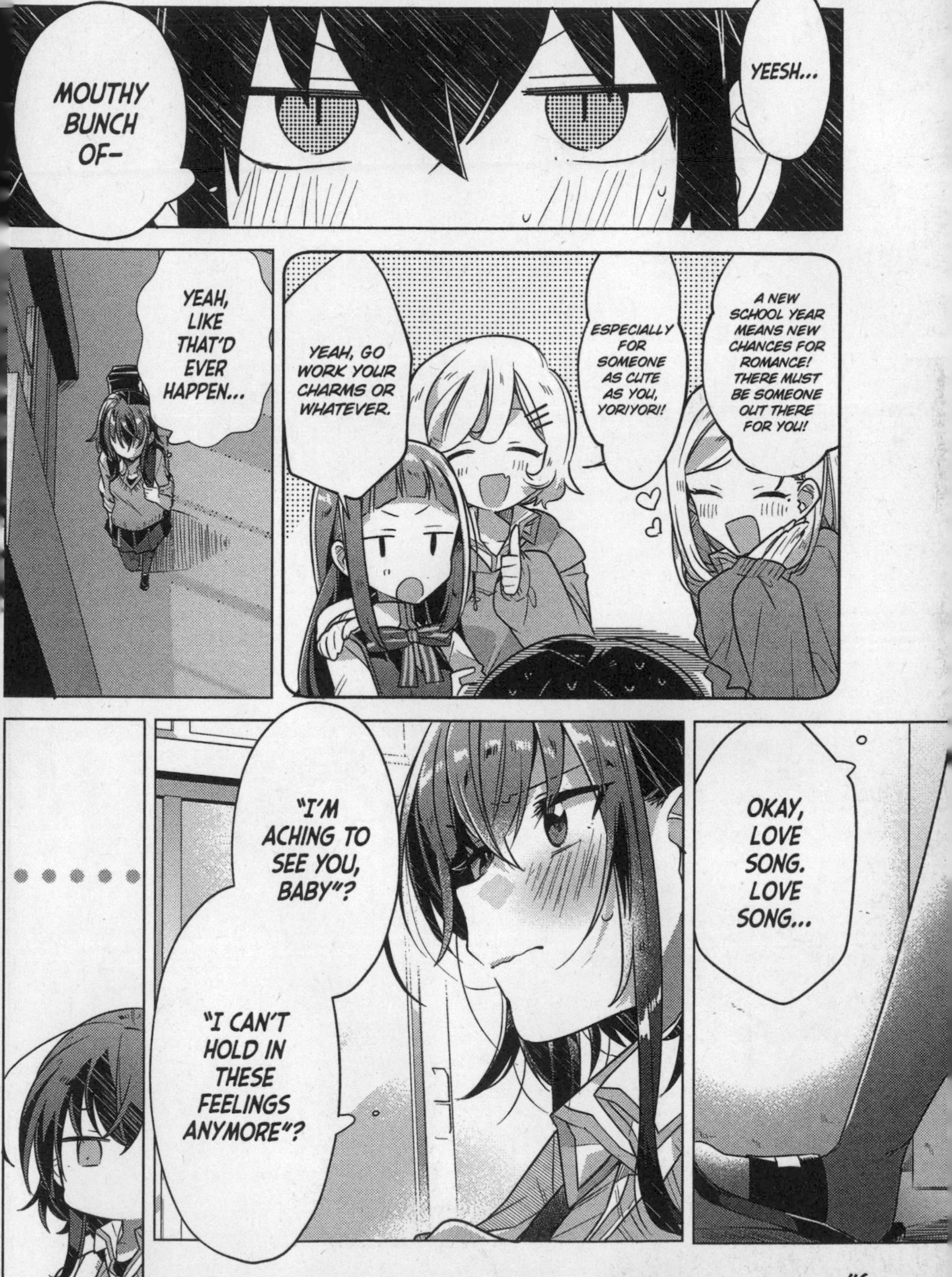
YEESH...
MOUTHY BUNCH OF–
A NEW SCHOOL YEAR MEANS NEW CHANCES FOR ROMANCE! THERE MUST BE SOMEONE OUT THERE FOR YOU!
ESPECIALLY FOR SOMEONE AS CUTE AS YOU, YORIYORI!
YEAH, GO WORK YOUR CHARMS OR WHATEVER.
YEAH, LIKE THAT'D EVER HAPPEN...
OKAY, LOVE SONG. LOVE SONG...
"I'M ACHING TO SEE YOU, BABY"?
"I CAN'T HOLD IN THESE FEELINGS ANYMORE"?
• • • • •

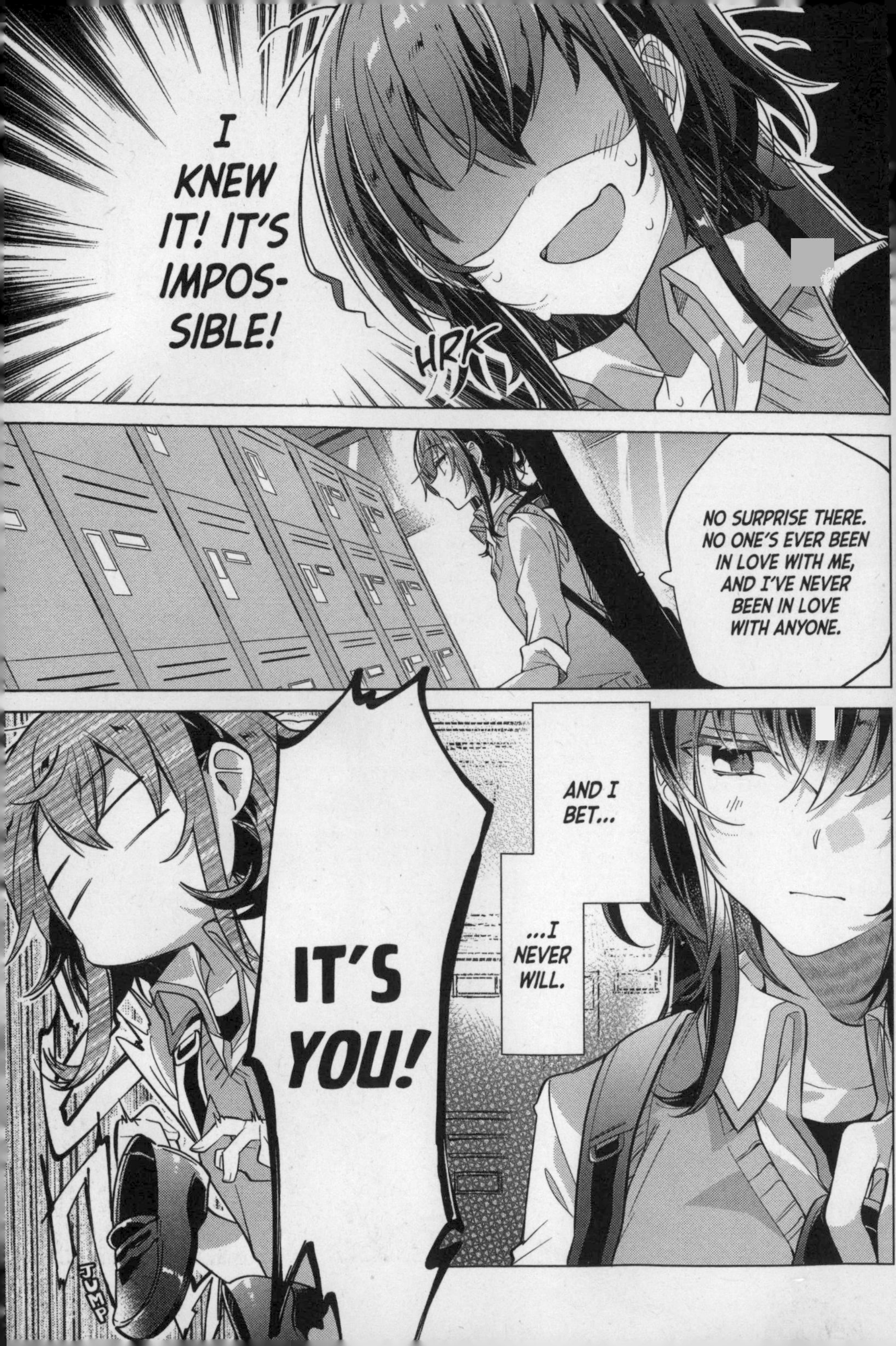
I KNEW IT! IT'S IMPOS-SIBLE!
HRK
NO SURPRISE THERE. NO ONE'S EVER BEEN IN LOVE WITH ME, AND I'VE NEVER BEEN IN LOVE WITH ANYONE.
AND I BET...
...I NEVER WILL.
IT'S YOU!
JUMP

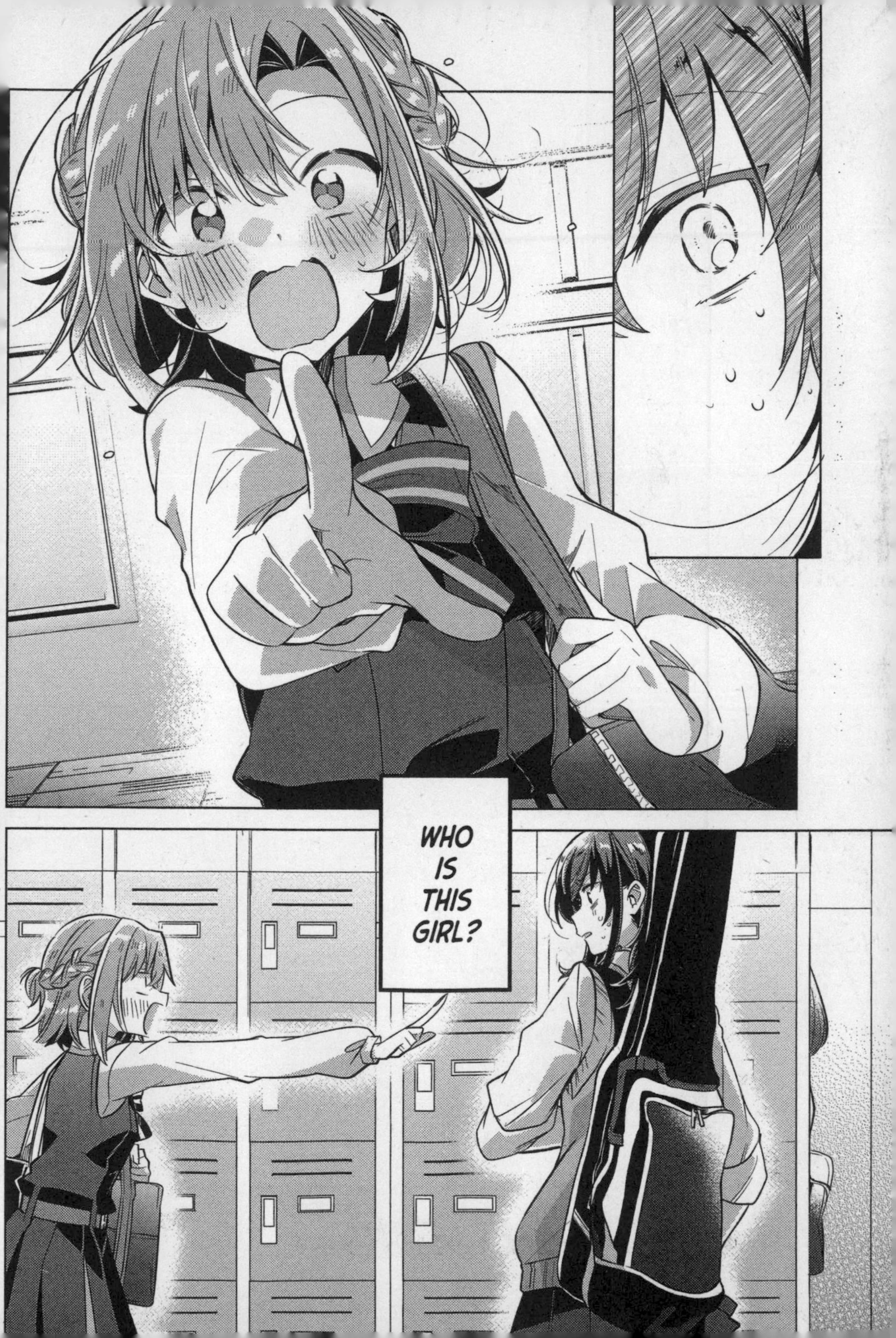
WHO IS THIS GIRL?

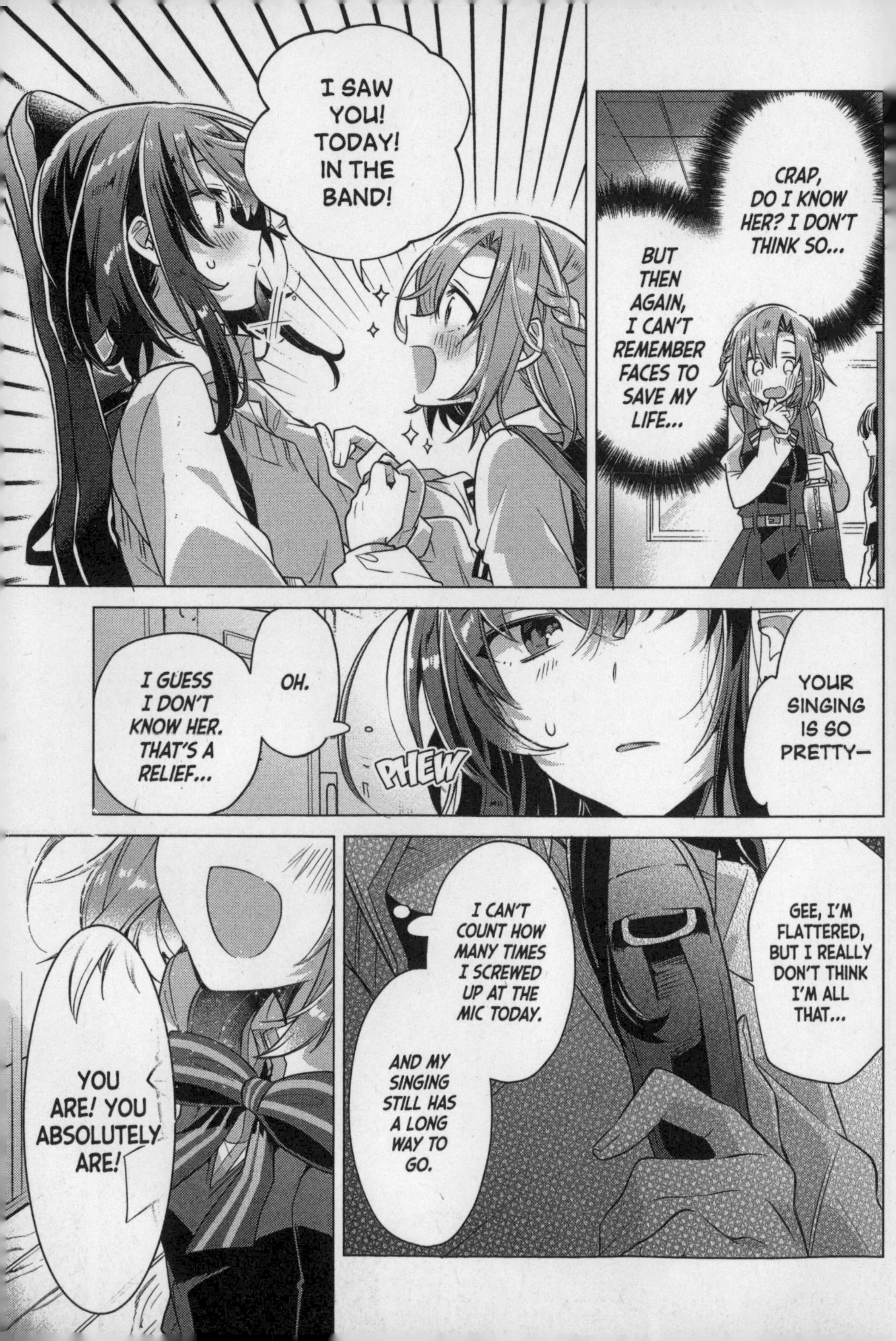
CRAP, DO I KNOW HER? I DON'T THINK SO...
BUT THEN AGAIN, I CAN'T REMEMBER FACES TO SAVE MY LIFE...
I SAW YOU! TODAY! IN THE BAND!
YOUR SINGING IS SO PRETTY—
OH.
PHEW
I GUESS I DON'T KNOW HER. THAT'S A RELIEF...
GEE, I'M FLATTERED, BUT I REALLY DON'T THINK I'M ALL THAT...
I CAN'T COUNT HOW MANY TIMES I SCREWED UP AT THE MIC TODAY.
AND MY SINGING STILL HAS A LONG WAY TO GO.
YOU ARE! YOU ABSOLUTELY ARE!

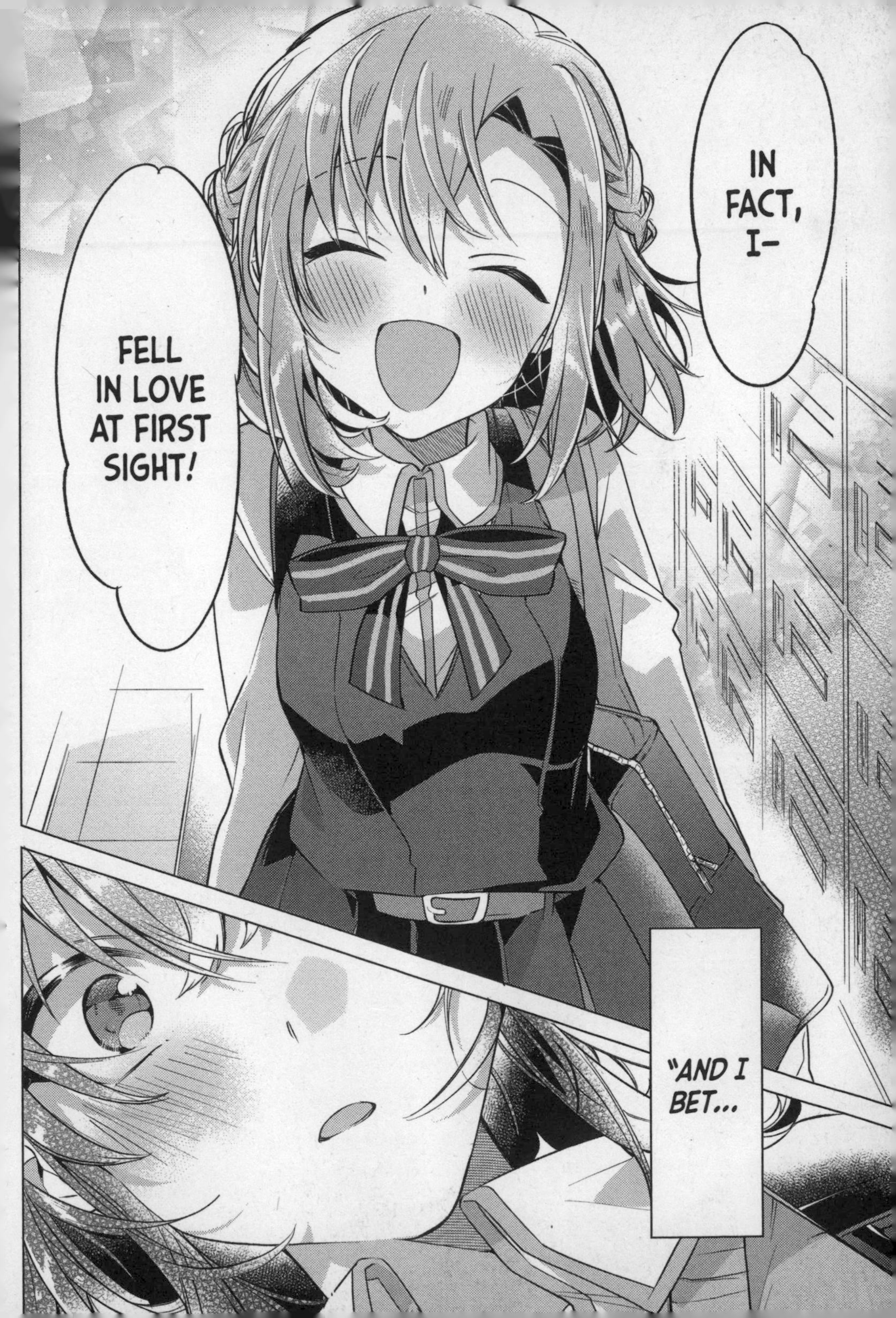
IN FACT, I-
FELL IN LOVE AT FIRST SIGHT!
"AND I BET...

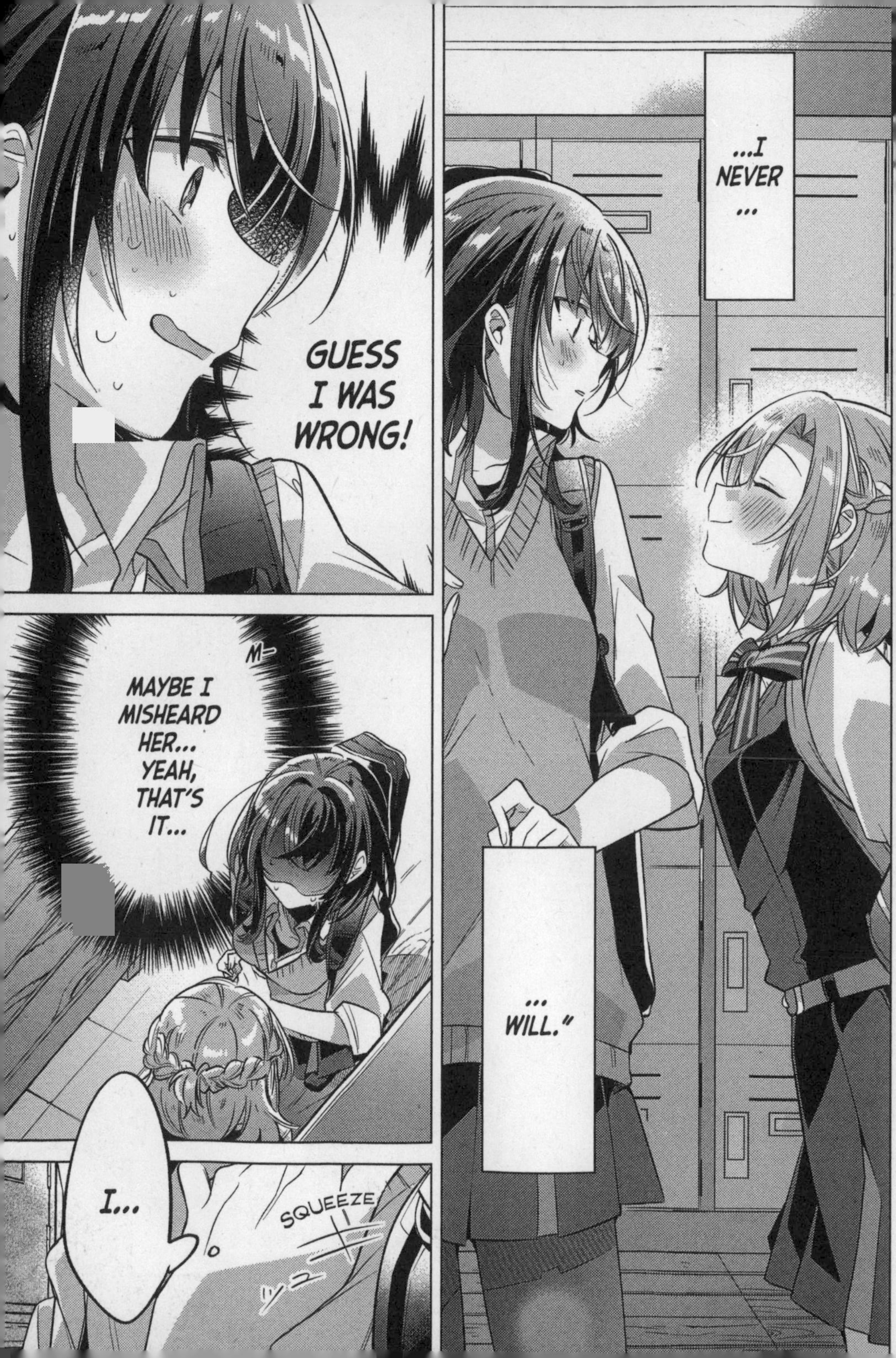
...I NEVER ...
... WILL."
GUESS I WAS WRONG!
M—
MAYBE I MISHEARD HER... YEAH, THAT'S IT...
I...
SQUEEZE

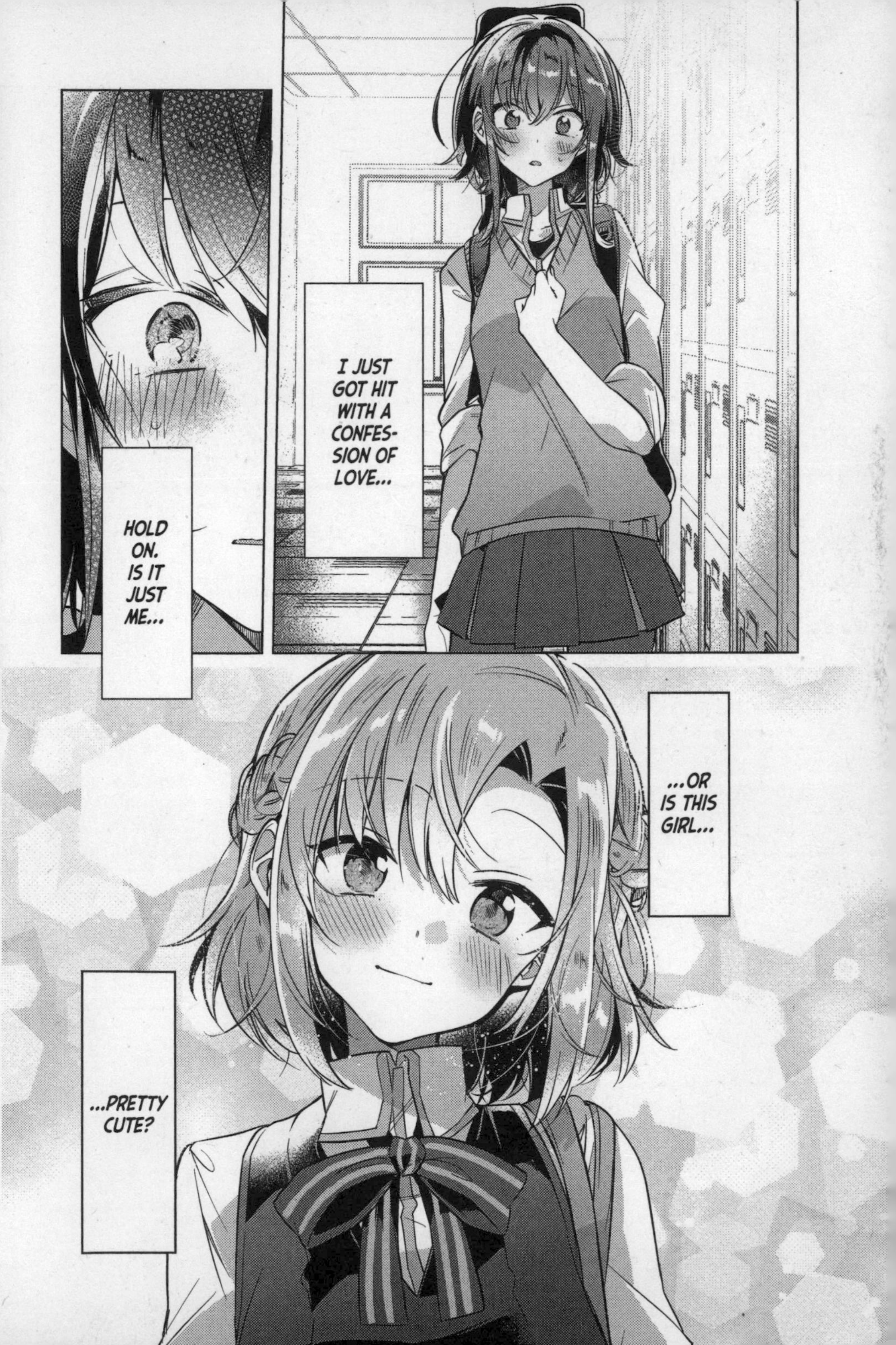
I JUST GOT HIT WITH A CONFESSION OF LOVE...
HOLD ON. IS IT JUST ME...
...OR IS THIS GIRL...
...PRETTY CUTE?

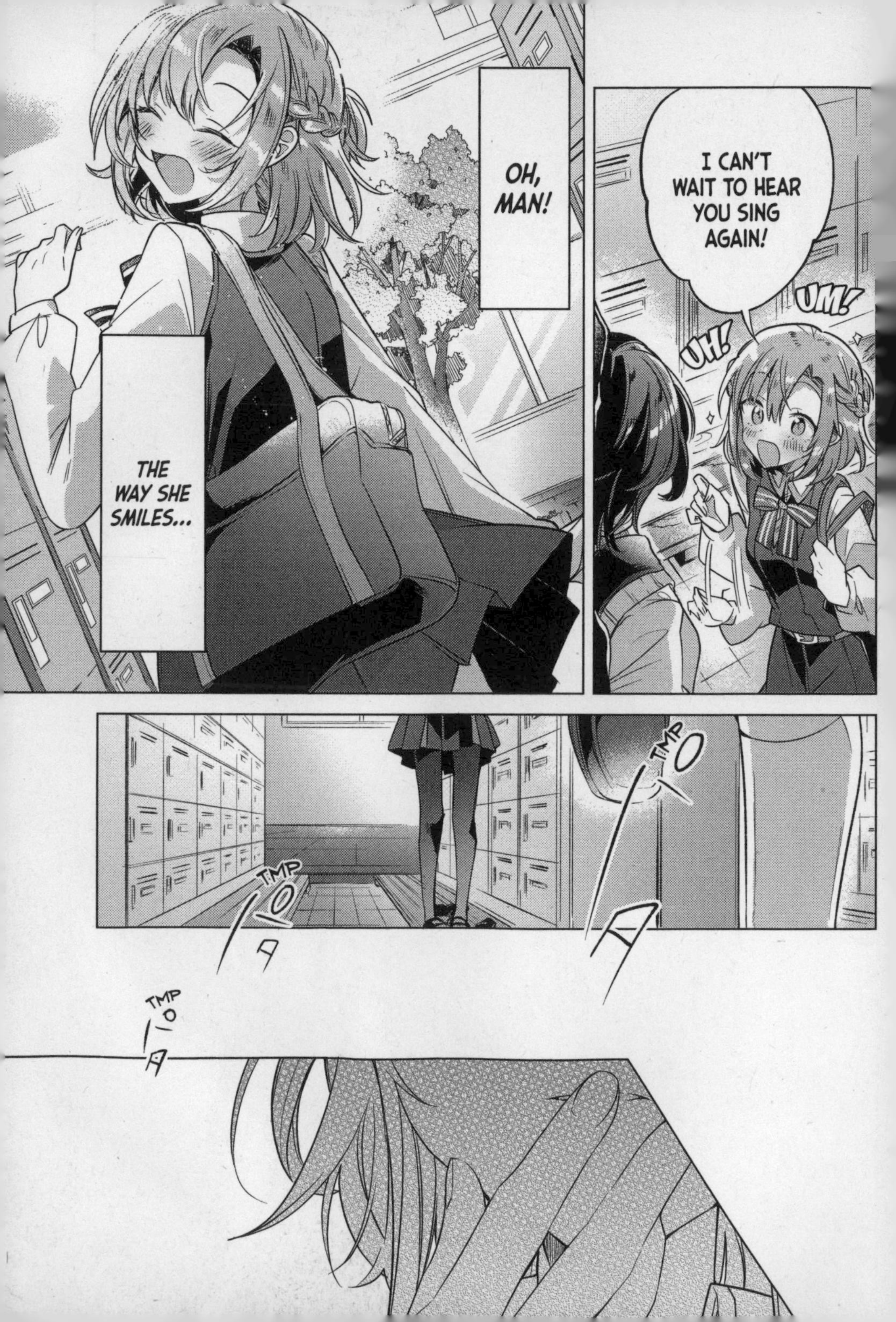
I CAN'T WAIT TO HEAR YOU SING AGAIN!
UH! UM!
OH, MAN!
THE WAY SHE SMILES...
TMP
TMP
TMP

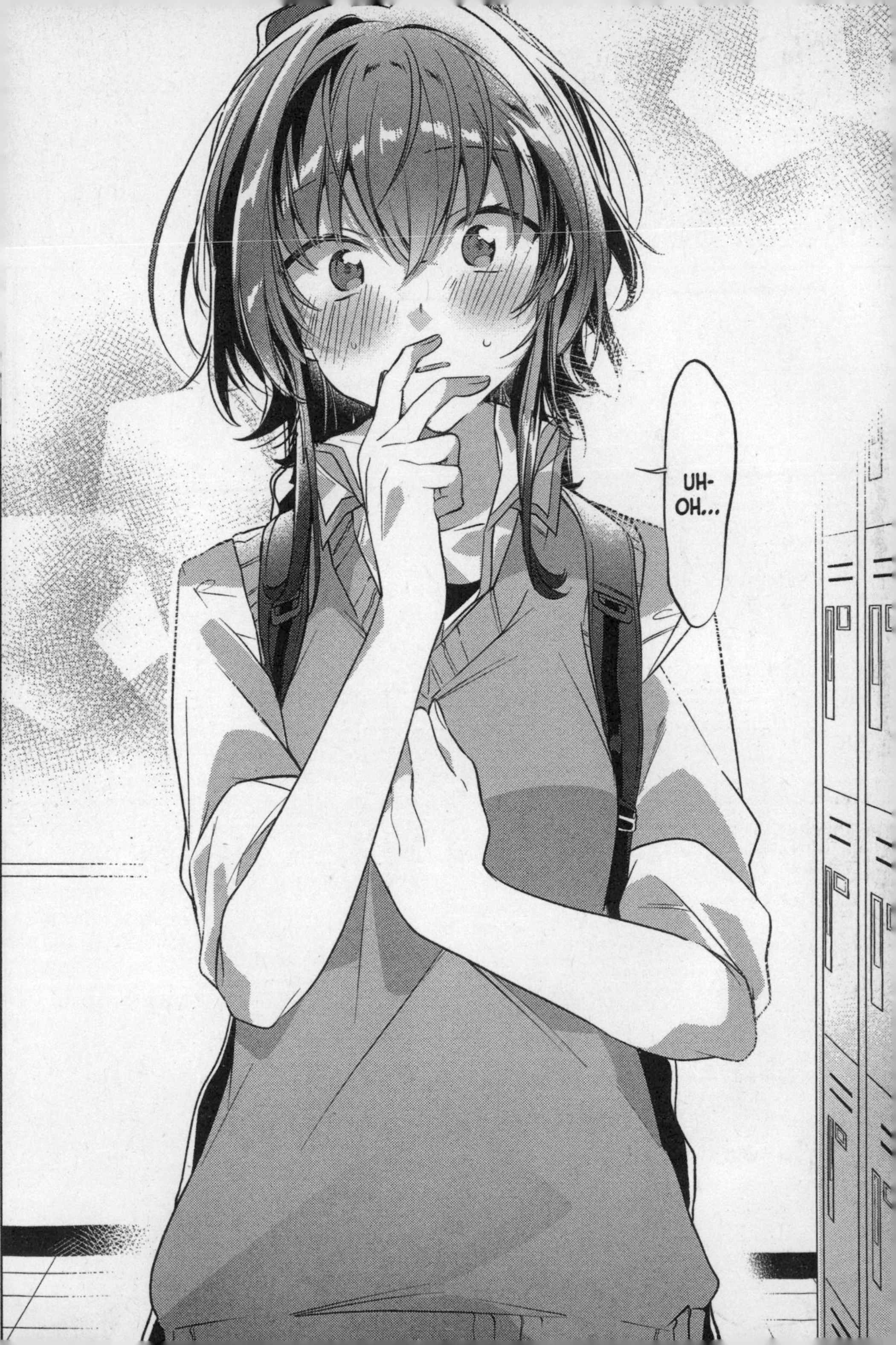
UH-
OH...

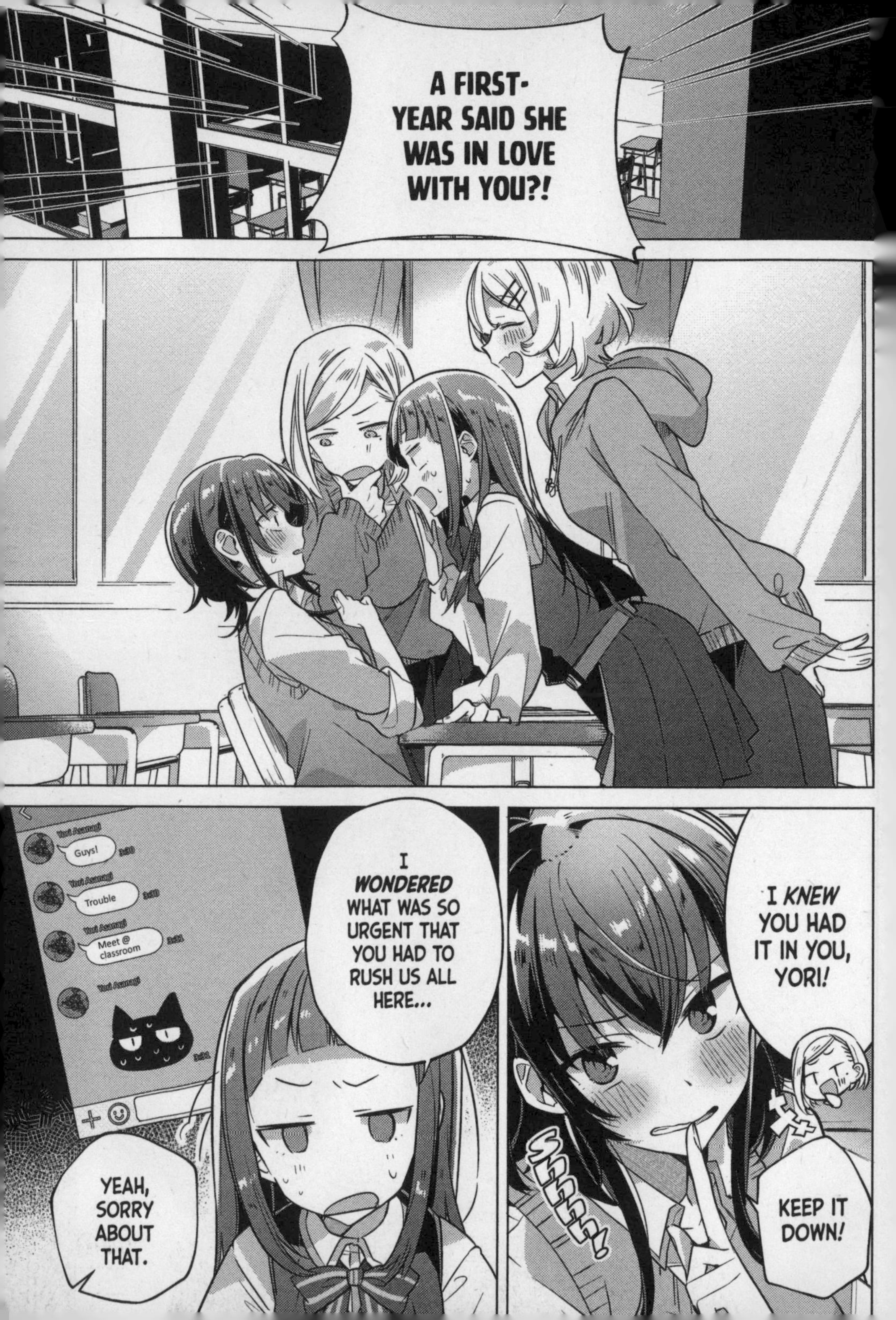
A FIRST-YEAR SAID SHE WAS IN LOVE WITH YOU?!
I *KNEW* YOU HAD IT IN YOU, YORI!
KEEP IT DOWN!
Yori Asanagi
Guys!
Yori Asanagi
Trouble
Yori Asanagi
Meet @ classroom
Yori Asanagi
I *WONDERED* WHAT WAS SO URGENT THAT YOU HAD TO RUSH US ALL HERE...
YEAH, SORRY ABOUT THAT.

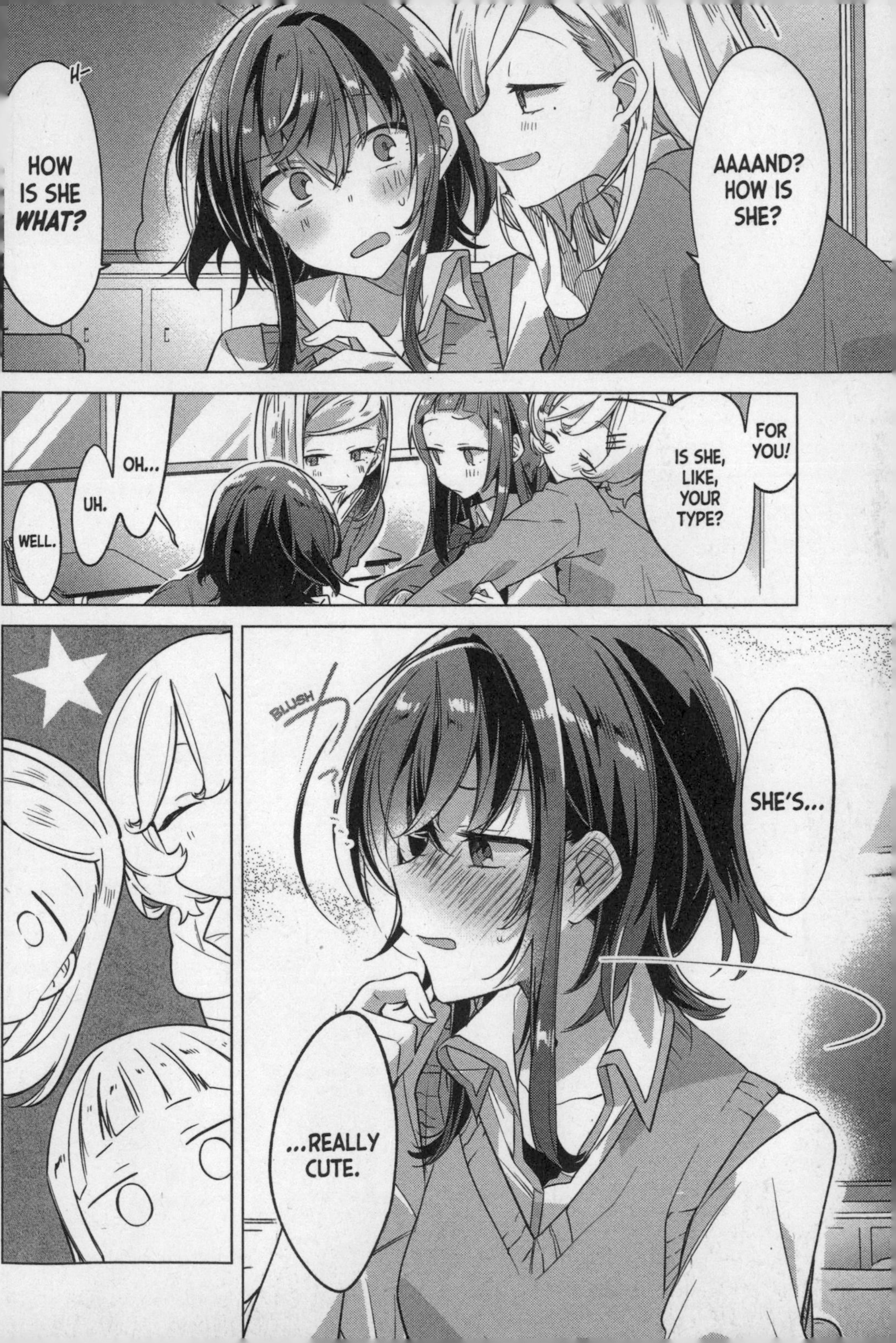
AAAAND? HOW IS SHE?
H–
HOW IS SHE *WHAT?*
IS SHE, LIKE, YOUR TYPE?
FOR YOU!
OH...
UH.
WELL.
BLUSH
SHE'S...
...REALLY CUTE.

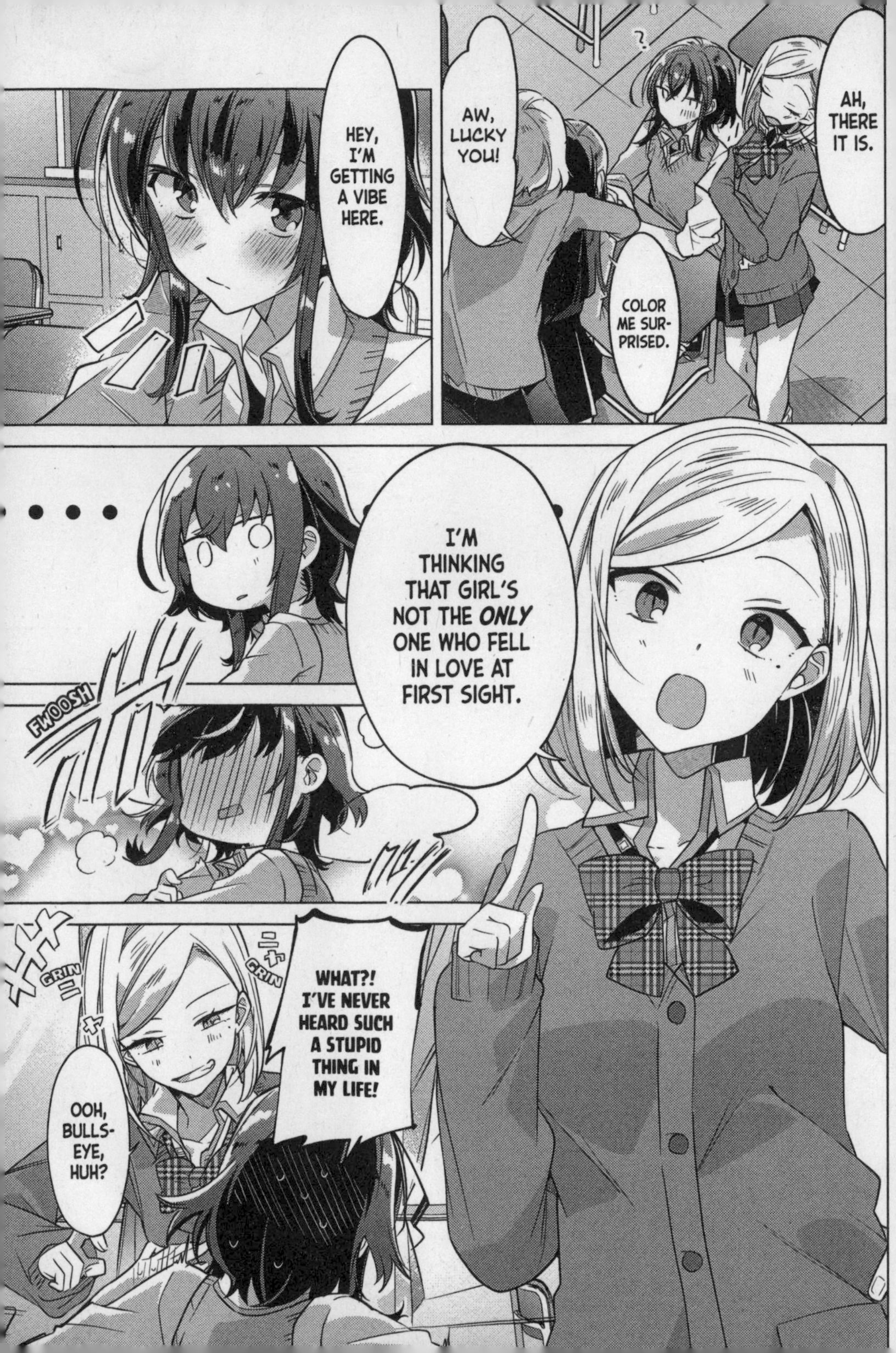
AH, THERE IT IS.
?
AW, LUCKY YOU!
COLOR ME SURPRISED.
HEY, I'M GETTING A VIBE HERE.
I'M THINKING THAT GIRL'S NOT THE *ONLY* ONE WHO FELL IN LOVE AT FIRST SIGHT.
• • •
FWOOSH
WHAT?! I'VE NEVER HEARD SUCH A STUPID THING IN MY LIFE!
GRIN
GRIN
OOH, BULLS-EYE, HUH?

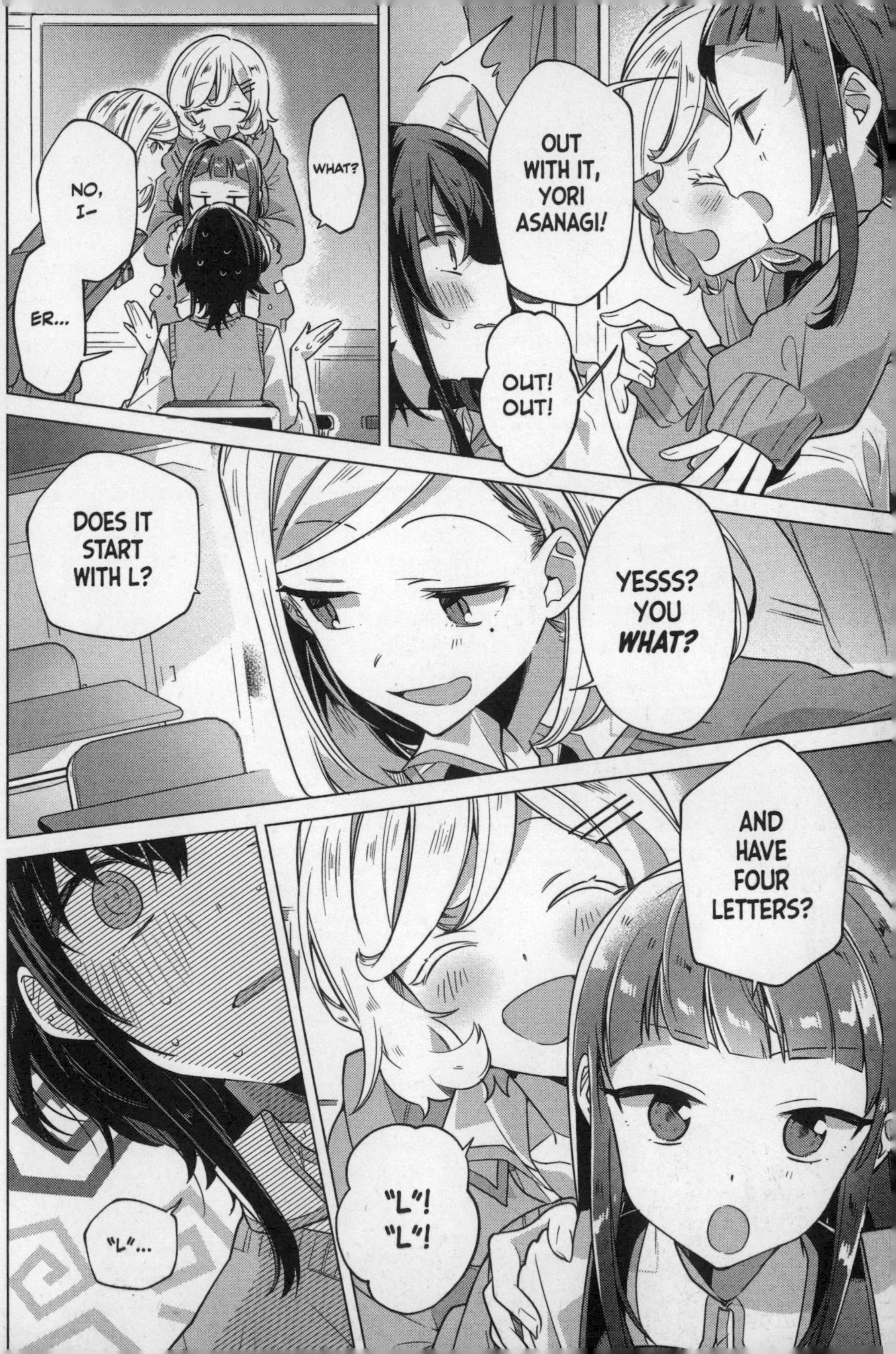
OUT WITH IT, YORI ASANAGI!
OUT! OUT!
WHAT?
NO, I—
ER...
YESSS? YOU *WHAT?*
DOES IT START WITH L?
AND HAVE FOUR LETTERS?
"L"! "L"!
"L"...

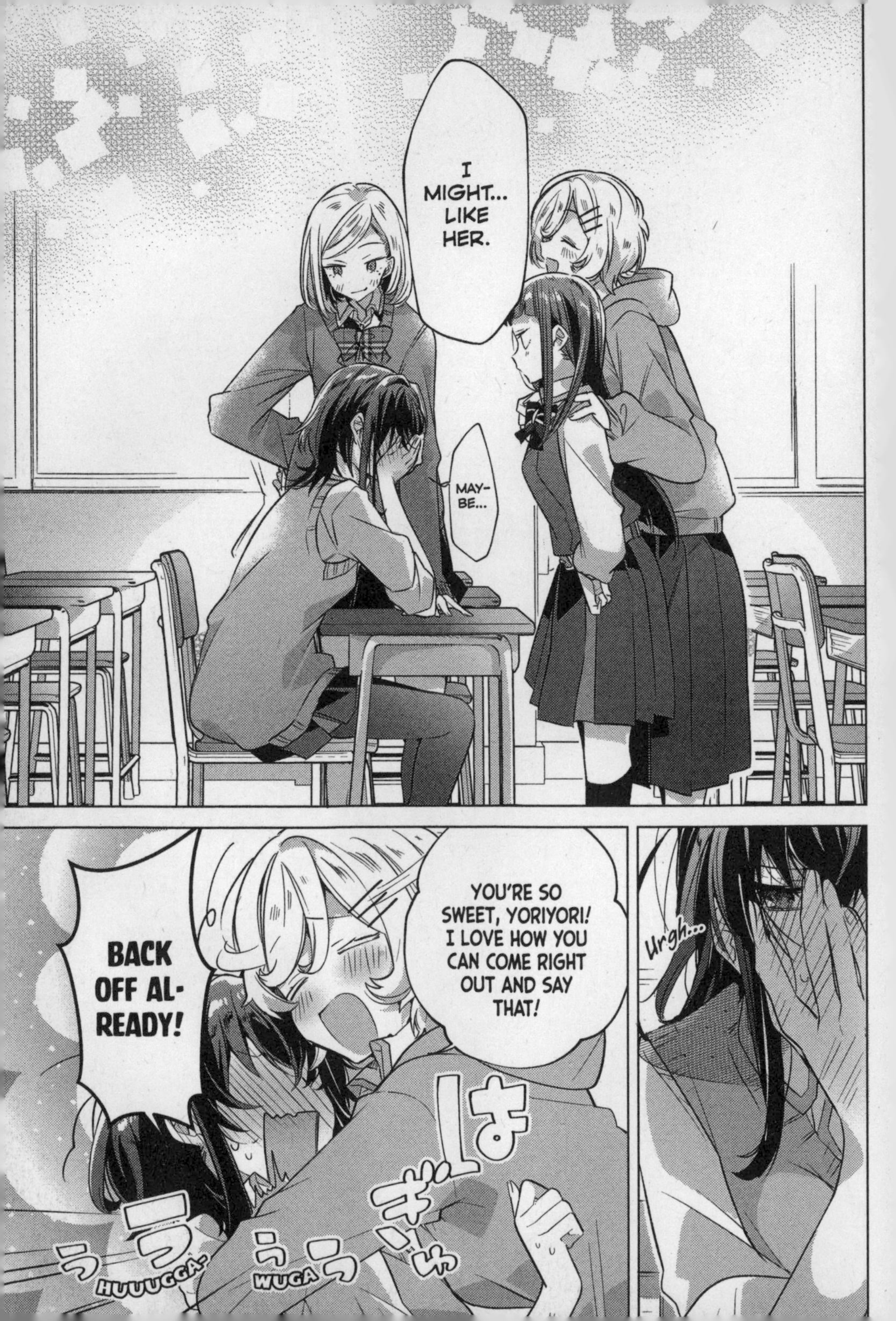
I MIGHT... LIKE HER.
MAY-BE...
Urgh...
YOU'RE SO SWEET, YORIYORI! I LOVE HOW YOU CAN COME RIGHT OUT AND SAY THAT!
BACK OFF AL-READY!
HUUUGGA-
WUGA

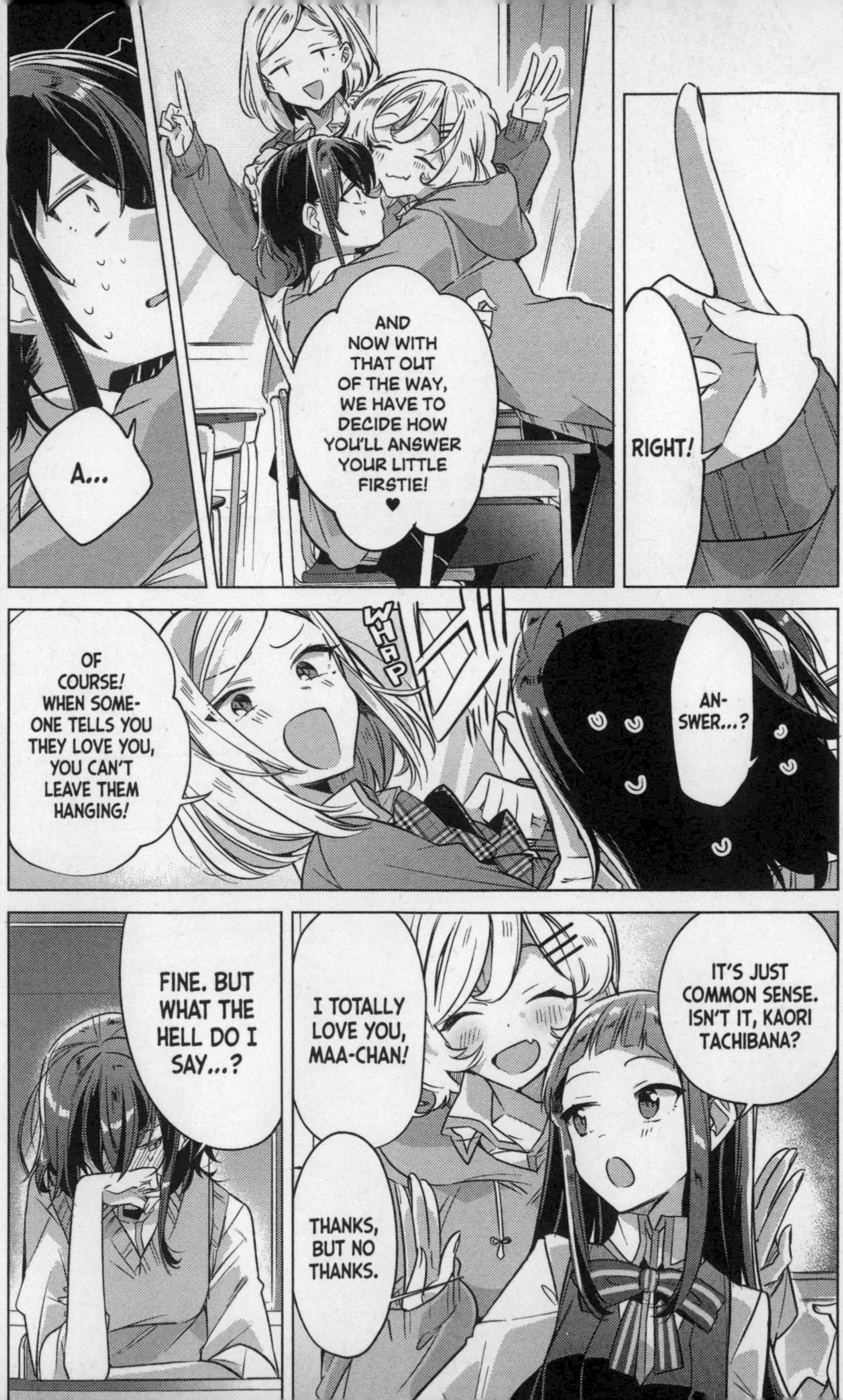
RIGHT!
AND NOW WITH THAT OUT OF THE WAY, WE HAVE TO DECIDE HOW YOU'LL ANSWER YOUR LITTLE FIRSTIE! ♥
A...
AN-SWER...?
WHAP
OF COURSE! WHEN SOME-ONE TELLS YOU THEY LOVE YOU, YOU CAN'T LEAVE THEM HANGING!
IT'S JUST COMMON SENSE. ISN'T IT, KAORI TACHIBANA?
I TOTALLY LOVE YOU, MAA-CHAN!
THANKS, BUT NO THANKS.
FINE. BUT WHAT THE HELL DO I SAY...?

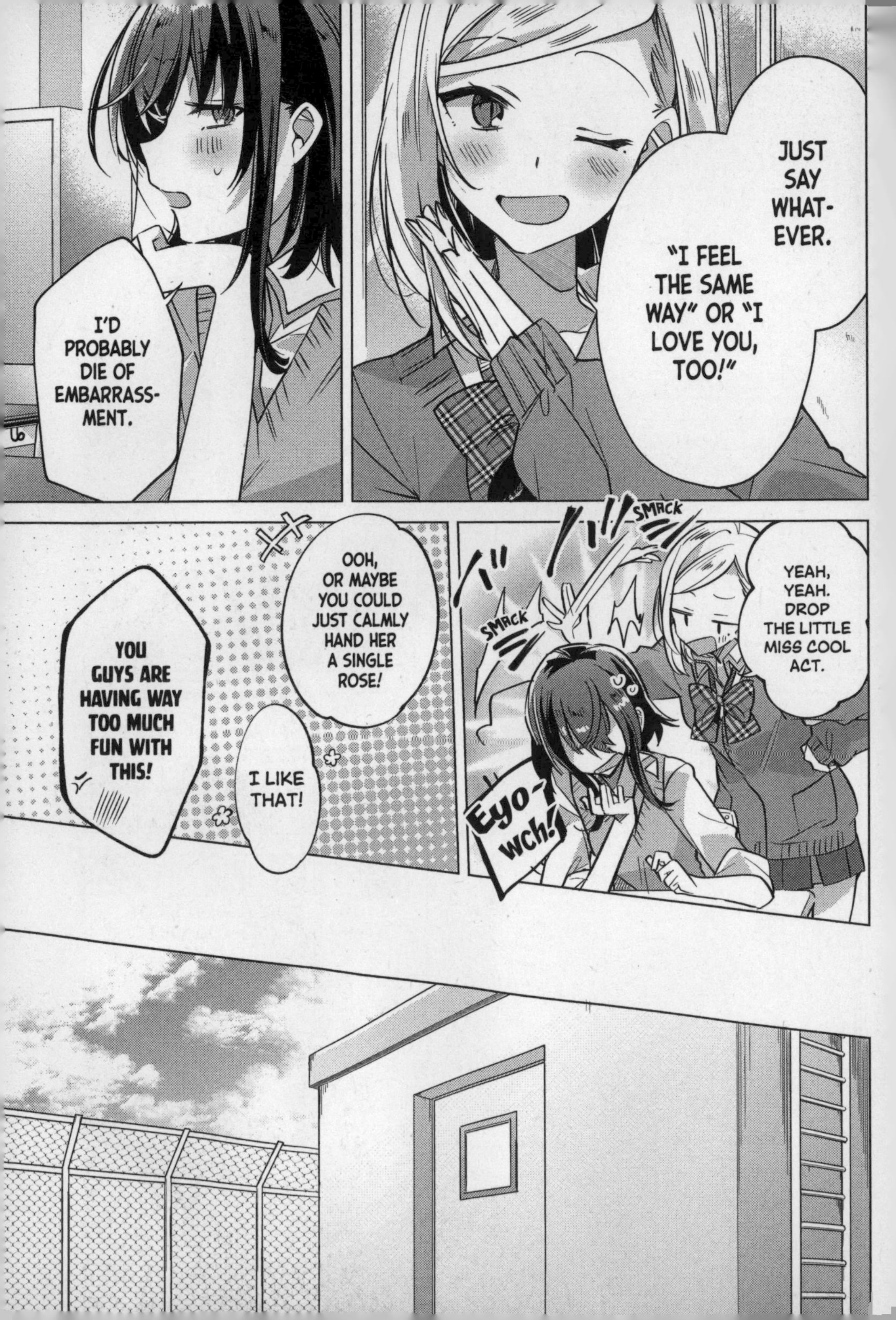
JUST SAY WHAT-EVER.
“I FEEL THE SAME WAY” OR “I LOVE YOU, TOO!”
I'D PROBABLY DIE OF EMBARRASS-MENT.
SMACK
YEAH, YEAH. DROP THE LITTLE MISS COOL ACT.
SMACK
Eyo-wch!
OOH, OR MAYBE YOU COULD JUST CALMLY HAND HER A SINGLE ROSE!
I LIKE THAT!
YOU GUYS ARE HAVING WAY TOO MUCH FUN WITH THIS!

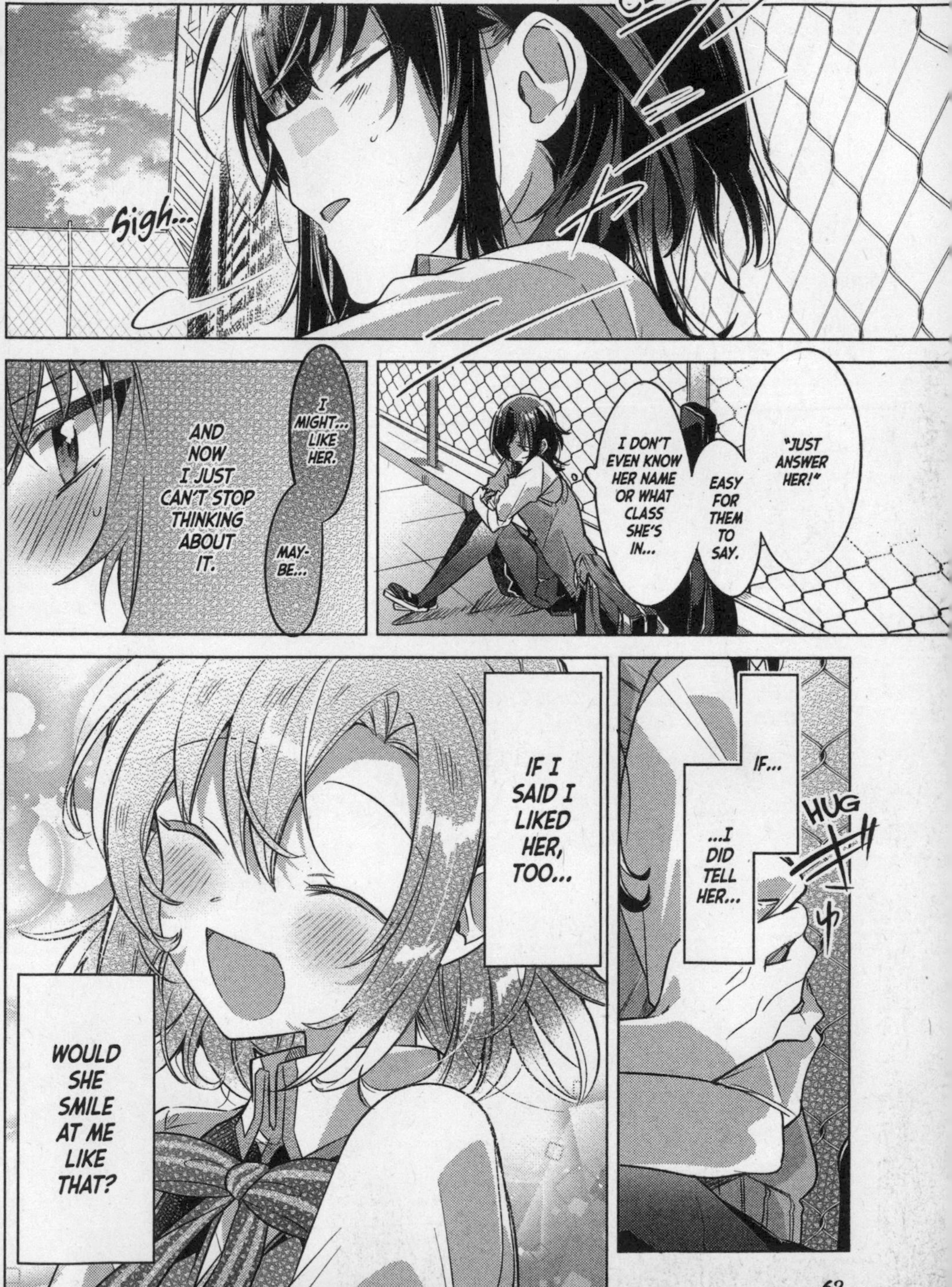
CLANK
Sigh...
"JUST ANSWER HER!"
EASY FOR THEM TO SAY.
I DON'T EVEN KNOW HER NAME OR WHAT CLASS SHE'S IN...
I MIGHT... LIKE HER.
MAY-BE...
AND NOW I JUST CAN'T STOP THINKING ABOUT IT.
IF...
...I DID TELL HER...
HUG
IF I SAID I LIKED HER, TOO...
WOULD SHE SMILE AT ME LIKE THAT?

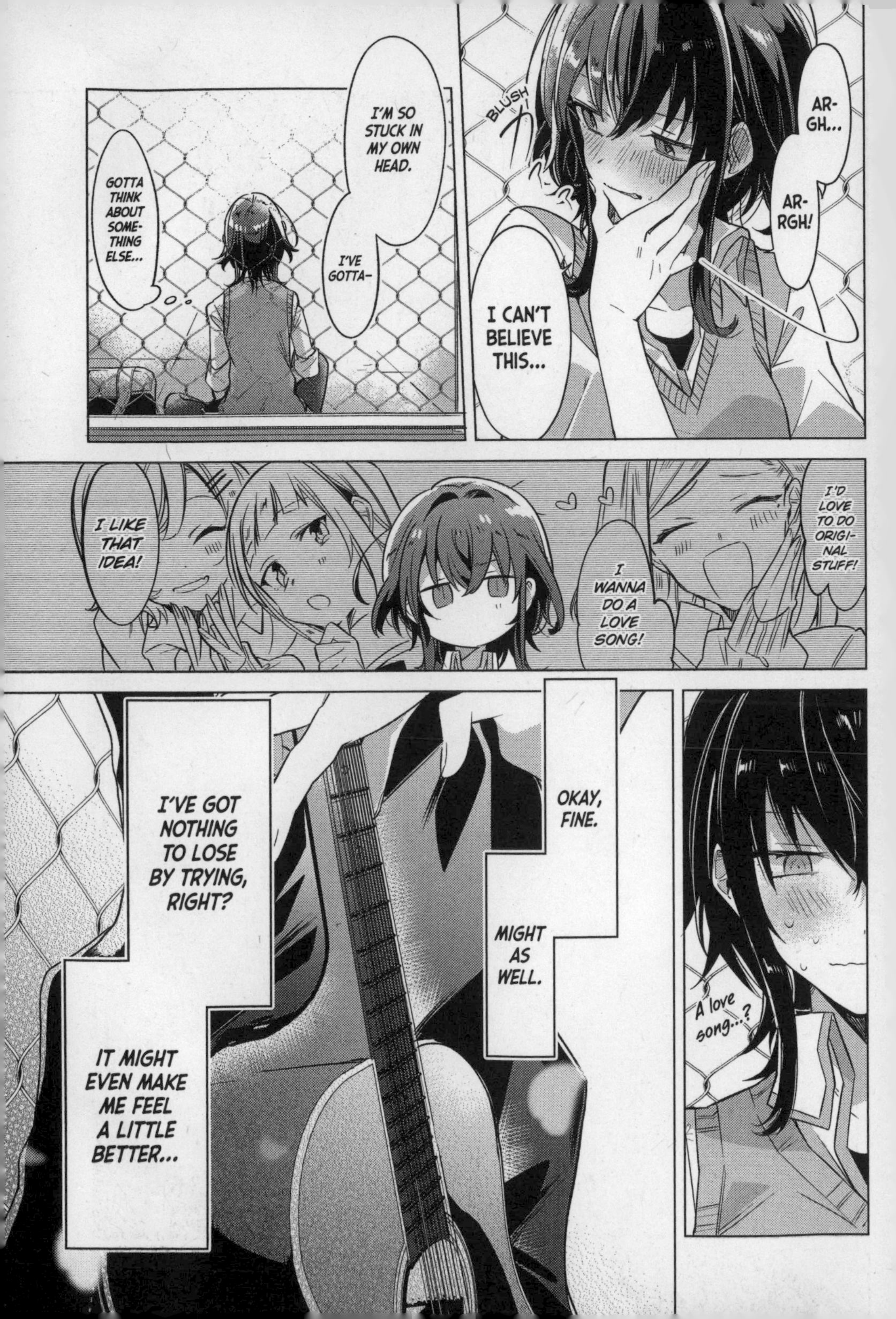
AR-GH...
AR-RGH!
BLUSH
I CAN'T BELIEVE THIS...
I'M SO STUCK IN MY OWN HEAD.
I'VE GOTTA-
GOTTA THINK ABOUT SOME-THING ELSE...
I'D LOVE TO DO ORIGI-NAL STUFF!
I WANNA DO A LOVE SONG!
I LIKE THAT IDEA!
A love song...?
OKAY, FINE.
MIGHT AS WELL.
I'VE GOT NOTHING TO LOSE BY TRYING, RIGHT?
IT MIGHT EVEN MAKE ME FEEL A LITTLE BETTER...

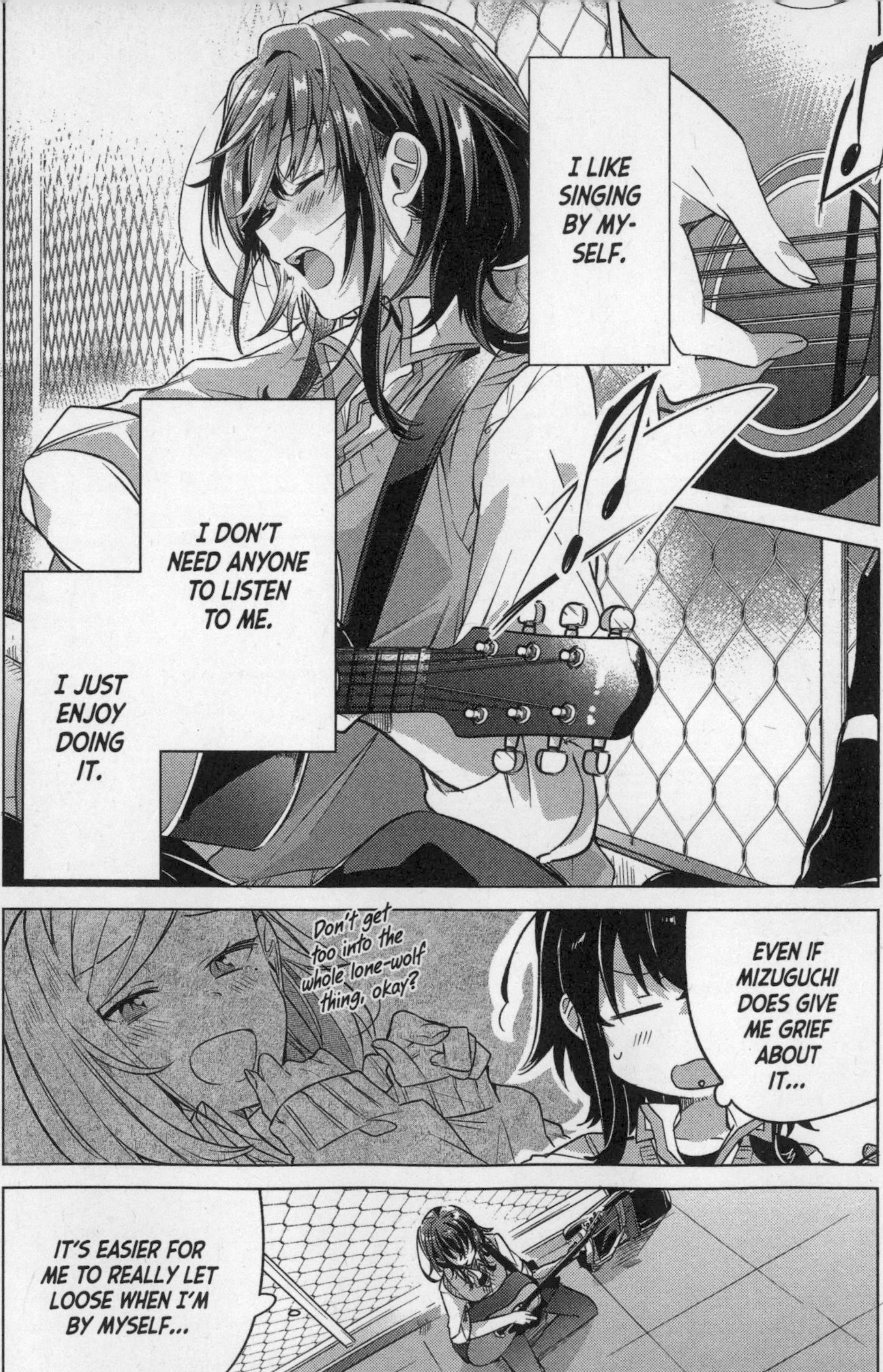
I LIKE SINGING BY MY-SELF.
I DON'T NEED ANYONE TO LISTEN TO ME.
I JUST ENJOY DOING IT.
EVEN IF MIZUGUCHI DOES GIVE ME GRIEF ABOUT IT...
Don't get too into the whole lone-wolf thing, okay?
IT'S EASIER FOR ME TO REALLY LET LOOSE WHEN I'M BY MYSELF...

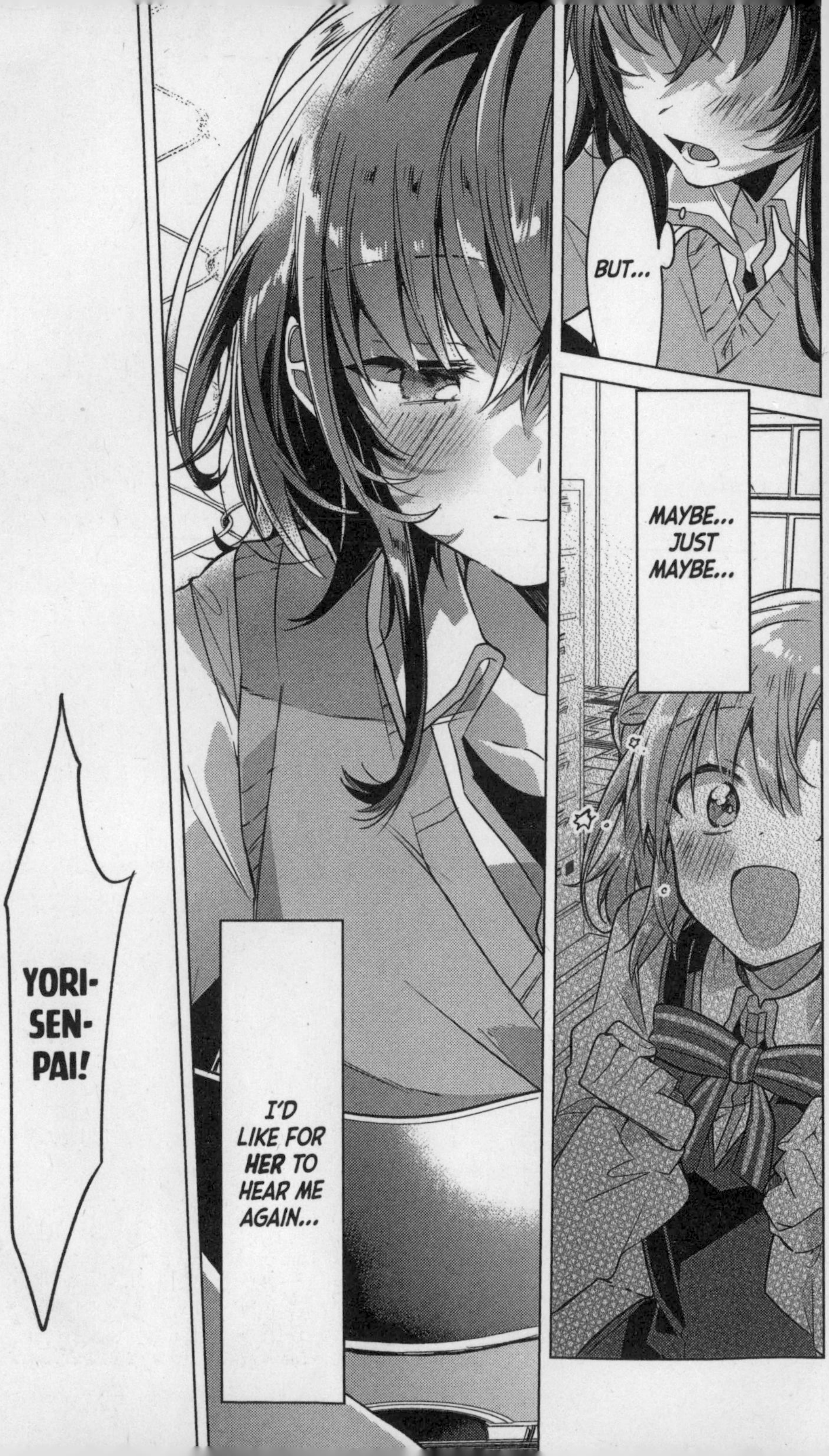
BUT...
MAYBE... JUST MAYBE...
I'D LIKE FOR HER TO HEAR ME AGAIN...
YORI-SENPAI!

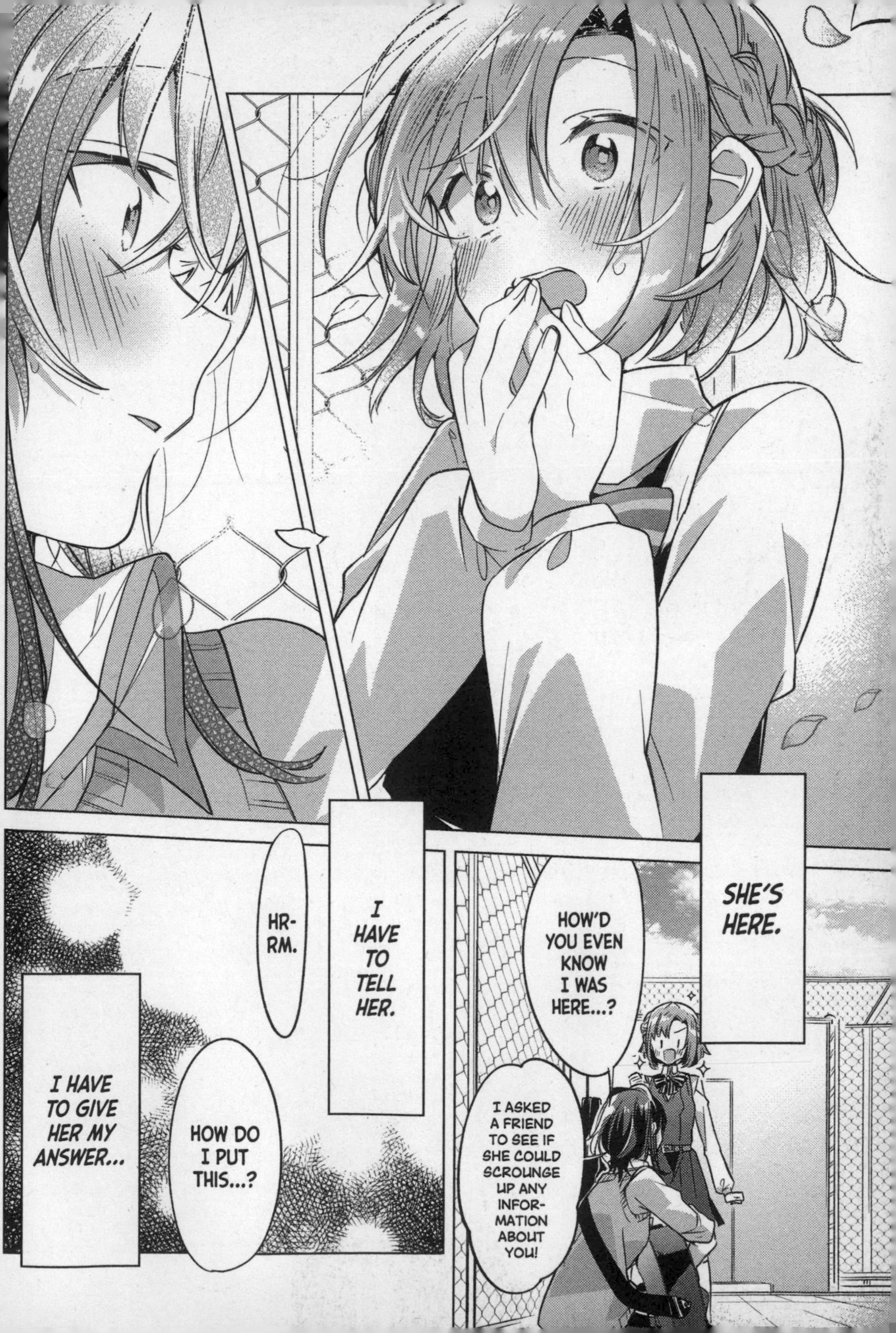
SHE'S HERE.
HOW'D YOU EVEN KNOW I WAS HERE...?
I ASKED A FRIEND TO SEE IF SHE COULD SCROUNGE UP ANY INFORMATION ABOUT YOU!
I HAVE TO TELL HER.
HR-RM.
HOW DO I PUT THIS...?
I HAVE TO GIVE HER MY ANSWER...

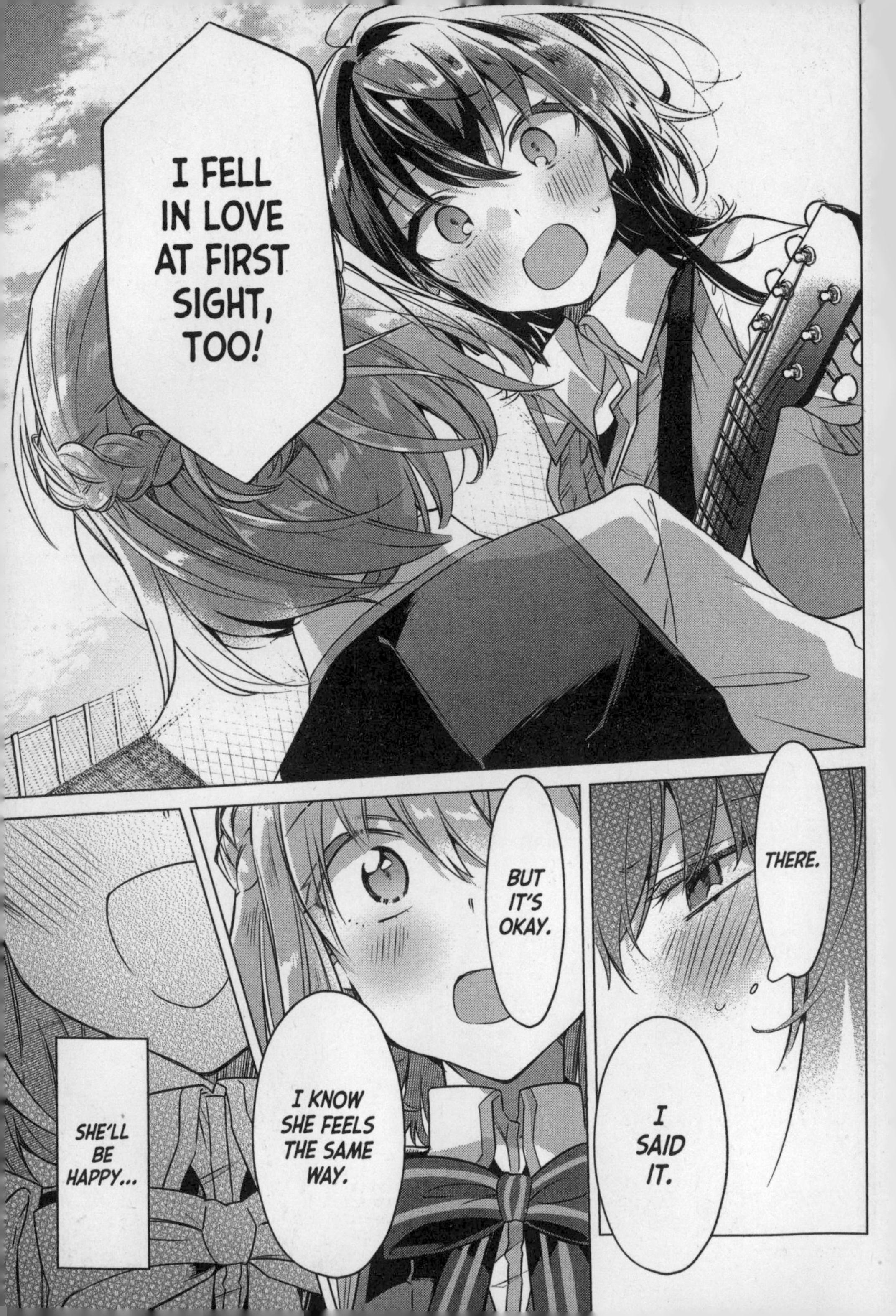
I FELL IN LOVE AT FIRST SIGHT, TOO!
THERE.
I SAID IT.
BUT IT'S OKAY.
I KNOW SHE FEELS THE SAME WAY.
SHE'LL BE HAPPY...

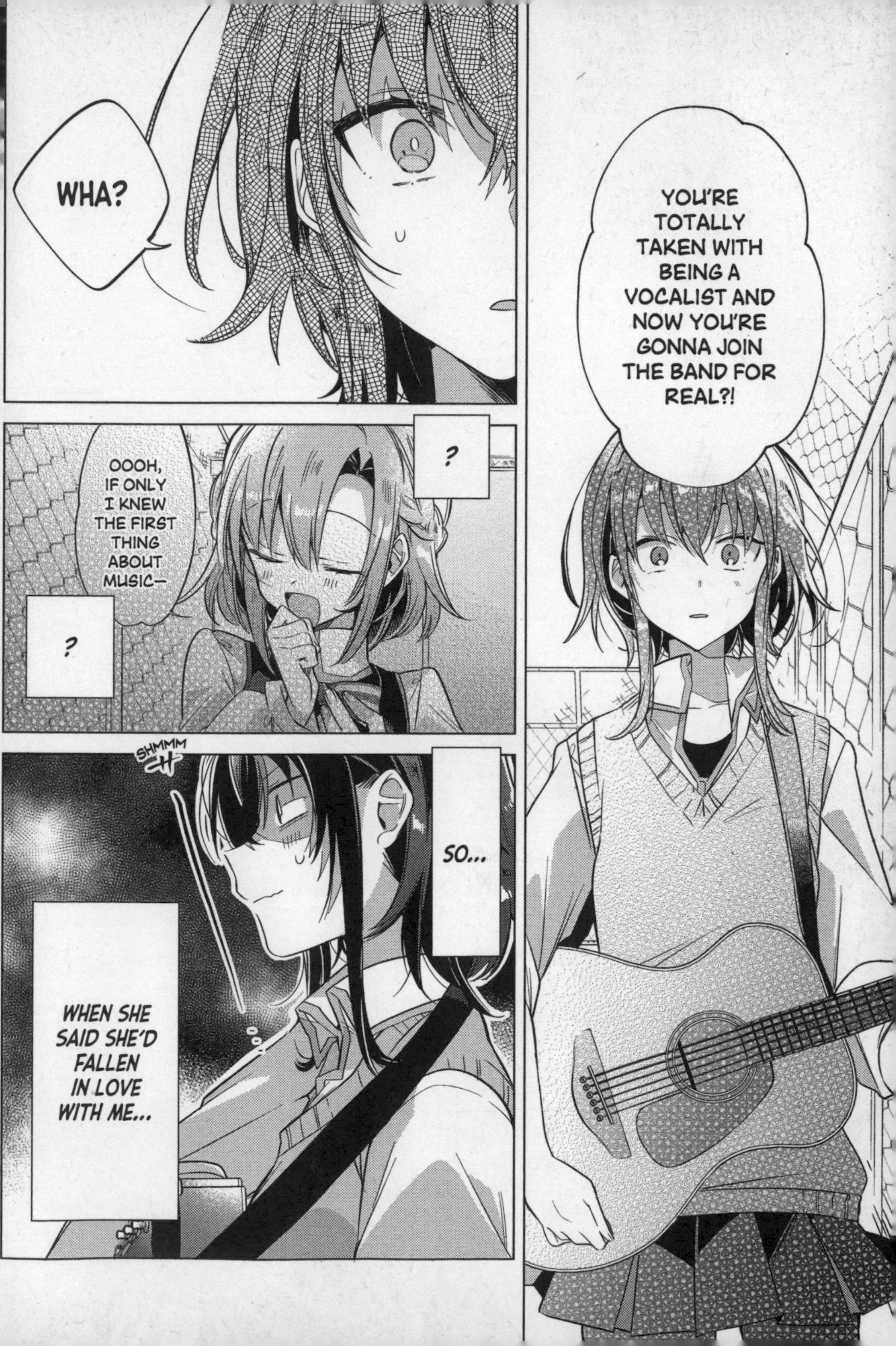
YOU'RE TOTALLY TAKEN WITH BEING A VOCALIST AND NOW YOU'RE GONNA JOIN THE BAND FOR REAL?!
WHA?
?
OOOH, IF ONLY I KNEW THE FIRST THING ABOUT MUSIC—
?
SHMMM
SO...
WHEN SHE SAID SHE'D FALLEN IN LOVE WITH ME...

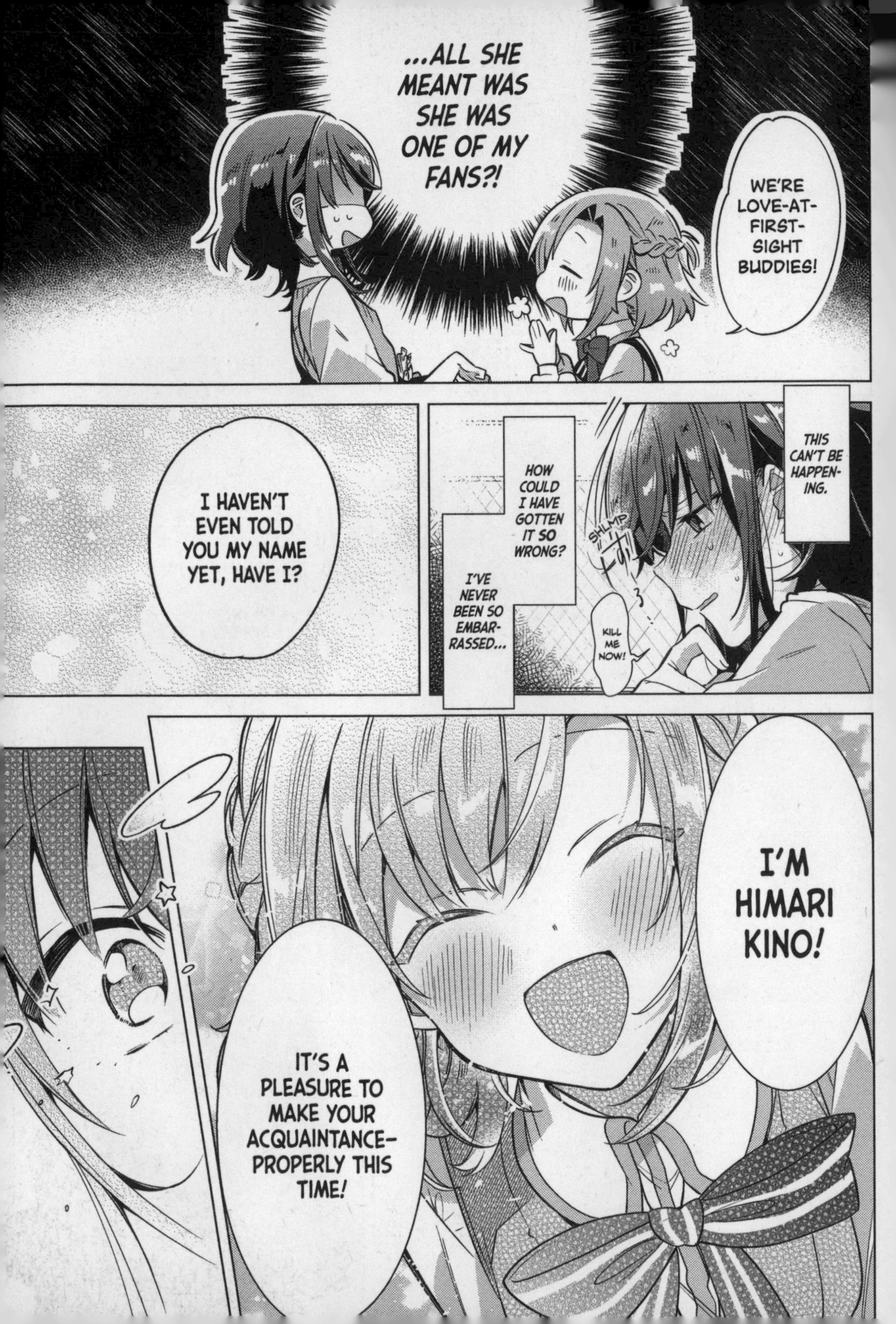
WE'RE LOVE-AT-FIRST-SIGHT BUDDIES!
...ALL SHE MEANT WAS SHE WAS ONE OF MY FANS?!
THIS CAN'T BE HAPPENING.
HOW COULD I HAVE GOTTEN IT SO WRONG?
SHLMP
I'VE NEVER BEEN SO EMBARRASSED...
KILL ME NOW!
I HAVEN'T EVEN TOLD YOU MY NAME YET, HAVE I?
I'M HIMARI KINO!
IT'S A PLEASURE TO MAKE YOUR ACQUAINTANCE—PROPERLY THIS TIME!

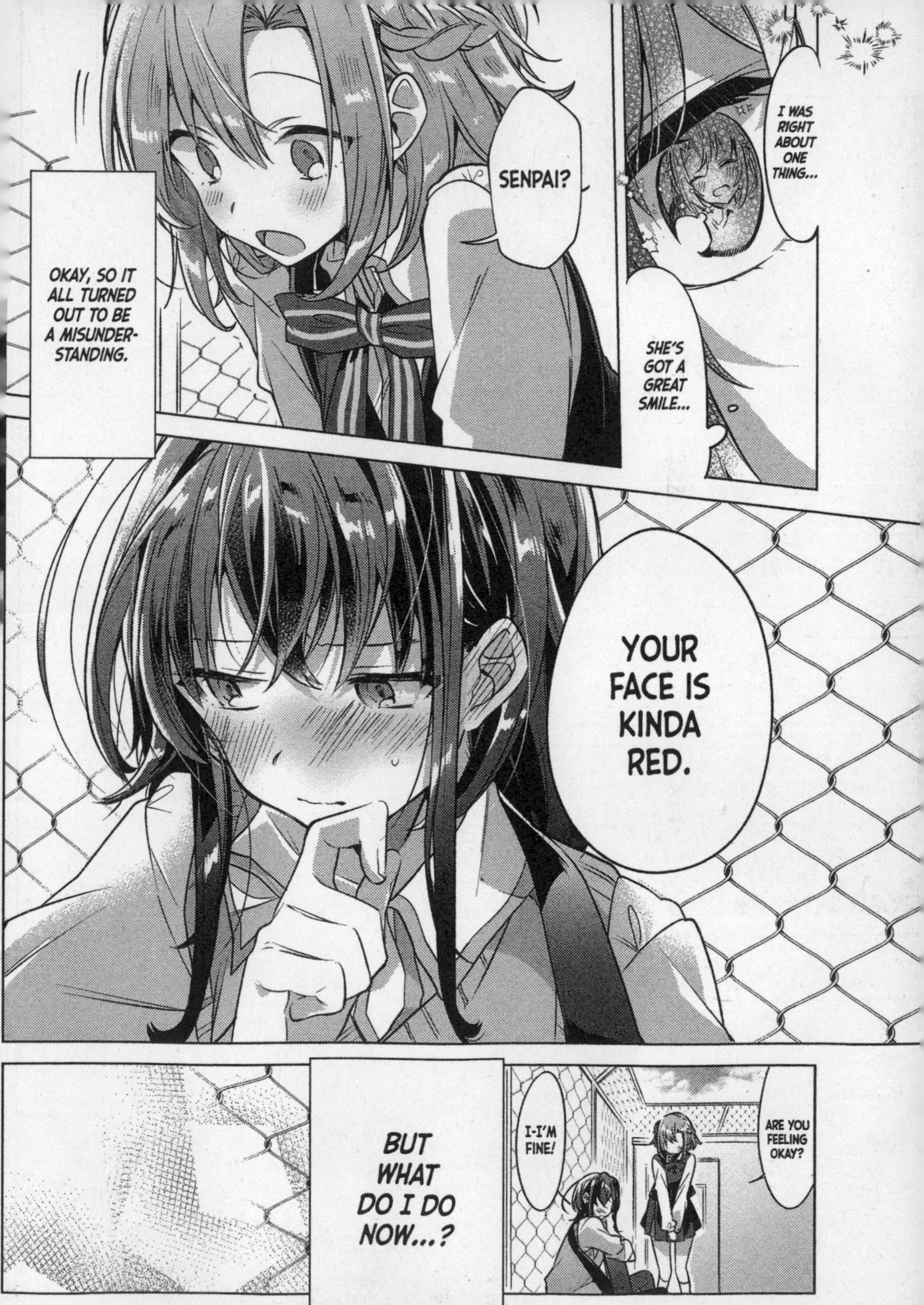
I WAS RIGHT ABOUT ONE THING...
SHE'S GOT A GREAT SMILE...
SENPAI?
OKAY, SO IT ALL TURNED OUT TO BE A MISUNDER-STANDING.
YOUR FACE IS KINDA RED.
ARE YOU FEELING OKAY?
I-I'M FINE!
BUT WHAT DO I DO NOW...?

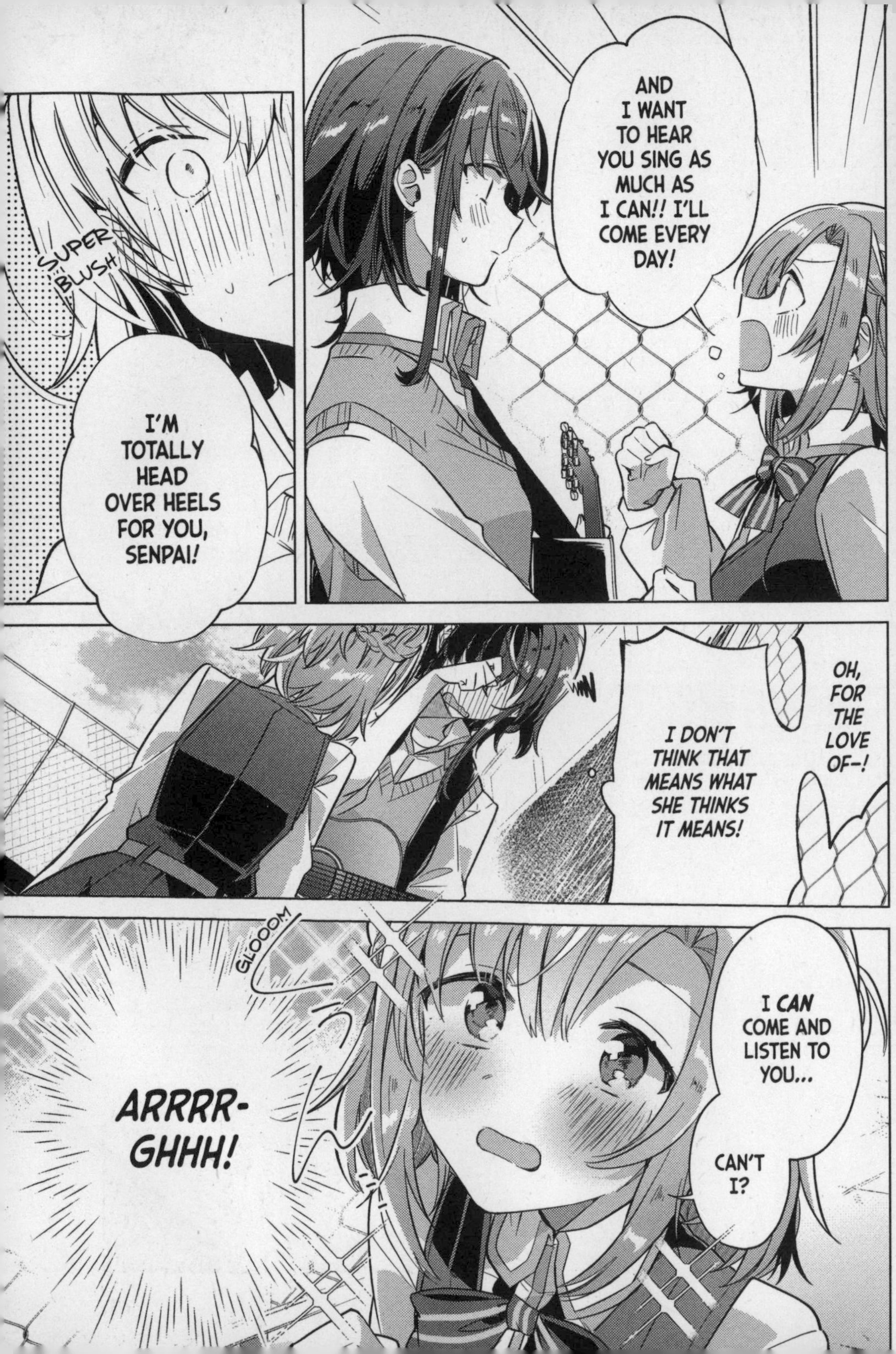
AND I WANT TO HEAR YOU SING AS MUCH AS I CAN!! I'LL COME EVERY DAY!
SUPER BLUSH
I'M TOTALLY HEAD OVER HEELS FOR YOU, SENPAI!
OH, FOR THE LOVE OF—!
I DON'T THINK THAT MEANS WHAT SHE THINKS IT MEANS!
I *CAN* COME AND LISTEN TO YOU...
CAN'T I?
GLOOOM
ARRRR-GHHH!

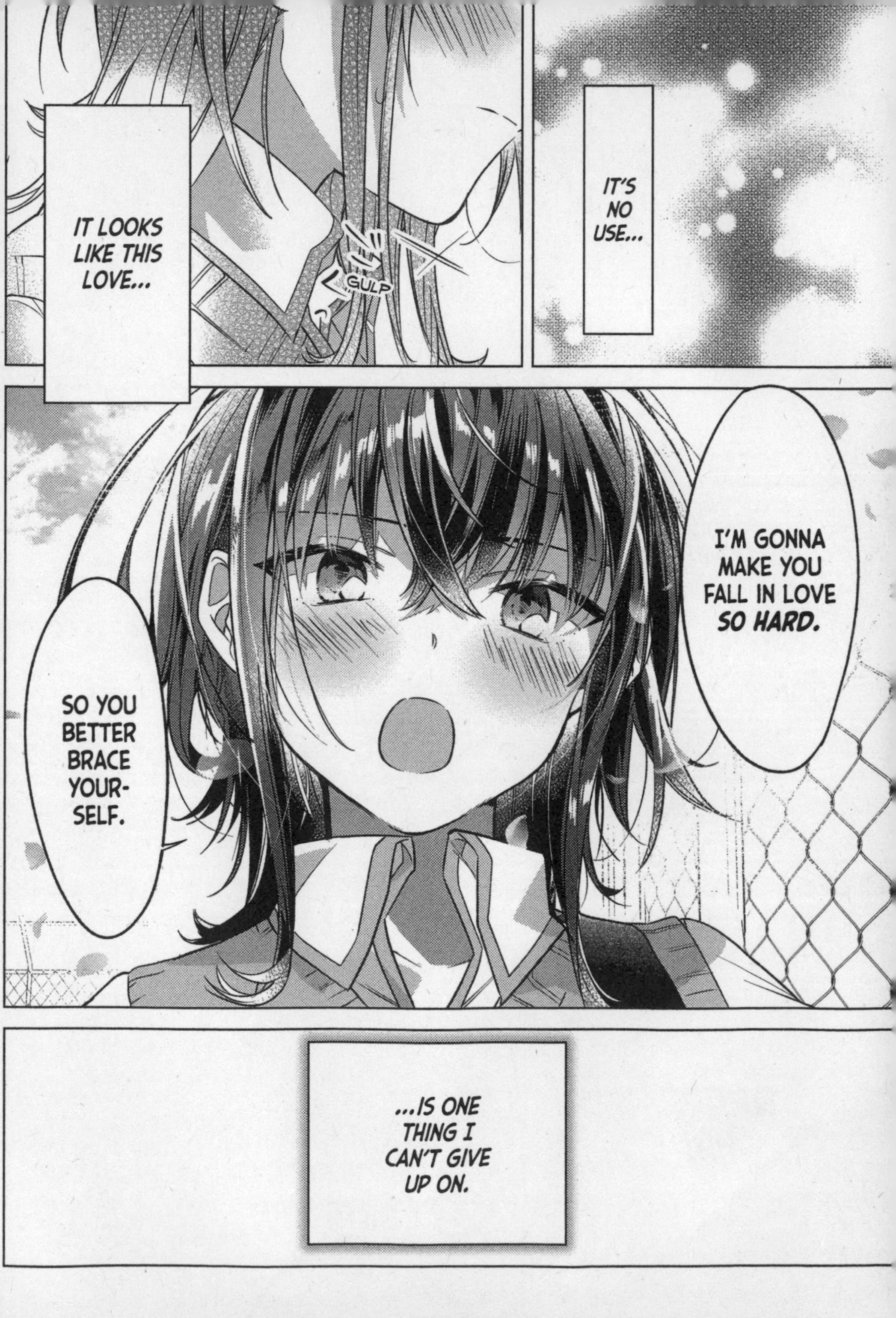
IT'S NO USE...
IT LOOKS LIKE THIS LOVE...
GULP
I'M GONNA MAKE YOU FALL IN LOVE SO HARD.
SO YOU BETTER BRACE YOUR-SELF.
...IS ONE THING I CAN'T GIVE UP ON.

Whisper Me
A Love Song
Eku
Takeshima

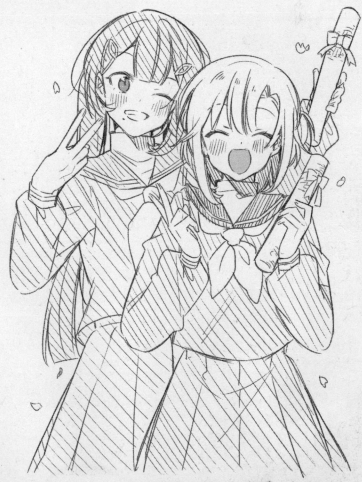

Himari & Miki @ middle school graduation

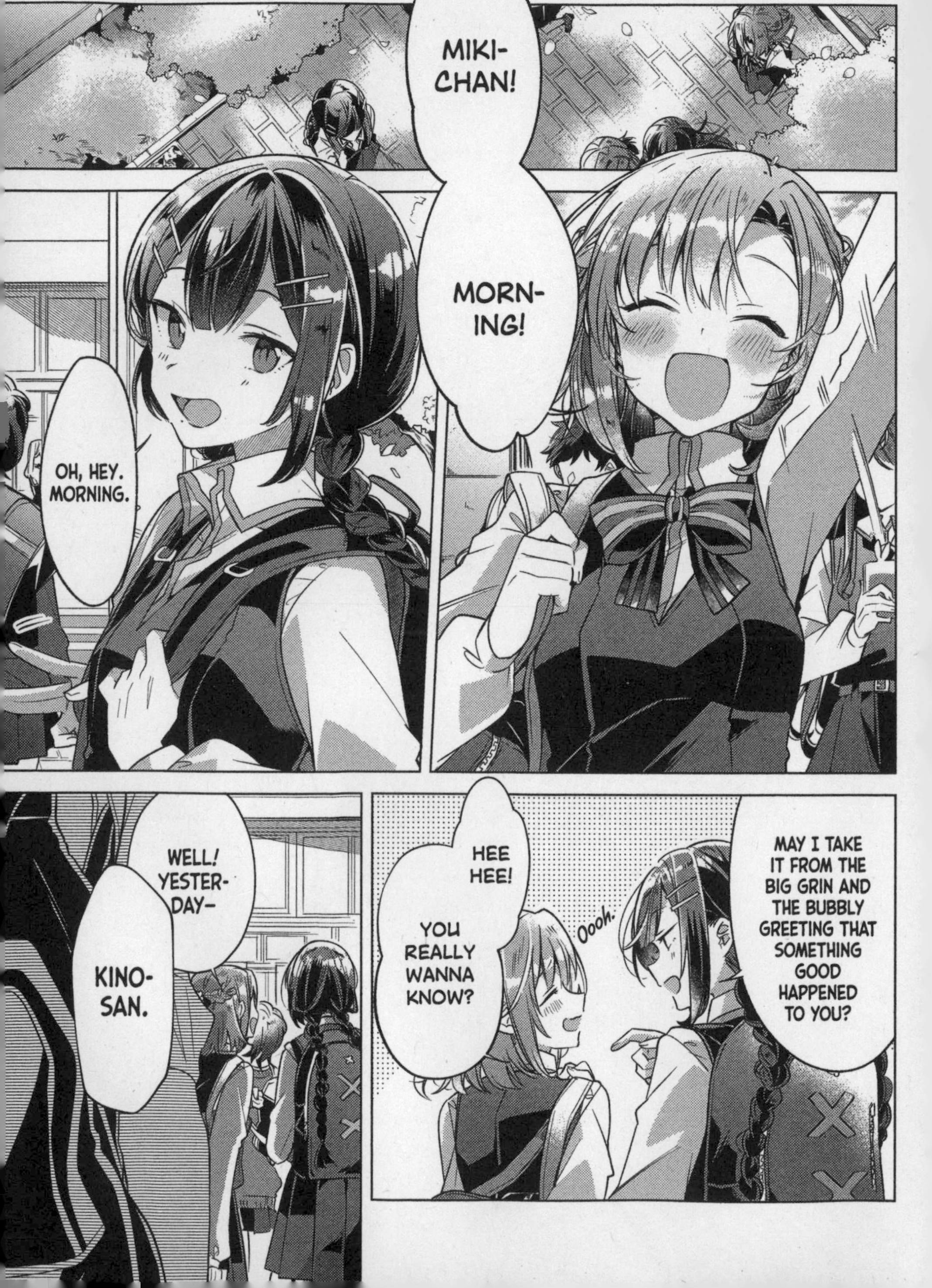
MIKI-CHAN!
MORNING!
OH, HEY. MORNING.
MAY I TAKE IT FROM THE BIG GRIN AND THE BUBBLY GREETING THAT SOMETHING GOOD HAPPENED TO YOU?
Oooh.
HEE HEE!
YOU REALLY WANNA KNOW?
WELL! YESTERDAY—
KINO-SAN.

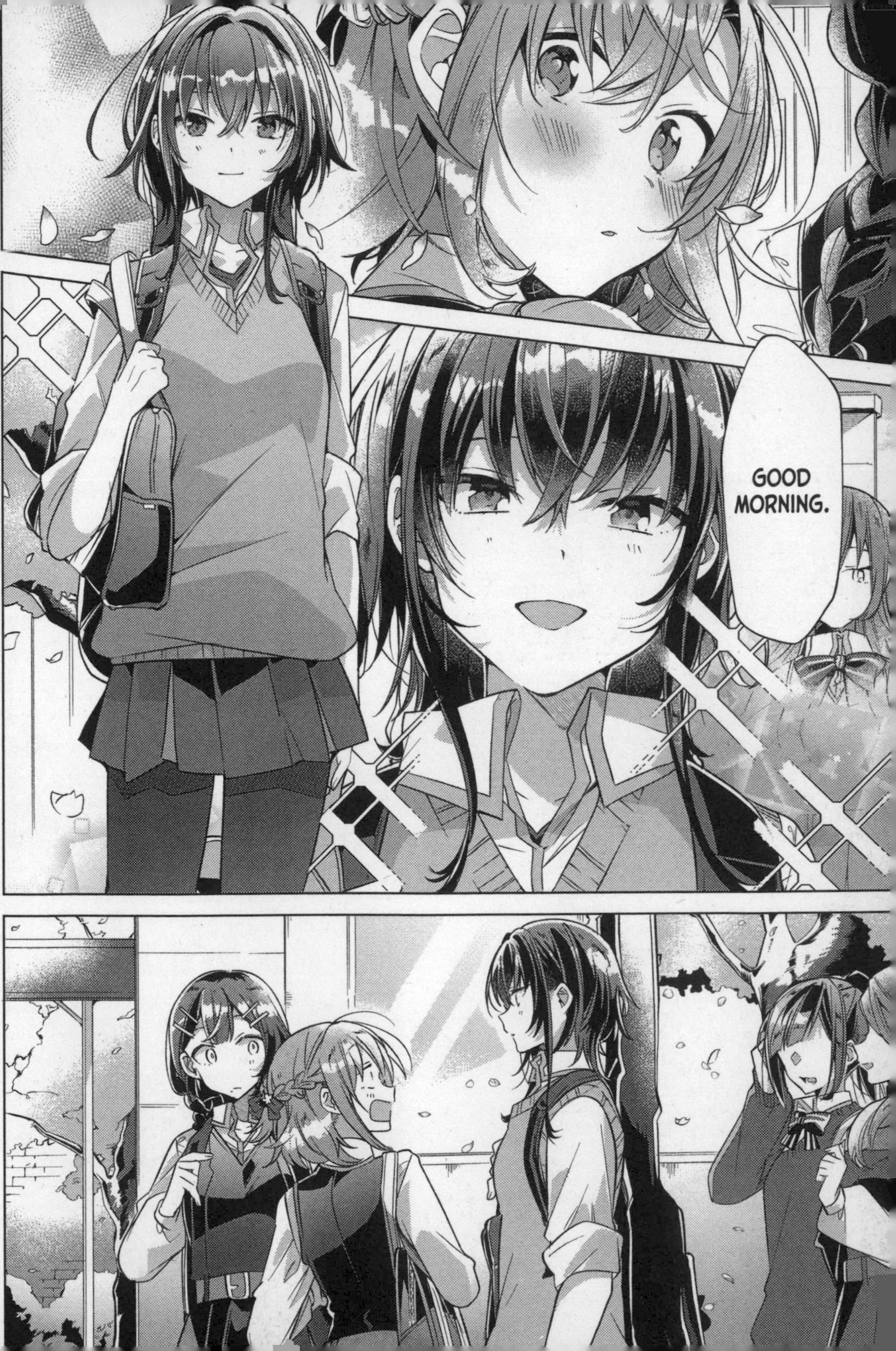
GOOD MORNING.

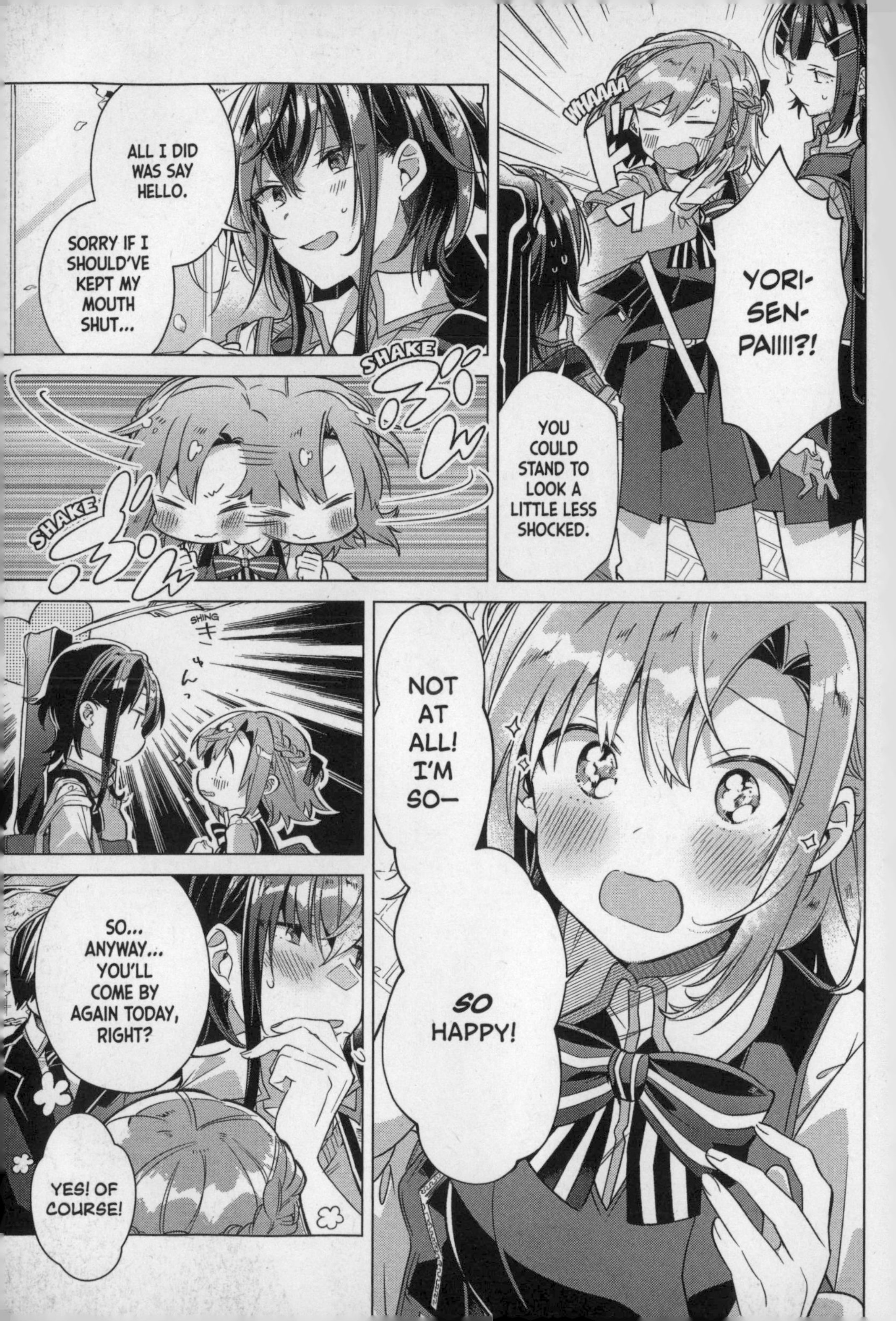
WHAAAA
YORI-SEN-PAIIII?!
YOU COULD STAND TO LOOK A LITTLE LESS SHOCKED.
ALL I DID WAS SAY HELLO.
SORRY IF I SHOULD'VE KEPT MY MOUTH SHUT...
SHAKE
SHAKE
NOT AT ALL! I'M SO—
SO HAPPY!
SHING
SO... ANYWAY... YOU'LL COME BY AGAIN TODAY, RIGHT?
YES! OF COURSE!

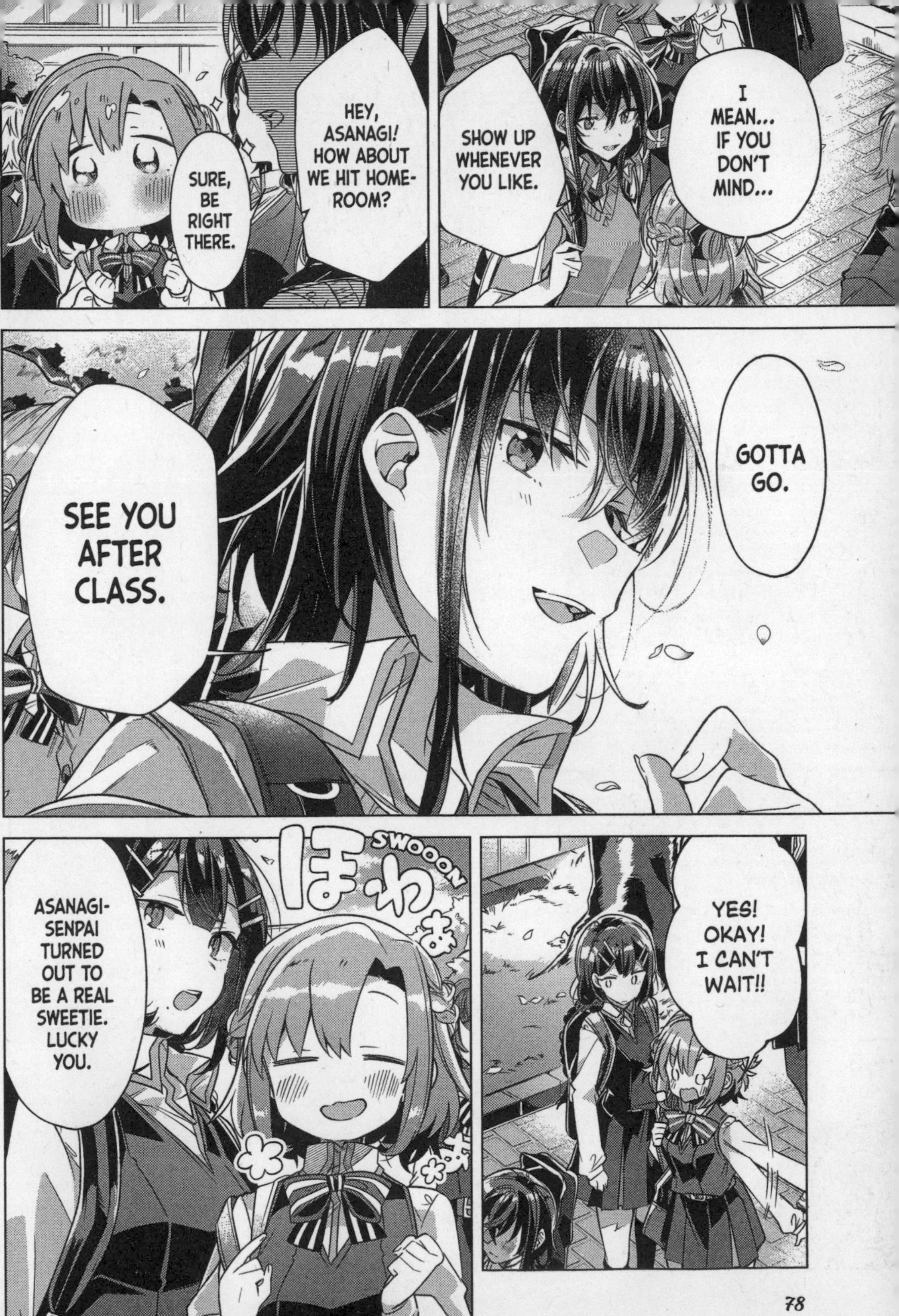
I MEAN... IF YOU DON'T MIND...
SHOW UP WHENEVER YOU LIKE.
HEY, ASANAGI! HOW ABOUT WE HIT HOME-ROOM?
SURE, BE RIGHT THERE.
GOTTA GO.
SEE YOU AFTER CLASS.
YES! OKAY! I CAN'T WAIT!!
SWOOON
ASANAGI-SENPAI TURNED OUT TO BE A REAL SWEETIE. LUCKY YOU.

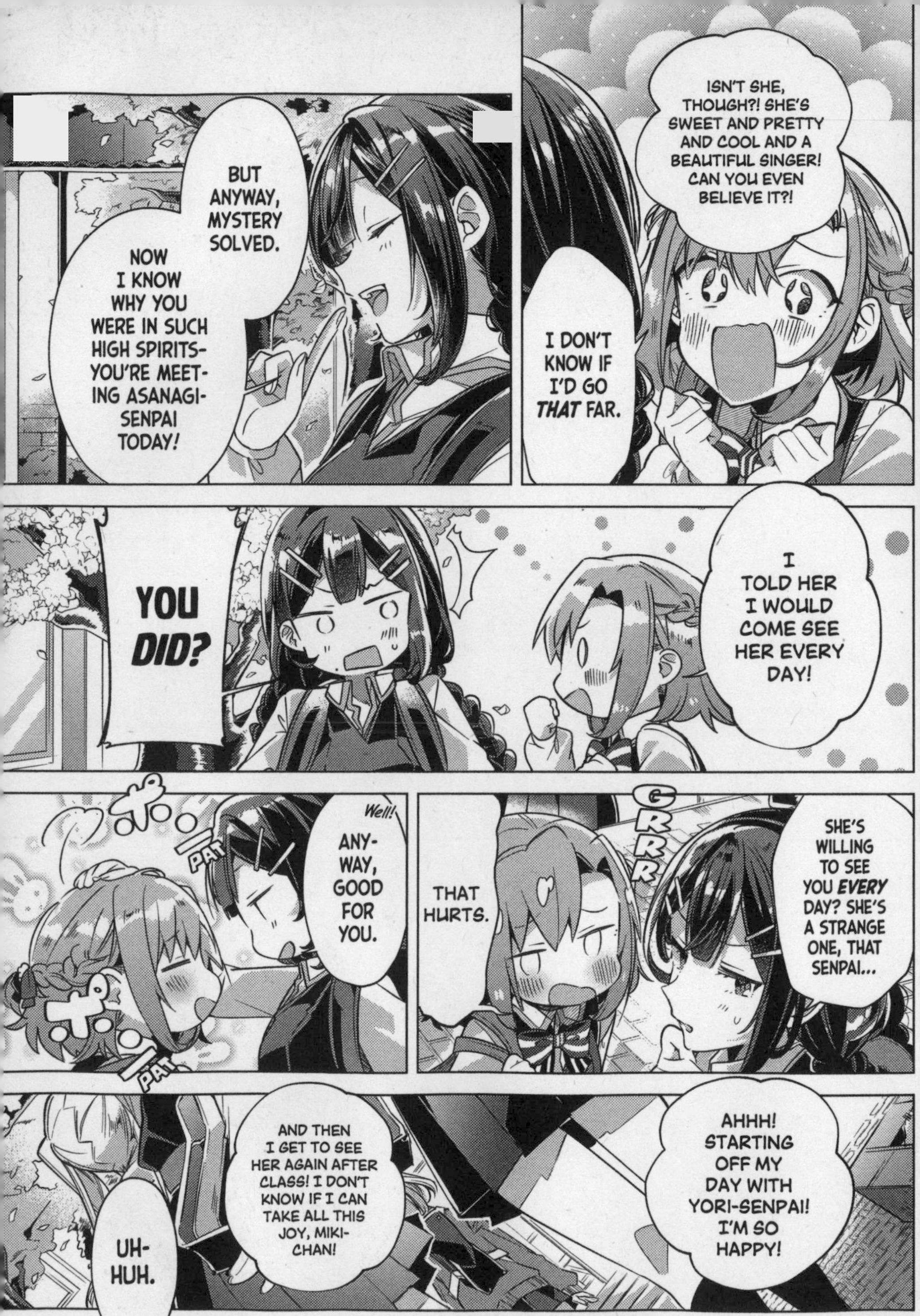
ISN'T SHE, THOUGH?! SHE'S SWEET AND PRETTY AND COOL AND A BEAUTIFUL SINGER! CAN YOU EVEN BELIEVE IT?!
I DON'T KNOW IF I'D GO *THAT* FAR.
BUT ANYWAY, MYSTERY SOLVED.
NOW I KNOW WHY YOU WERE IN SUCH HIGH SPIRITS- YOU'RE MEET-ING ASANAGI-SENPAI TODAY!
I TOLD HER I WOULD COME SEE HER EVERY DAY!
YOU *DID?*
CRRR
SHE'S WILLING TO SEE YOU *EVERY* DAY? SHE'S A STRANGE ONE, THAT SENPAI...
THAT HURTS.
Well!
ANY-WAY, GOOD FOR YOU.
PAT
PAT
AHHH! STARTING OFF MY DAY WITH YORI-SENPAI! I'M SO HAPPY!
AND THEN I GET TO SEE HER AGAIN AFTER CLASS! I DON'T KNOW IF I CAN TAKE ALL THIS JOY, MIKI-CHAN!
UH-HUH.

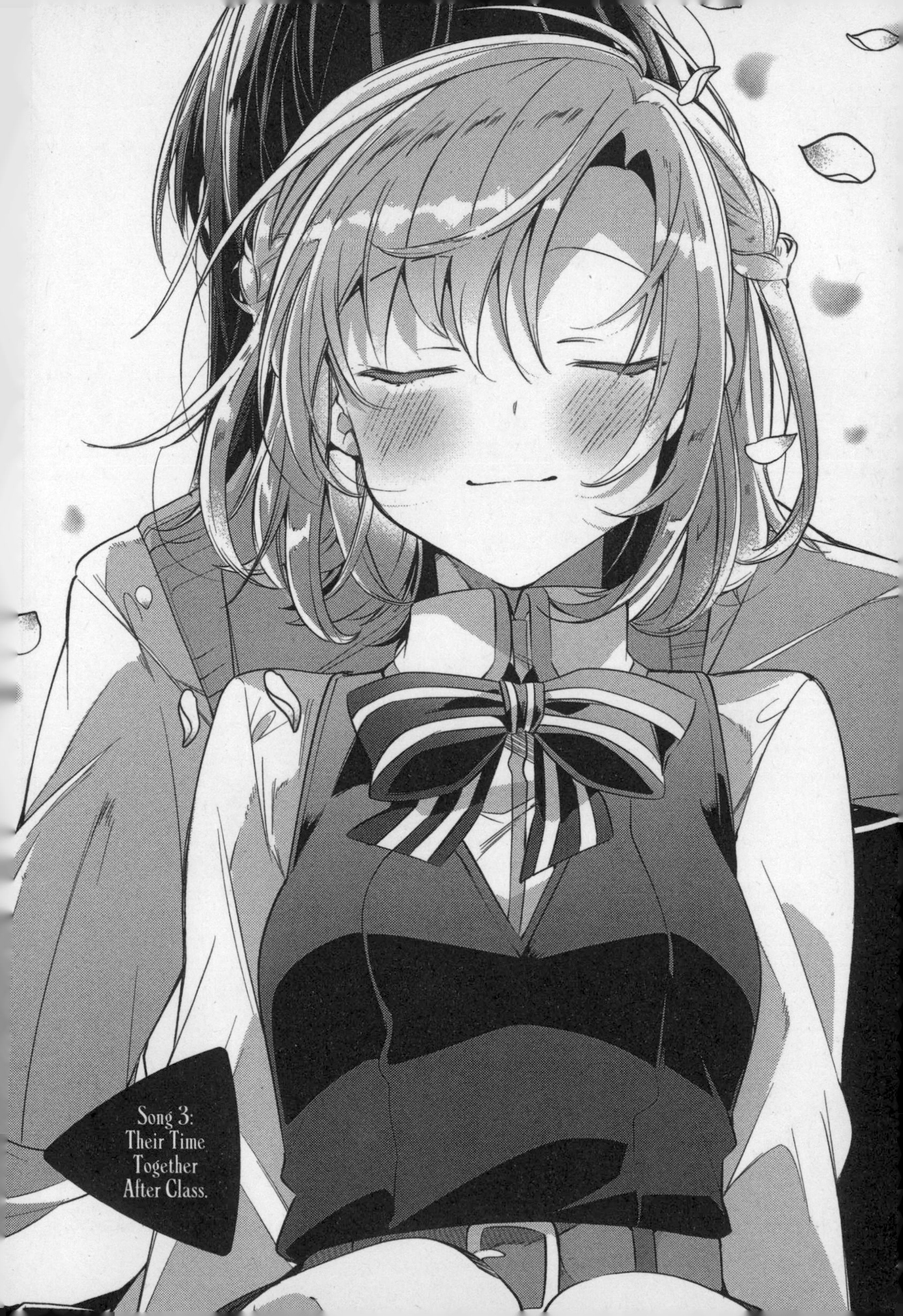
Song 3:
Their Time
Together
After Class.

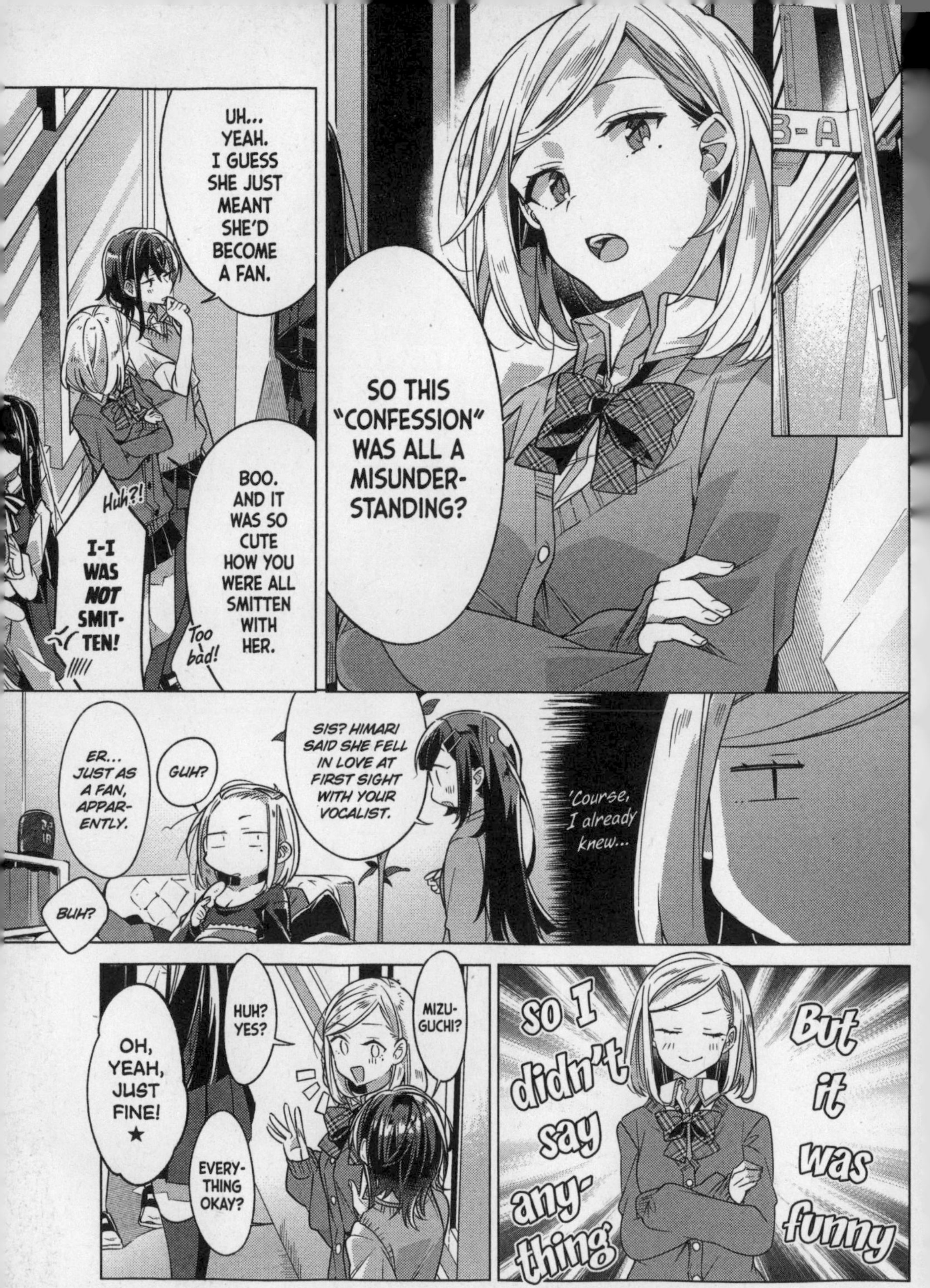
SO THIS "CONFESSION" WAS ALL A MISUNDERSTANDING?
UH... YEAH. I GUESS SHE JUST MEANT SHE'D BECOME A FAN.
BOO. AND IT WAS SO CUTE HOW YOU WERE ALL SMITTEN WITH HER.
Too bad!
Huh?!
I-I WAS NOT SMITTEN!
'Course, I already knew...
SIS? HIMARI SAID SHE FELL IN LOVE AT FIRST SIGHT WITH YOUR VOCALIST.
GUH?
ER... JUST AS A FAN, APPARENTLY.
BUH?
But it was funny
so I didn't say anything
MIZUGUCHI?
HUH? YES?
EVERYTHING OKAY?
OH, YEAH, JUST FINE! ★

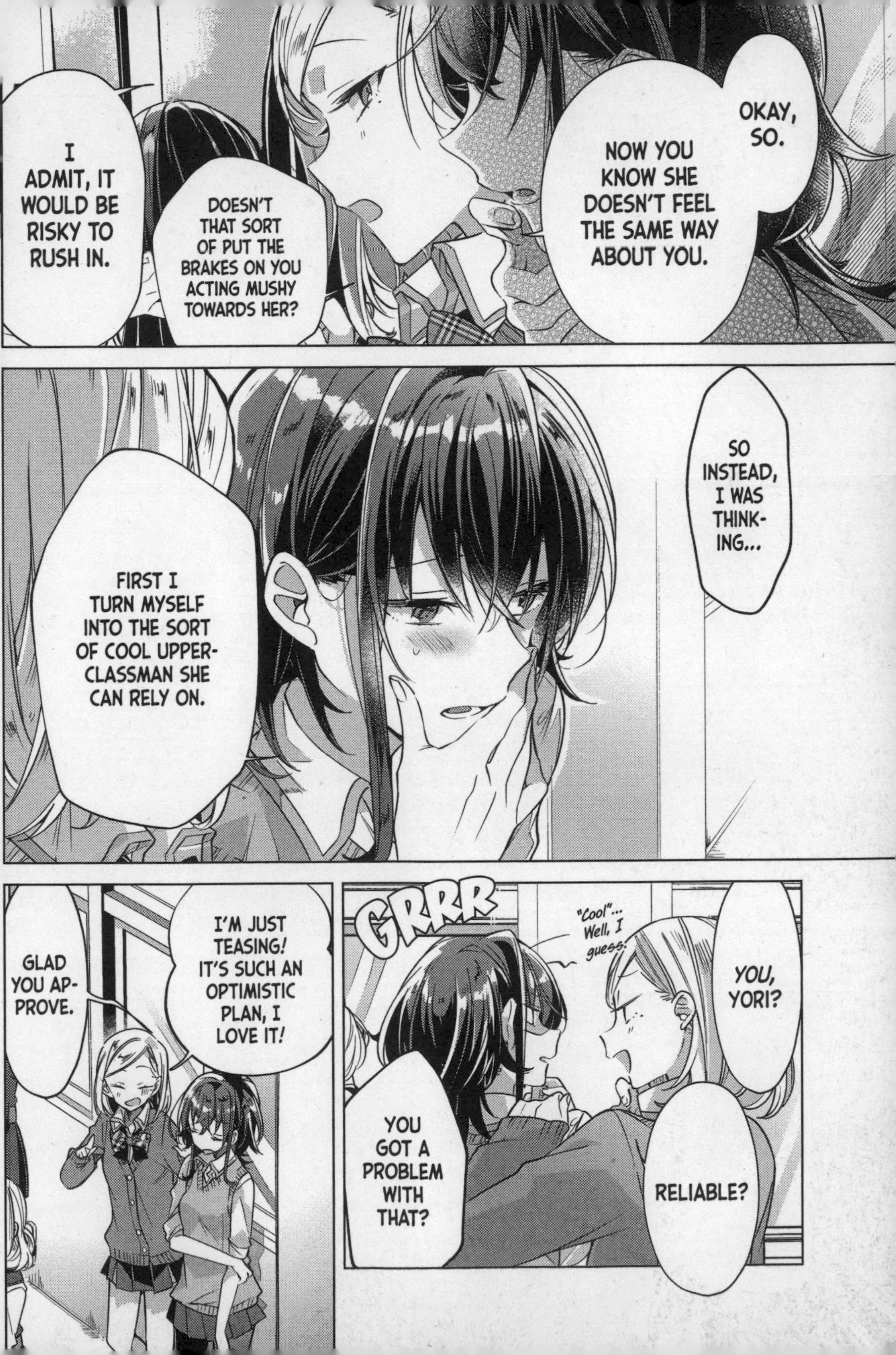
OKAY, SO.
NOW YOU KNOW SHE DOESN'T FEEL THE SAME WAY ABOUT YOU.
DOESN'T THAT SORT OF PUT THE BRAKES ON YOU ACTING MUSHY TOWARDS HER?
I ADMIT, IT WOULD BE RISKY TO RUSH IN.
SO INSTEAD, I WAS THINKING...
FIRST I TURN MYSELF INTO THE SORT OF COOL UPPERCLASSMAN SHE CAN RELY ON.
YOU, YORI?
RELIABLE?
"Cool"... Well, I guess.
GRRR
YOU GOT A PROBLEM WITH THAT?
I'M JUST TEASING! IT'S SUCH AN OPTIMISTIC PLAN, I LOVE IT!
GLAD YOU APPROVE.

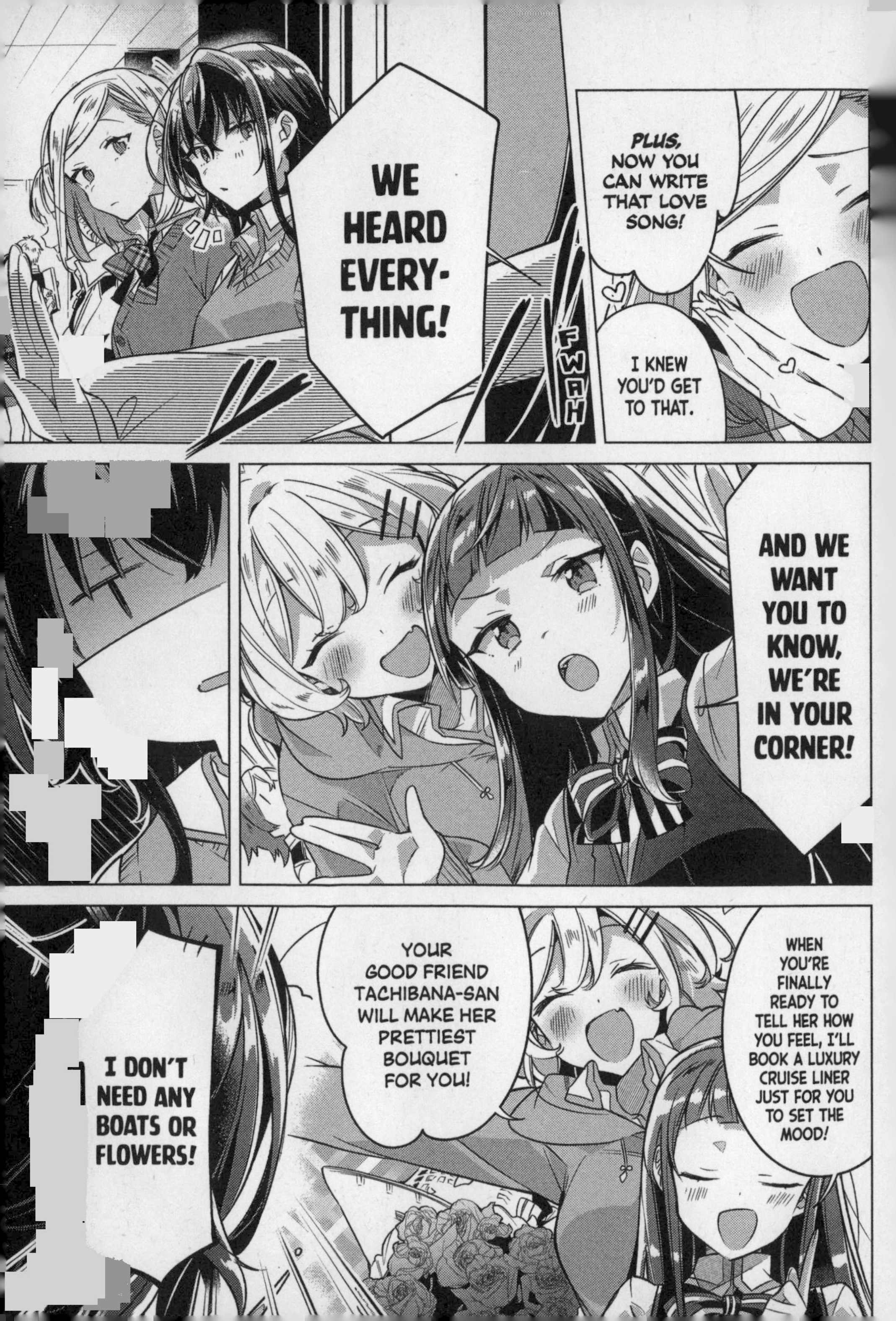
PLUS, NOW YOU CAN WRITE THAT LOVE SONG!
FWAH
I KNEW YOU'D GET TO THAT.
WE HEARD EVERYTHING!
AND WE WANT YOU TO KNOW, WE'RE IN YOUR CORNER!
WHEN YOU'RE FINALLY READY TO TELL HER HOW YOU FEEL, I'LL BOOK A LUXURY CRUISE LINER JUST FOR YOU TO SET THE MOOD!
YOUR GOOD FRIEND TACHIBANA-SAN WILL MAKE HER PRETTIEST BOUQUET FOR YOU!
I DON'T NEED ANY BOATS OR FLOWERS!

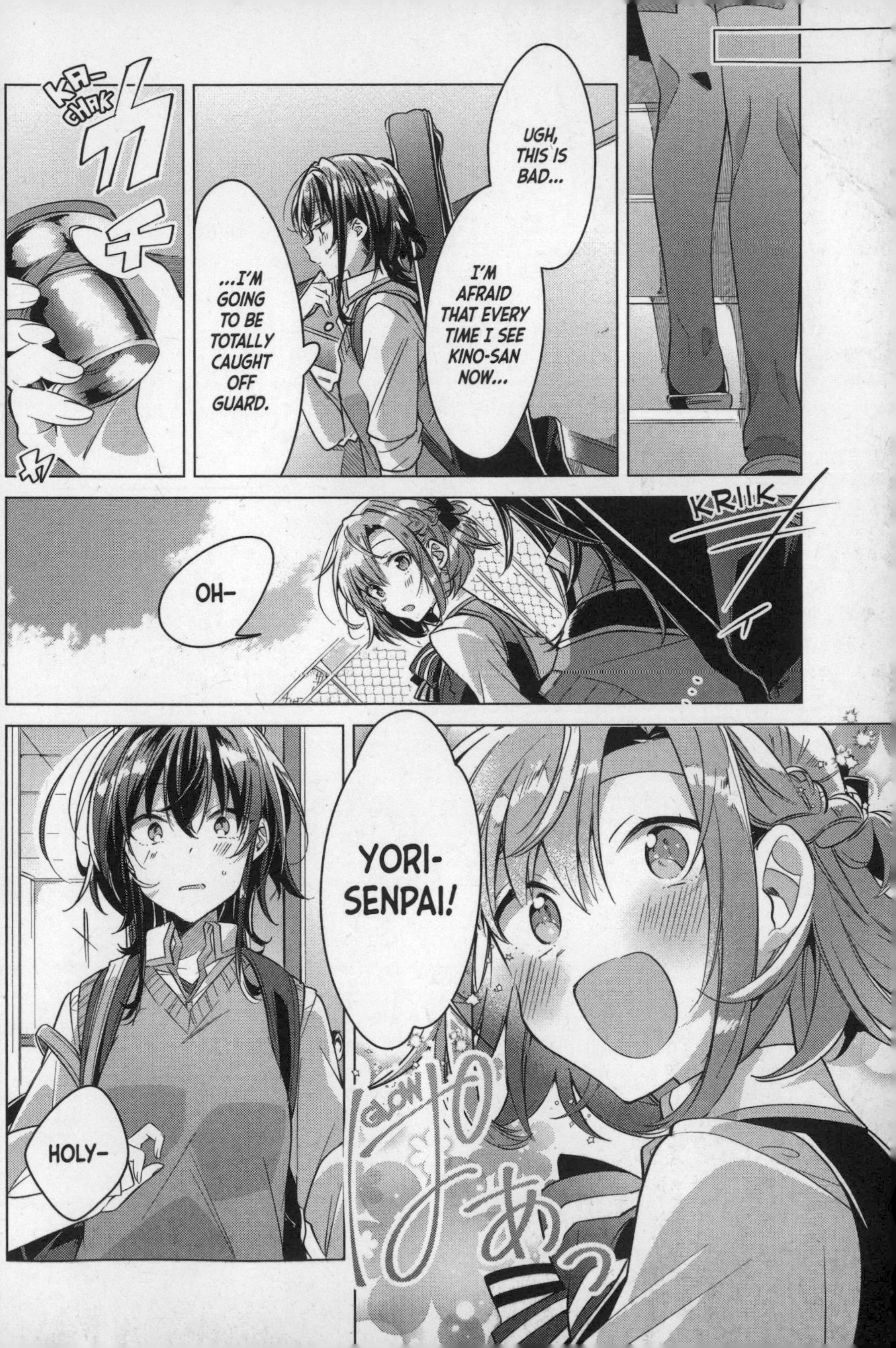
UGH, THIS IS BAD...
I'M AFRAID THAT EVERY TIME I SEE KINO-SAN NOW...
...I'M GOING TO BE TOTALLY CAUGHT OFF GUARD.
KA-CHAK
KRIIK
OH-
YORI-SENPAI!
GLOW
HOLY-

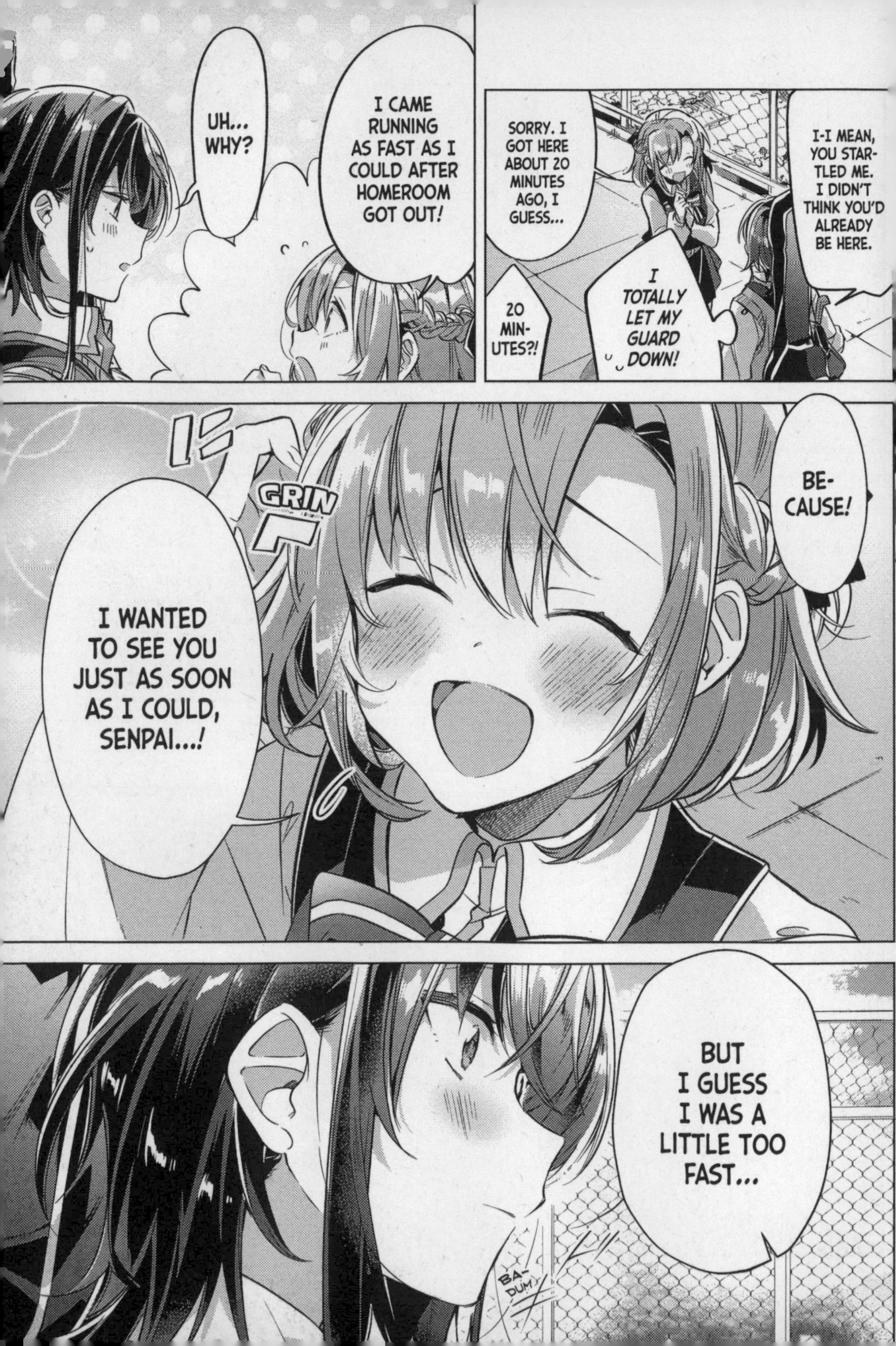
I-I MEAN, YOU STAR-TLED ME. I DIDN'T THINK YOU'D ALREADY BE HERE.
SORRY. I GOT HERE ABOUT 20 MINUTES AGO, I GUESS...
I TOTALLY LET MY GUARD DOWN!
20 MIN-UTES?!
I CAME RUNNING AS FAST AS I COULD AFTER HOMEROOM GOT OUT!
UH... WHY?
BE-CAUSE!
GRIN
I WANTED TO SEE YOU JUST AS SOON AS I COULD, SENPAI...!
BUT I GUESS I WAS A LITTLE TOO FAST...
BA-DUM

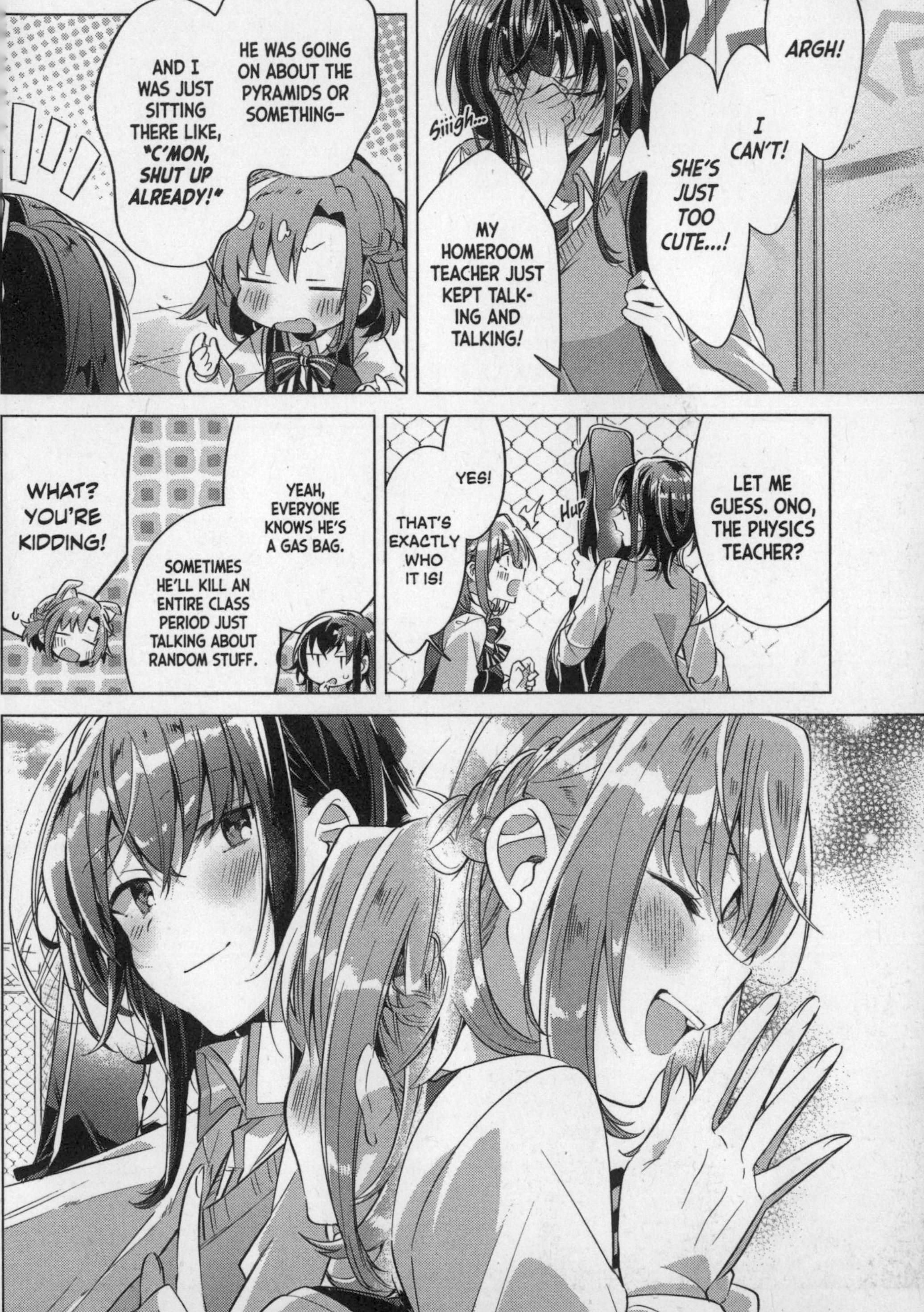
ARGH!
I CAN'T!
SHE'S JUST TOO CUTE...!
Siiigh...
MY HOMEROOM TEACHER JUST KEPT TALKING AND TALKING!
HE WAS GOING ON ABOUT THE PYRAMIDS OR SOMETHING–
AND I WAS JUST SITTING THERE LIKE, "C'MON, SHUT UP ALREADY!"
LET ME GUESS. ONO, THE PHYSICS TEACHER?
Hup
YES!
THAT'S EXACTLY WHO IT IS!
YEAH, EVERYONE KNOWS HE'S A GAS BAG.
SOMETIMES HE'LL KILL AN ENTIRE CLASS PERIOD JUST TALKING ABOUT RANDOM STUFF.
WHAT? YOU'RE KIDDING!

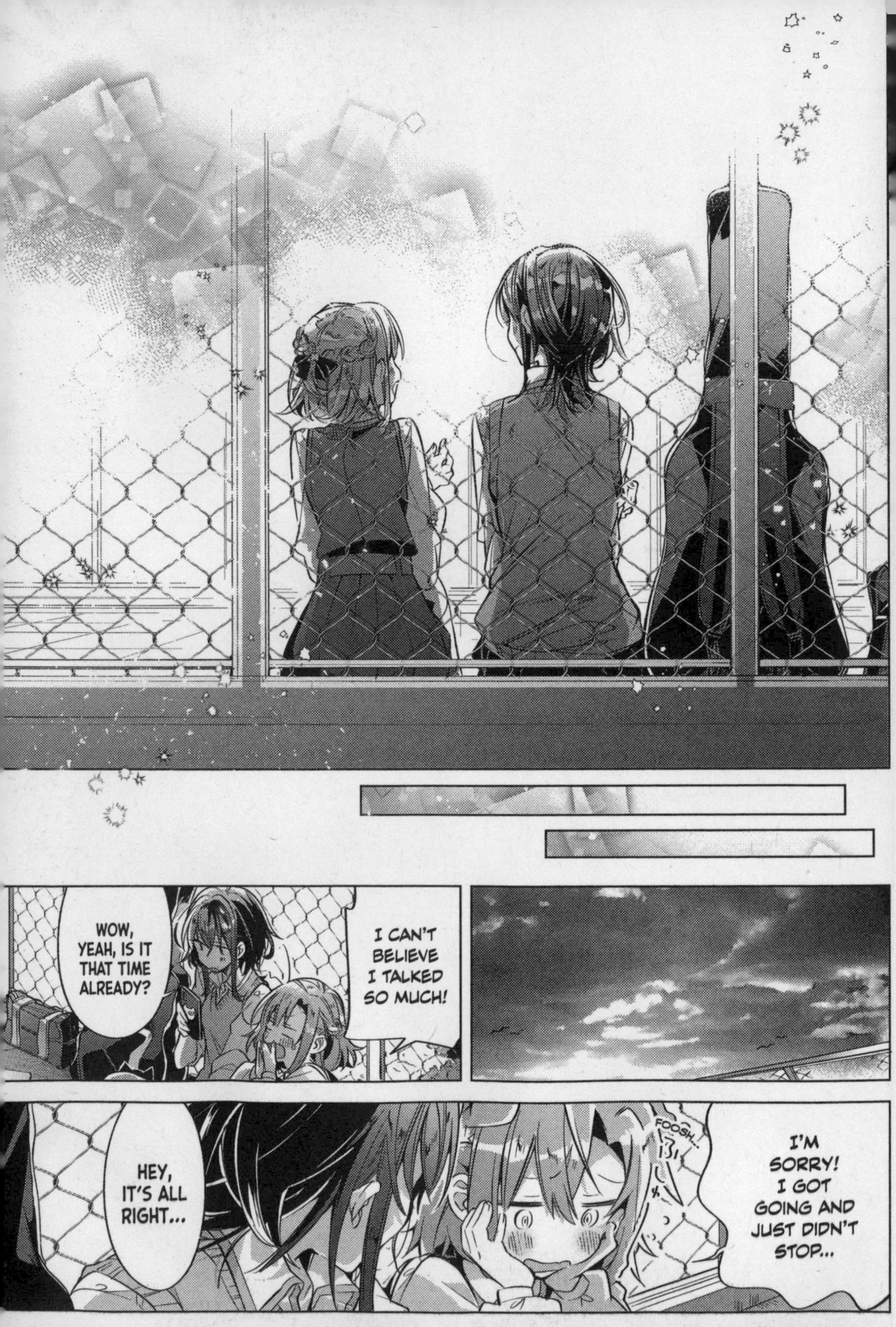
I CAN'T BELIEVE I TALKED SO MUCH!
WOW, YEAH, IS IT THAT TIME ALREADY?
I'M SORRY! I GOT GOING AND JUST DIDN'T STOP...
FOOSH...
HEY, IT'S ALL RIGHT...

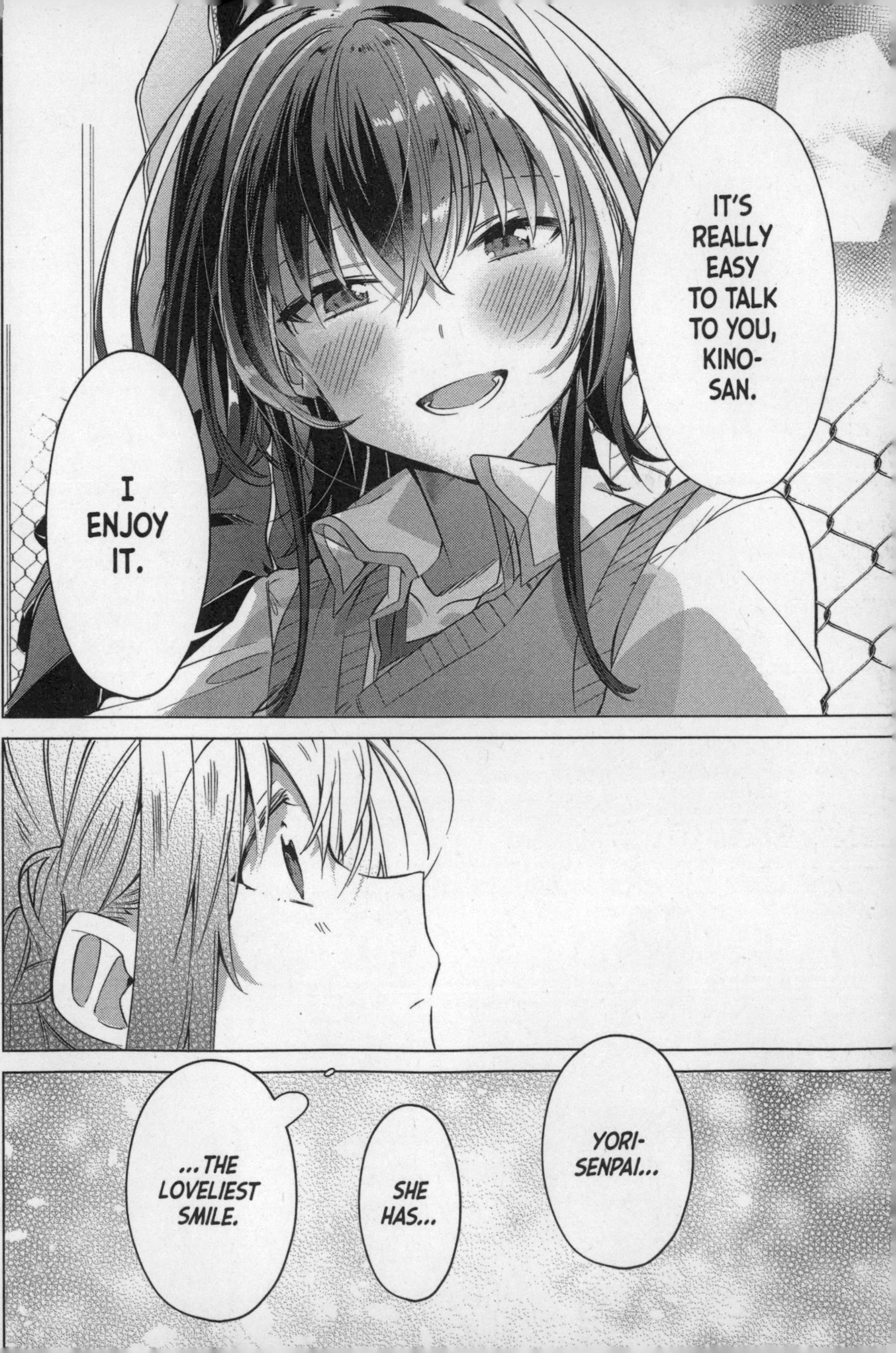
IT'S REALLY EASY TO TALK TO YOU, KINO-SAN.
I ENJOY IT.
YORI-SENPAI...
SHE HAS...
...THE LOVELIEST SMILE.

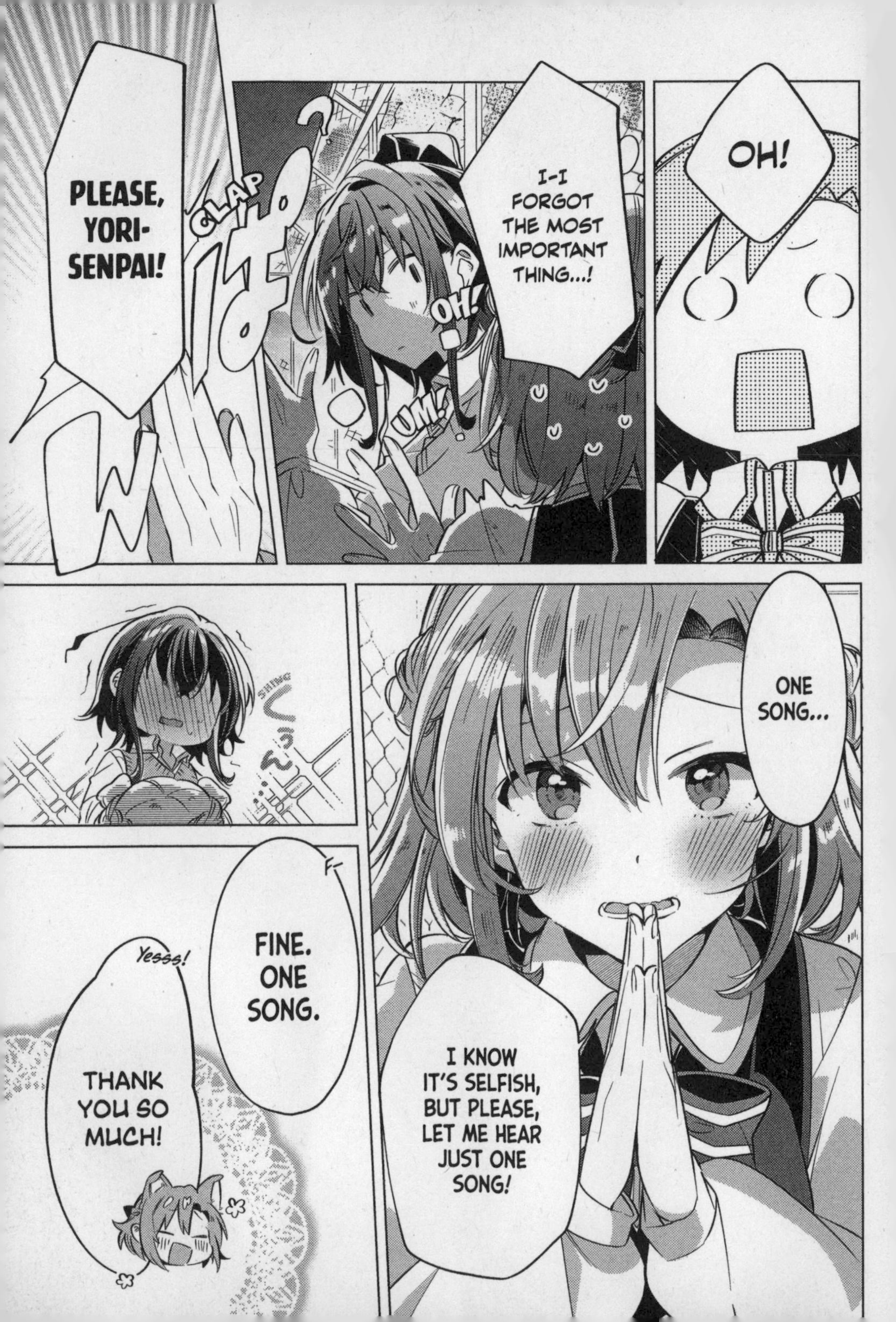
OH!
I-I FORGOT THE MOST IMPORTANT THING...!
OH!
UM!
PLEASE, YORI-SENPAI!
CLAP
ONE SONG...
I KNOW IT'S SELFISH, BUT PLEASE, LET ME HEAR JUST ONE SONG!
SHING
F-
FINE. ONE SONG.
Yessss!
THANK YOU SO MUCH!

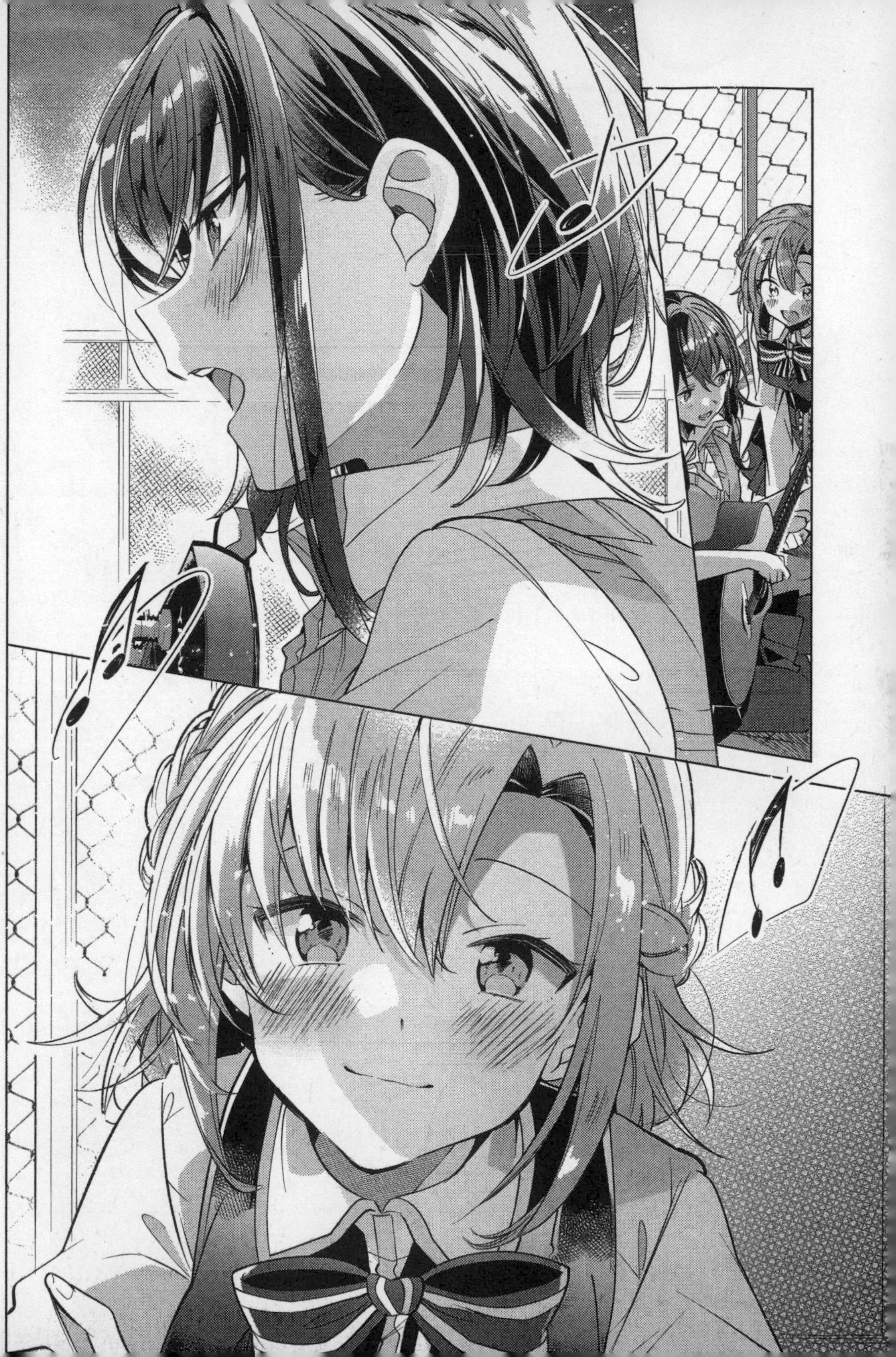

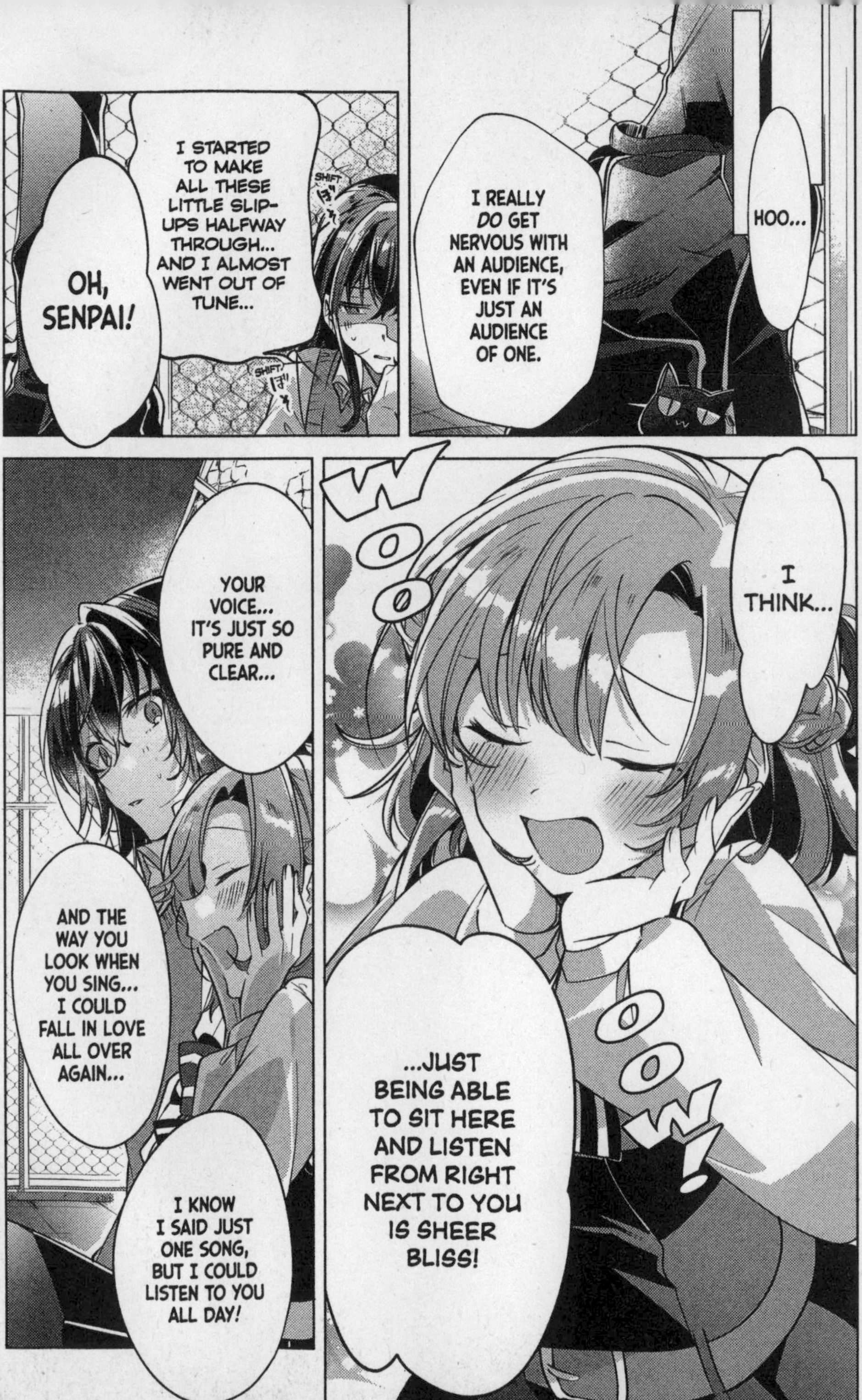
HOO...
I REALLY *DO* GET NERVOUS WITH AN AUDIENCE, EVEN IF IT'S JUST AN AUDIENCE OF ONE.
I STARTED TO MAKE ALL THESE LITTLE SLIP-UPS HALFWAY THROUGH... AND I ALMOST WENT OUT OF TUNE...
SHIFT
SHIFT
OH, SENPAI!
I THINK...
WOOOOOW!
...JUST BEING ABLE TO SIT HERE AND LISTEN FROM RIGHT NEXT TO YOU IS SHEER BLISS!
YOUR VOICE... IT'S JUST SO PURE AND CLEAR...
AND THE WAY YOU LOOK WHEN YOU SING... I COULD FALL IN LOVE ALL OVER AGAIN...
I KNOW I SAID JUST ONE SONG, BUT I COULD LISTEN TO YOU ALL DAY!

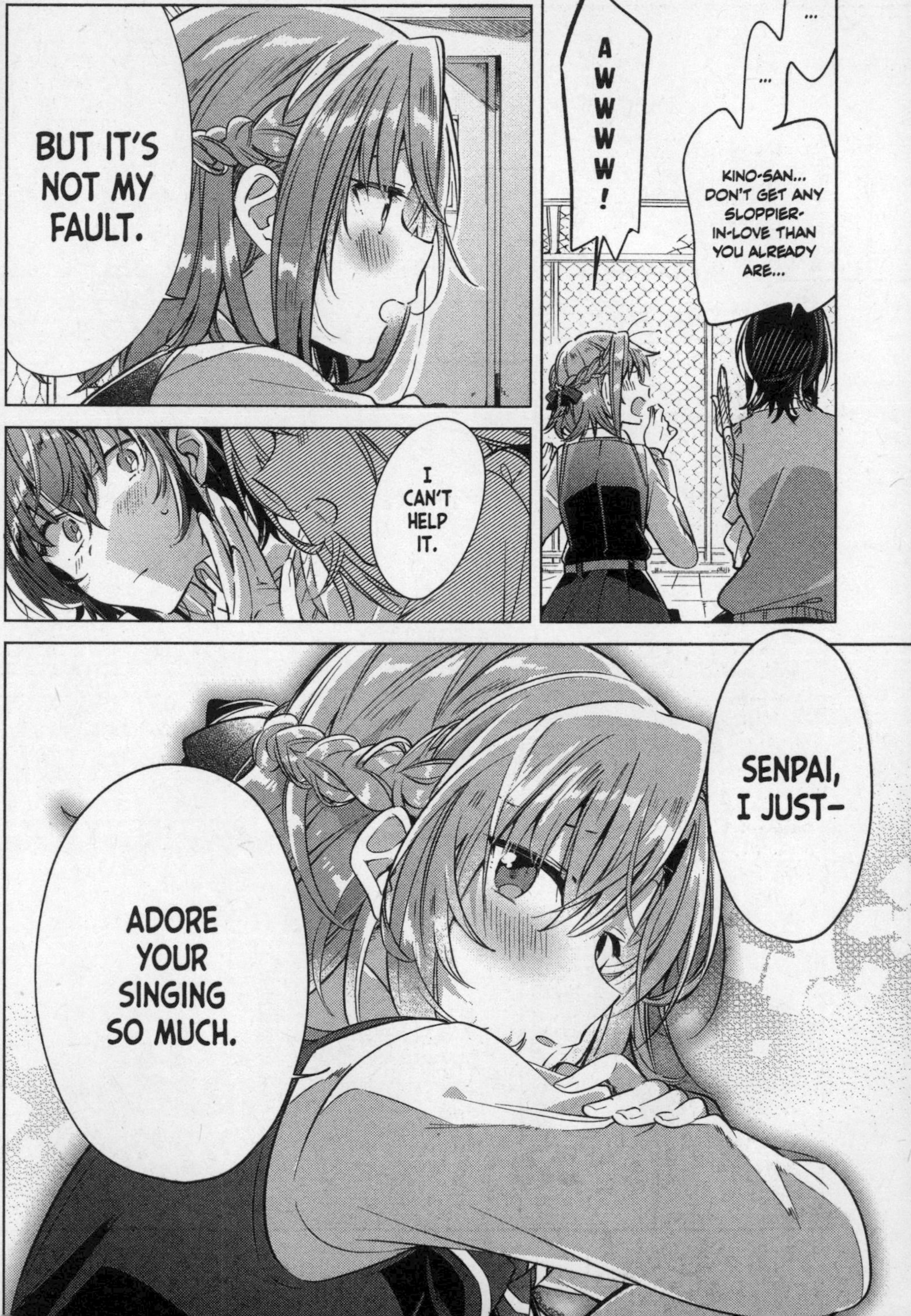
...
...
KINO-SAN... DON'T GET ANY SLOPPIER-IN-LOVE THAN YOU ALREADY ARE...
AWWWWW!
BUT IT'S NOT MY FAULT.
I CAN'T HELP IT.
SENPAI, I JUST-
ADORE YOUR SINGING SO MUCH.

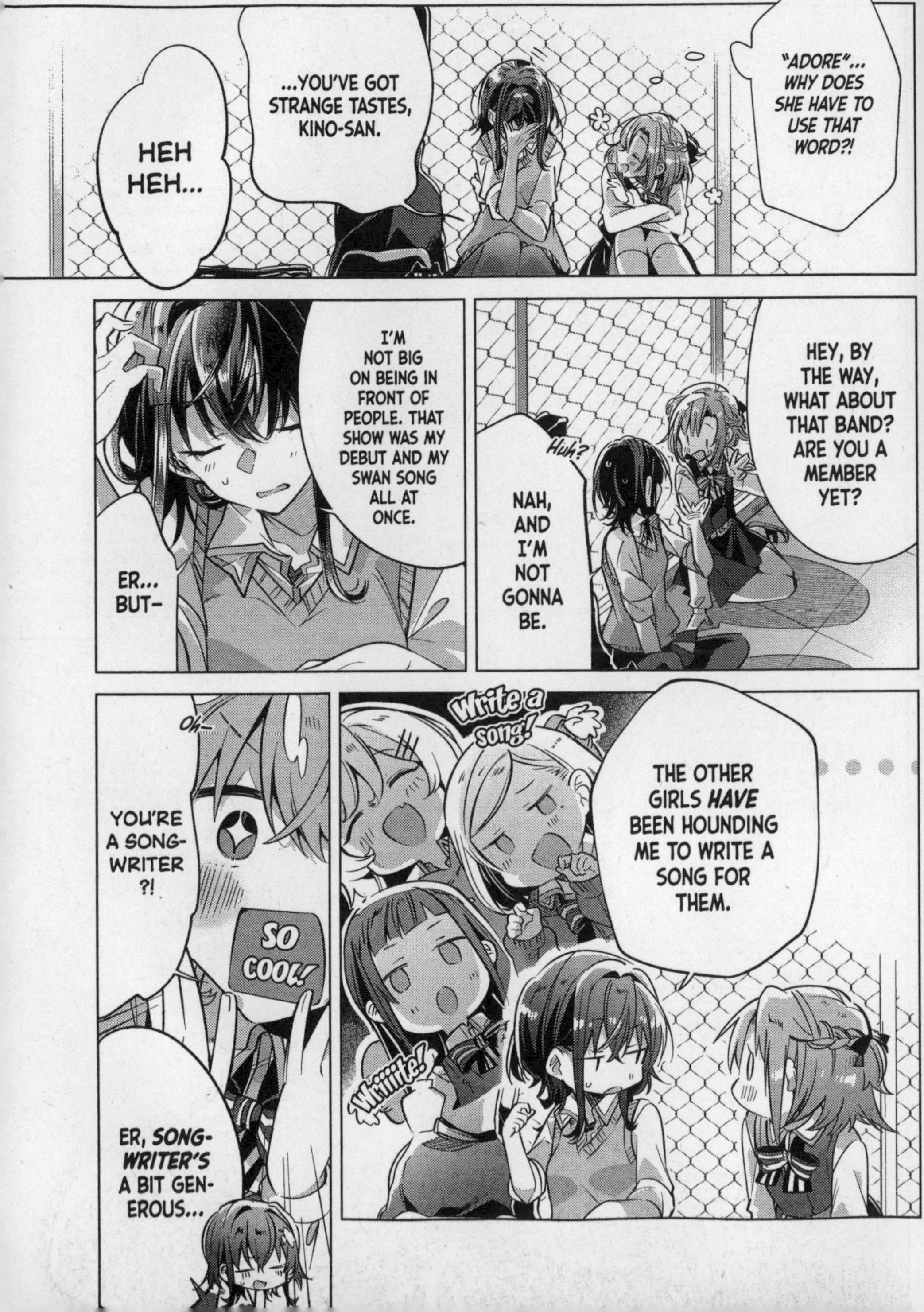
"ADORE"... WHY DOES SHE HAVE TO USE THAT WORD?!
...YOU'VE GOT STRANGE TASTES, KINO-SAN.
HEH HEH...
HEY, BY THE WAY, WHAT ABOUT THAT BAND? ARE YOU A MEMBER YET?
Huh?
NAH, AND I'M NOT GONNA BE.
I'M NOT BIG ON BEING IN FRONT OF PEOPLE. THAT SHOW WAS MY DEBUT AND MY SWAN SONG ALL AT ONCE.
ER... BUT–
THE OTHER GIRLS HAVE BEEN HOUNDING ME TO WRITE A SONG FOR THEM.
Write a song!
Wriiiite!
Oh–
YOU'RE A SONG-WRITER?!
SO COOL!
ER, SONG-WRITER'S A BIT GEN-EROUS...

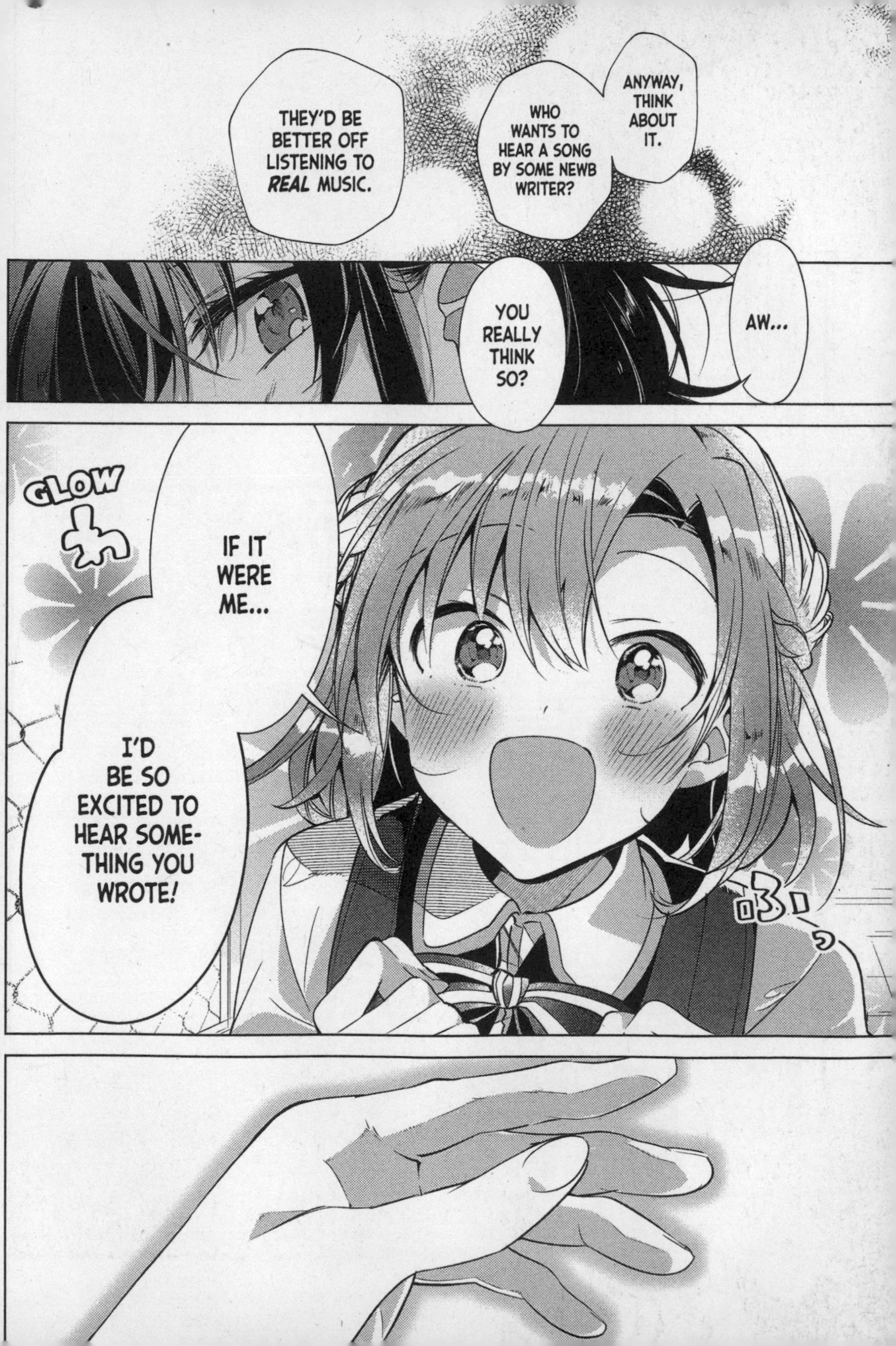
ANYWAY, THINK ABOUT IT.
WHO WANTS TO HEAR A SONG BY SOME NEWB WRITER?
THEY'D BE BETTER OFF LISTENING TO *REAL* MUSIC.
AW...
YOU REALLY THINK SO?
IF IT WERE ME...
I'D BE SO EXCITED TO HEAR SOME-THING YOU WROTE!
GLOW

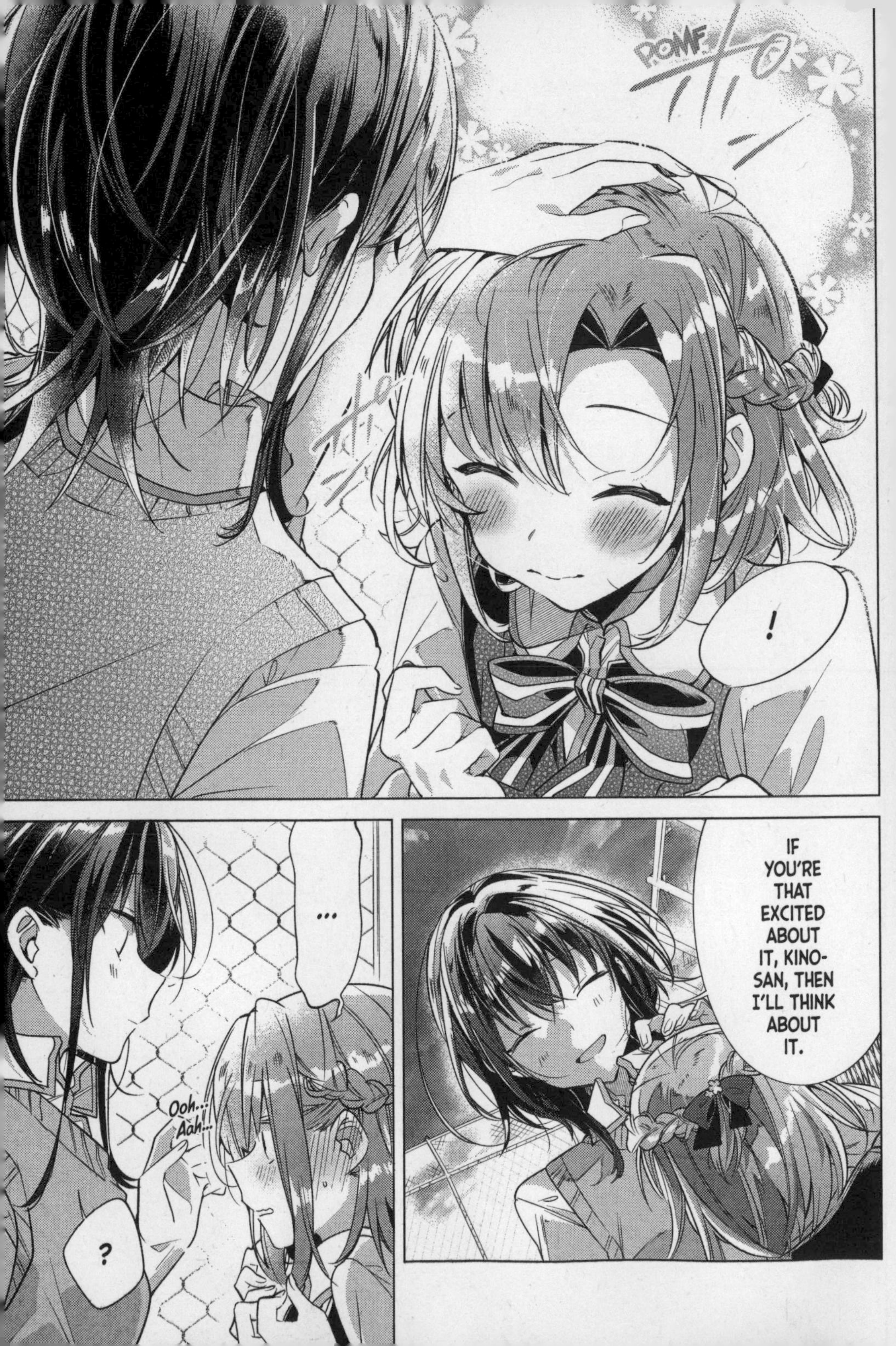
POMF
!
IF YOU'RE THAT EXCITED ABOUT IT, KINO-SAN, THEN I'LL THINK ABOUT IT.
...
Ooh... Aah...
?

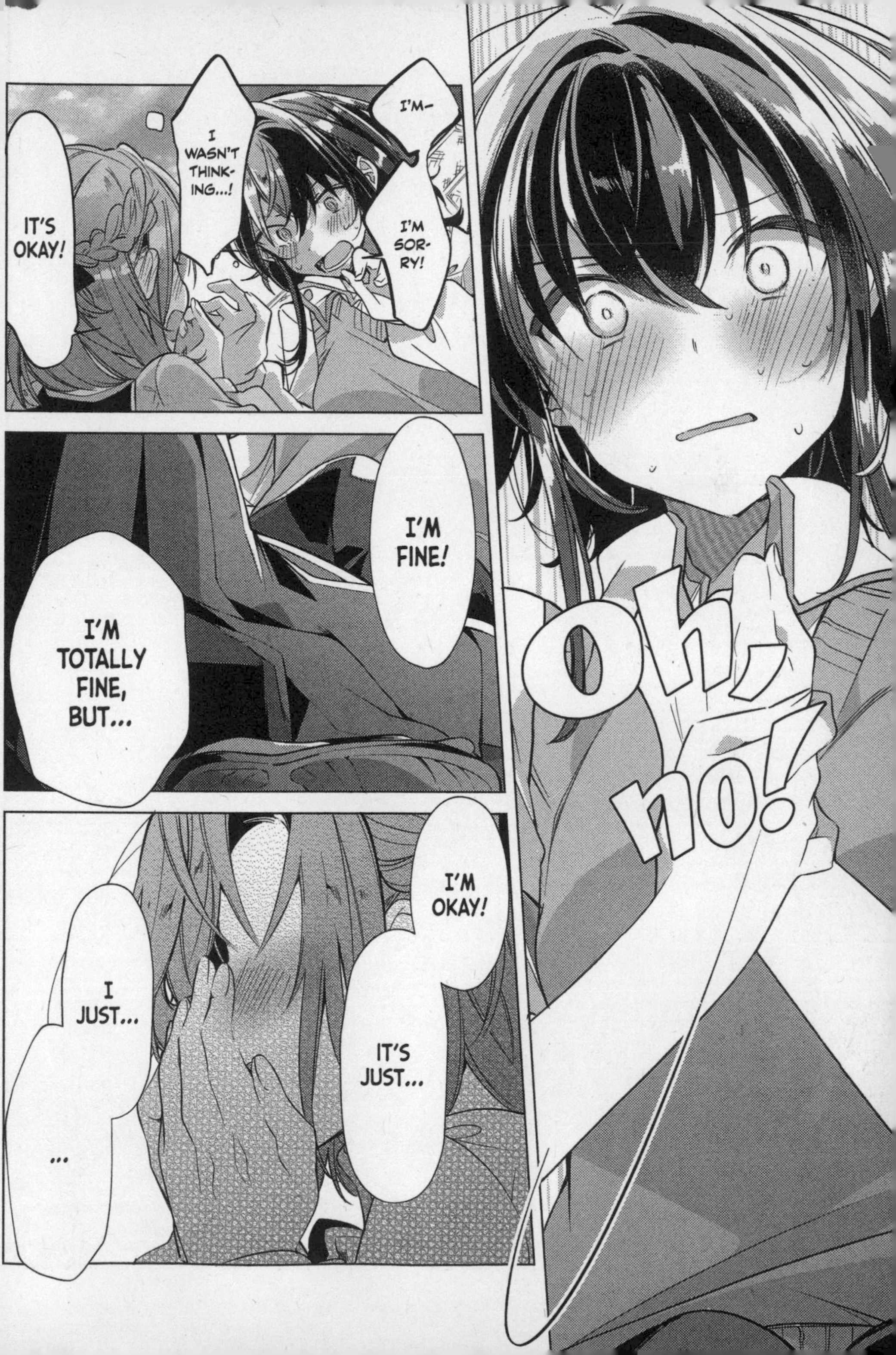
Oh, no!
I'M—
I WASN'T THINKING...!
I'M SORRY!
IT'S OKAY!
I'M FINE!
I'M TOTALLY FINE, BUT...
I'M OKAY!
IT'S JUST...
I JUST...
...

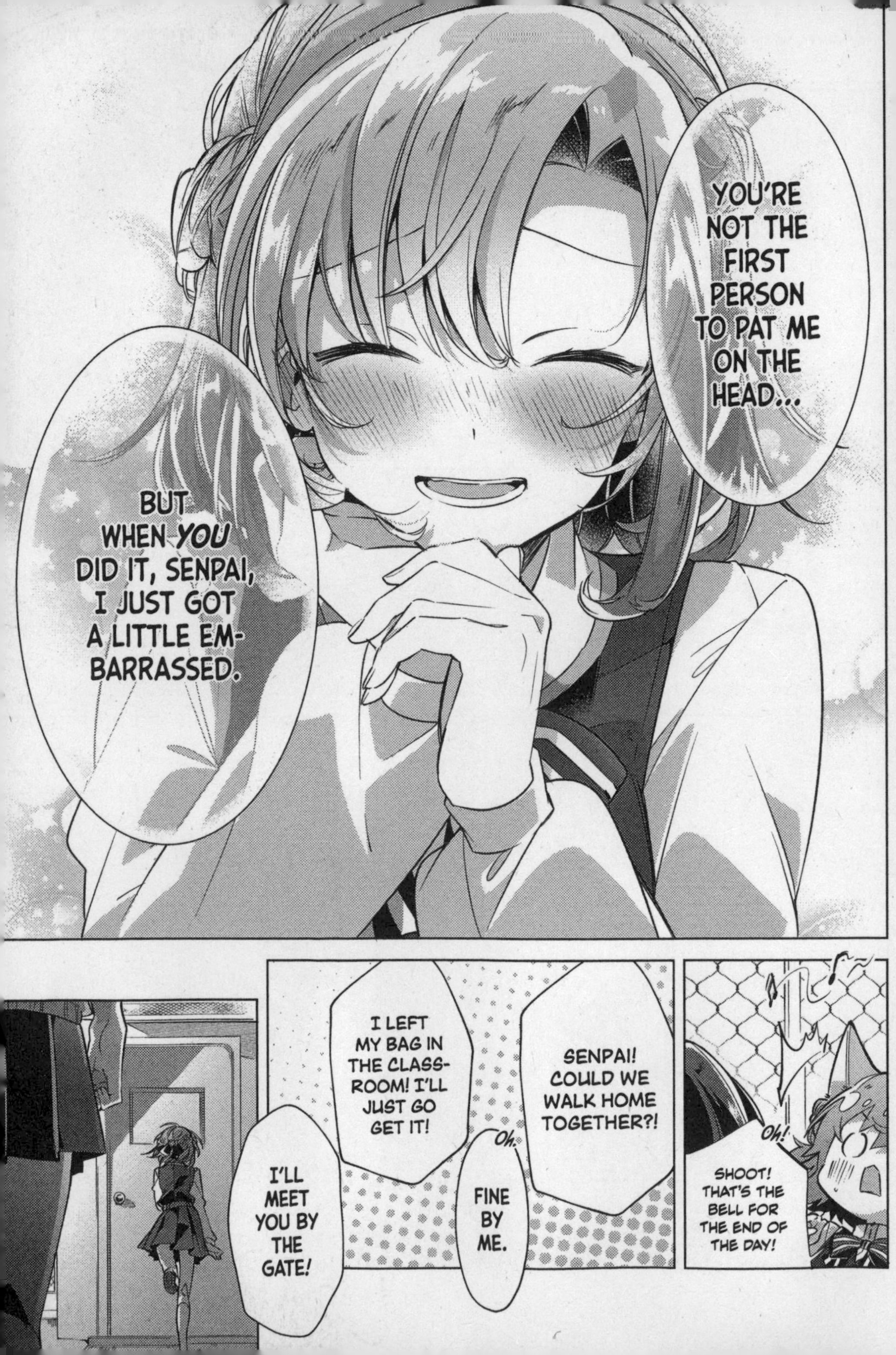
YOU'RE NOT THE FIRST PERSON TO PAT ME ON THE HEAD...
BUT WHEN *YOU* DID IT, SENPAI, I JUST GOT A LITTLE EM-BARRASSED.
Oh!
SHOOT! THAT'S THE BELL FOR THE END OF THE DAY!
SENPAI! COULD WE WALK HOME TOGETHER?!
Oh.
FINE BY ME.
I LEFT MY BAG IN THE CLASS-ROOM! I'LL JUST GO GET IT!
I'LL MEET YOU BY THE GATE!

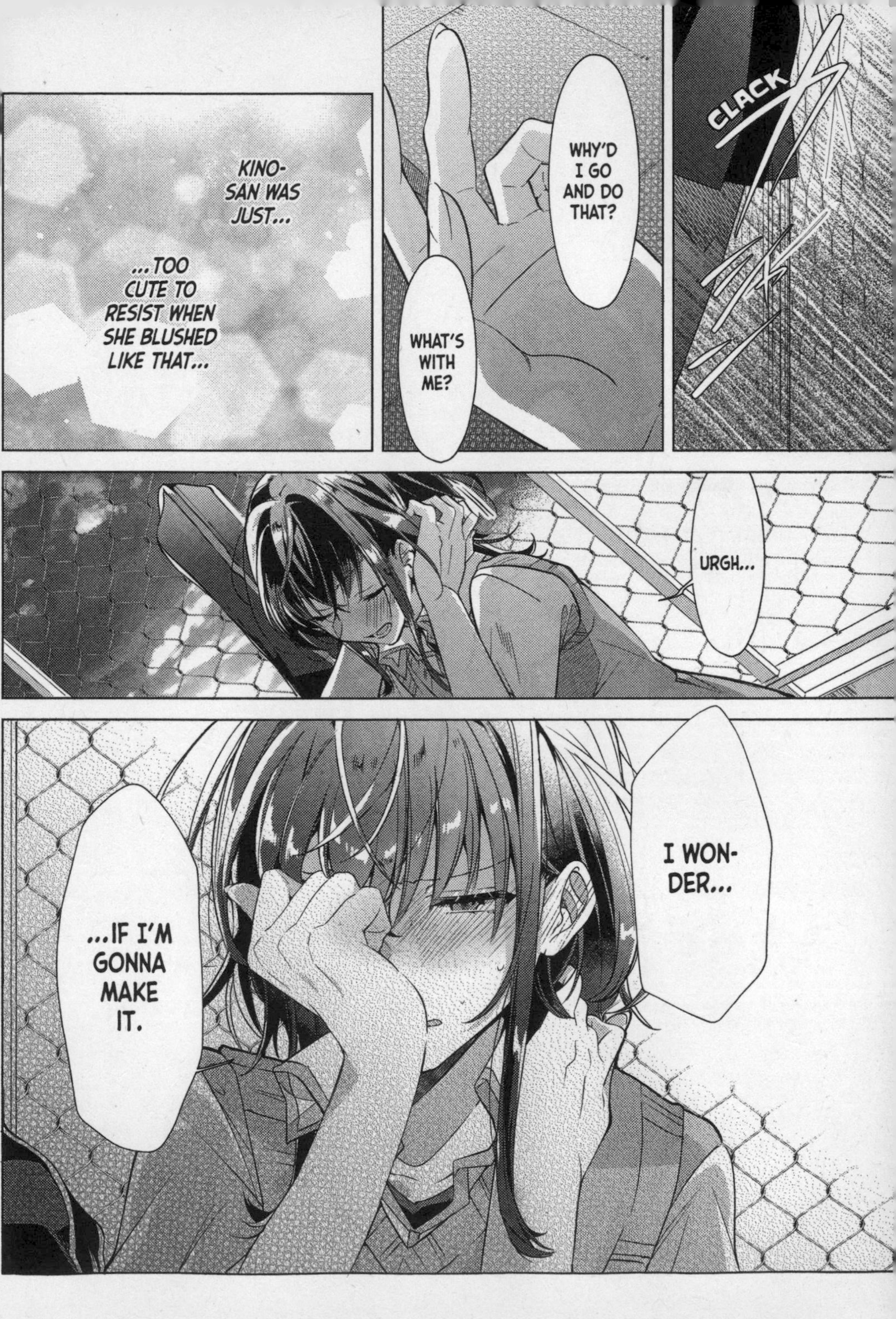
CLACK
WHY'D I GO AND DO THAT?
WHAT'S WITH ME?
KINO-SAN WAS JUST...
...TOO CUTE TO RESIST WHEN SHE BLUSHED LIKE THAT...
URGH...
I WONDER...
...IF I'M GONNA MAKE IT.

Whisper Me
A Love Song

Eku
Takeshima

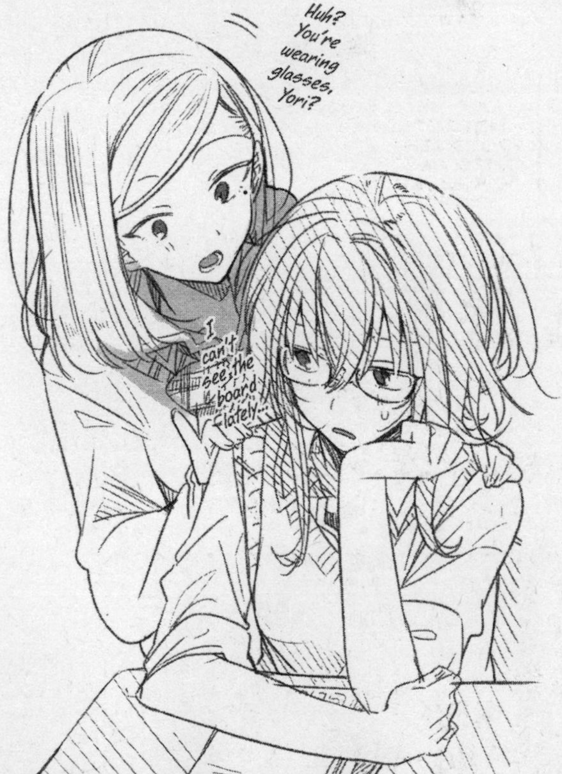
Huh? You're wearing glasses, Yori?
I can't see the board lately...

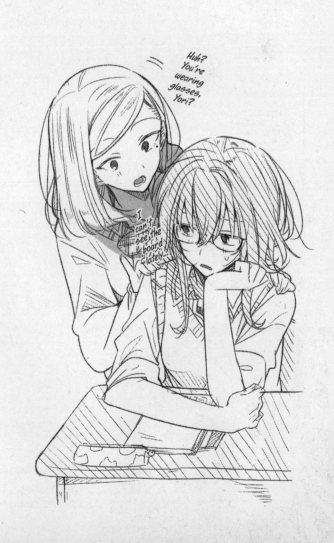

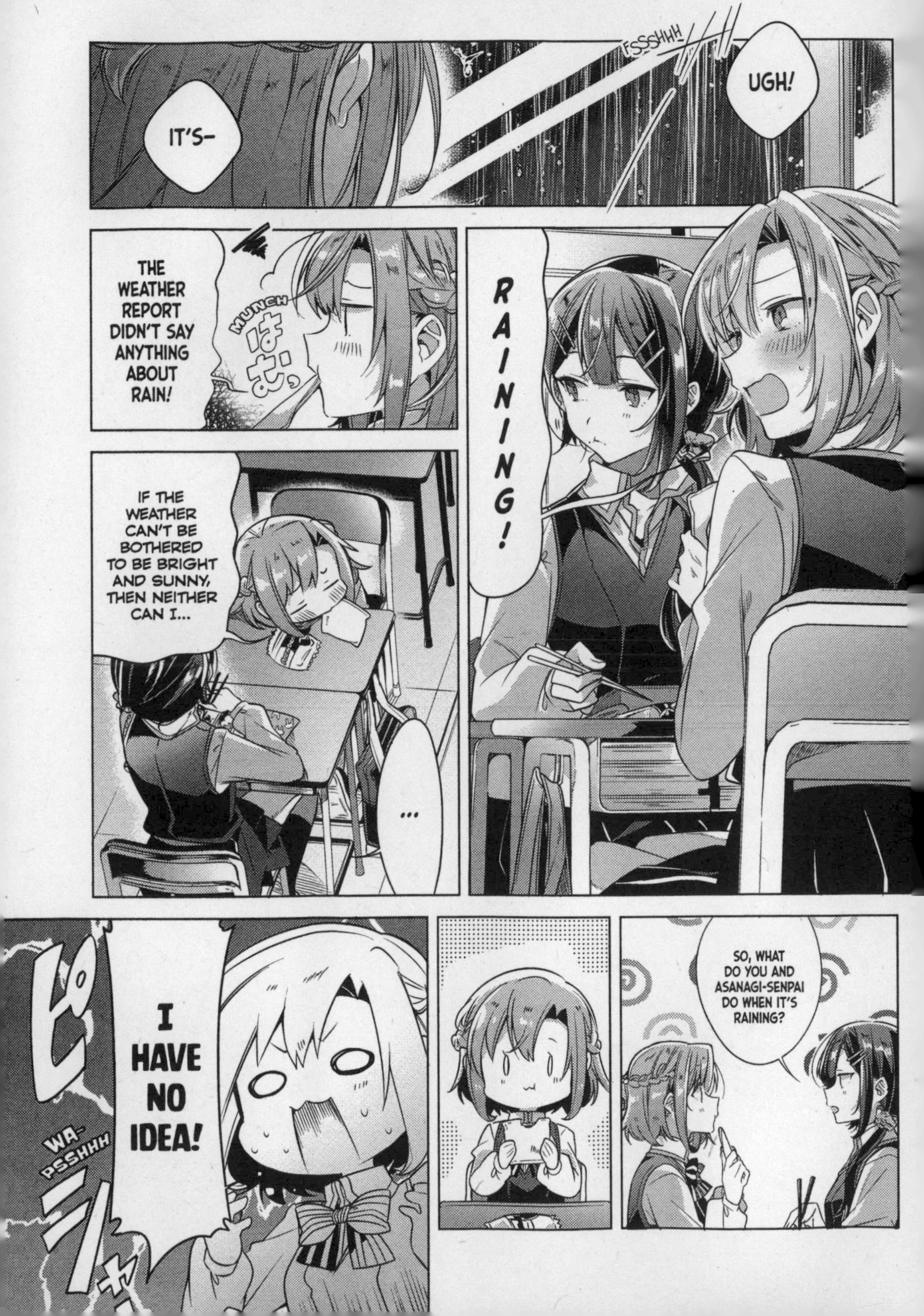
UGH!
FSSSHHH
IT'S-
RAINING!
MUNCH
はむっ
THE WEATHER REPORT DIDN'T SAY ANYTHING ABOUT RAIN!
IF THE WEATHER CAN'T BE BOTHERED TO BE BRIGHT AND SUNNY, THEN NEITHER CAN I...
...
SO, WHAT DO YOU AND ASANAGI-SENPAI DO WHEN IT'S RAINING?
I HAVE NO IDEA!
WA-PSSHHH

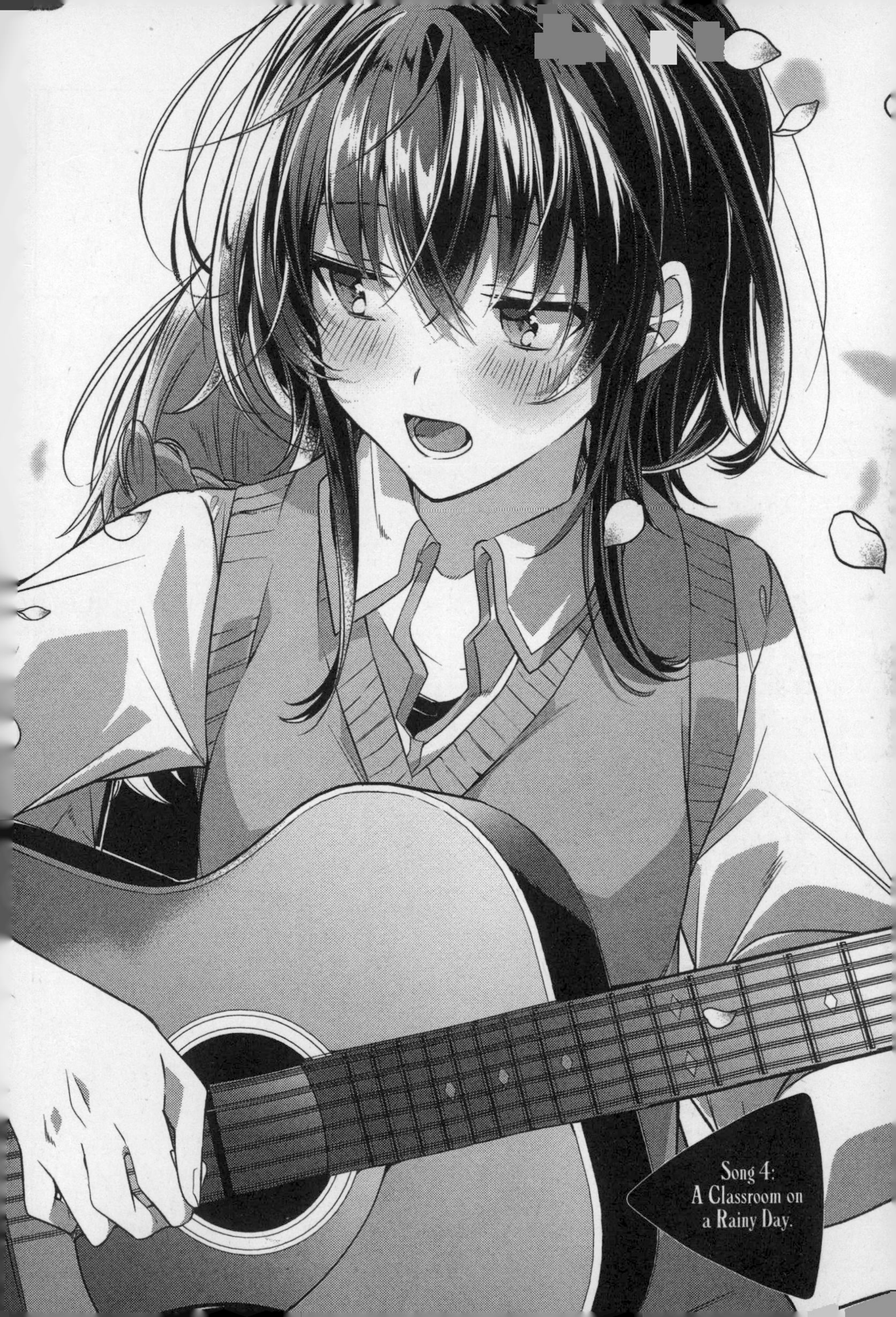
Song 4:
A Classroom on
a Rainy Day.

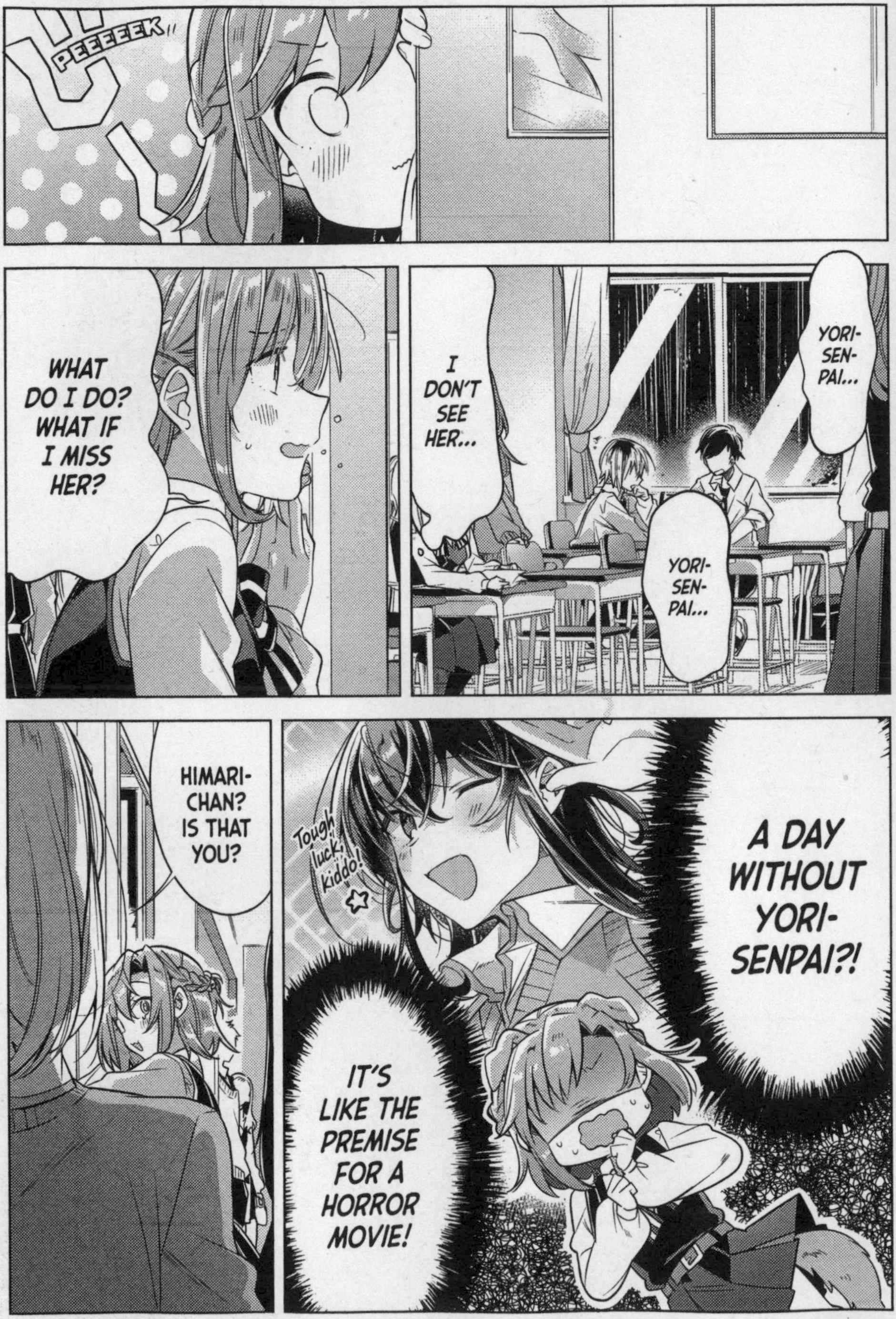
PEEEEEK
YORI-SENPAI...
I DON'T SEE HER...
YORI-SENPAI...
WHAT DO I DO? WHAT IF I MISS HER?
A DAY WITHOUT YORI-SENPAI?!
Tough luck, kiddo!
IT'S LIKE THE PREMISE FOR A HORROR MOVIE!
HIMARI-CHAN? IS THAT YOU?

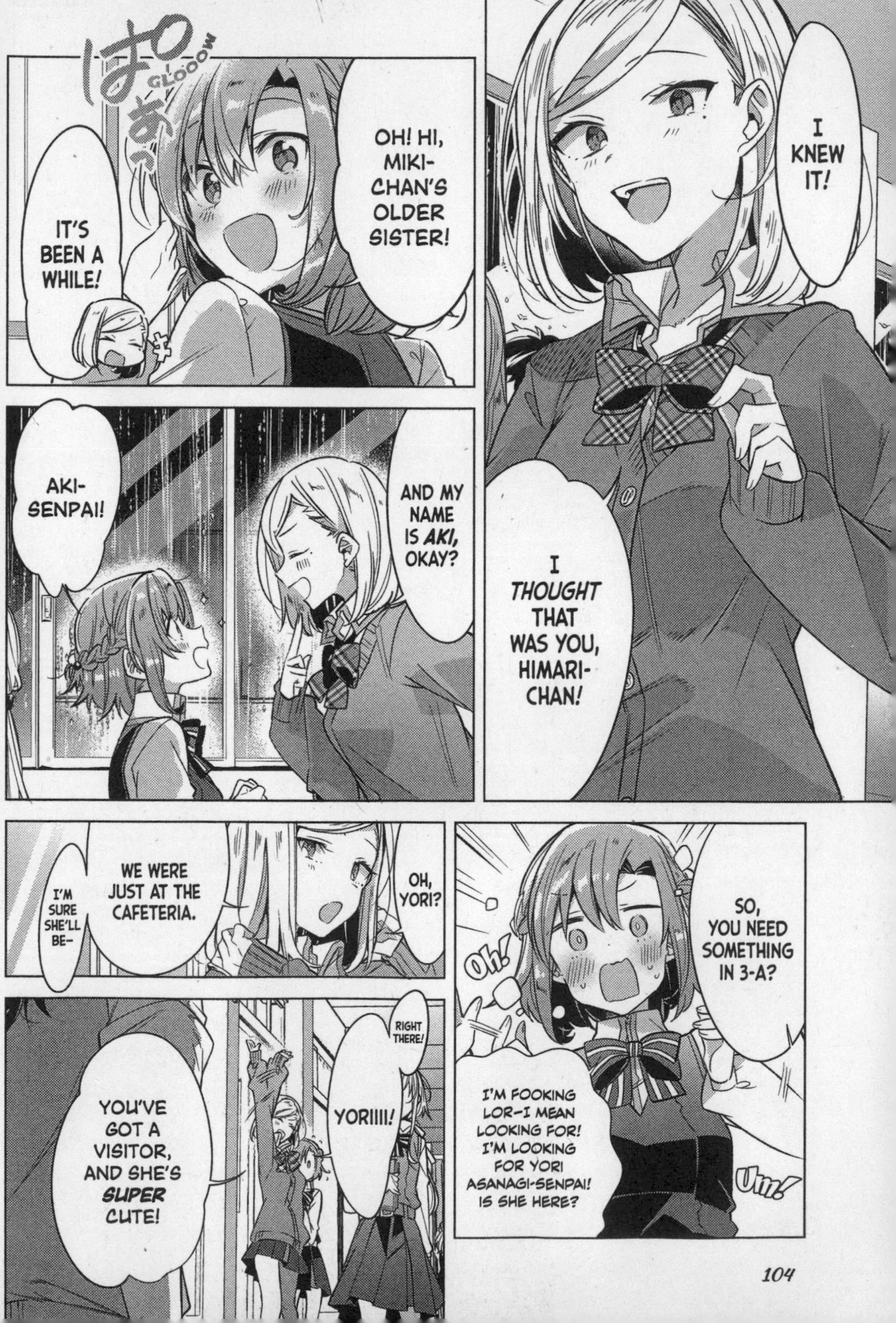
I KNEW IT!
I THOUGHT THAT WAS YOU, HIMARI-CHAN!
ぱあっ
GLOOOW
OH! HI, MIKI-CHAN'S OLDER SISTER!
IT'S BEEN A WHILE!
AND MY NAME IS AKI, OKAY?
AKI-SENPAI!
SO, YOU NEED SOMETHING IN 3-A?
Oh!
I'M FOOKING LOR–I MEAN LOOKING FOR! I'M LOOKING FOR YORI ASANAGI-SENPAI! IS SHE HERE?
Um!
OH, YORI?
WE WERE JUST AT THE CAFETERIA.
I'M SURE SHE'LL BE-
YORIIII!
RIGHT THERE!
YOU'VE GOT A VISITOR, AND SHE'S SUPER CUTE!

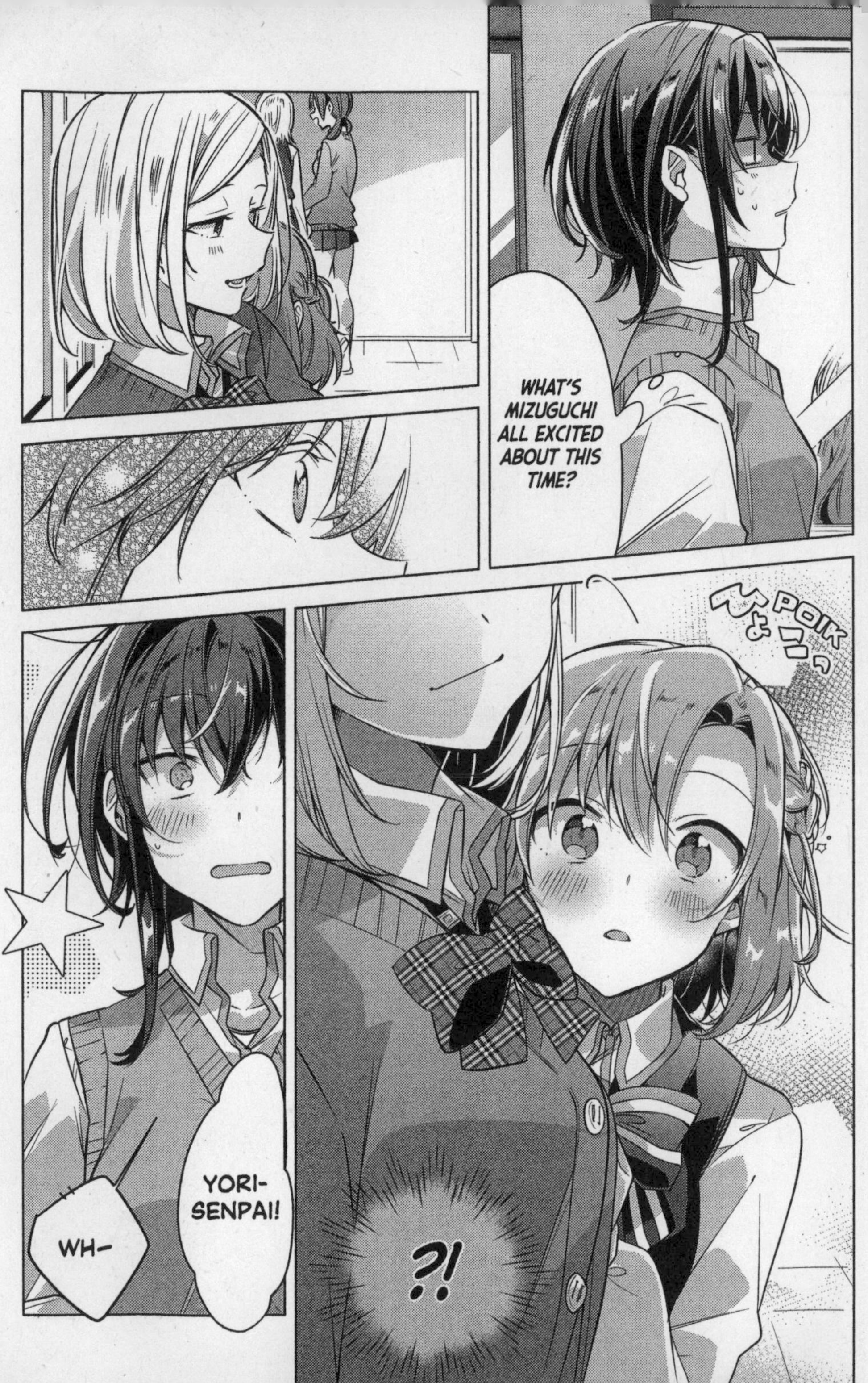
WHAT'S MIZUGUCHI ALL EXCITED ABOUT THIS TIME?
ぴょこっ
POIK
?!
YORI-SENPAI!
WH-

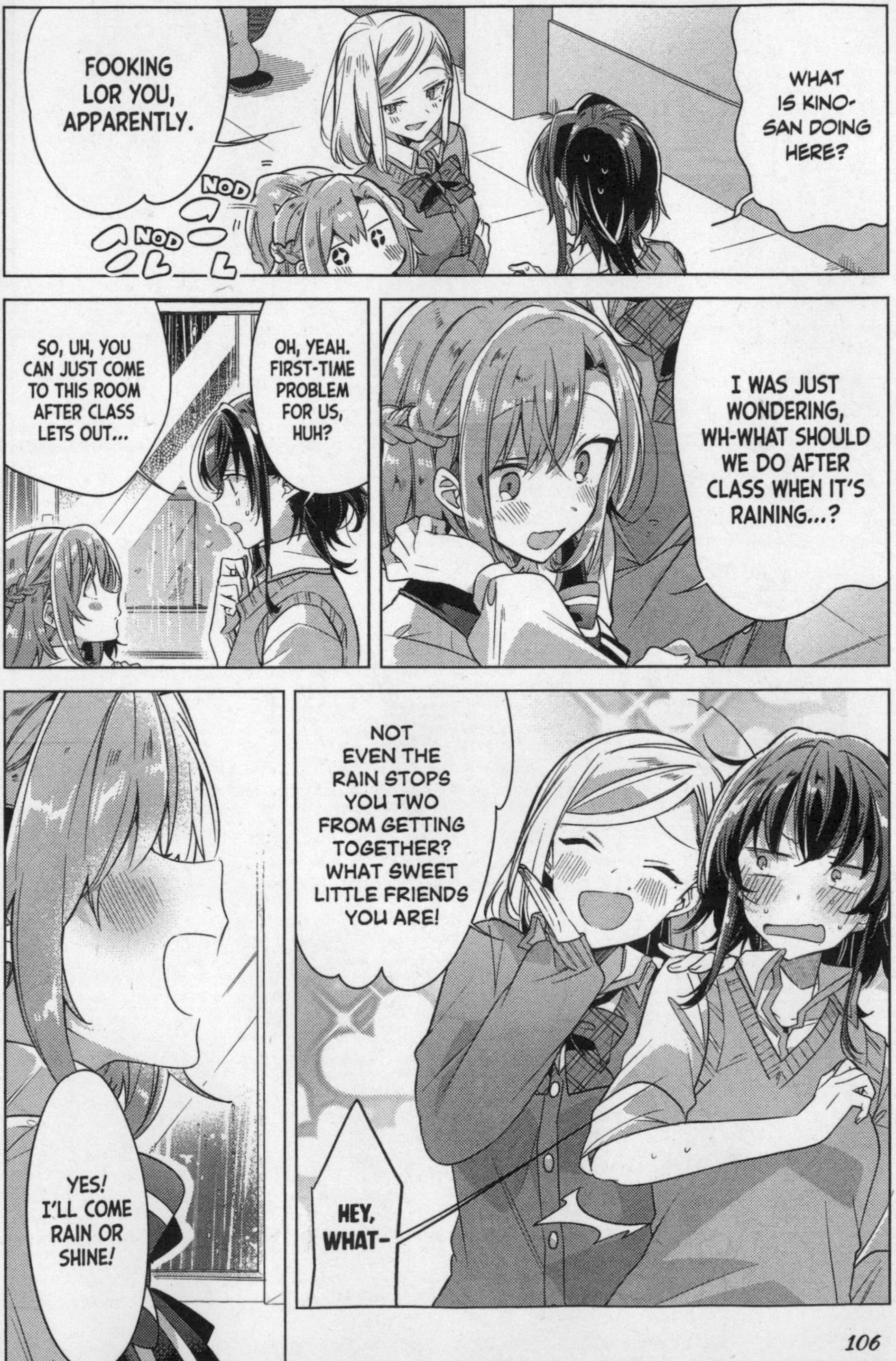
WHAT IS KINO-SAN DOING HERE?
FOOKING LOR YOU, APPARENTLY.
NOD
NOD
I WAS JUST WONDERING, WH-WHAT SHOULD WE DO AFTER CLASS WHEN IT'S RAINING...?
OH, YEAH. FIRST-TIME PROBLEM FOR US, HUH?
SO, UH, YOU CAN JUST COME TO THIS ROOM AFTER CLASS LETS OUT...
NOT EVEN THE RAIN STOPS YOU TWO FROM GETTING TOGETHER? WHAT SWEET LITTLE FRIENDS YOU ARE!
HEY, WHAT-
YES! I'LL COME RAIN OR SHINE!

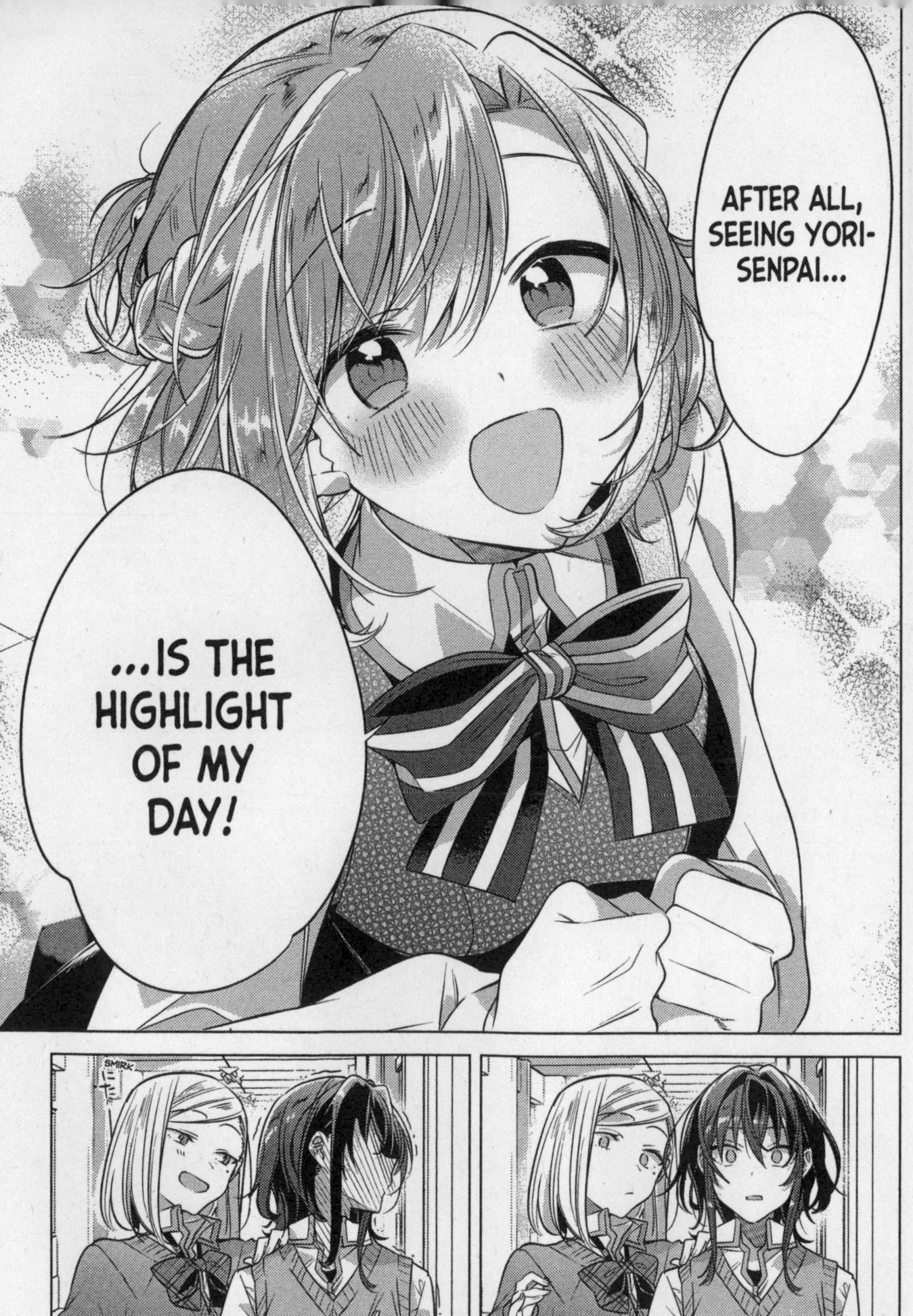
AFTER ALL, SEEING YORI-SENPAI...
...IS THE HIGHLIGHT OF MY DAY!
SMIRK

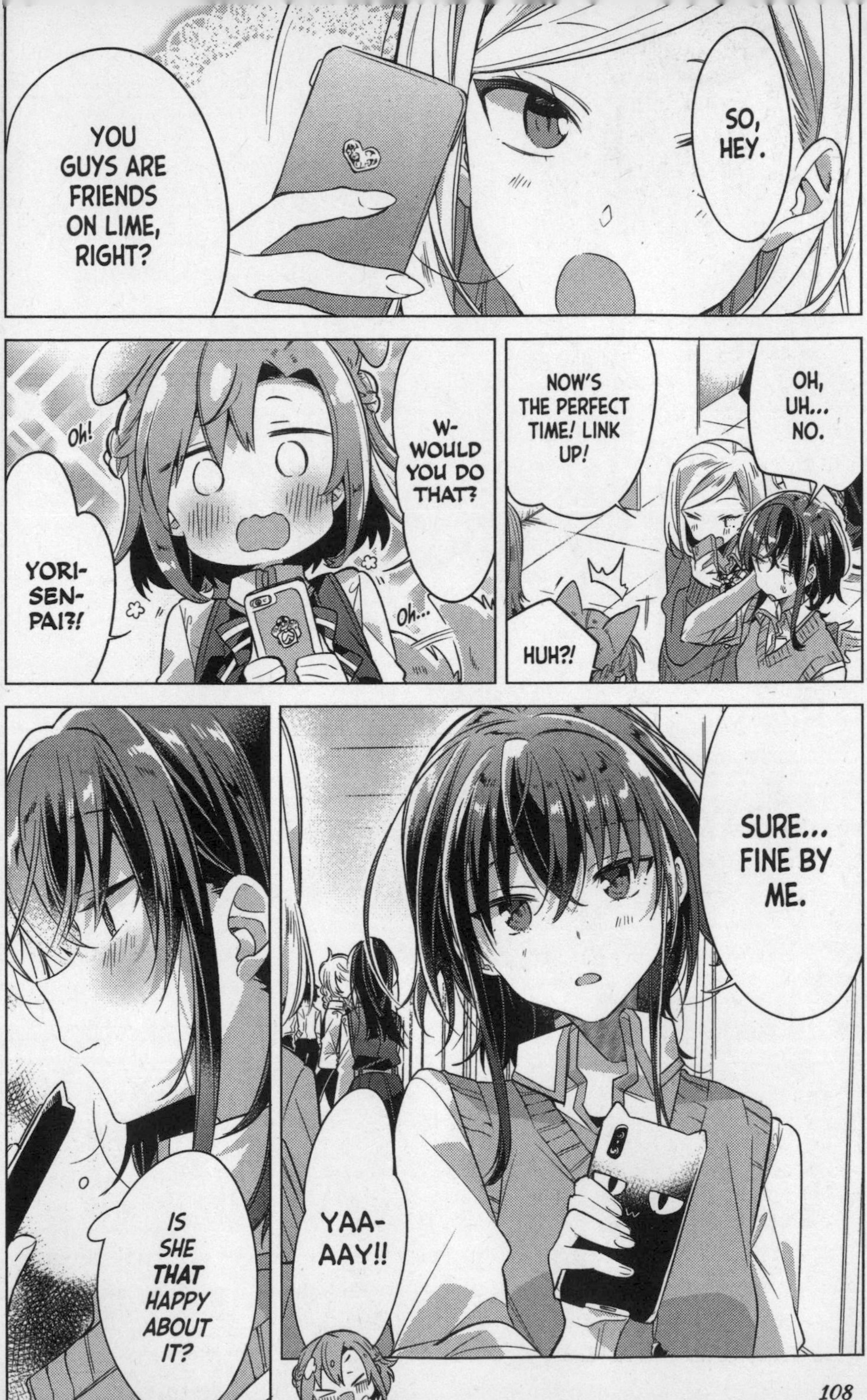
SO, HEY.
YOU GUYS ARE FRIENDS ON LIME, RIGHT?
OH, UH... NO.
NOW'S THE PERFECT TIME! LINK UP!
HUH?!
W-WOULD YOU DO THAT?
Oh!
Oh...
YORI-SENPAI?!
SURE... FINE BY ME.
YAA-AAY!!
IS SHE THAT HAPPY ABOUT IT?

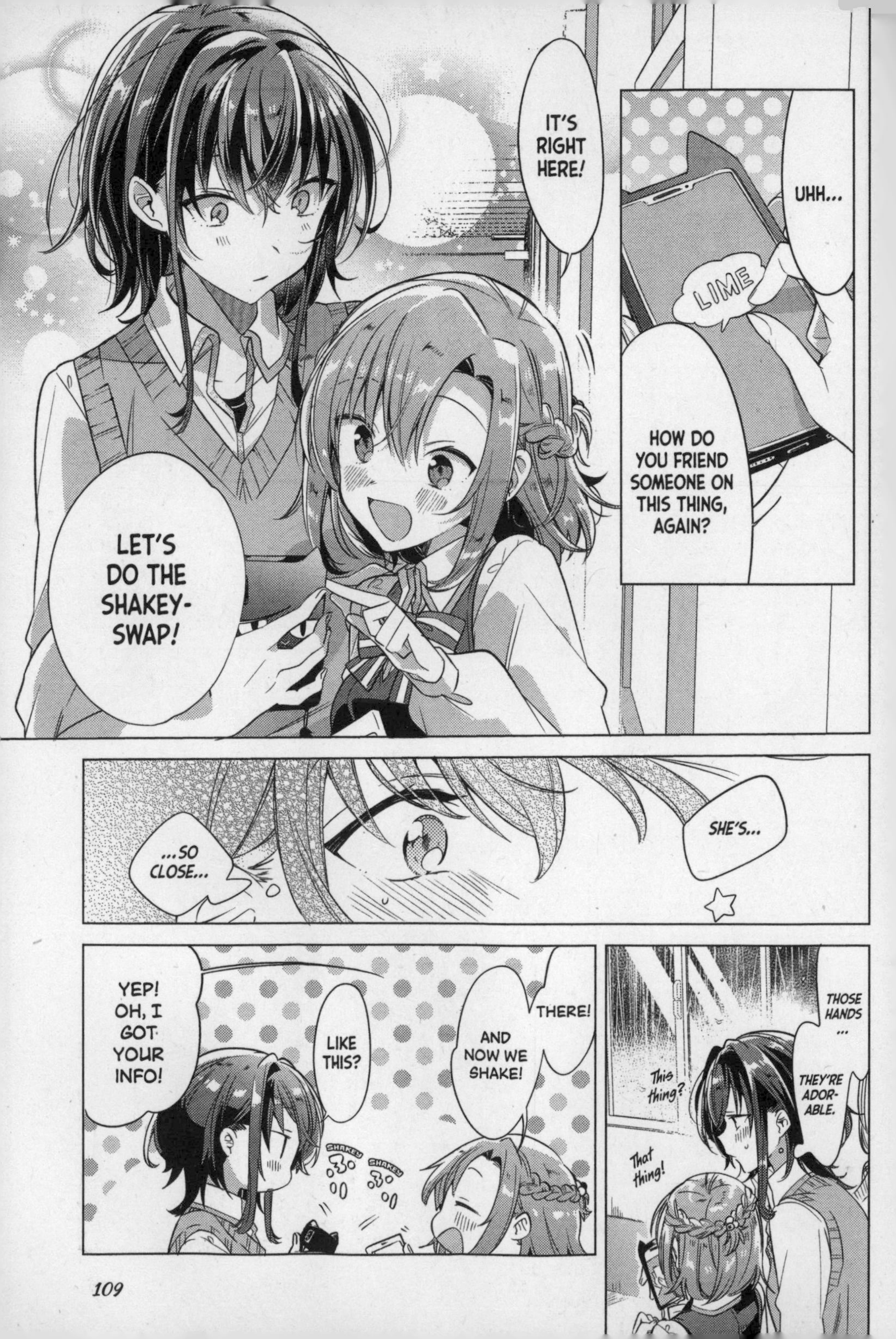
UHH...
LIME
HOW DO YOU FRIEND SOMEONE ON THIS THING, AGAIN?
IT'S RIGHT HERE!
LET'S DO THE SHAKEY-SWAP!
SHE'S...
...SO CLOSE...
THOSE HANDS...
This thing?
That thing!
THEY'RE ADORABLE.
THERE!
AND NOW WE SHAKE!
LIKE THIS?
SHAKEY SHAKEY
YEP! OH, I GOT YOUR INFO!

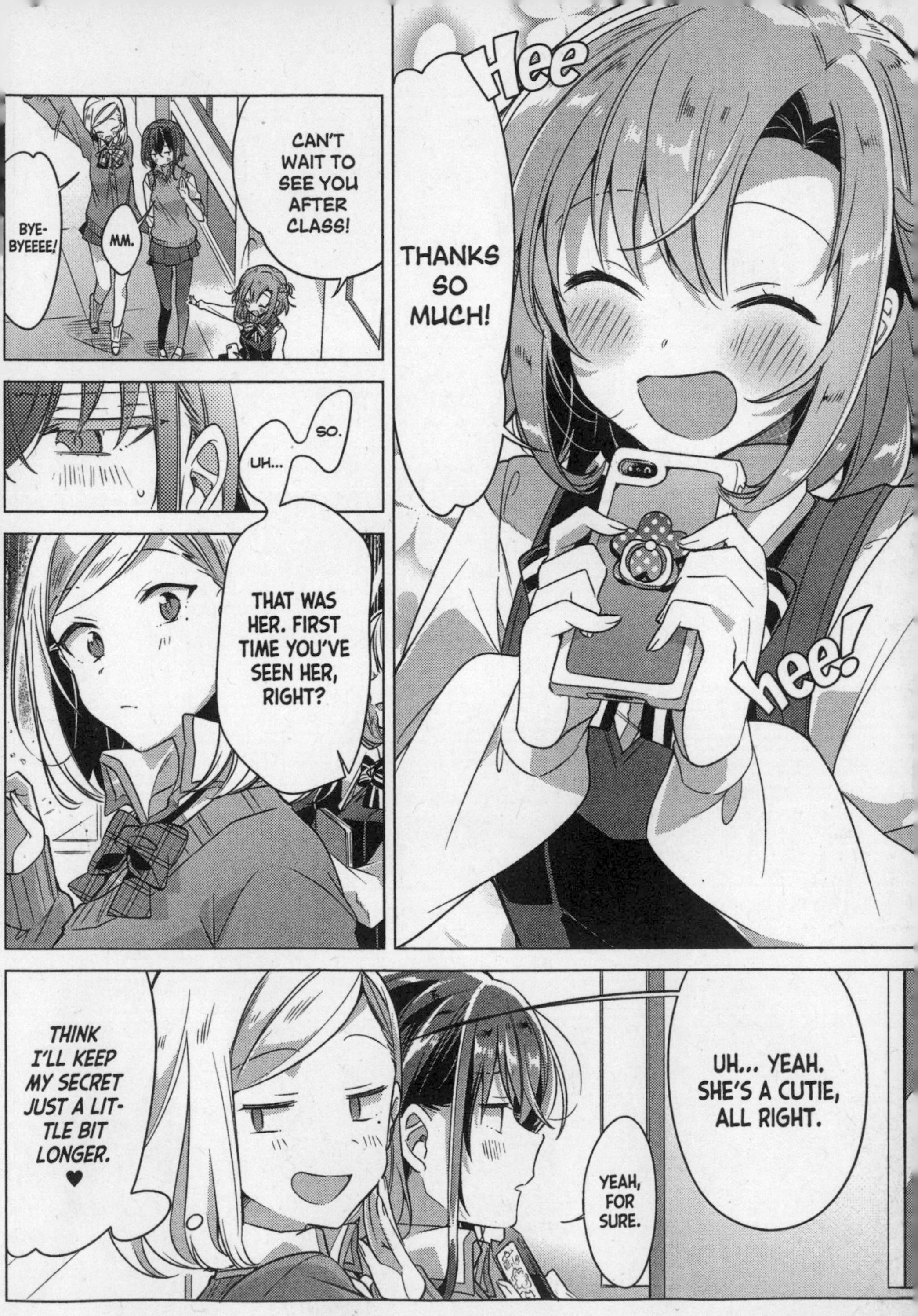
Hee
THANKS SO MUCH!
hee!
CAN'T WAIT TO SEE YOU AFTER CLASS!
MM.
BYE-BYEEEE!
SO.
UH...
THAT WAS HER. FIRST TIME YOU'VE SEEN HER, RIGHT?
UH... YEAH. SHE'S A CUTIE, ALL RIGHT.
YEAH, FOR SURE.
THINK I'LL KEEP MY SECRET JUST A LIT-TLE BIT LONGER. ♥

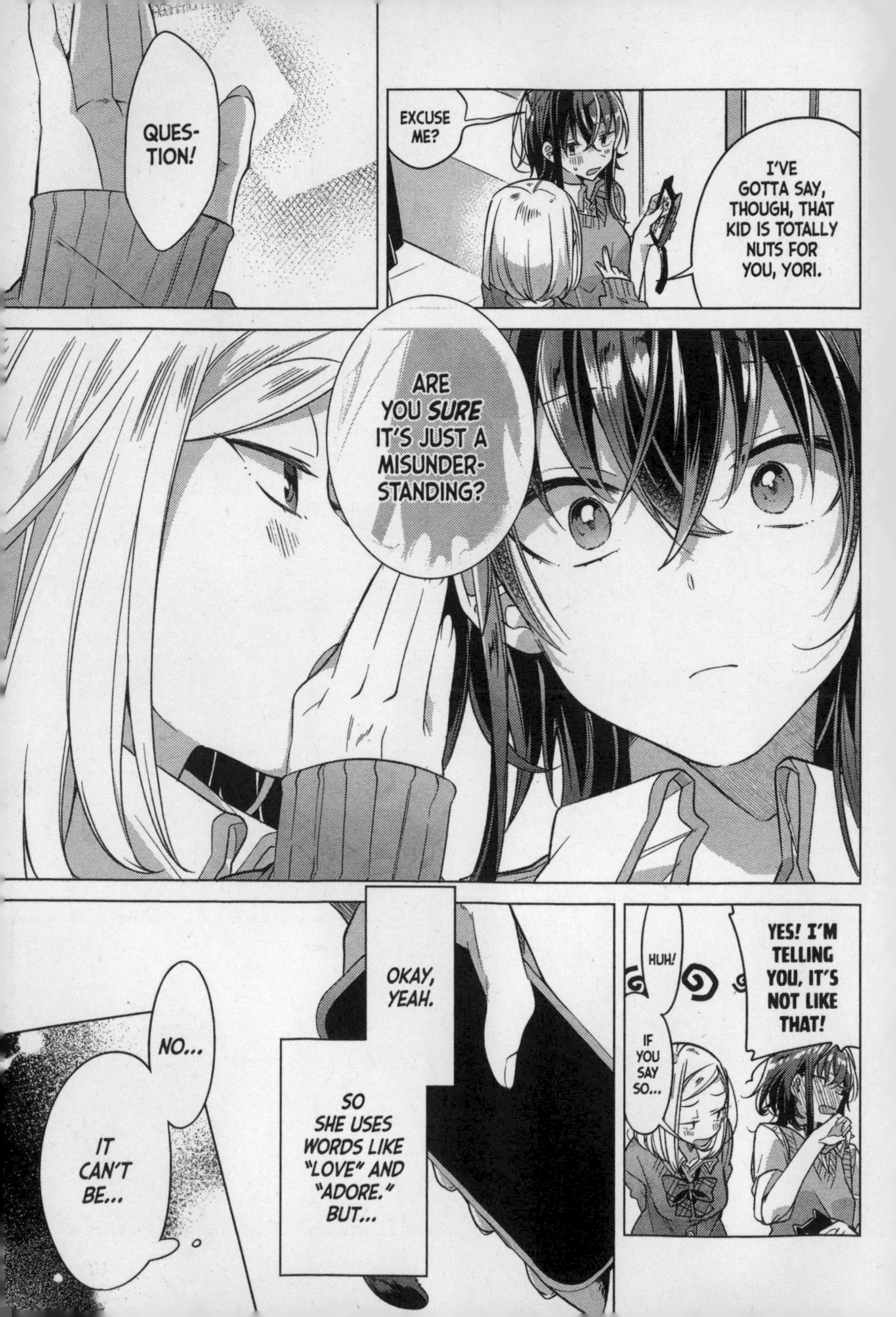
I'VE GOTTA SAY, THOUGH, THAT KID IS TOTALLY NUTS FOR YOU, YORI.
EXCUSE ME?
QUES-TION!
ARE YOU *SURE* IT'S JUST A MISUNDER-STANDING?
YES! I'M TELLING YOU, IT'S NOT LIKE THAT!
HUH!
IF YOU SAY SO...
OKAY, YEAH.
SO SHE USES WORDS LIKE "LOVE" AND "ADORE." BUT...
NO...
IT CAN'T BE...

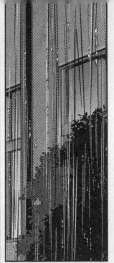

HOORAY, CLASS IS OVER!

NOW TO SEE YORI-SENPAI! ♪

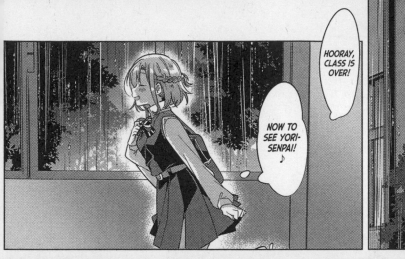

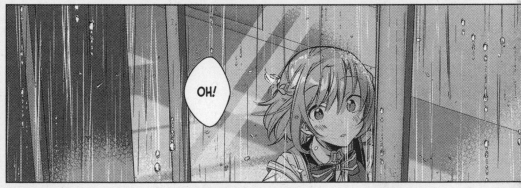

OH!

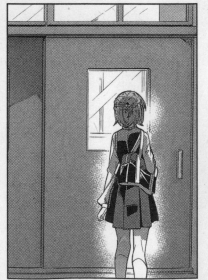

3 - A

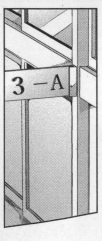

I'M SUPPOSED TO GO TO HER HOMEROOM TODAY.

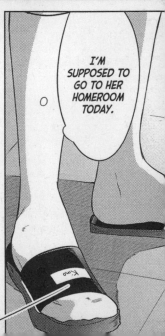

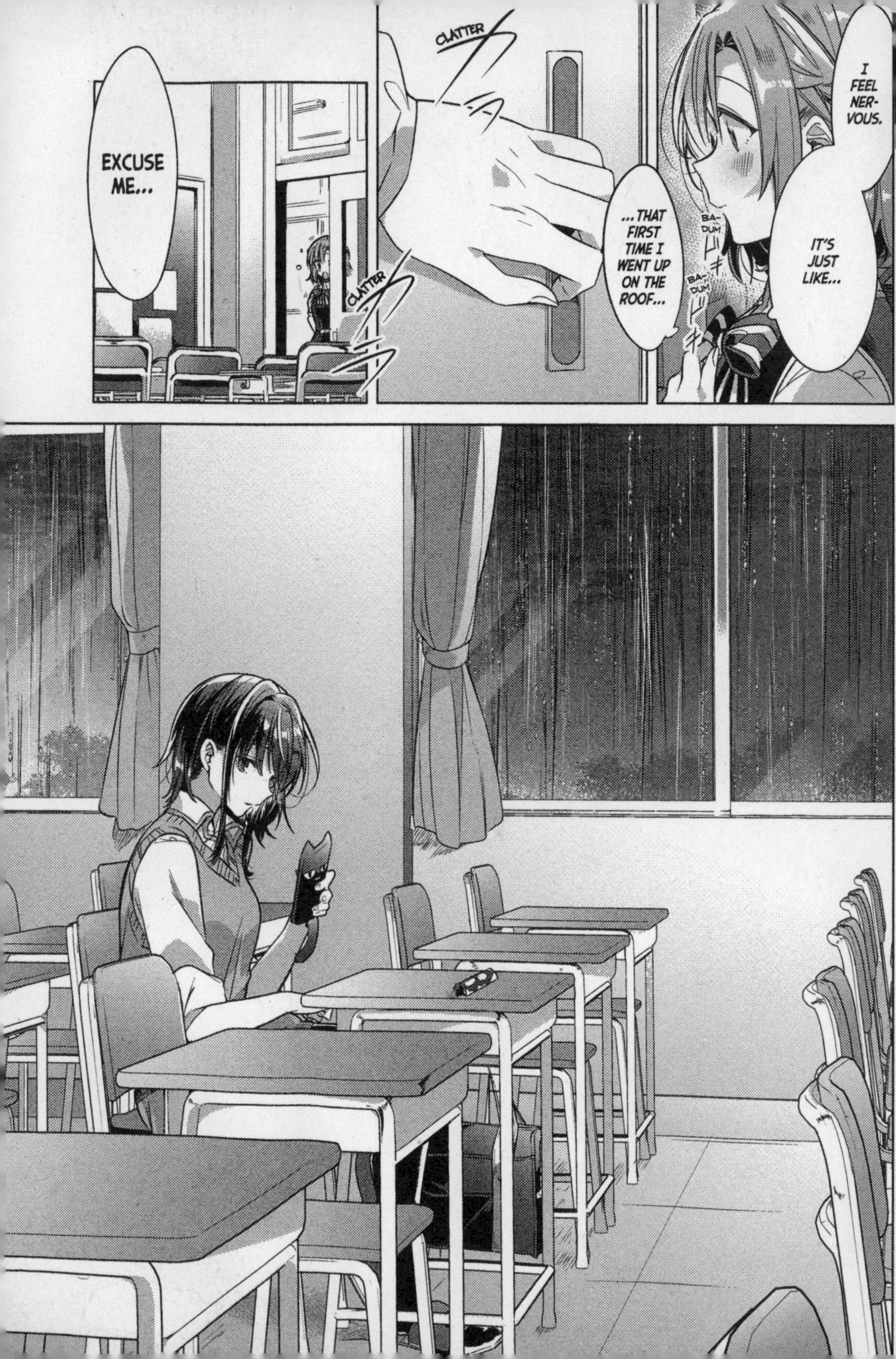
I FEEL NER-VOUS.
IT'S JUST LIKE...
...THAT FIRST TIME I WENT UP ON THE ROOF...
BA-DUM
BA-DUM
CLATTER
CLATTER
EXCUSE ME...

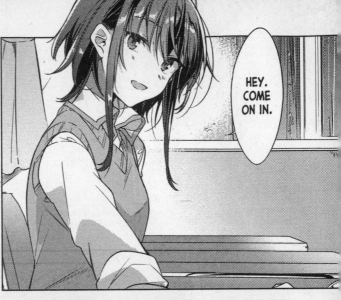

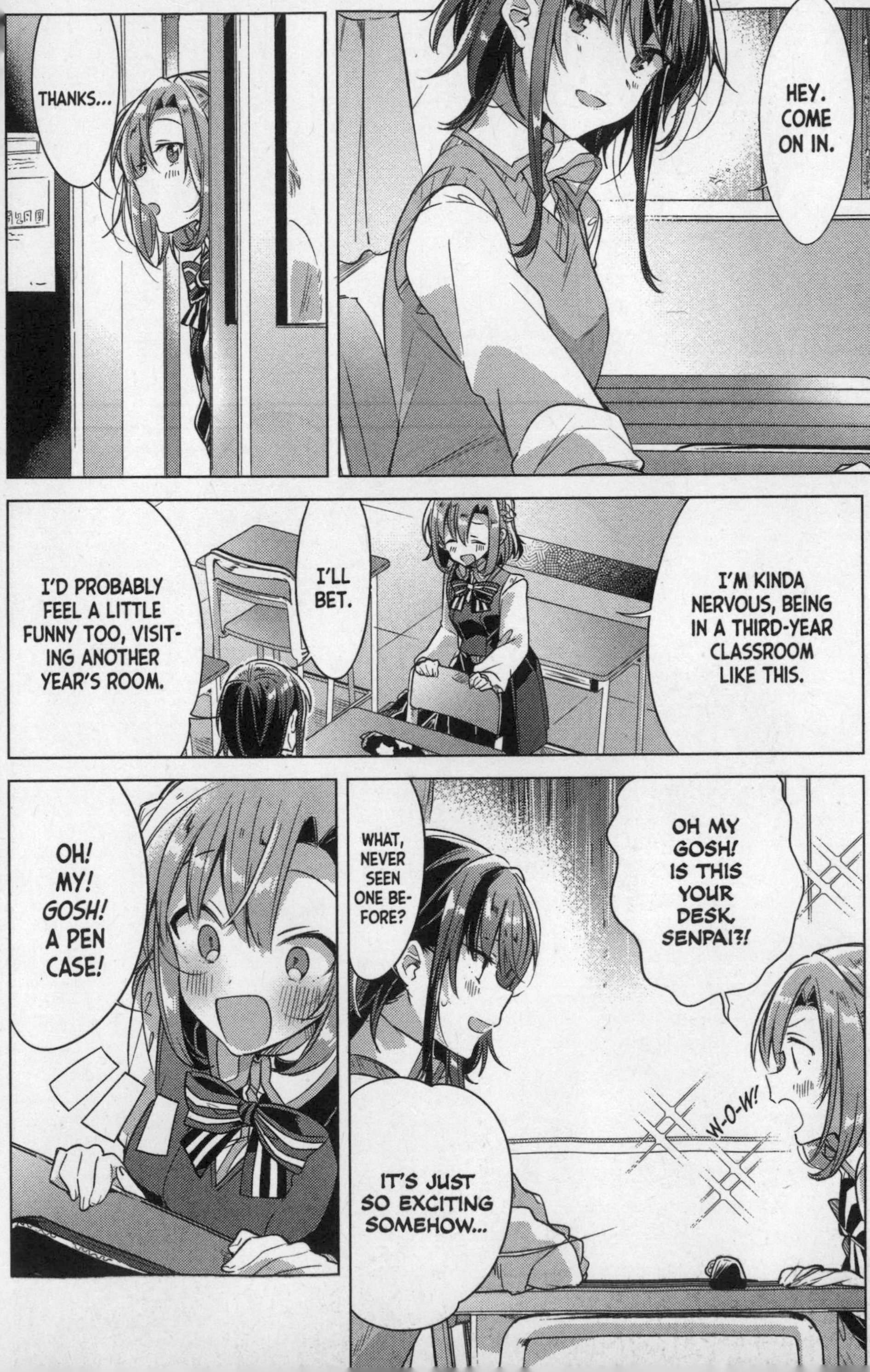
HEY. COME ON IN.
THANKS...
I'M KINDA NERVOUS, BEING IN A THIRD-YEAR CLASSROOM LIKE THIS.
I'LL BET.
I'D PROBABLY FEEL A LITTLE FUNNY TOO, VISIT-ING ANOTHER YEAR'S ROOM.
OH MY GOSH! IS THIS YOUR DESK, SENPAI?!
W-O-W!
WHAT, NEVER SEEN ONE BE-FORE?
IT'S JUST SO EXCITING SOMEHOW...
OH! MY! GOSH! A PEN CASE!

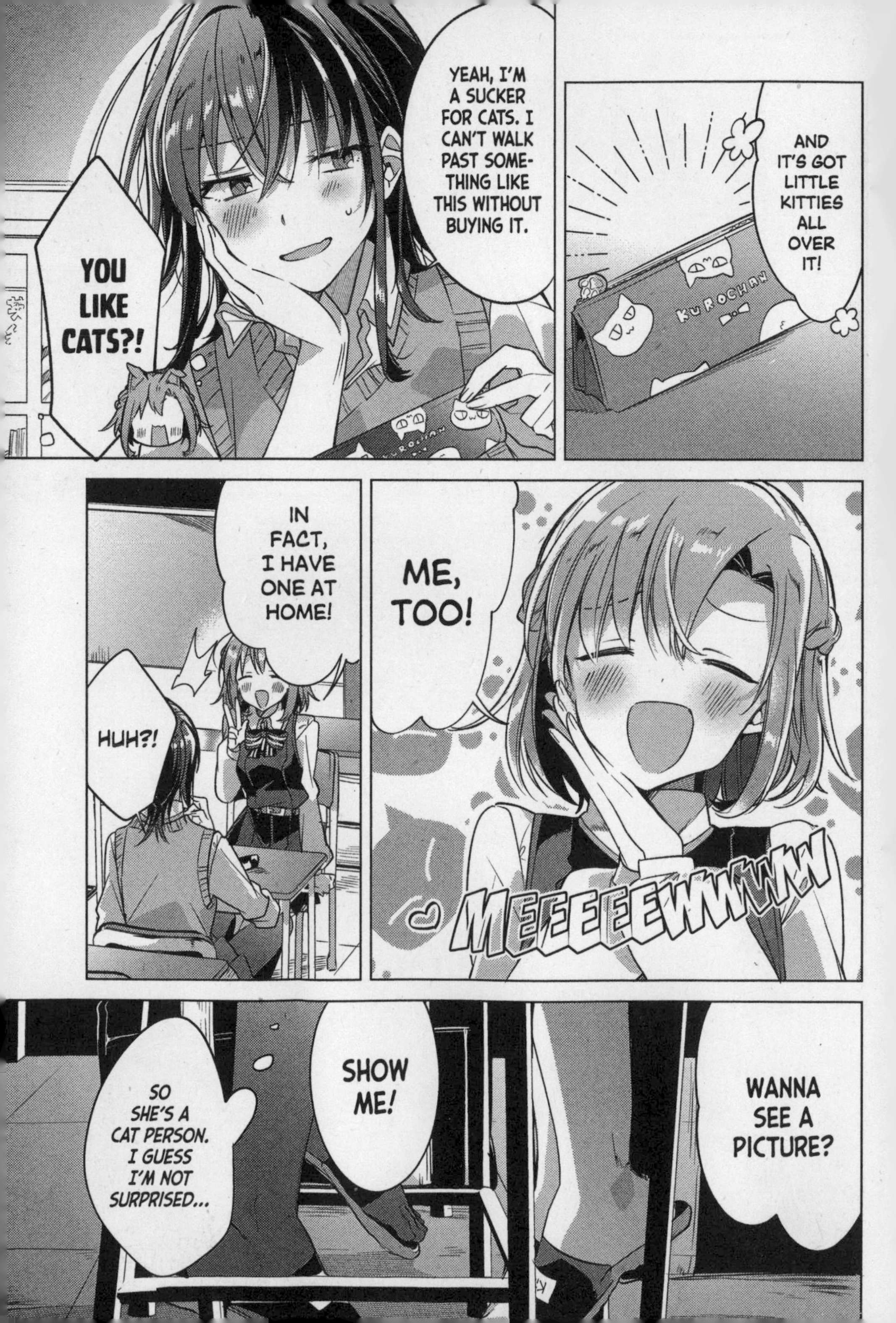
AND IT'S GOT LITTLE KITTIES ALL OVER IT!
KUROCHAN
YEAH, I'M A SUCKER FOR CATS. I CAN'T WALK PAST SOME-THING LIKE THIS WITHOUT BUYING IT.
YOU LIKE CATS?!
ME, TOO!
MEEEEEWWWWW
IN FACT, I HAVE ONE AT HOME!
HUH?!
WANNA SEE A PICTURE?
SHOW ME!
SO SHE'S A CAT PERSON. I GUESS I'M NOT SURPRISED...

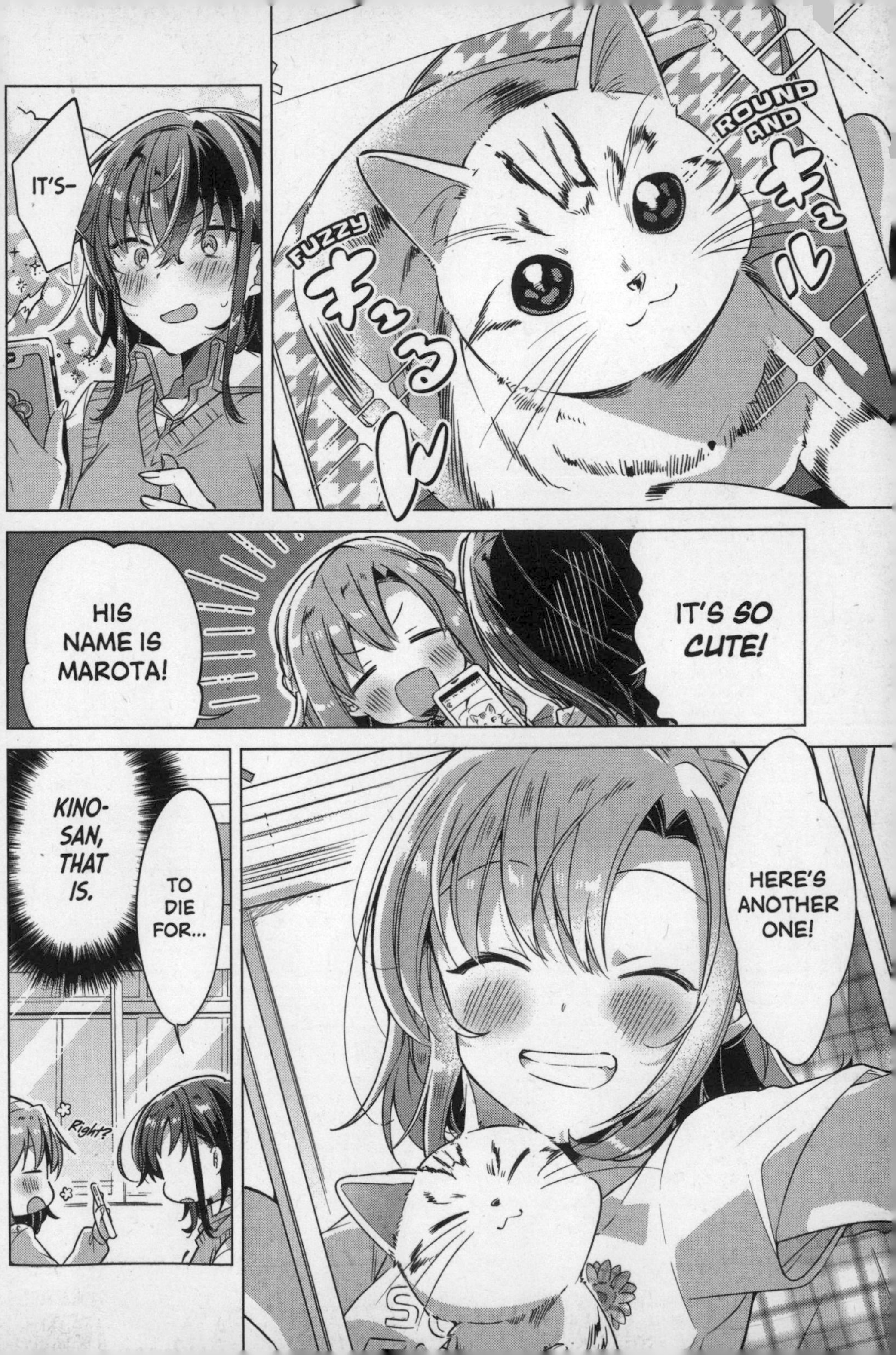
ROUND AND キュル
FUZZY キュるん
IT'S-
IT'S SO CUTE!
HIS NAME IS MAROTA!
HERE'S ANOTHER ONE!
TO DIE FOR...
KINO-SAN, THAT IS.
Right?

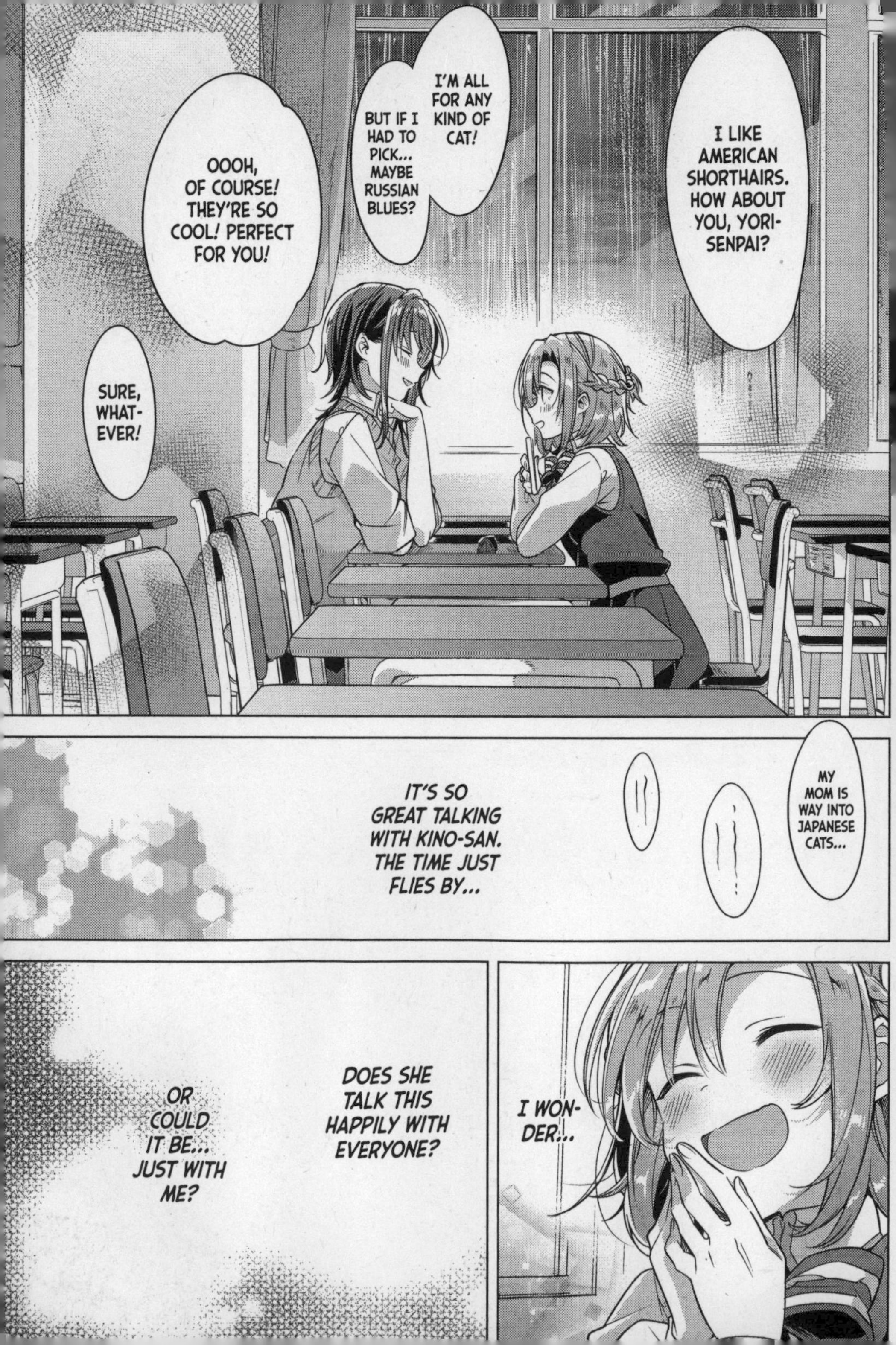
I LIKE AMERICAN SHORTHAIRS. HOW ABOUT YOU, YORI-SENPAI?
I'M ALL FOR ANY KIND OF CAT!
BUT IF I HAD TO PICK... MAYBE RUSSIAN BLUES?
OOOH, OF COURSE! THEY'RE SO COOL! PERFECT FOR YOU!
SURE, WHAT-EVER!
MY MOM IS WAY INTO JAPANESE CATS...
IT'S SO GREAT TALKING WITH KINO-SAN. THE TIME JUST FLIES BY...
I WON-DER...
DOES SHE TALK THIS HAPPILY WITH EVERYONE?
OR COULD IT BE... JUST WITH ME?

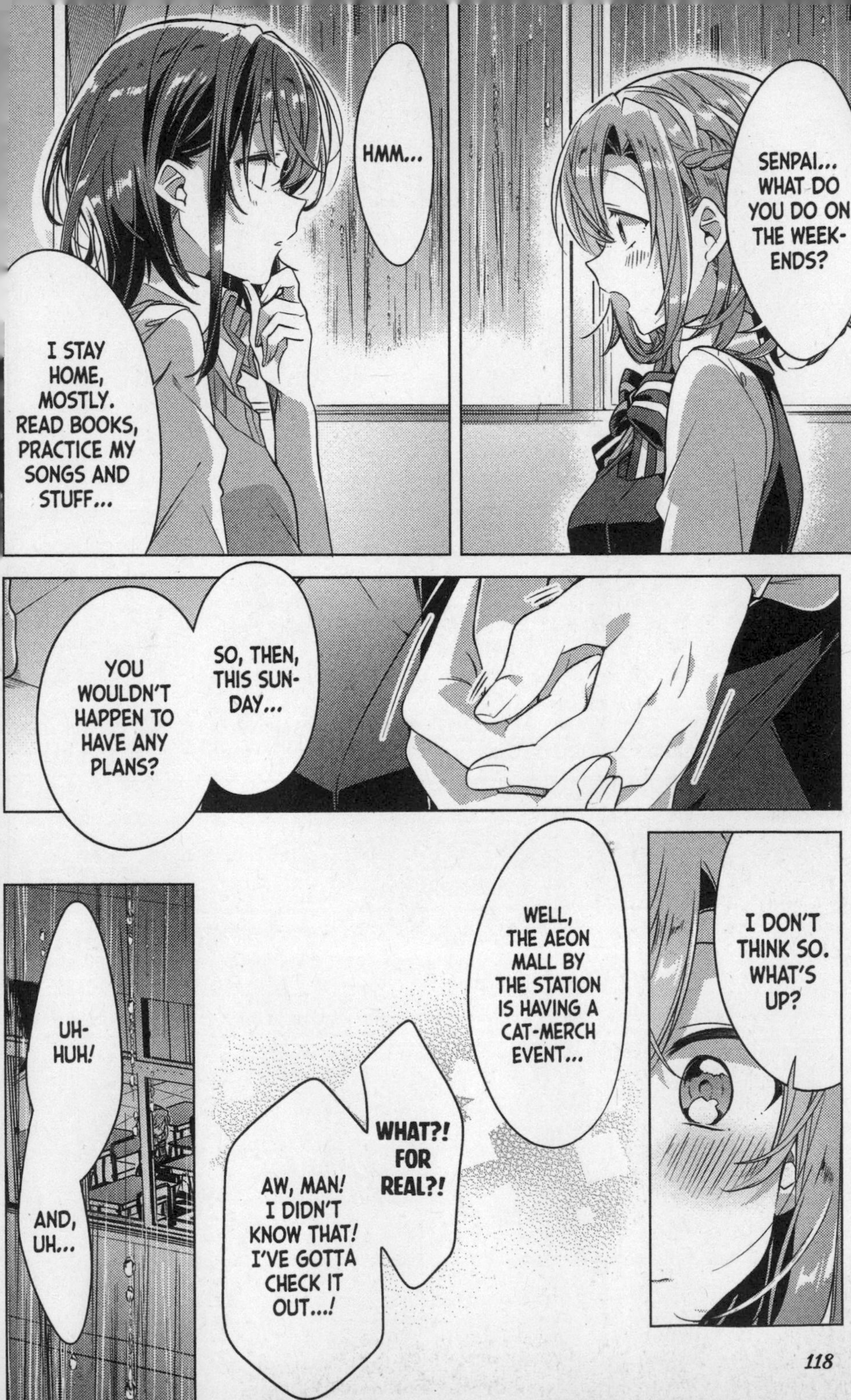
SENPAI... WHAT DO YOU DO ON THE WEEK-ENDS?
HMM...
I STAY HOME, MOSTLY. READ BOOKS, PRACTICE MY SONGS AND STUFF...
SO, THEN, THIS SUN-DAY...
YOU WOULDN'T HAPPEN TO HAVE ANY PLANS?
I DON'T THINK SO. WHAT'S UP?
WELL, THE AEON MALL BY THE STATION IS HAVING A CAT-MERCH EVENT...
WHAT?! FOR REAL?!
AW, MAN! I DIDN'T KNOW THAT! I'VE GOTTA CHECK IT OUT...!
UH-HUH!
AND, UH...

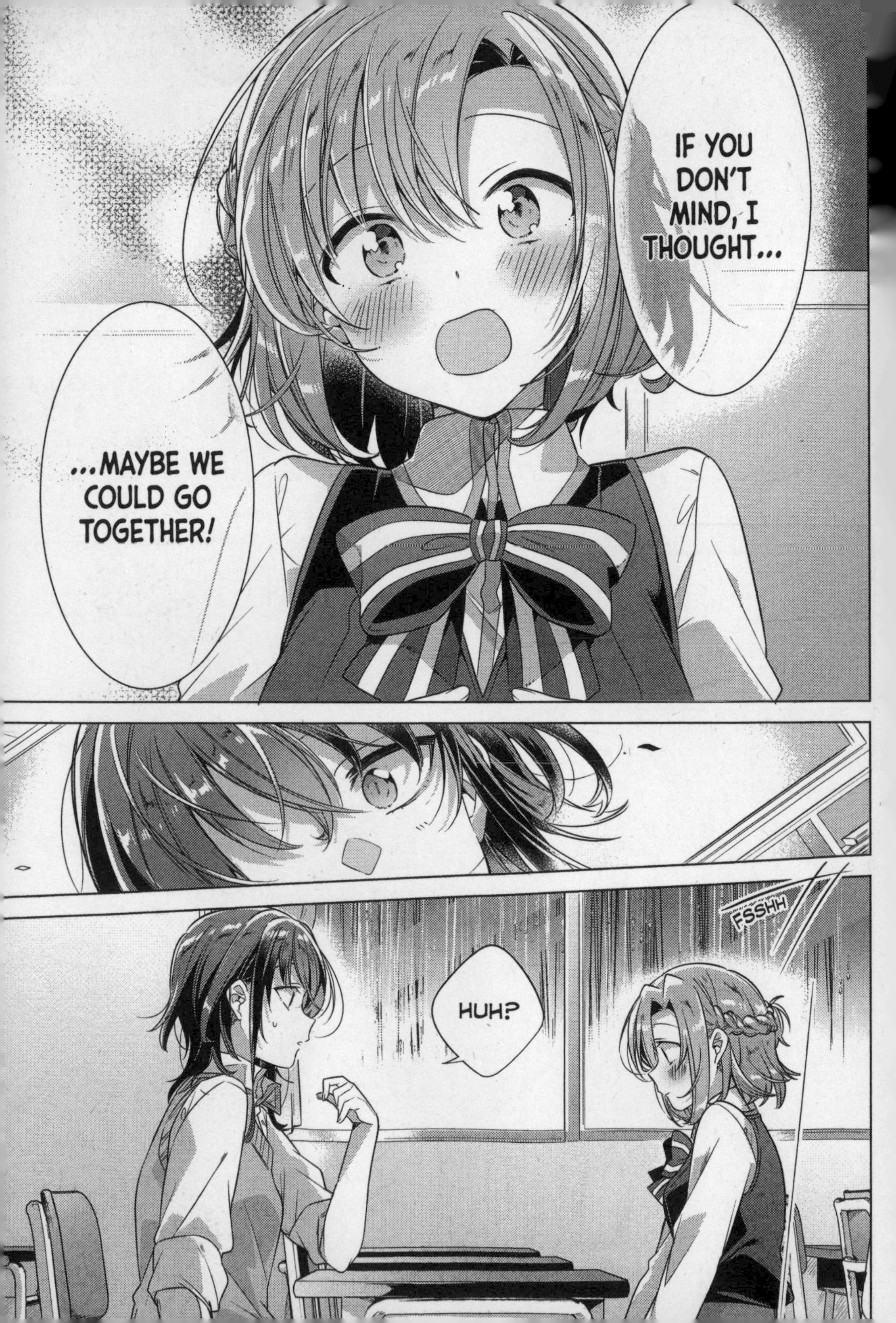
IF YOU DON'T MIND, I THOUGHT...
...MAYBE WE COULD GO TOGETHER!
FSSHH
HUH?

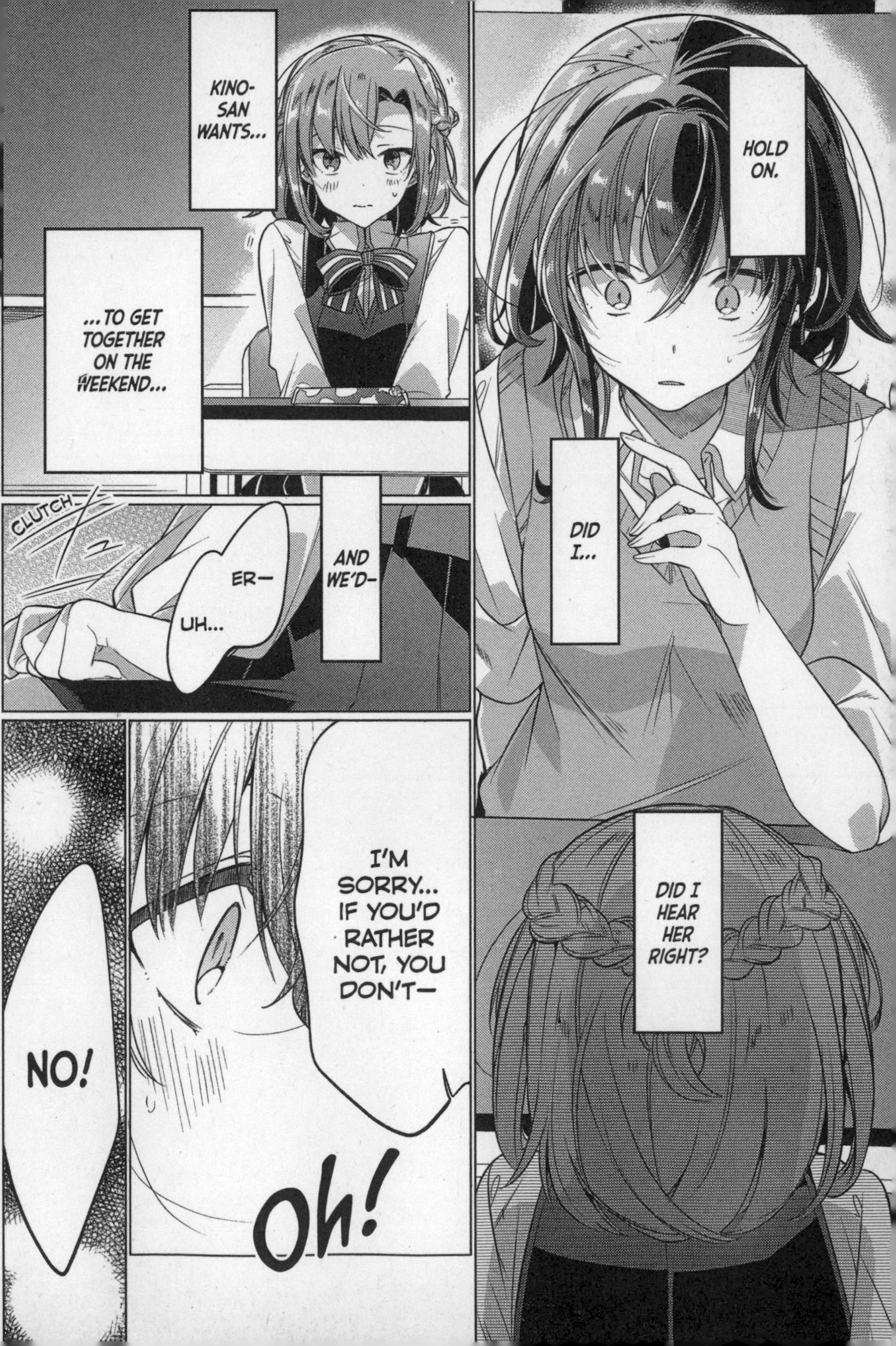
HOLD ON.
DID I...
KINO-SAN WANTS...
...TO GET TOGETHER ON THE WEEKEND...
AND WE'D—
CLUTCH
ER—
UH...
DID I HEAR HER RIGHT?
I'M SORRY... IF YOU'D RATHER NOT, YOU DON'T—
Oh!
NO!

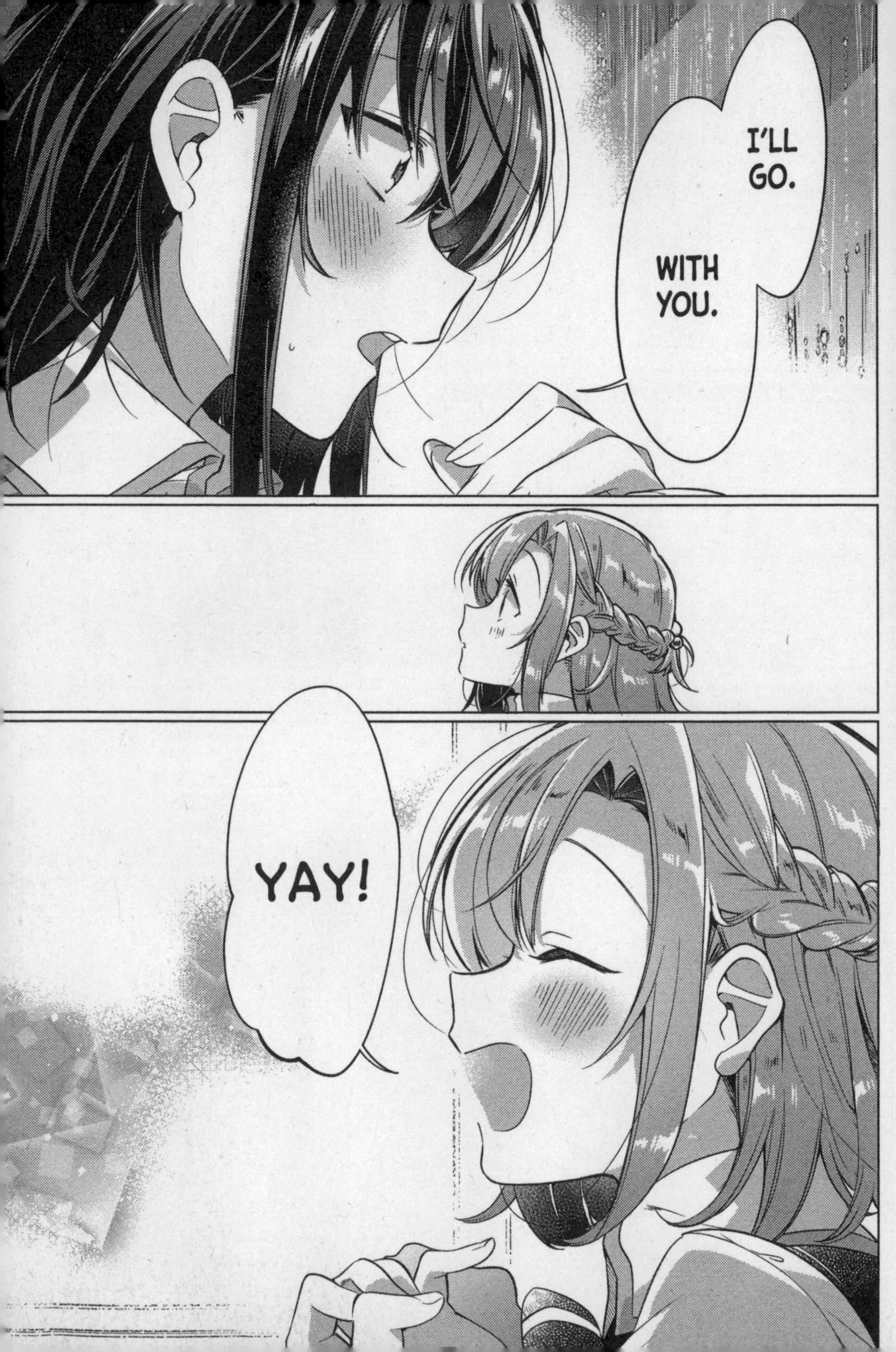
I'LL GO.
WITH YOU.
YAY!

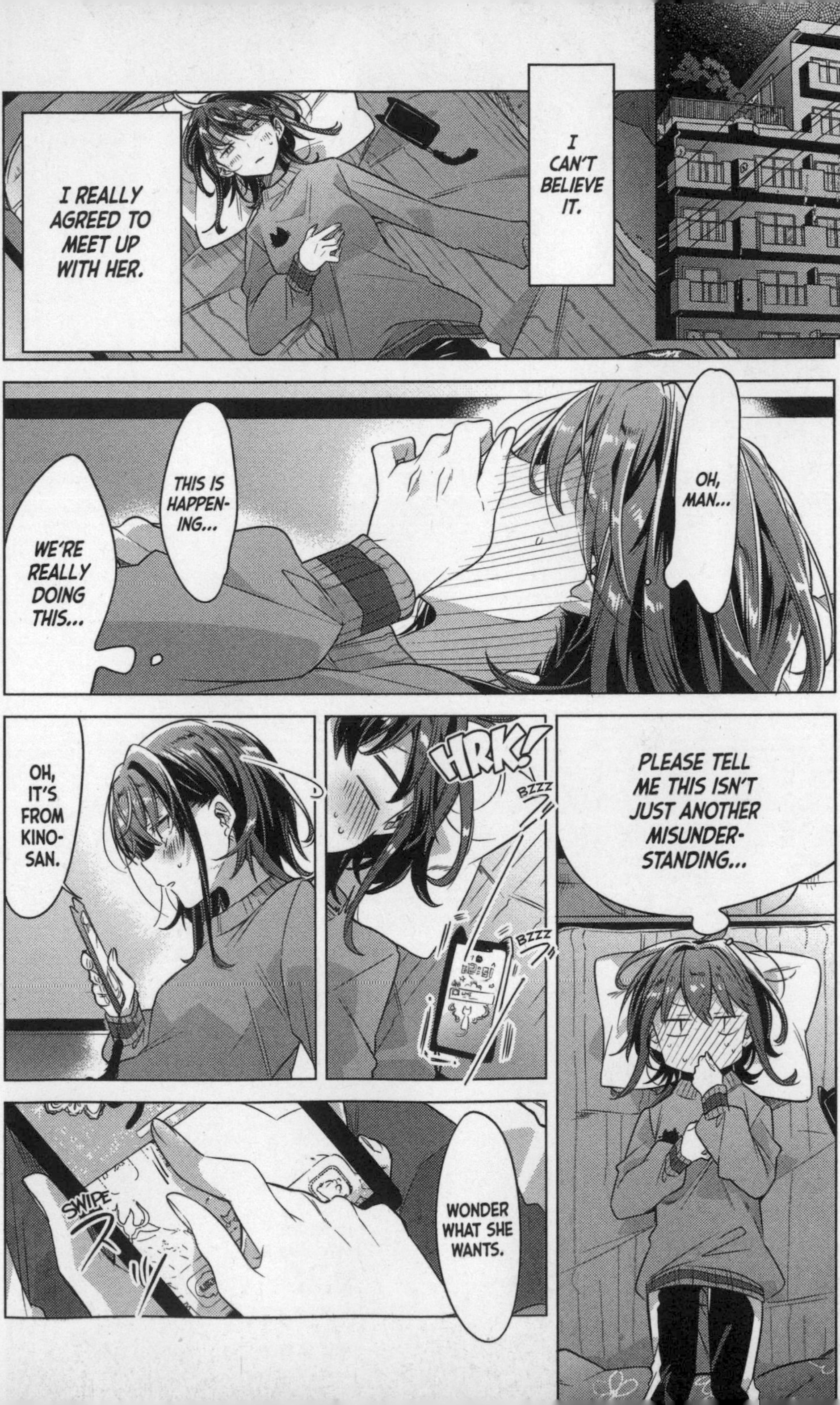
I CAN'T BELIEVE IT.
I REALLY AGREED TO MEET UP WITH HER.
OH, MAN...
THIS IS HAPPENING...
WE'RE REALLY DOING THIS...
PLEASE TELL ME THIS ISN'T JUST ANOTHER MISUNDERSTANDING...
HRK!
BZZZ
BZZZ
OH, IT'S FROM KINO-SAN.
WONDER WHAT SHE WANTS.
SWIPE

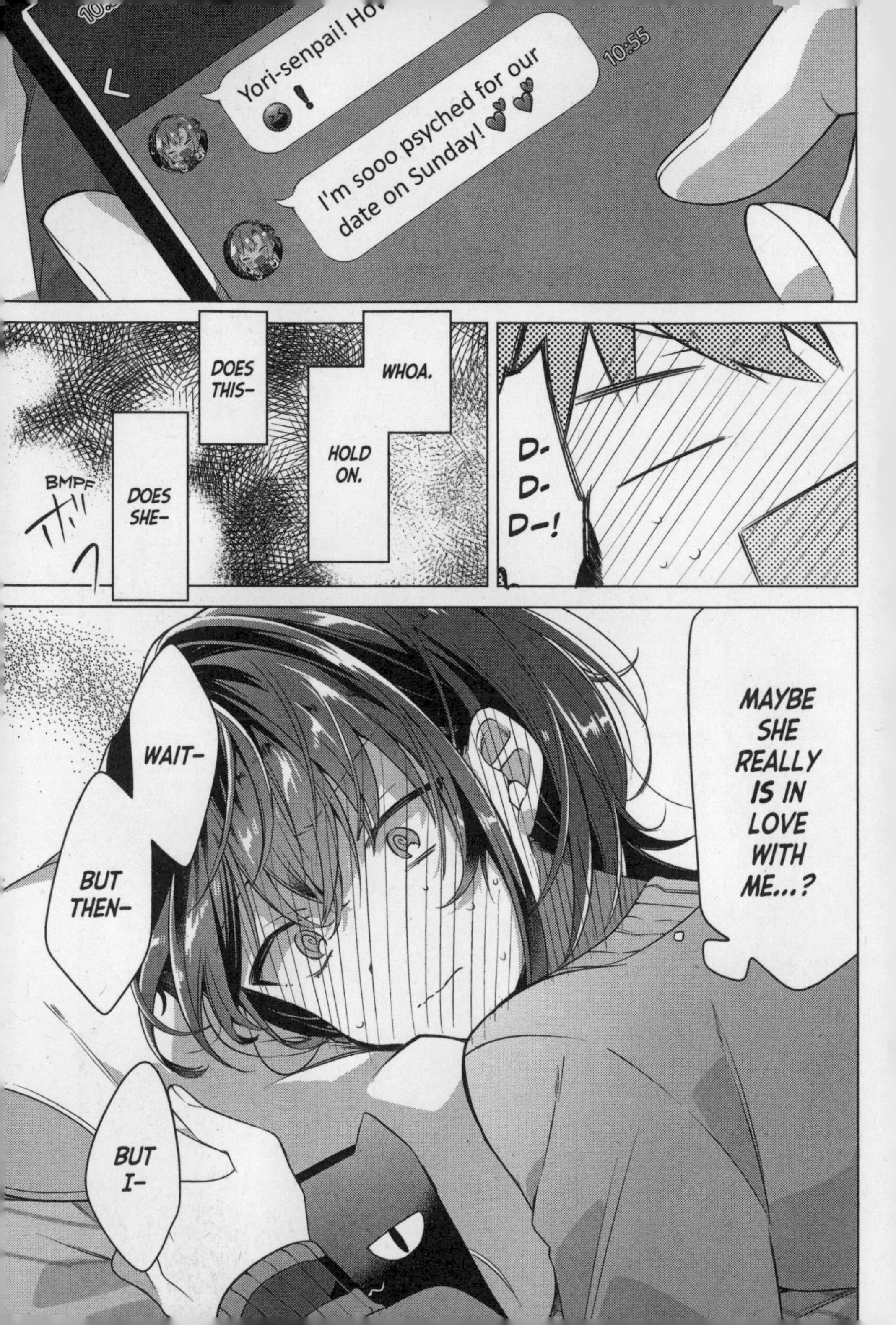
10:55
Yori-senpai!
!
I'm sooo psyched for our date on Sunday!
D- D- D-!
WHOA.
HOLD ON.
DOES THIS-
DOES SHE-
BMPF
MAYBE SHE REALLY IS IN LOVE WITH ME...?
WAIT-
BUT THEN-
BUT I-

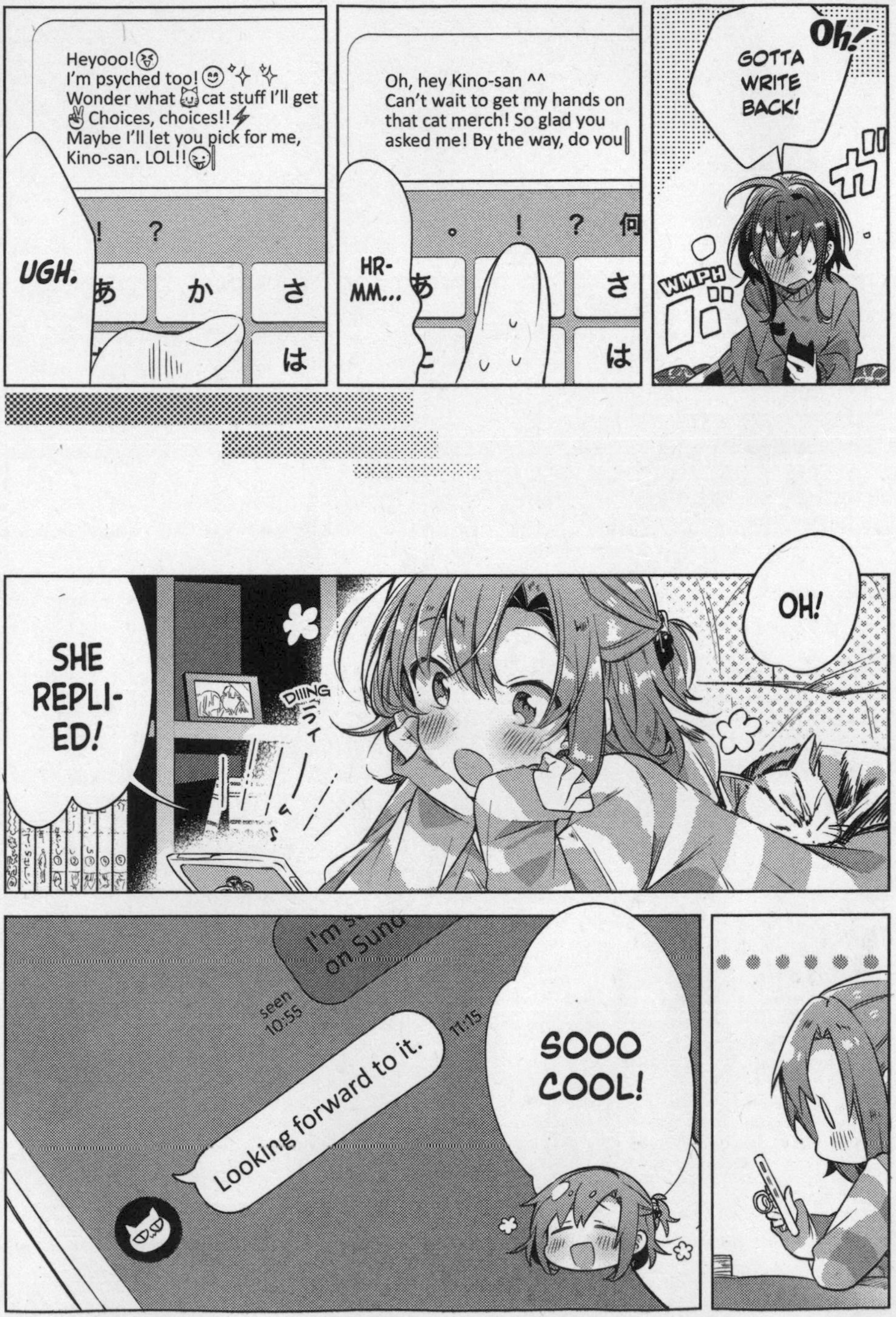
GOTTA WRITE BACK!
Oh!
ガ
WMPH
Oh, hey Kino-san ^^
Can't wait to get my hands on that cat merch! So glad you asked me! By the way, do you
HR-MM...
Heyooo!
I'm psyched too!
Wonder what cat stuff I'll get
Choices, choices!!
Maybe I'll let you pick for me, Kino-san. LOL!!
UGH.
OH!
DIIING
SHE REPLIED!
I'm s
on Sund
seen 10:55
11:15
Looking forward to it.
SOOO COOL!

Whisper Me
A Love Song

Eku
Takeshima

lounging mode

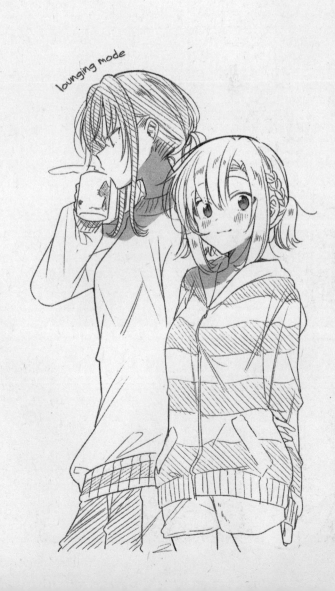

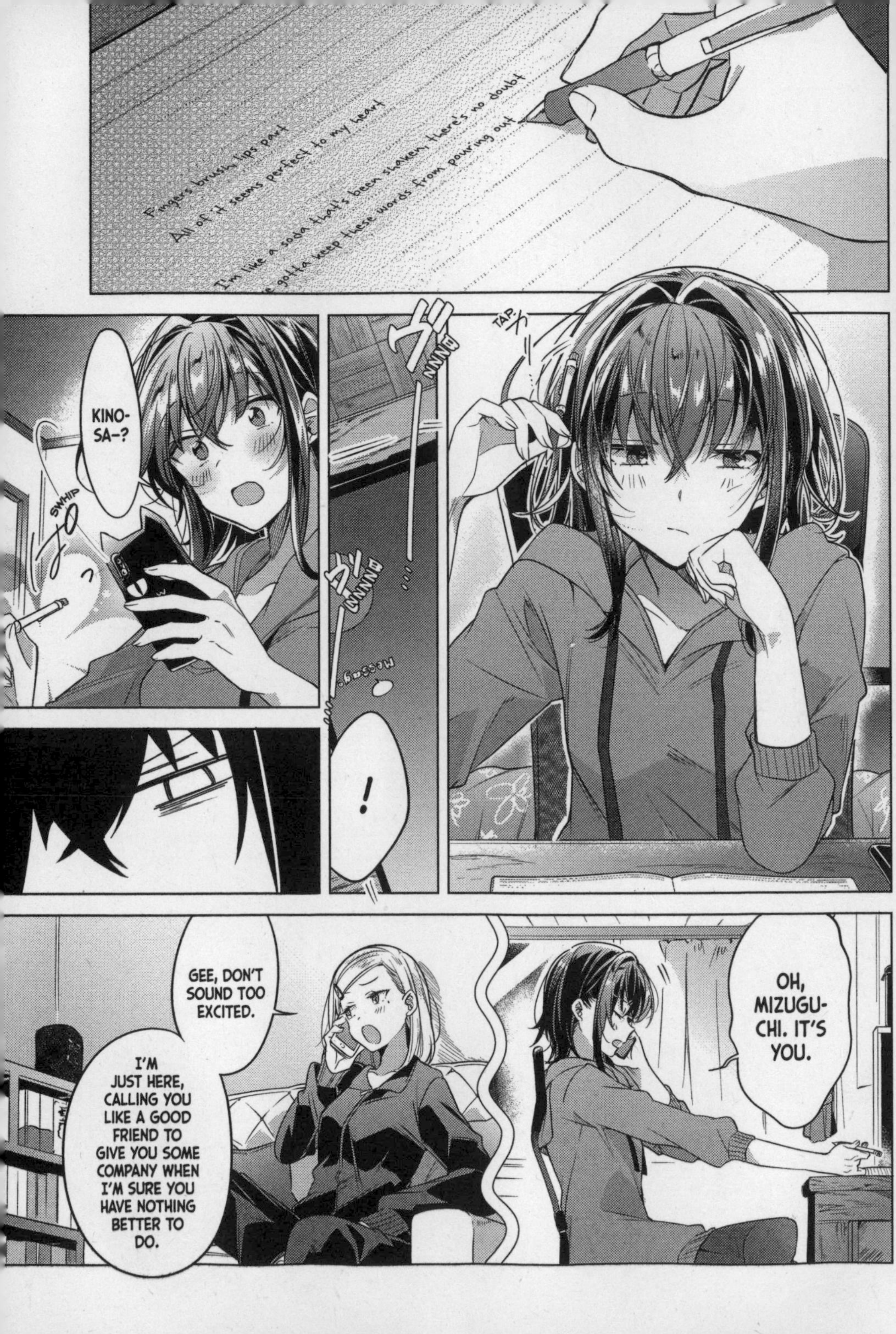
Fingers brush, lips part
All of it seems perfect to my heart
I'm like a soda that's been shaken, there's no doubt
gotta keep these words from pouring out
TAP
BZZZZ
BZZZZ
!
KINO-SA-?
SWHIP
OH, MIZUGU-CHI. IT'S YOU.
GEE, DON'T SOUND TOO EXCITED.
I'M JUST HERE, CALLING YOU LIKE A GOOD FRIEND TO GIVE YOU SOME COMPANY WHEN I'M SURE YOU HAVE NOTHING BETTER TO DO.

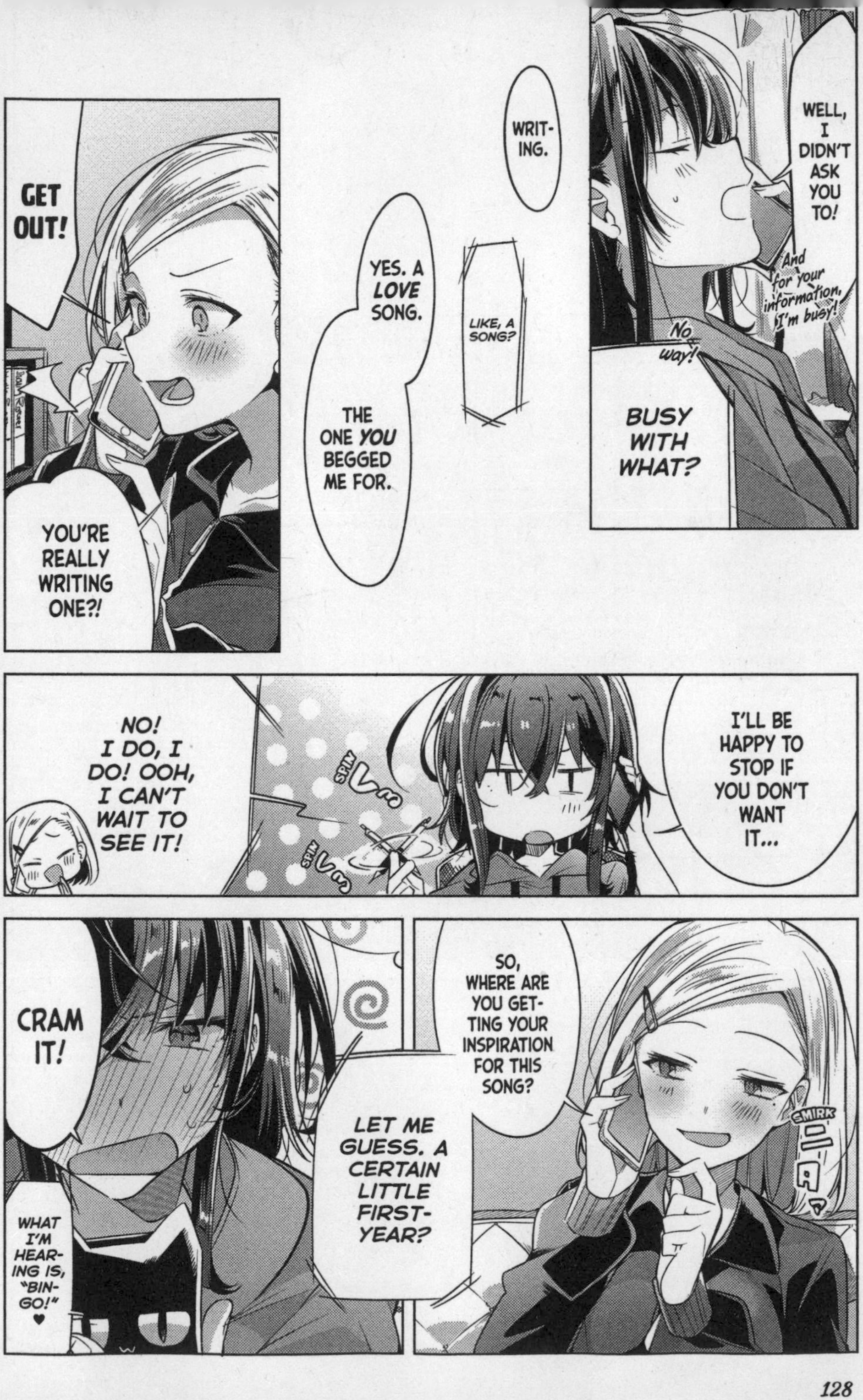
WELL, I DIDN'T ASK YOU TO!
And for your information, I'm busy!
No way!
BUSY WITH WHAT?
WRITING.
LIKE, A SONG?
YES. A *LOVE* SONG.
THE ONE *YOU* BEGGED ME FOR.
GET OUT!
YOU'RE REALLY WRITING ONE?!
I'LL BE HAPPY TO STOP IF YOU DON'T WANT IT...
SPIN
SPIN
NO! I DO, I DO! OOH, I CAN'T WAIT TO SEE IT!
SO, WHERE ARE YOU GETTING YOUR INSPIRATION FOR THIS SONG?
SMIRK
LET ME GUESS. A CERTAIN LITTLE FIRST-YEAR?
CRAM IT!
WHAT I'M HEARING IS, "BINGO!" ♥

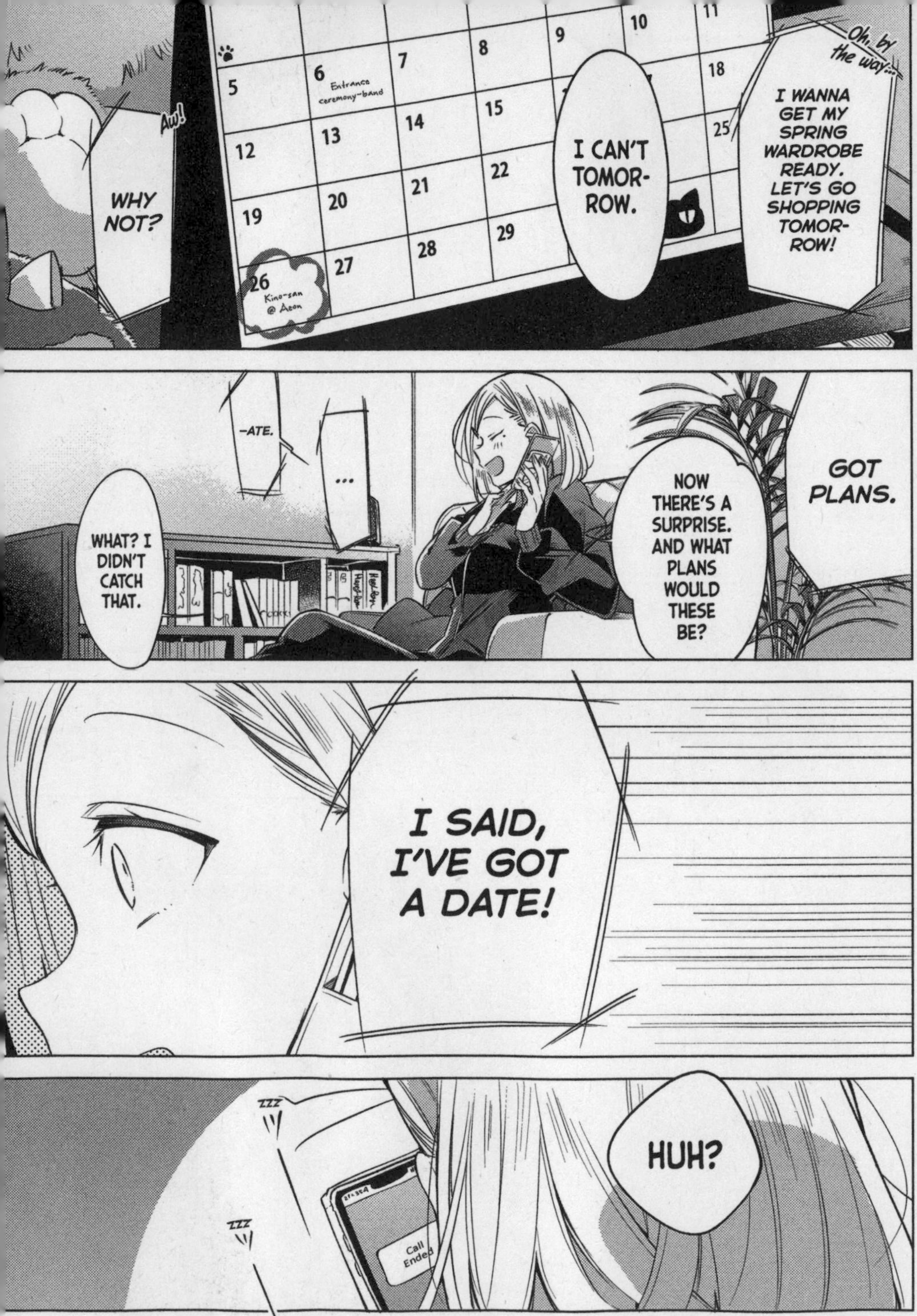

Oh, by the way...
I WANNA GET MY SPRING WARDROBE READY. LET'S GO SHOPPING TOMORROW!
I CAN'T TOMORROW.
Entrance ceremony-band
Kino-san @ Aeon
Aw!
WHY NOT?
GOT PLANS.
NOW THERE'S A SURPRISE. AND WHAT PLANS WOULD THESE BE?
...
-ATE.
WHAT? I DIDN'T CATCH THAT.
I SAID, I'VE GOT A DATE!
HUH?
Call Ended
ZZZ
ZZZ

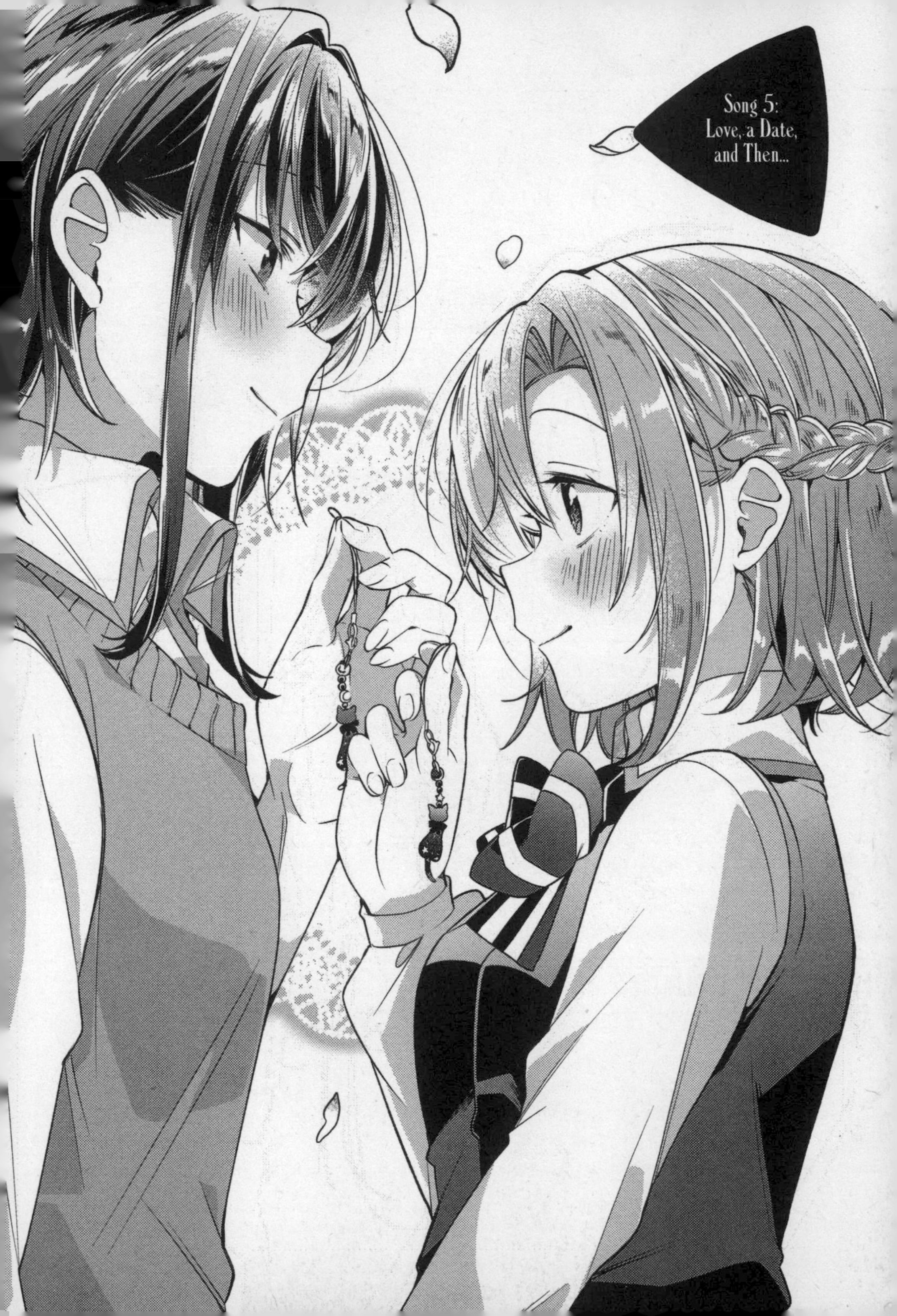
Song 5:
Love, a Date,
and Then...

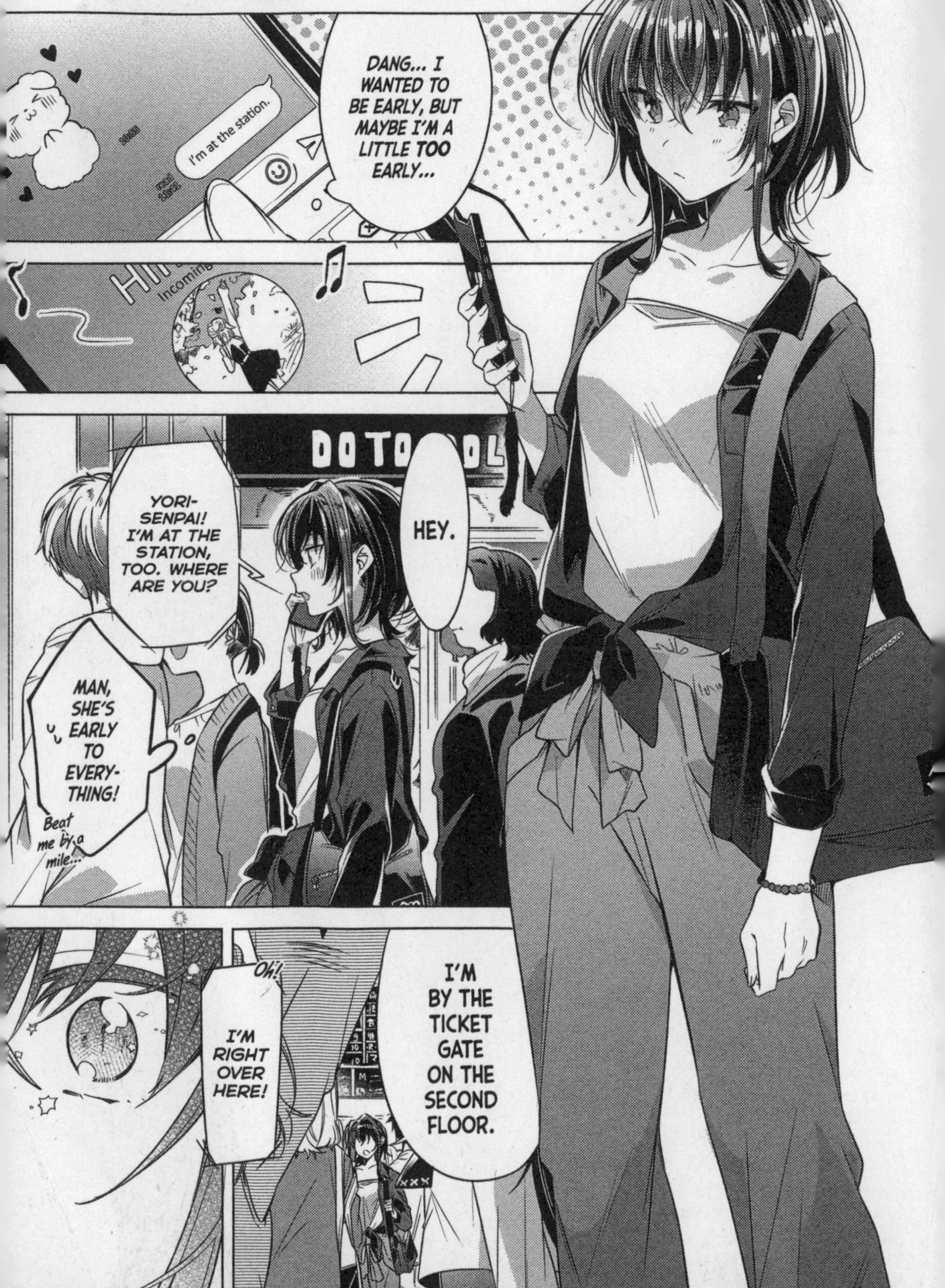
DANG... I WANTED TO BE EARLY, BUT MAYBE I'M A LITTLE TOO EARLY...
I'm at the station.
Incoming
HEY.
YORI-SENPAI! I'M AT THE STATION, TOO. WHERE ARE YOU?
MAN, SHE'S EARLY TO EVERY-THING!
Beat me by a mile...
I'M BY THE TICKET GATE ON THE SECOND FLOOR.
Oh!
I'M RIGHT OVER HERE!

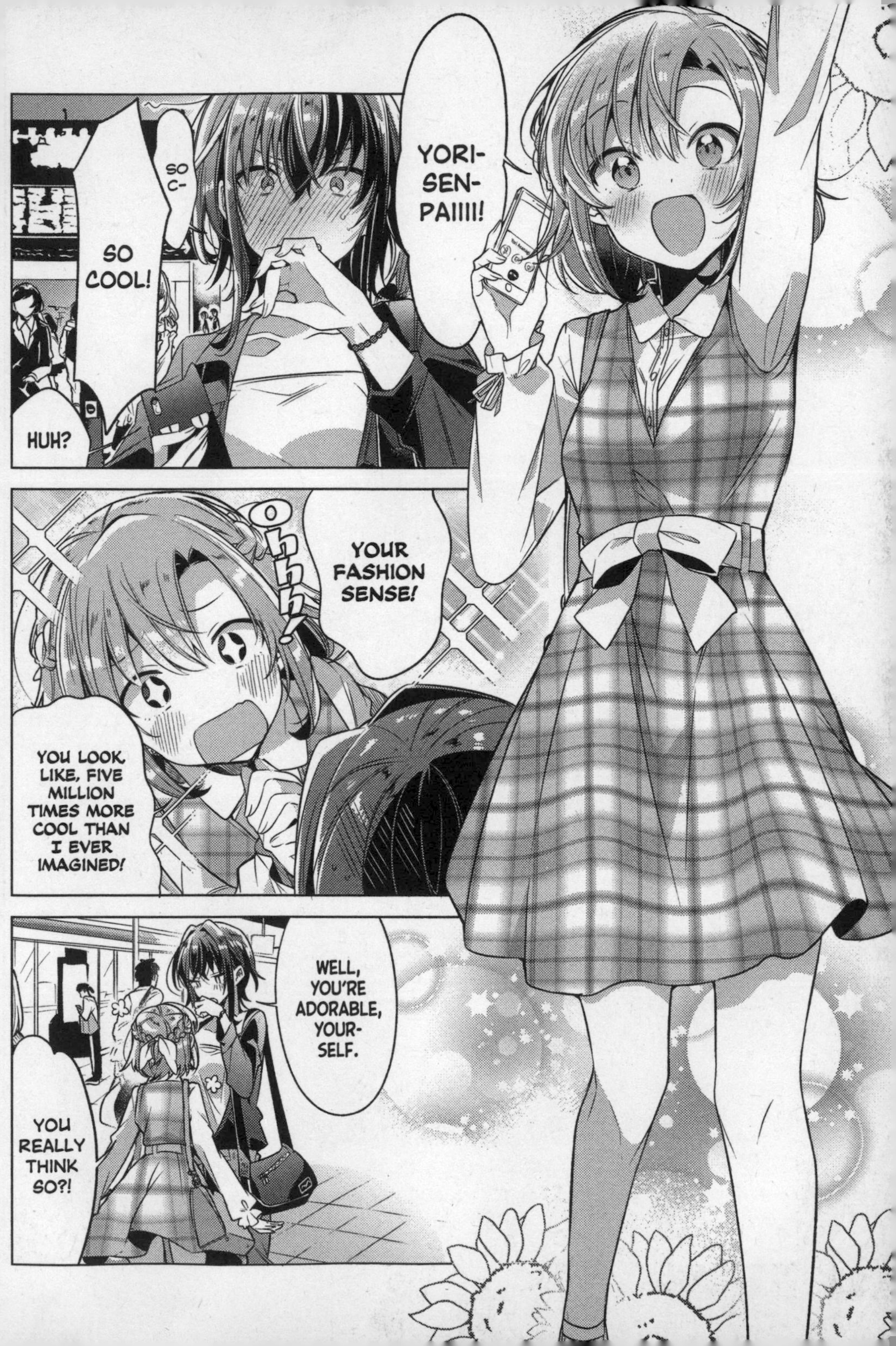
YORI-SEN-PAIIIII!
SO C-
SO COOL!
HUH?
Ohhh!
YOUR FASHION SENSE!
YOU LOOK LIKE, FIVE MILLION TIMES MORE COOL THAN I EVER IMAGINED!
WELL, YOU'RE ADORABLE, YOUR-SELF.
YOU REALLY THINK SO?!

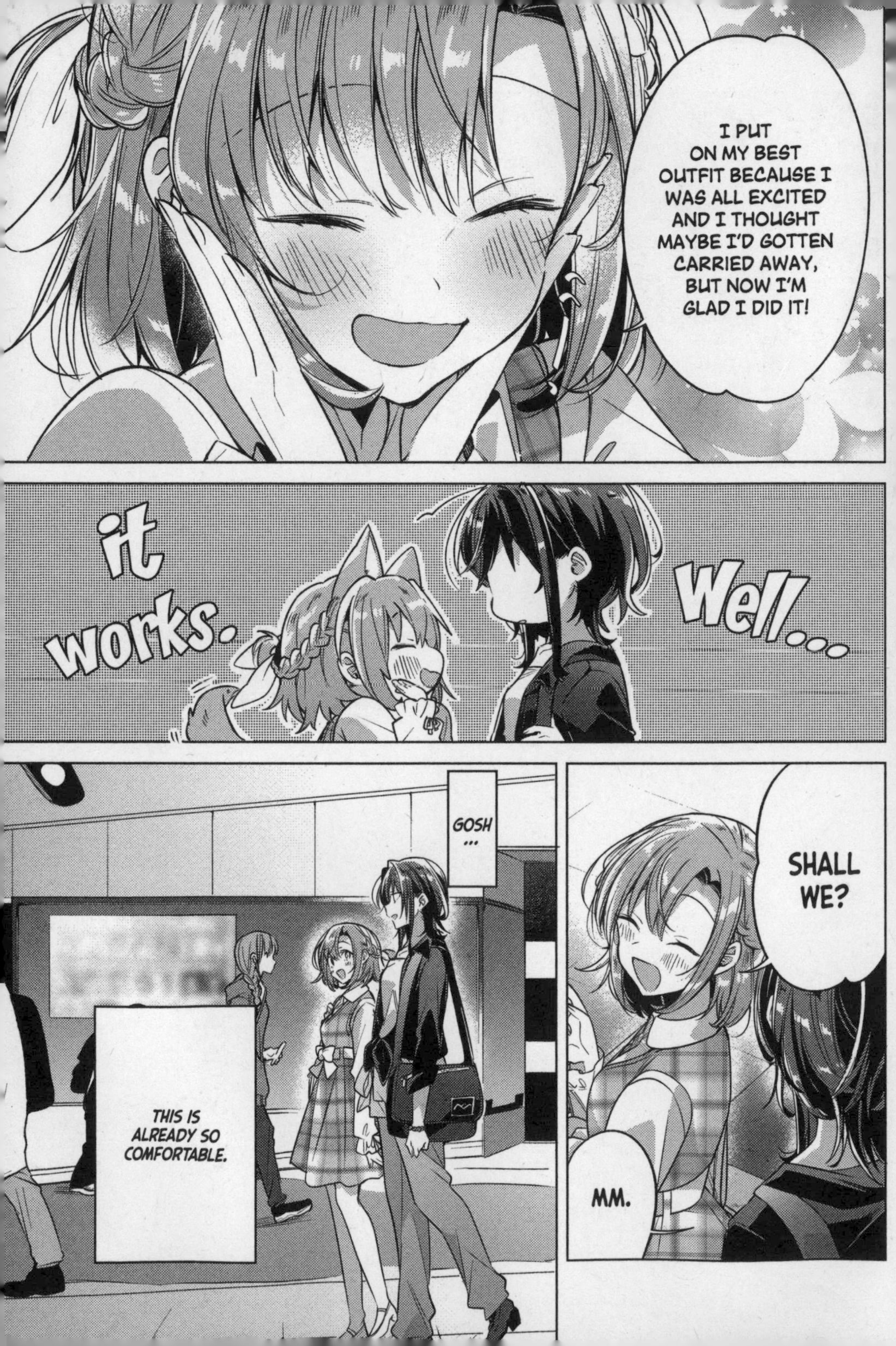
I PUT ON MY BEST OUTFIT BECAUSE I WAS ALL EXCITED AND I THOUGHT MAYBE I'D GOTTEN CARRIED AWAY, BUT NOW I'M GLAD I DID IT!
Well...
it works.
SHALL WE?
MM.
GOSH...
THIS IS ALREADY SO COMFORTABLE.

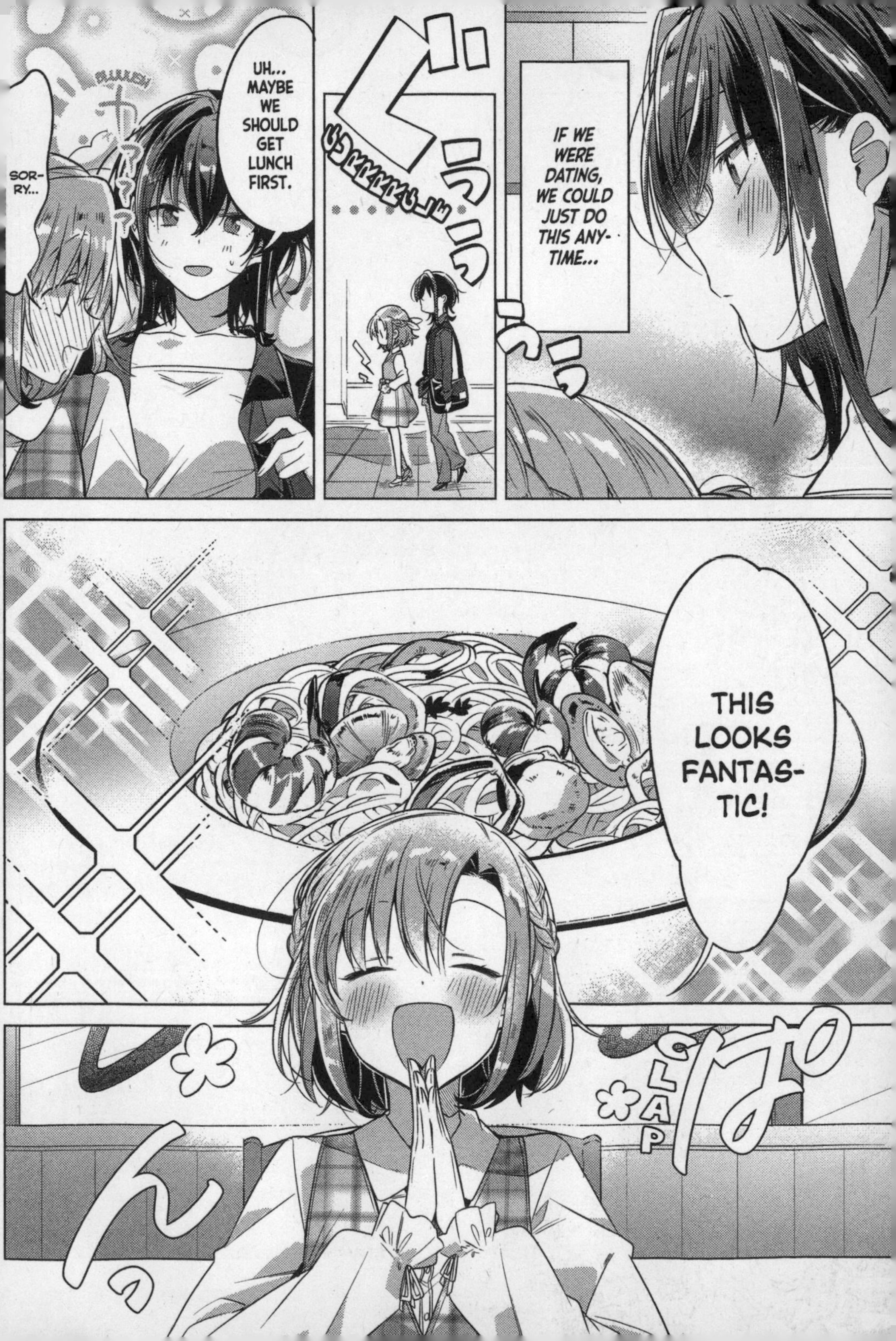
IF WE WERE DATING, WE COULD JUST DO THIS ANY-TIME...
GRUMMMBLE
UH... MAYBE WE SHOULD GET LUNCH FIRST.
SOR-RY...
THIS LOOKS FANTAS-TIC!
CLAP

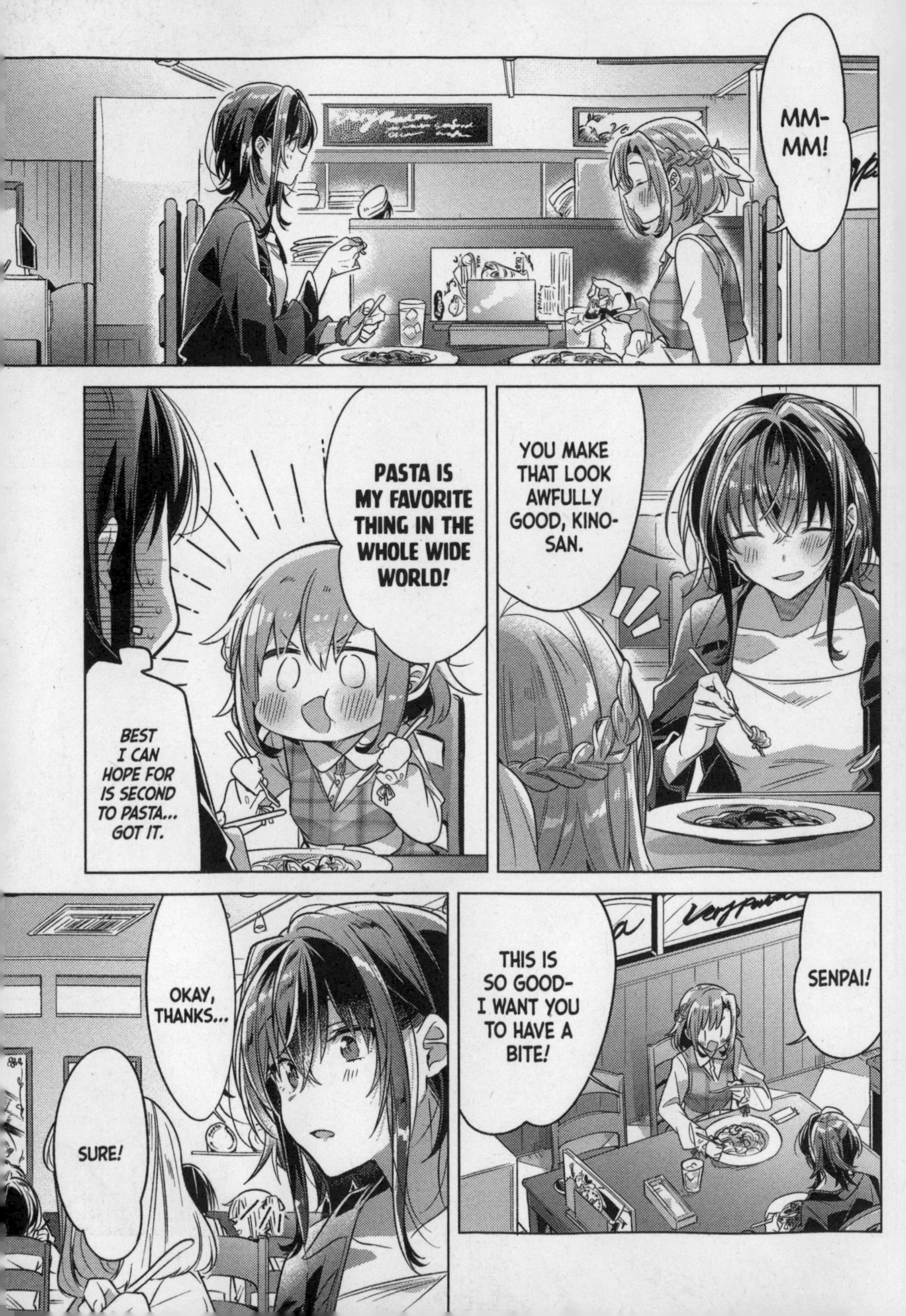
MM-MM!
YOU MAKE THAT LOOK AWFULLY GOOD, KINO-SAN.
PASTA IS MY FAVORITE THING IN THE WHOLE WIDE WORLD!
BEST I CAN HOPE FOR IS SECOND TO PASTA... GOT IT.
SENPAI!
THIS IS SO GOOD- I WANT YOU TO HAVE A BITE!
OKAY, THANKS...
SURE!

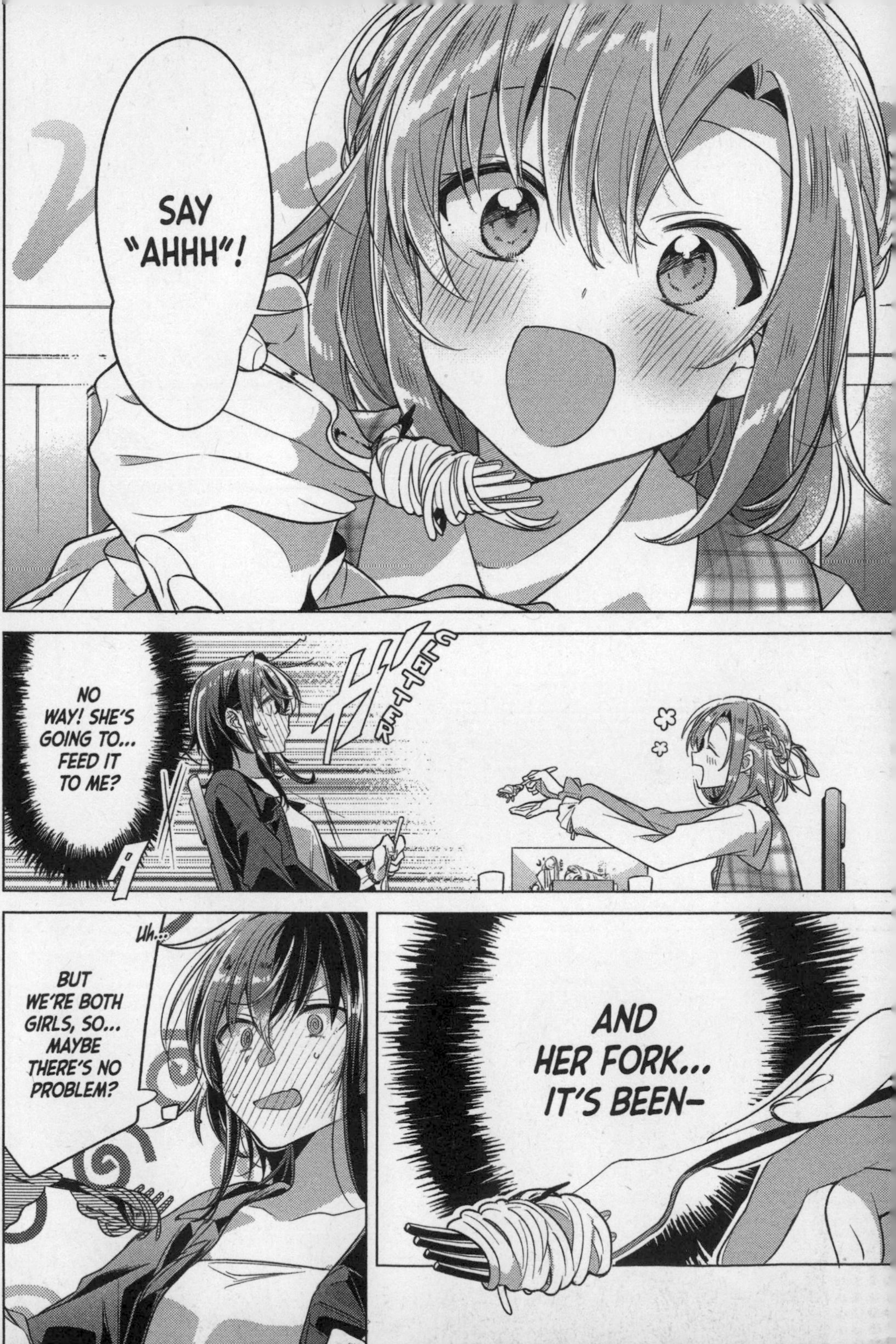
SAY "AHHH"!
NO WAY! SHE'S GOING TO... FEED IT TO ME?
AND HER FORK... IT'S BEEN–
Uh...
BUT WE'RE BOTH GIRLS, SO... MAYBE THERE'S NO PROBLEM?

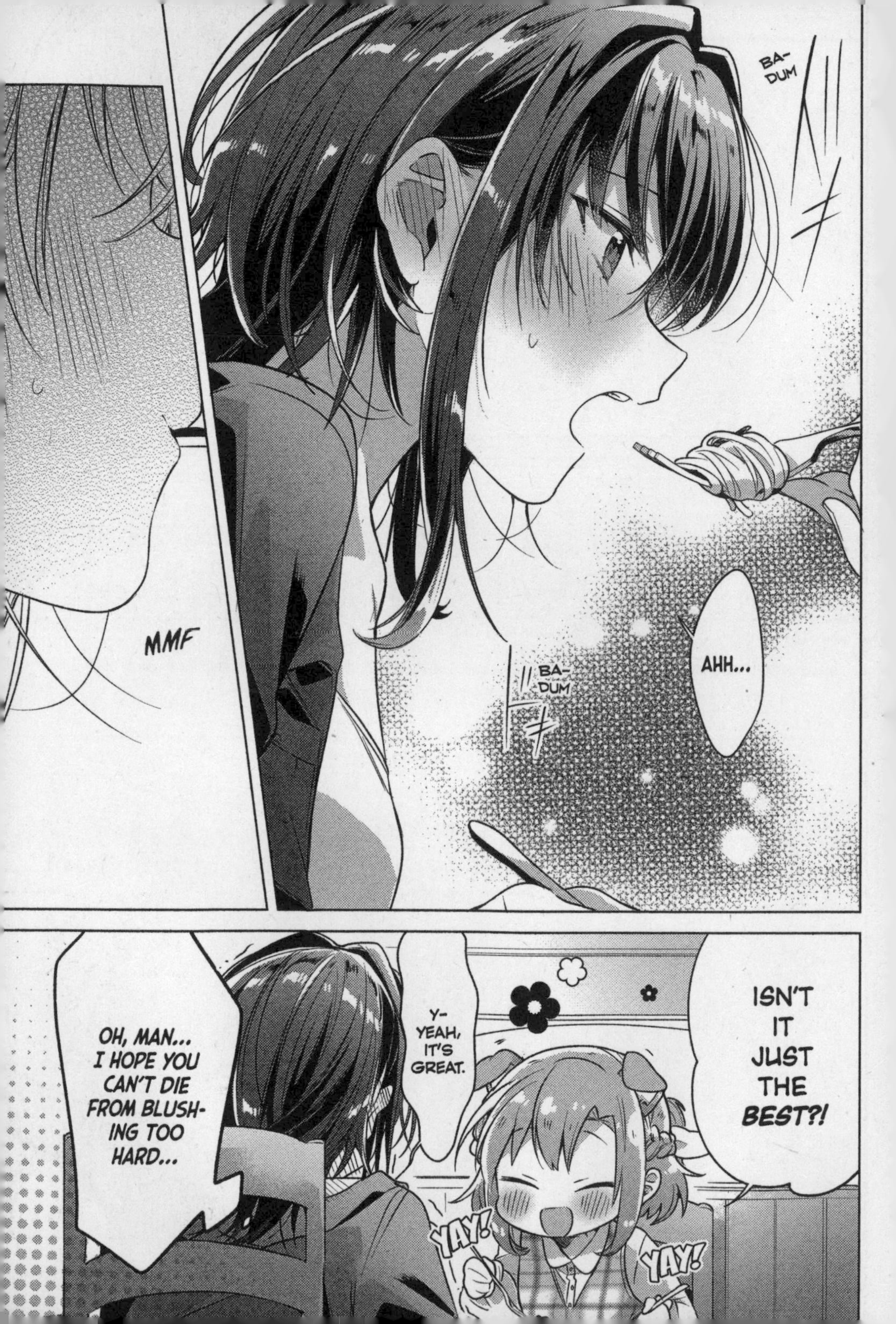
BA-DUM
AHH...
BA-DUM
MMF
ISN'T IT JUST THE BEST?!
Y-YEAH, IT'S GREAT.
OH, MAN... I HOPE YOU CAN'T DIE FROM BLUSHING TOO HARD...
YAY!
YAY!

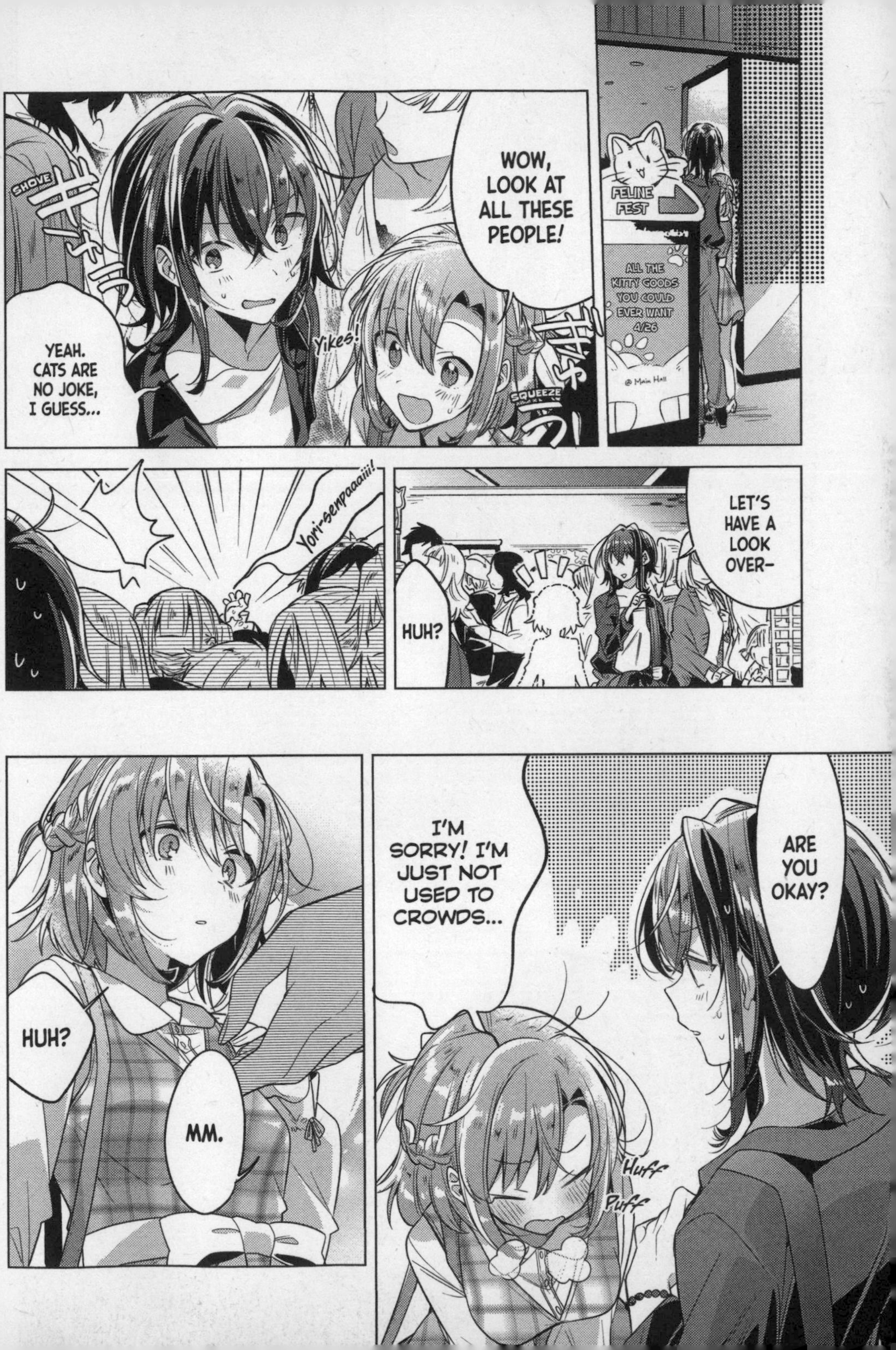
FELINE FEST
ALL THE KITTY GOODS YOU COULD EVER WANT 4/26
@ Main Hall
WOW, LOOK AT ALL THESE PEOPLE!
SHOVE
Yikes!
SQUEEZE
YEAH. CATS ARE NO JOKE, I GUESS...
LET'S HAVE A LOOK OVER–
HUH?
Yori-senpaaaiii!
ARE YOU OKAY?
I'M SORRY! I'M JUST NOT USED TO CROWDS...
Huff
Puff
HUH?
MM.

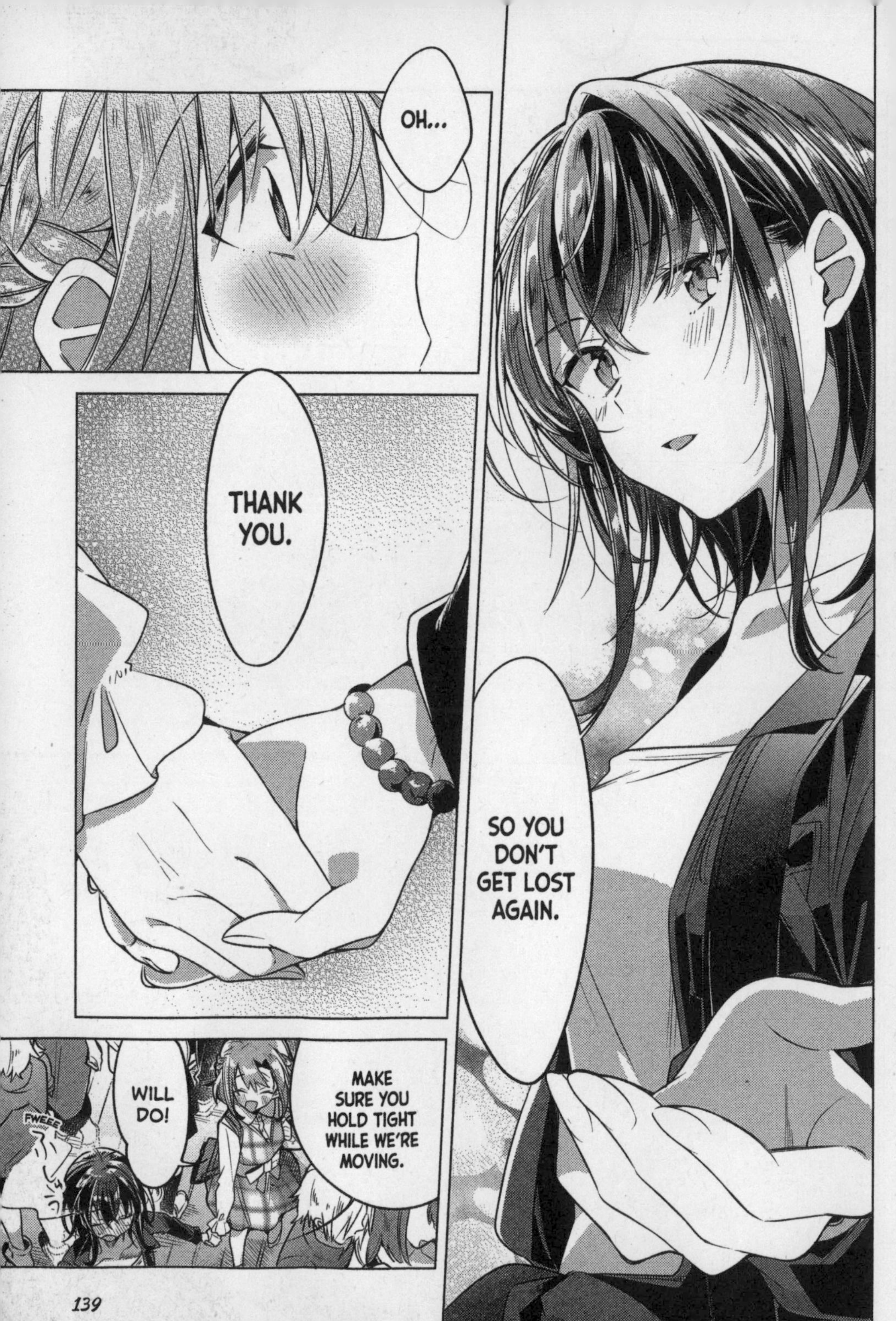

SO YOU DON'T GET LOST AGAIN.
OH...
THANK YOU.
MAKE SURE YOU HOLD TIGHT WHILE WE'RE MOVING.
WILL DO!
FWEEE

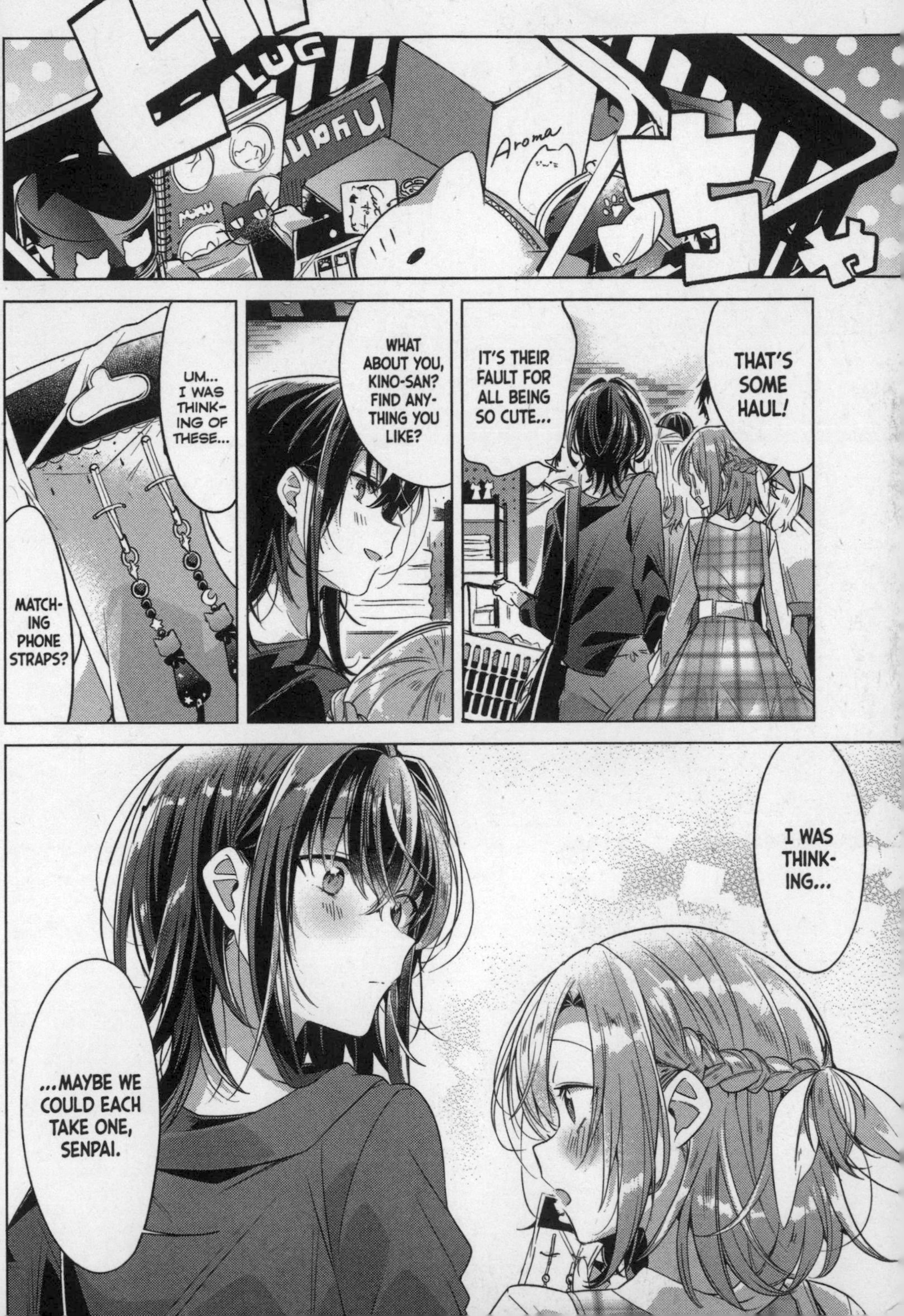
LUG
Aroma
THAT'S SOME HAUL!
IT'S THEIR FAULT FOR ALL BEING SO CUTE...
WHAT ABOUT YOU, KINO-SAN? FIND ANYTHING YOU LIKE?
UM... I WAS THINKING OF THESE...
MATCHING PHONE STRAPS?
I WAS THINKING...
...MAYBE WE COULD EACH TAKE ONE, SENPAI.

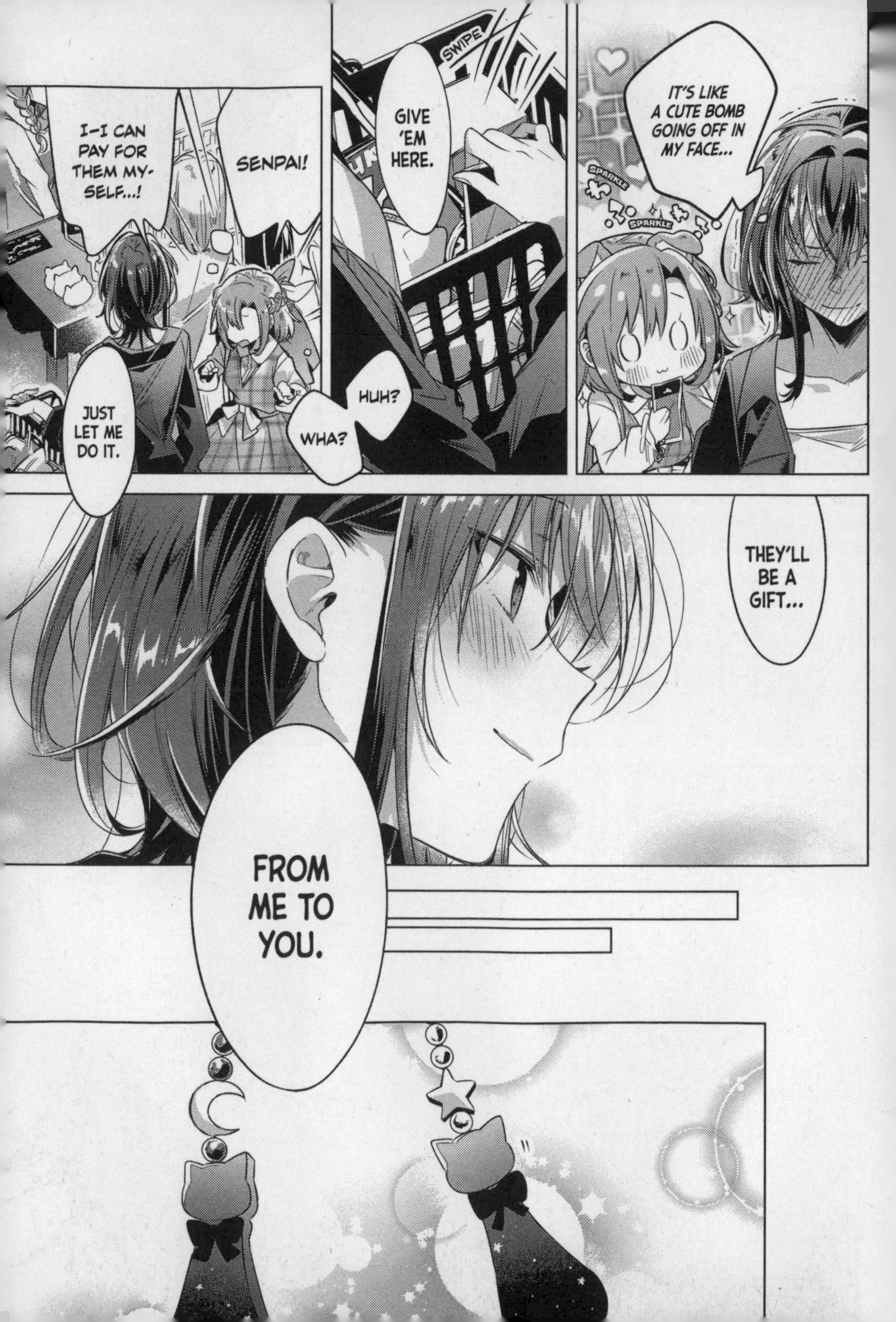
IT'S LIKE A CUTE BOMB GOING OFF IN MY FACE...
SPARKLE
SPARKLE
SWIPE
GIVE 'EM HERE.
HUH?
WHA?
SENPAI!
I-I CAN PAY FOR THEM MY-SELF...!
JUST LET ME DO IT.
THEY'LL BE A GIFT...
FROM ME TO YOU.

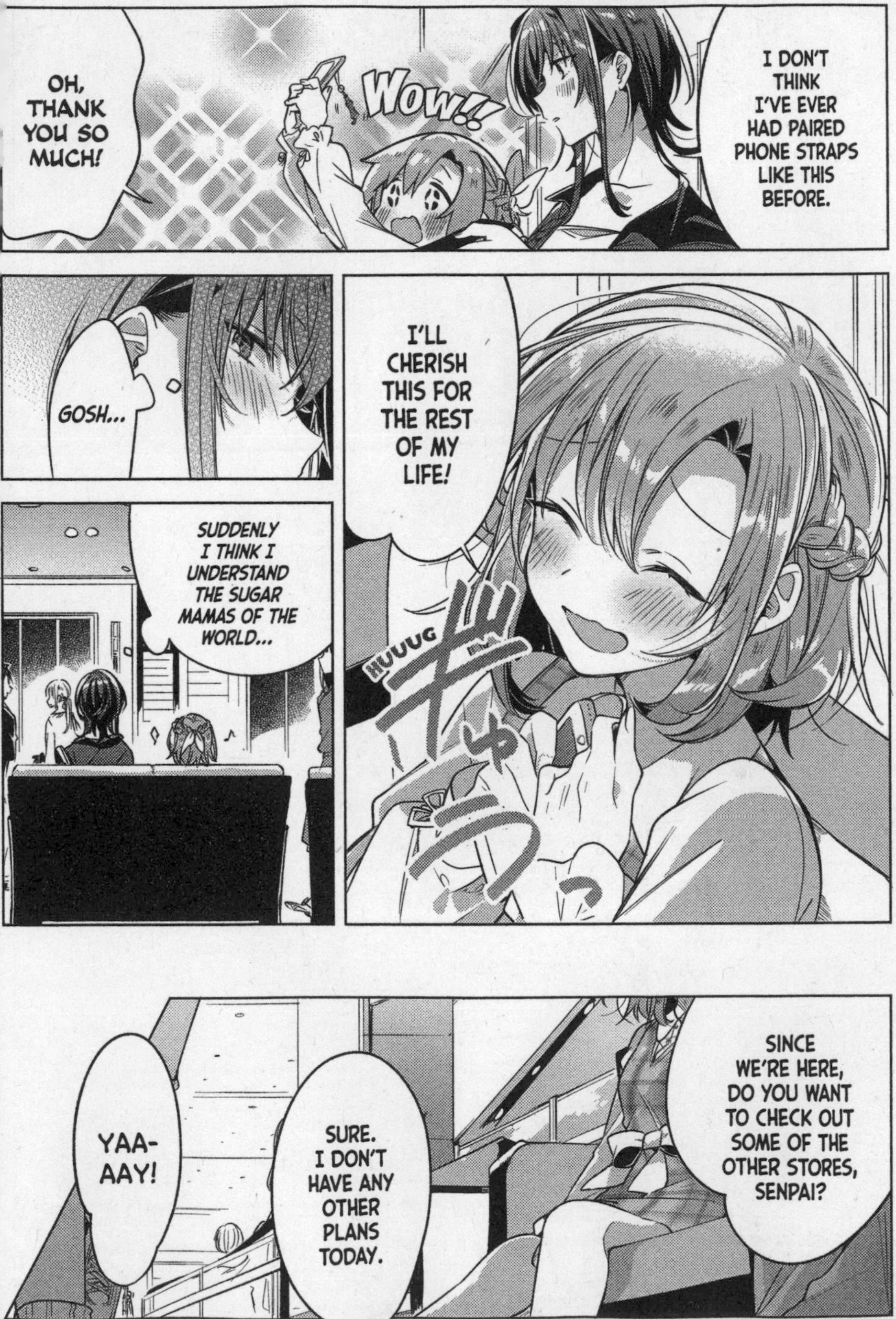
I DON'T THINK I'VE EVER HAD PAIRED PHONE STRAPS LIKE THIS BEFORE.
WOW!!
OH, THANK YOU SO MUCH!
I'LL CHERISH THIS FOR THE REST OF MY LIFE!
HUUUG
GOSH...
SUDDENLY I THINK I UNDERSTAND THE SUGAR MAMAS OF THE WORLD...
SINCE WE'RE HERE, DO YOU WANT TO CHECK OUT SOME OF THE OTHER STORES, SENPAI?
SURE. I DON'T HAVE ANY OTHER PLANS TODAY.
YAA-AAY!

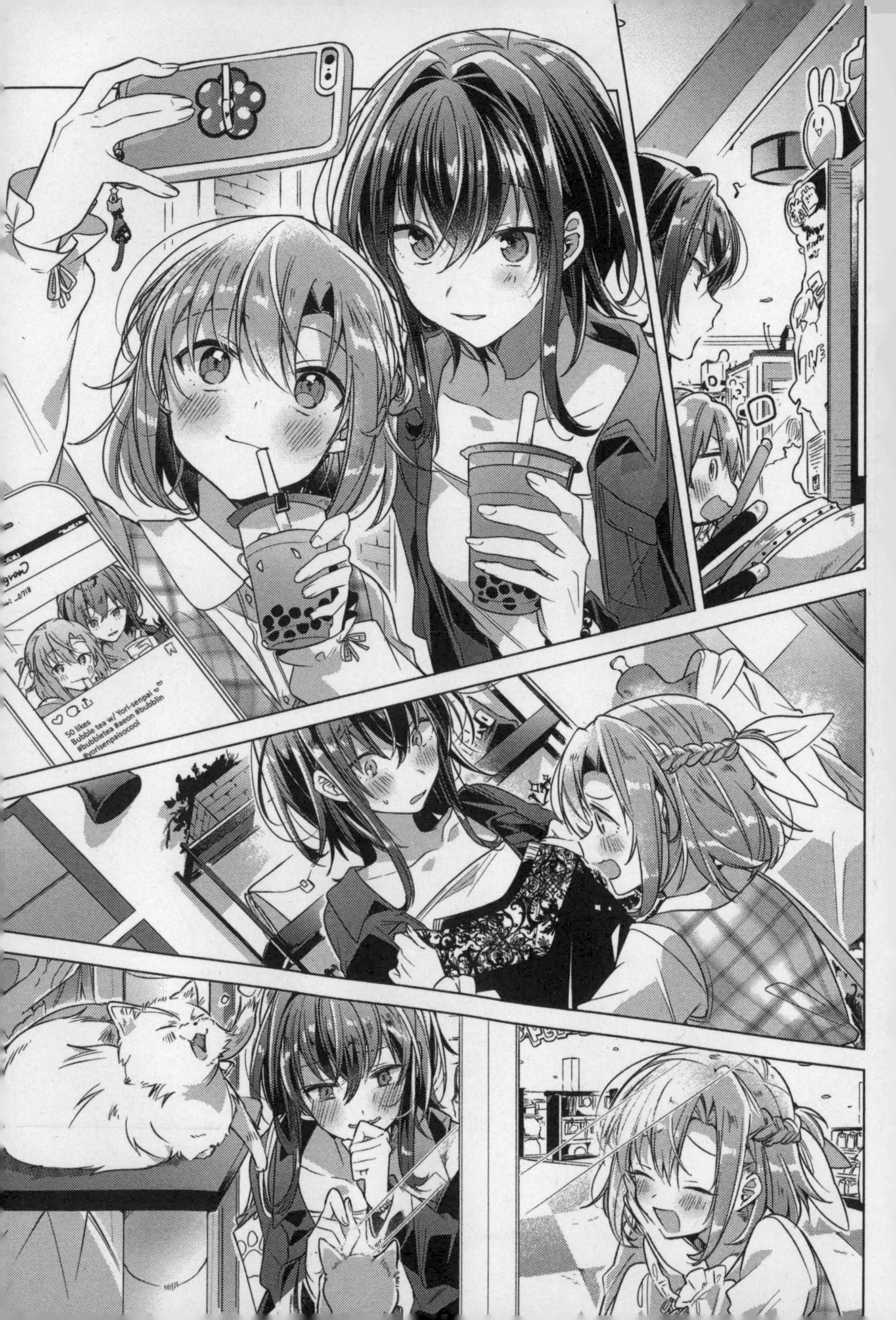
50 likes
Bubble tea w/ Yori-senpai
#bubbletea #aeon #bubblin
#yorisenpaisocool

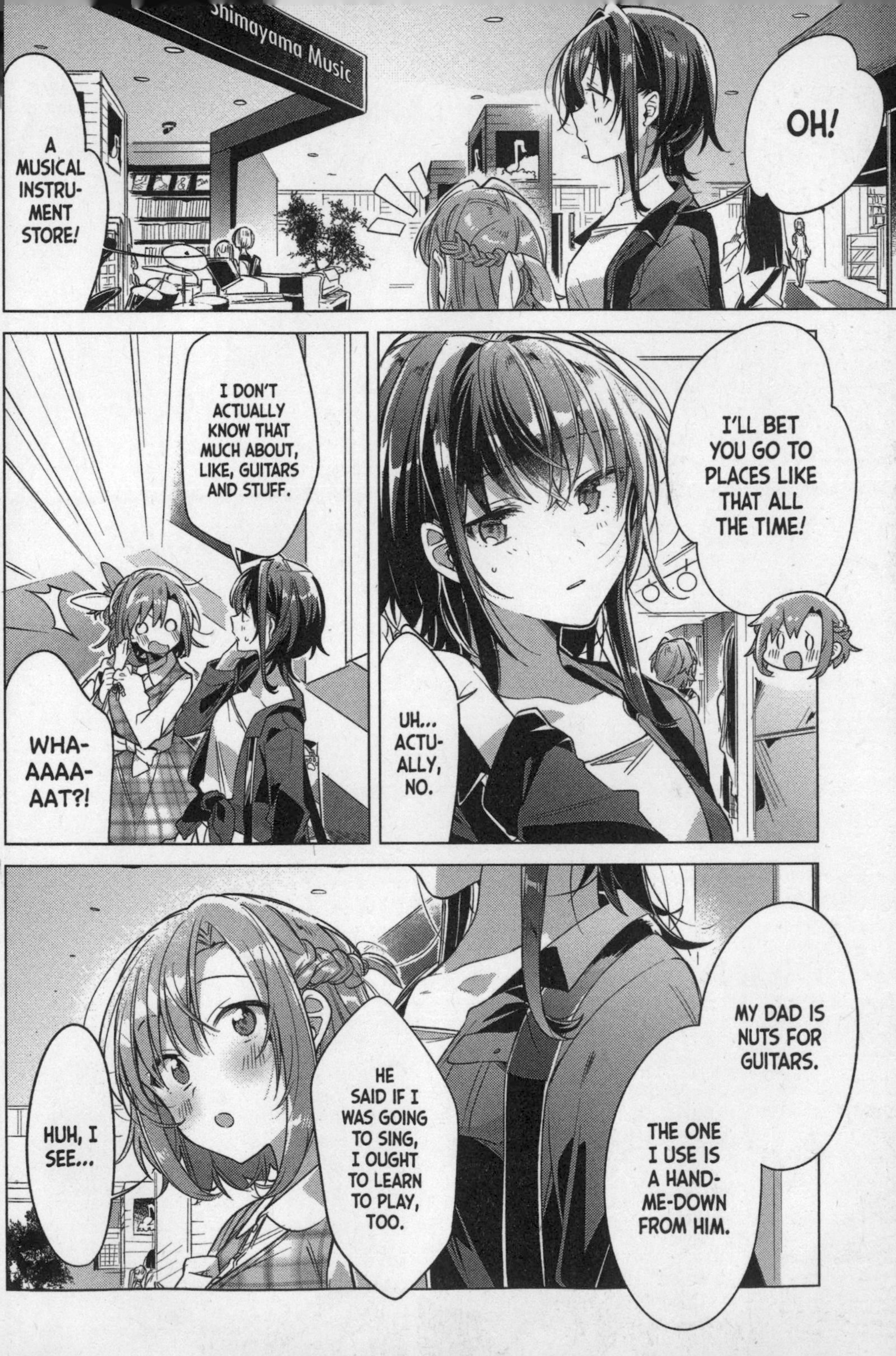
OH!
Shimayama Music
A MUSICAL INSTRUMENT STORE!
I'LL BET YOU GO TO PLACES LIKE THAT ALL THE TIME!
UH... ACTUALLY, NO.
I DON'T ACTUALLY KNOW THAT MUCH ABOUT, LIKE, GUITARS AND STUFF.
WHAAAAAAT?!
MY DAD IS NUTS FOR GUITARS.
THE ONE I USE IS A HAND-ME-DOWN FROM HIM.
HE SAID IF I WAS GOING TO SING, I OUGHT TO LEARN TO PLAY, TOO.
HUH, I SEE...

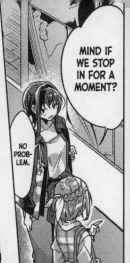

MIND IF WE STOP IN FOR A MOMENT?

NO PROB-LEM.

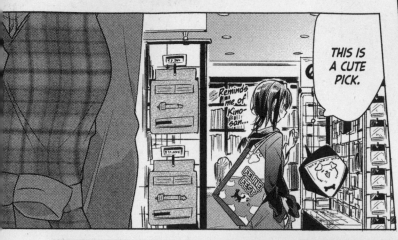

THIS IS A CUTE PICK.

Reminds me of Kino-chan...

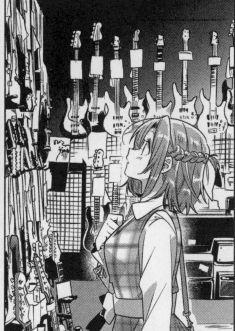

WHAT'S UP? CHECKING OUT THE ELECTRICS?

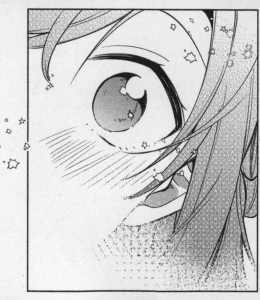

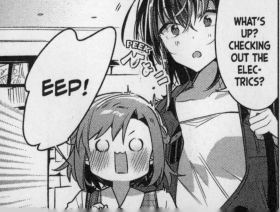

PEEK

EEP!

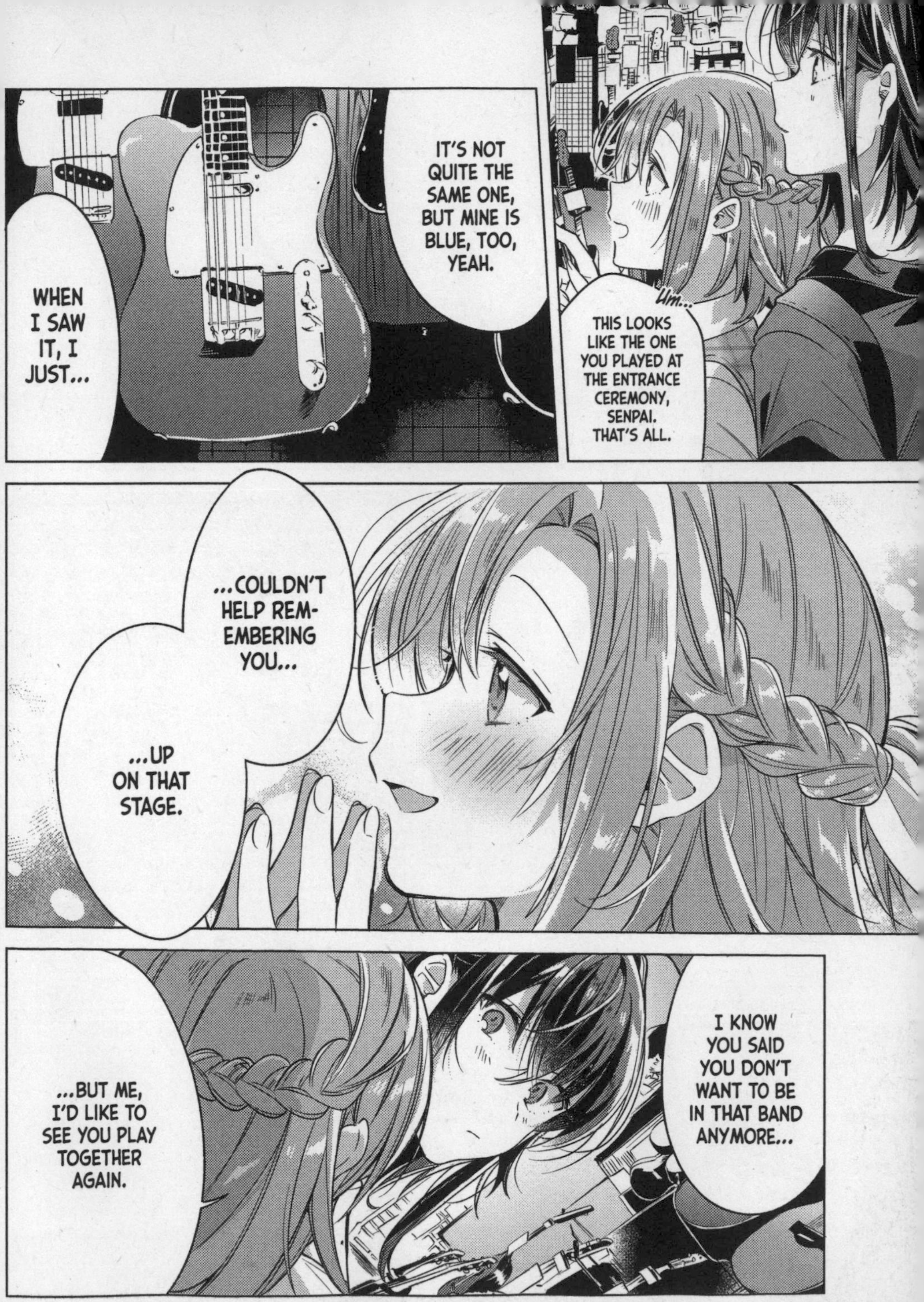
Um...
THIS LOOKS LIKE THE ONE YOU PLAYED AT THE ENTRANCE CEREMONY, SENPAI. THAT'S ALL.
IT'S NOT QUITE THE SAME ONE, BUT MINE IS BLUE, TOO, YEAH.
WHEN I SAW IT, I JUST...
...COULDN'T HELP REM-EMBERING YOU...
...UP ON THAT STAGE.
I KNOW YOU SAID YOU DON'T WANT TO BE IN THAT BAND ANYMORE...
...BUT ME, I'D LIKE TO SEE YOU PLAY TOGETHER AGAIN.

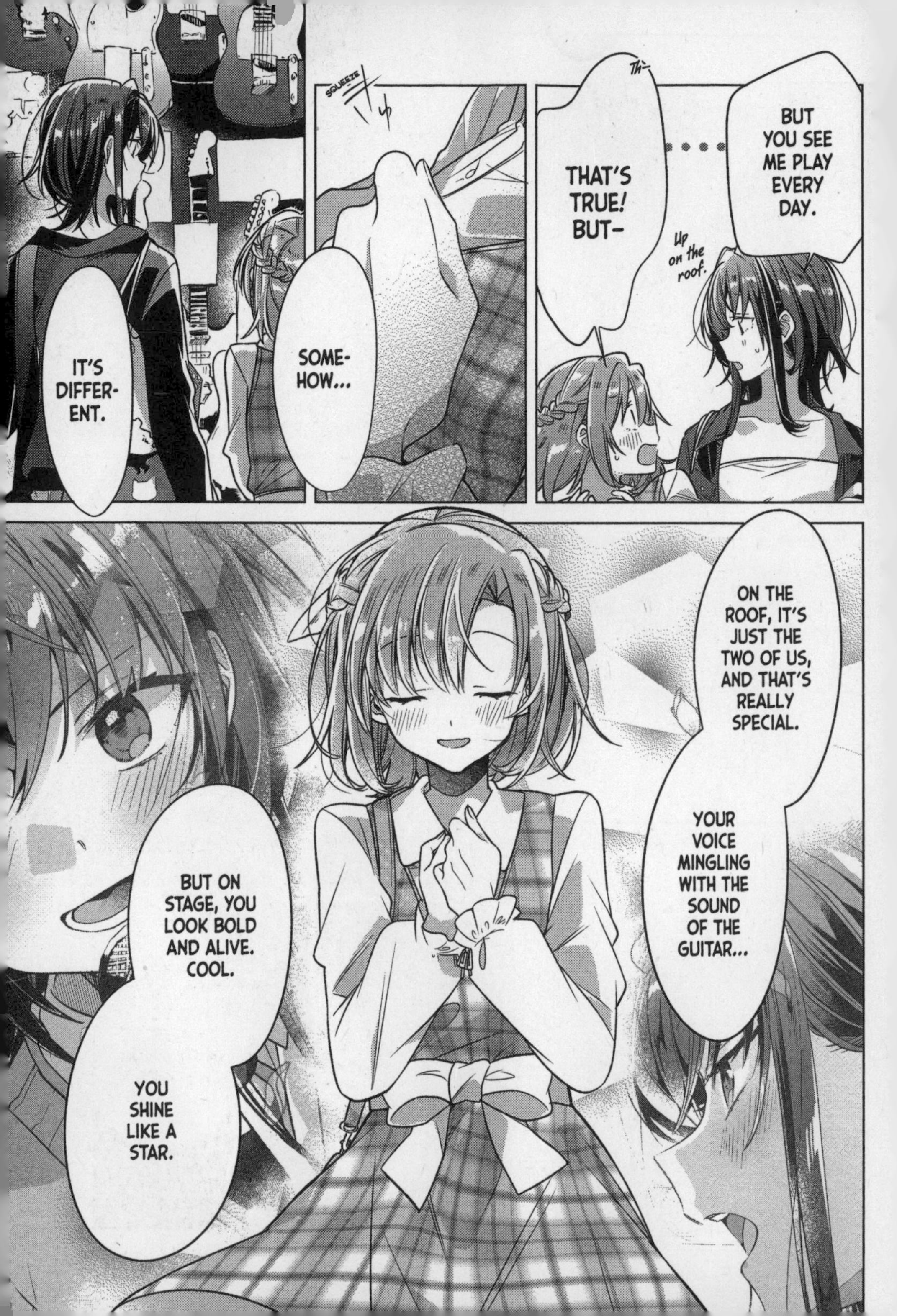
BUT YOU SEE ME PLAY EVERY DAY.
Up on the roof.
......
Th-
THAT'S TRUE! BUT-
SQUEEZE
SOME-HOW...
IT'S DIFFER-ENT.
ON THE ROOF, IT'S JUST THE TWO OF US, AND THAT'S REALLY SPECIAL.
YOUR VOICE MINGLING WITH THE SOUND OF THE GUITAR...
BUT ON STAGE, YOU LOOK BOLD AND ALIVE. COOL.
YOU SHINE LIKE A STAR.

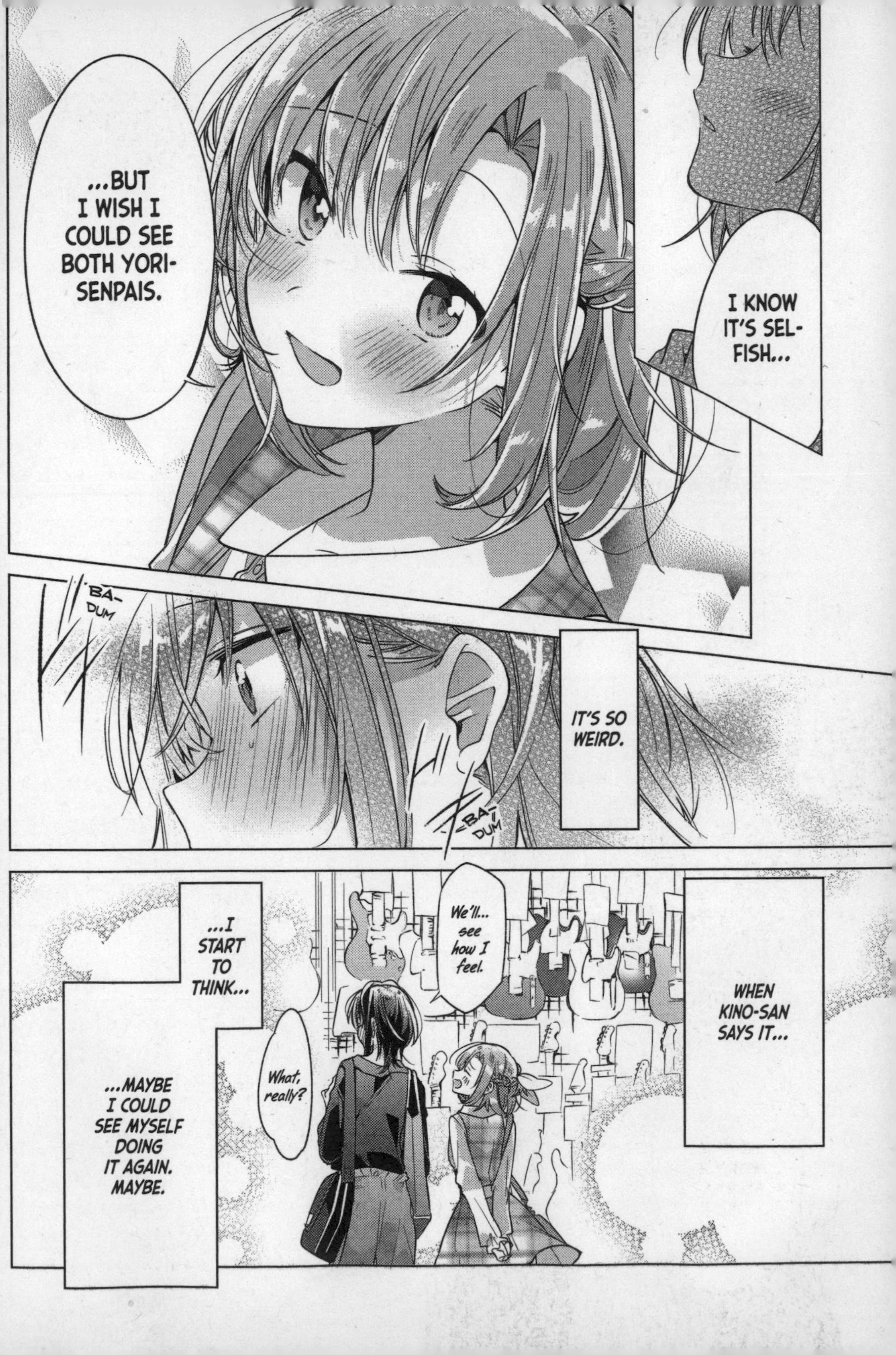
I KNOW IT'S SEL-FISH...
...BUT I WISH I COULD SEE BOTH YORI-SENPAIS.
IT'S SO WEIRD.
BA-DUM
BA-DUM
WHEN KINO-SAN SAYS IT...
We'll... see how I feel.
What, really?
...I START TO THINK...
...MAYBE I COULD SEE MYSELF DOING IT AGAIN. MAYBE.

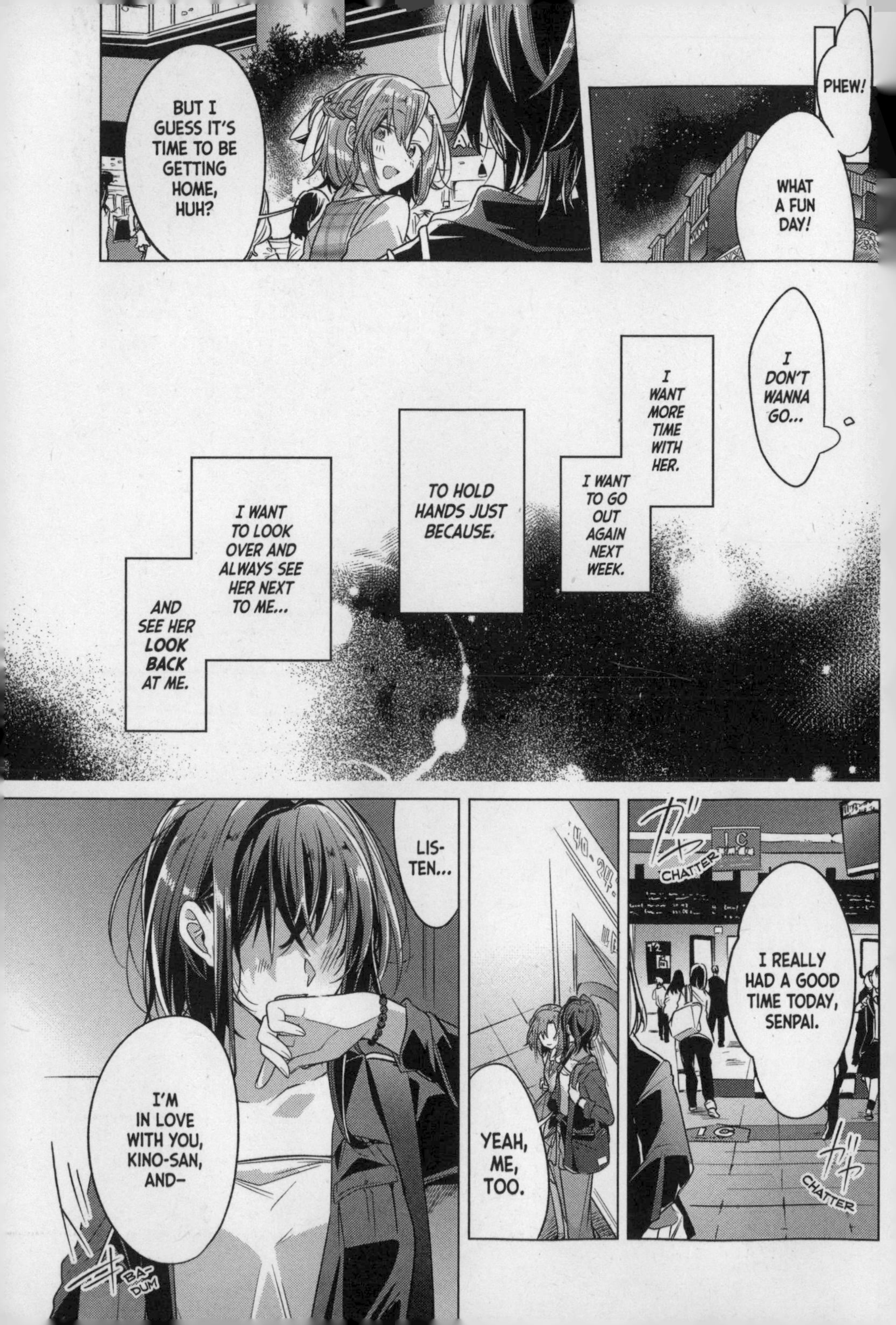
PHEW!
WHAT A FUN DAY!
BUT I GUESS IT'S TIME TO BE GETTING HOME, HUH?
I DON'T WANNA GO...
I WANT MORE TIME WITH HER.
I WANT TO GO OUT AGAIN NEXT WEEK.
TO HOLD HANDS JUST BECAUSE.
I WANT TO LOOK OVER AND ALWAYS SEE HER NEXT TO ME...
AND SEE HER LOOK BACK AT ME.
CHATTER
I REALLY HAD A GOOD TIME TODAY, SENPAI.
CHATTER
YEAH, ME, TOO.
LIS-TEN...
I'M IN LOVE WITH YOU, KINO-SAN, AND—
BA-DUM

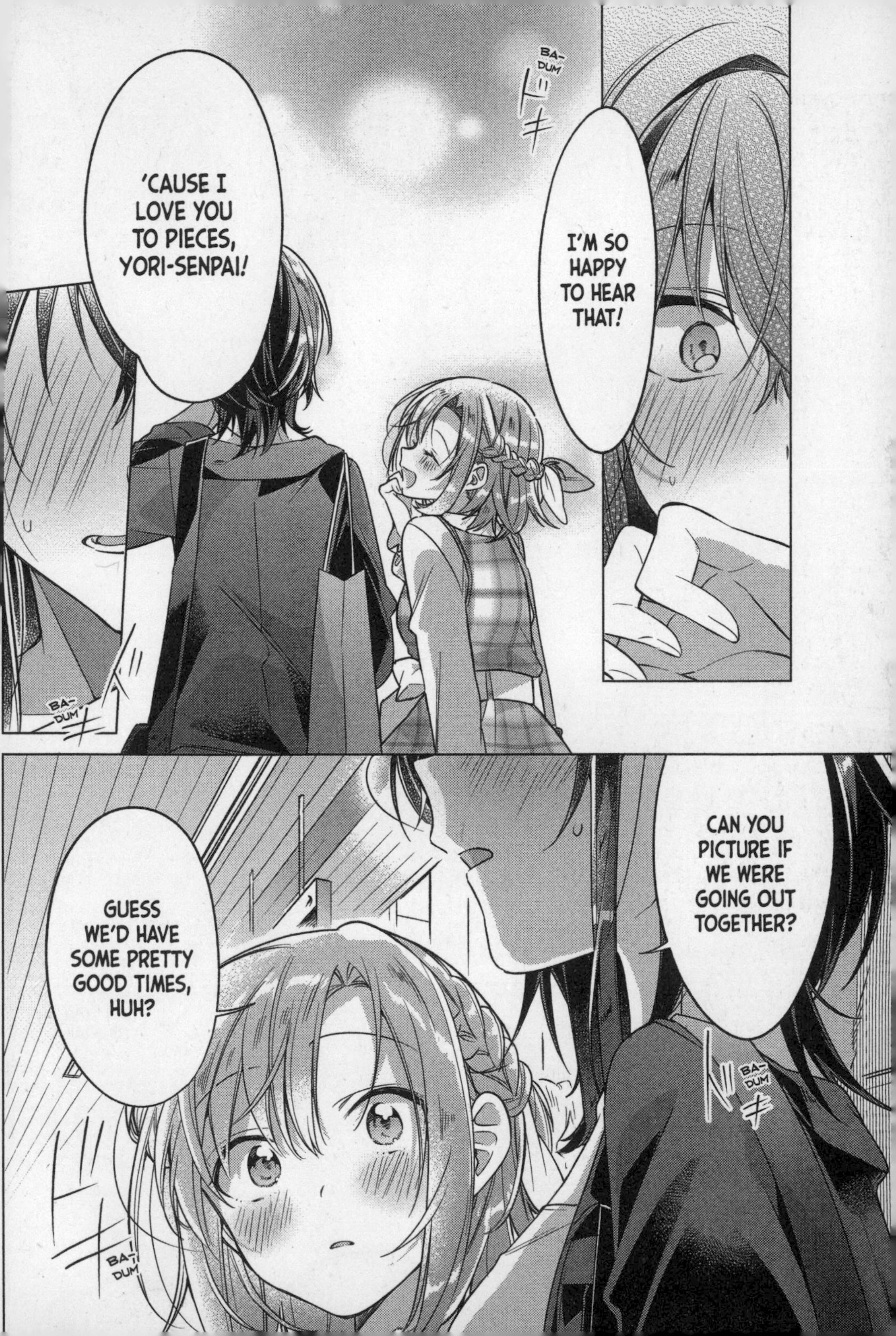
I'M SO HAPPY TO HEAR THAT!
BA-DUM
'CAUSE I LOVE YOU TO PIECES, YORI-SENPAI!
BA-DUM
CAN YOU PICTURE IF WE WERE GOING OUT TOGETHER?
BA-DUM
GUESS WE'D HAVE SOME PRETTY GOOD TIMES, HUH?
BA-DUM

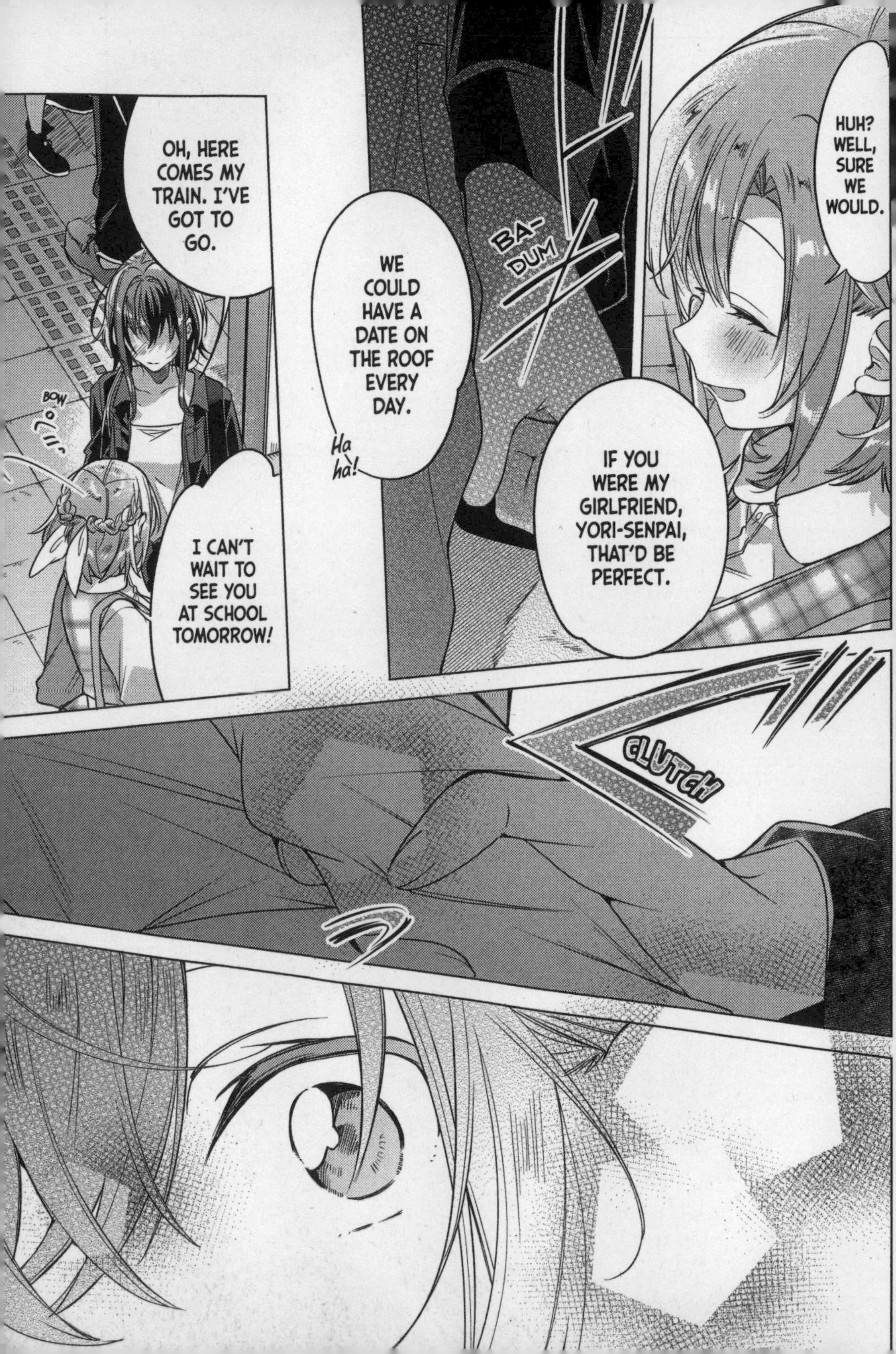
HUH? WELL, SURE WE WOULD.
IF YOU WERE MY GIRLFRIEND, YORI-SENPAI, THAT'D BE PERFECT.
BA-DUM
WE COULD HAVE A DATE ON THE ROOF EVERY DAY.
Ha ha!
OH, HERE COMES MY TRAIN. I'VE GOT TO GO.
BOW
I CAN'T WAIT TO SEE YOU AT SCHOOL TOMORROW!
CLUTCH

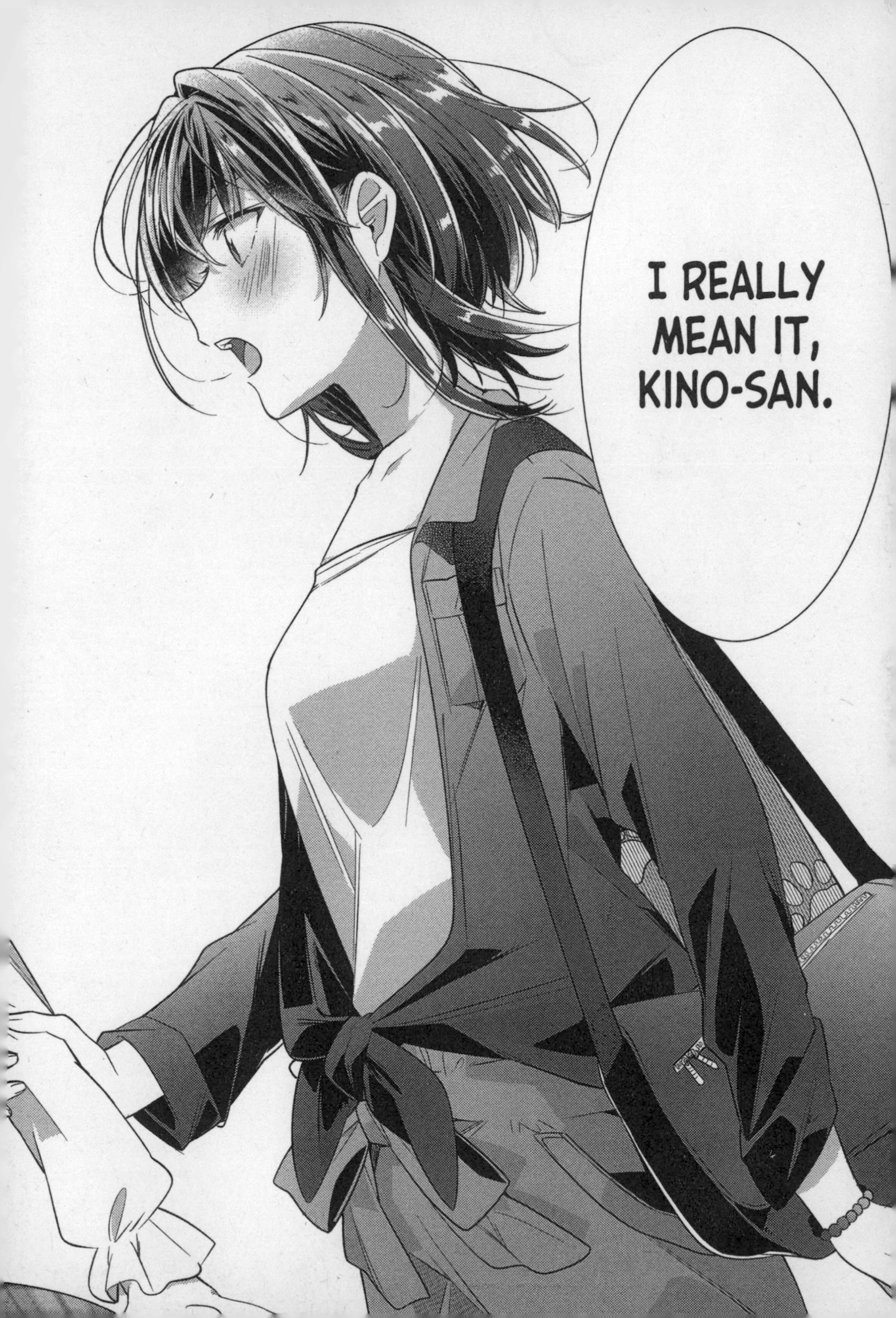
I REALLY MEAN IT, KINO-SAN.

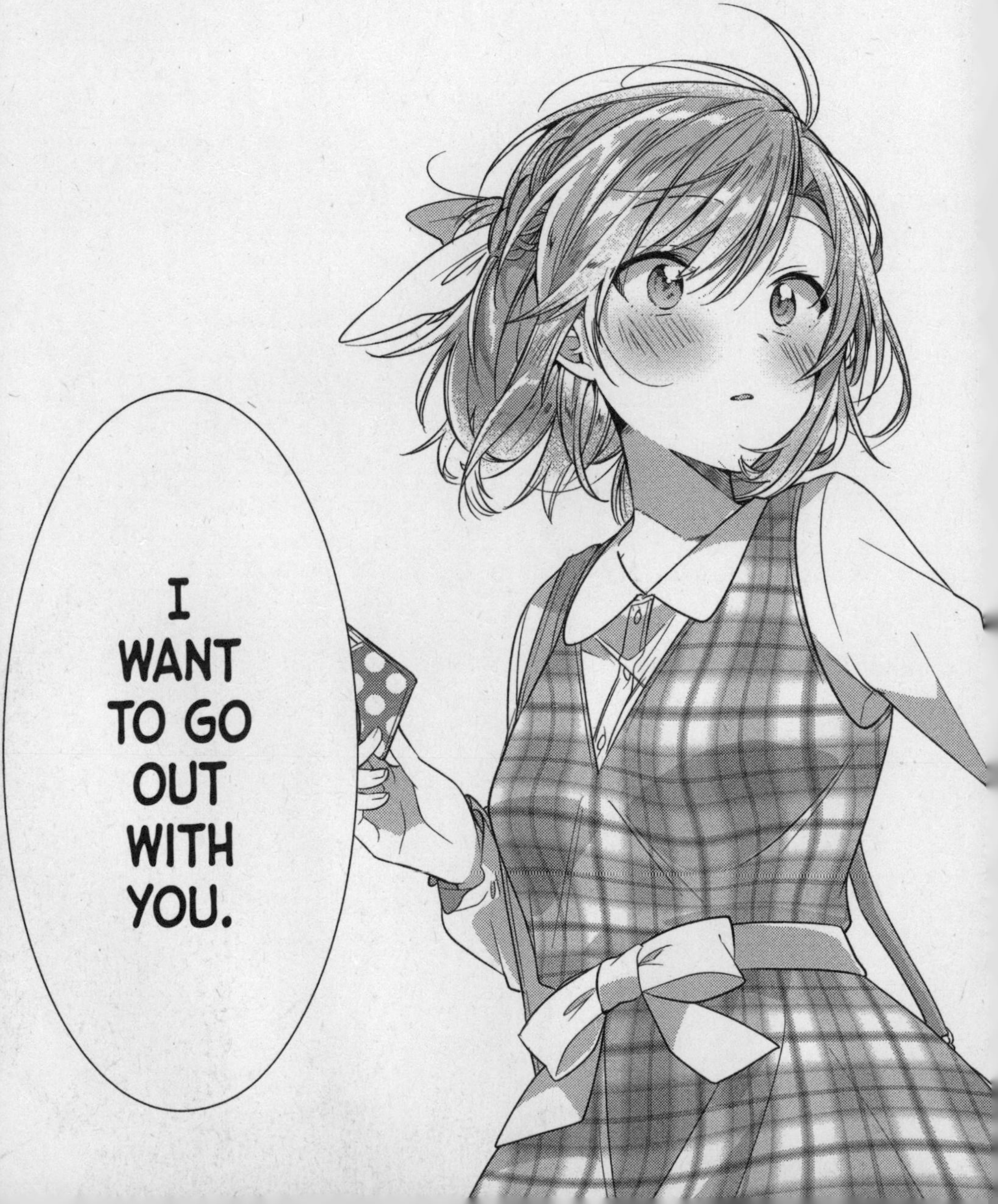
I WANT TO GO OUT WITH YOU.

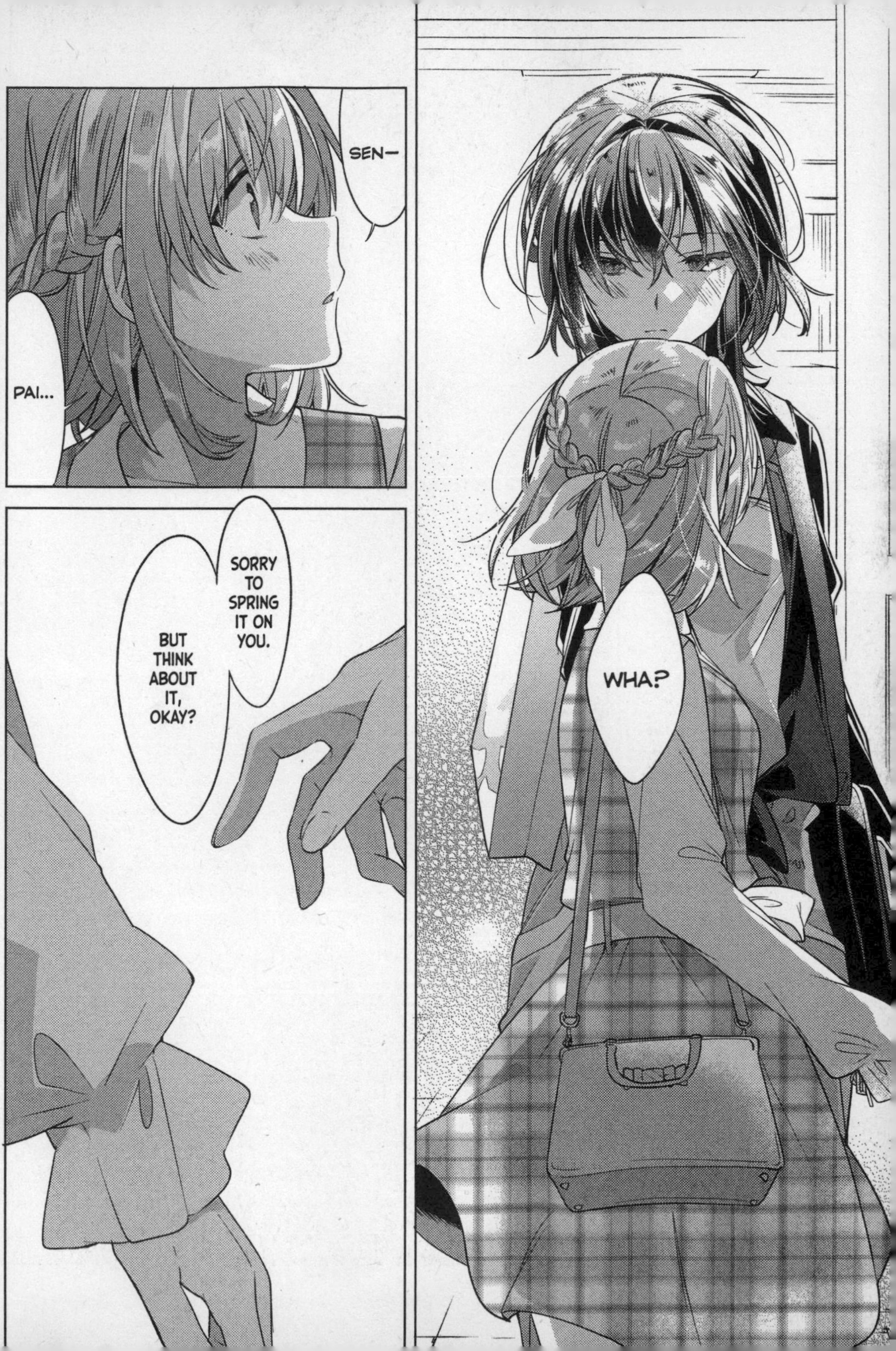
WHA?
SEN—
PAI...
SORRY TO SPRING IT ON YOU.
BUT THINK ABOUT IT, OKAY?

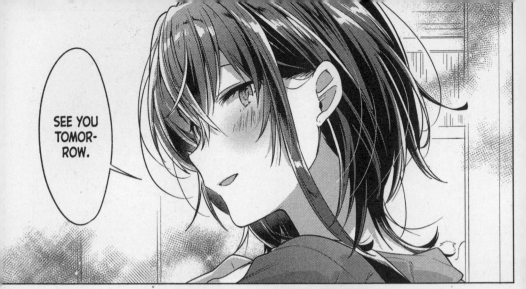

SEE YOU TOMOR-ROW.

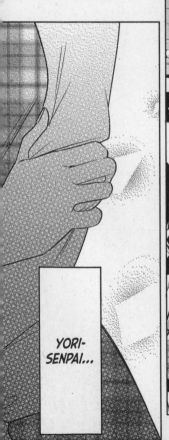

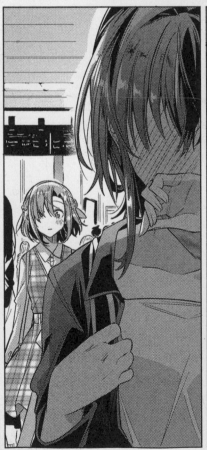

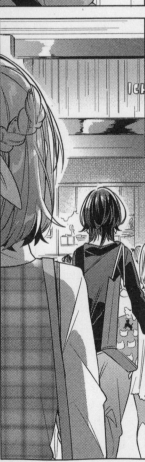

YORI-SENPAI...

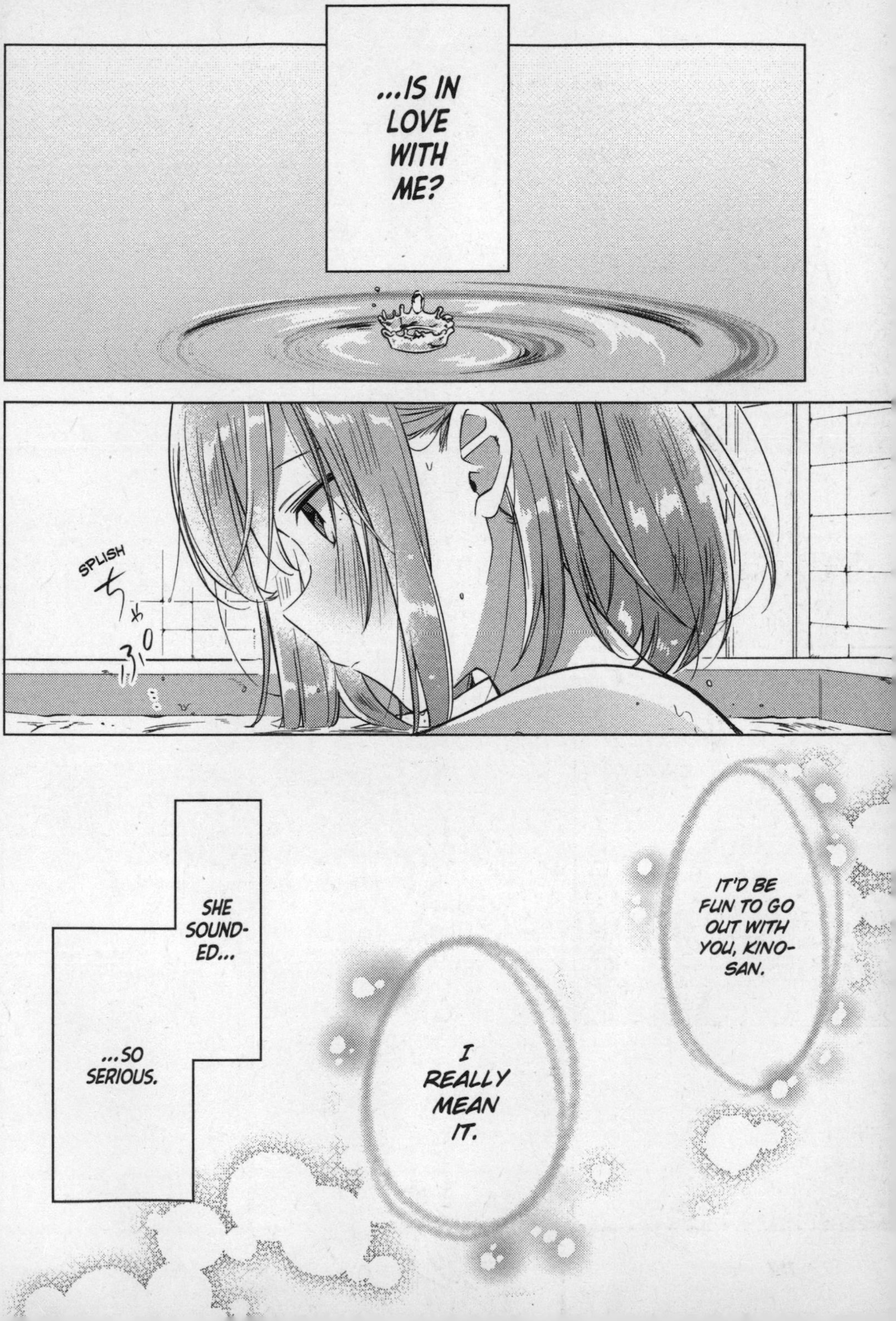
...IS IN LOVE WITH ME?
SPLISH
IT'D BE FUN TO GO OUT WITH YOU, KINO-SAN.
I REALLY MEAN IT.
SHE SOUND-ED...
...SO SERIOUS.

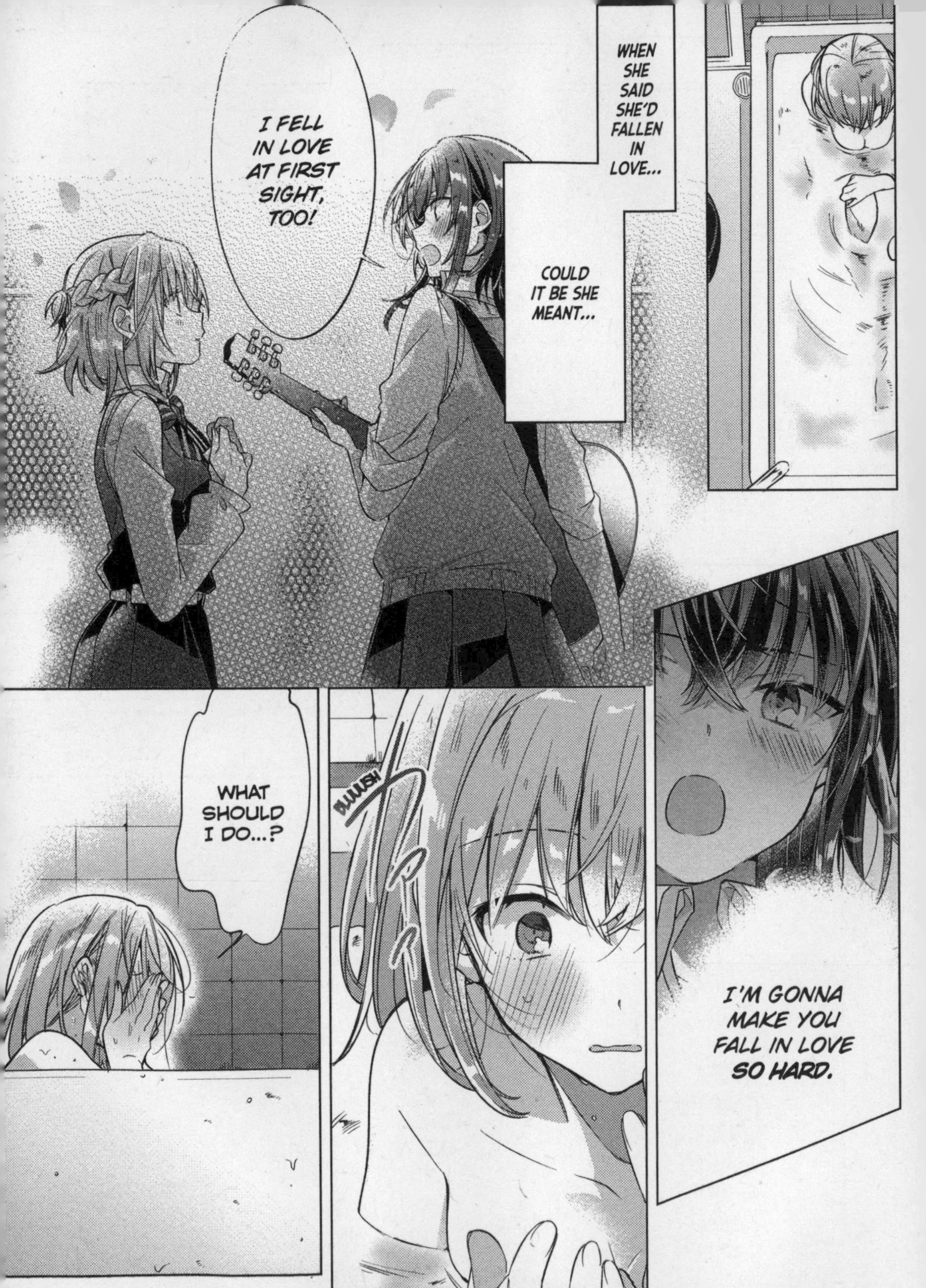
WHEN SHE SAID SHE'D FALLEN IN LOVE...
COULD IT BE SHE MEANT...
I FELL IN LOVE AT FIRST SIGHT, TOO!
I'M GONNA MAKE YOU FALL IN LOVE SO HARD.
BLUUUSH
WHAT SHOULD I DO...?

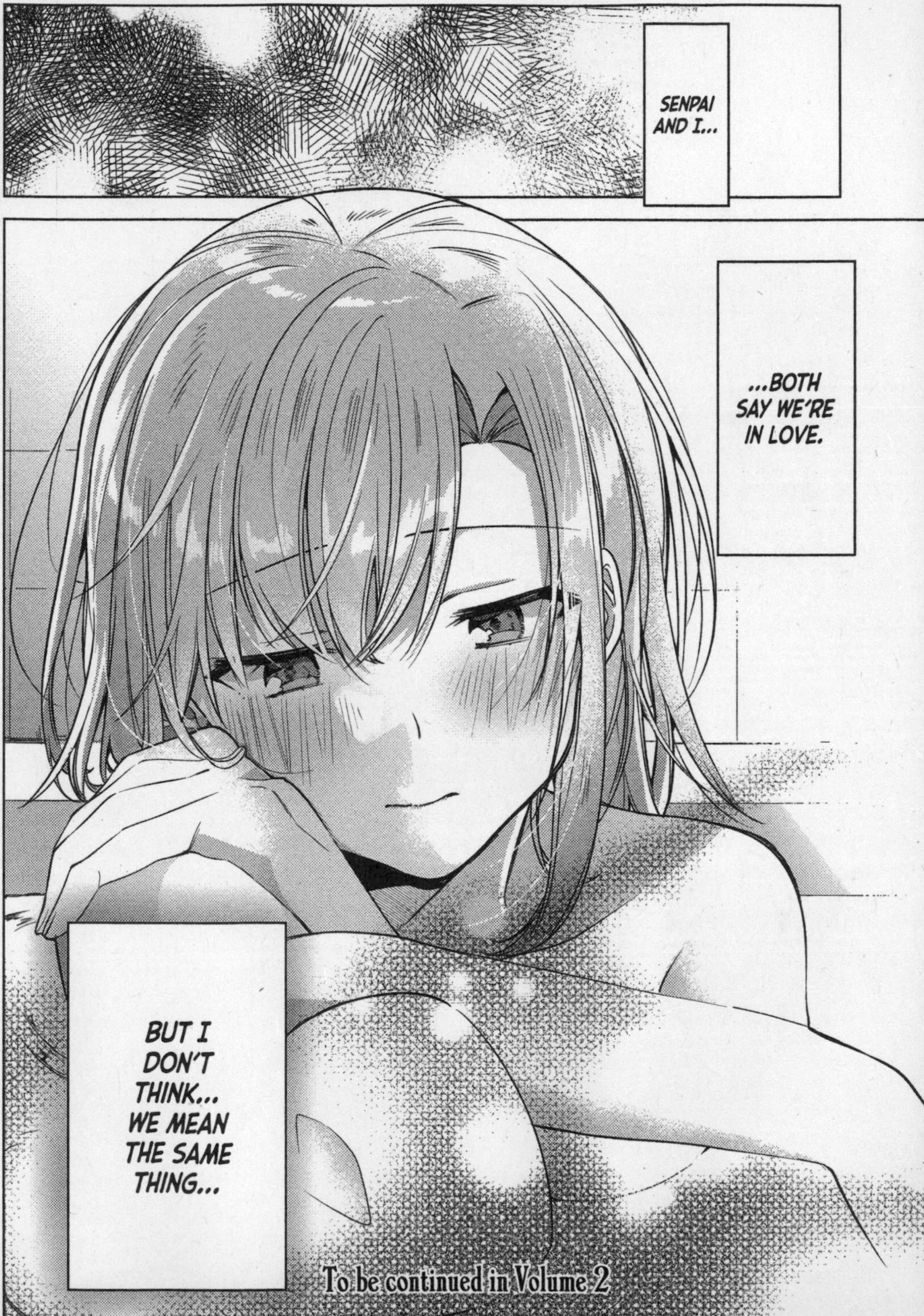
SENPAI AND I...
...BOTH SAY WE'RE IN LOVE.
BUT I DON'T THINK... WE MEAN THE SAME THING...
To be continued in Volume 2

Whisper Me
A Love Song
Eku
Takeshima

Bonus 1
Love Song

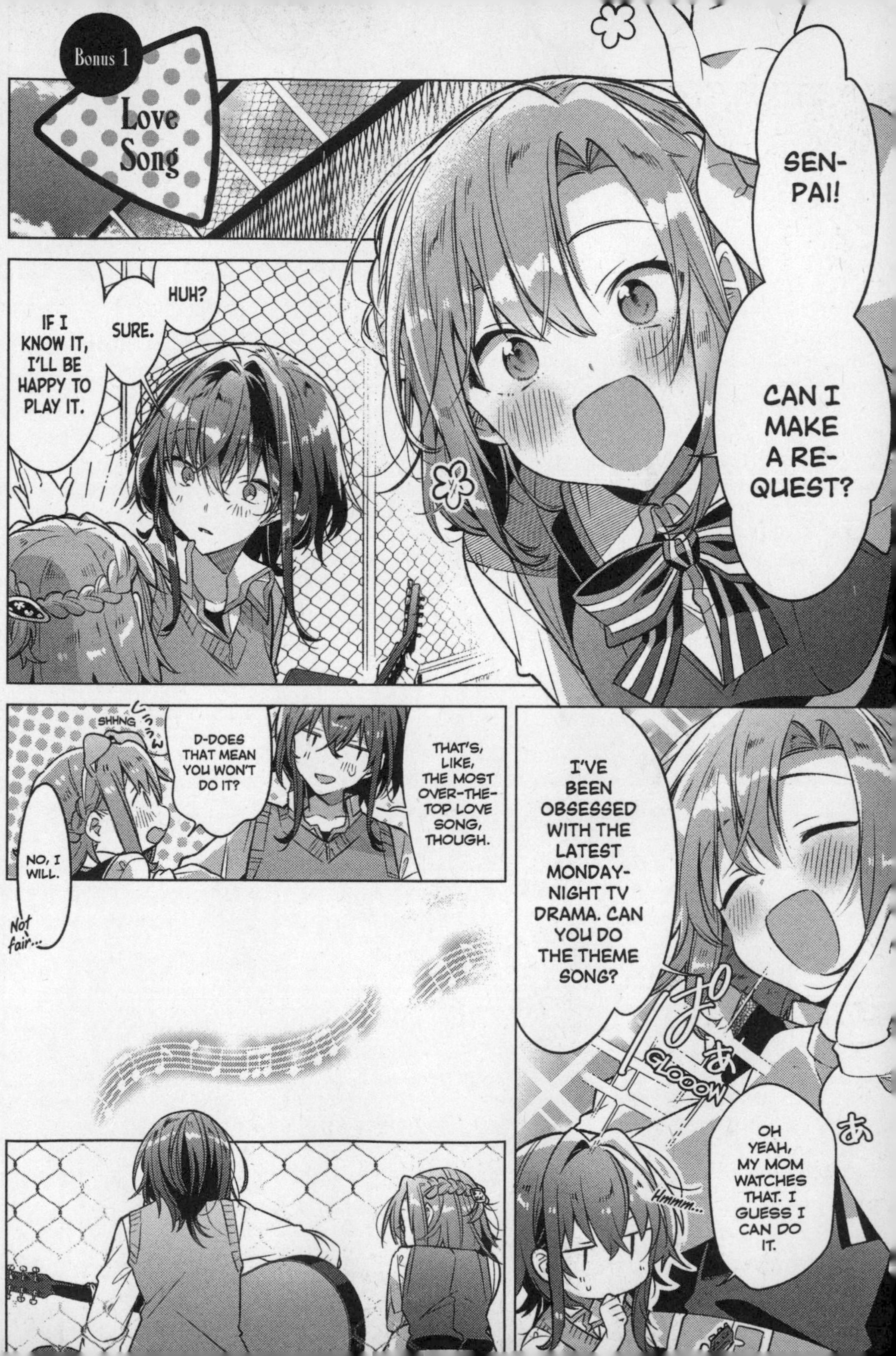
SEN-PAI!
CAN I MAKE A RE-QUEST?
HUH?
SURE.
IF I KNOW IT, I'LL BE HAPPY TO PLAY IT.
I'VE BEEN OBSESSED WITH THE LATEST MONDAY-NIGHT TV DRAMA. CAN YOU DO THE THEME SONG?
GLOOOW
OH YEAH, MY MOM WATCHES THAT. I GUESS I CAN DO IT.
Hmmm...
THAT'S, LIKE, THE MOST OVER-THE-TOP LOVE SONG, THOUGH.
D-DOES THAT MEAN YOU WON'T DO IT?
SHHNG
NO, I WILL.
Not fair...

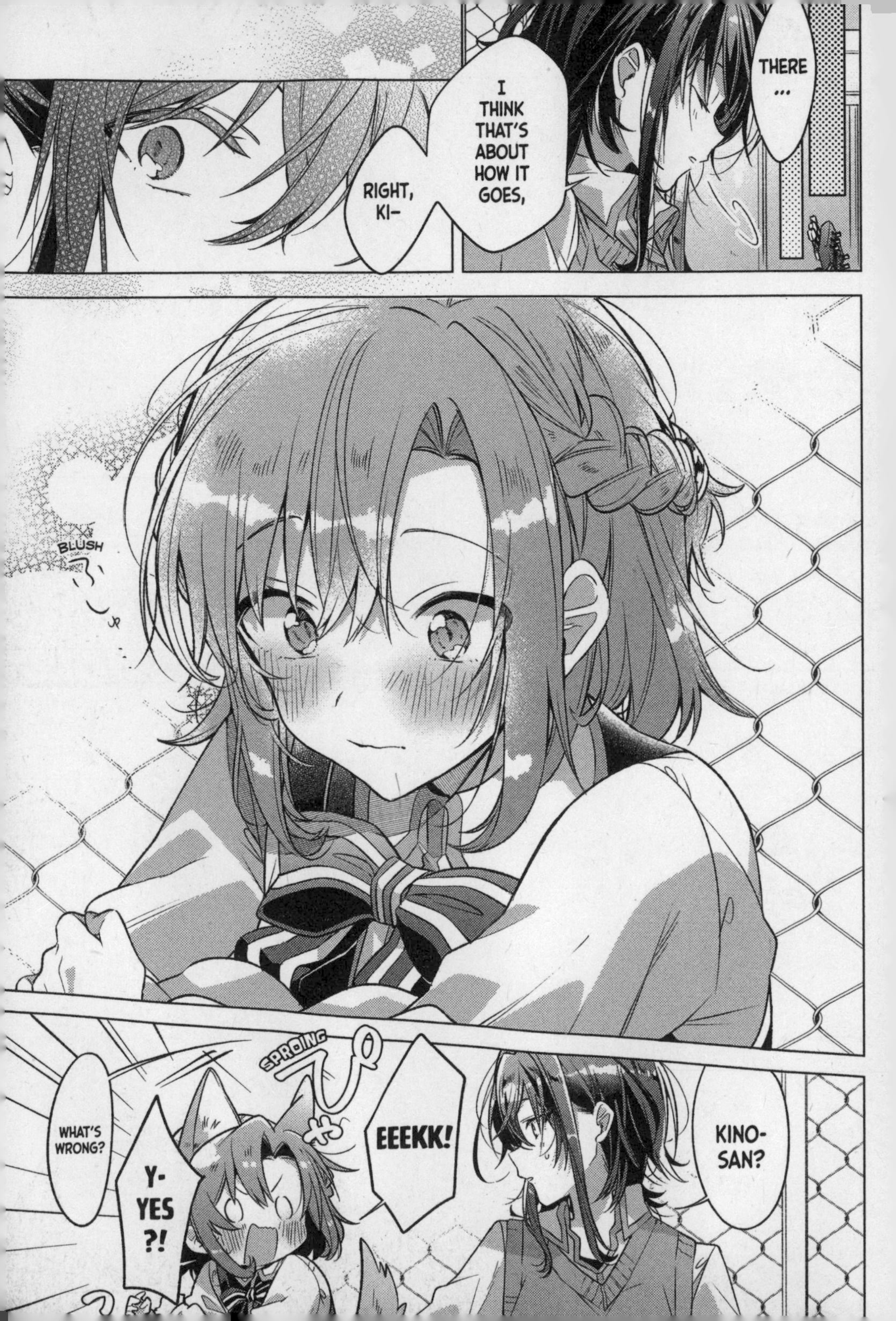
THERE...
I THINK THAT'S ABOUT HOW IT GOES,
RIGHT, KI-
BLUSH
KINO-SAN?
EEEKK!
SPROING
Y-YES?!
WHAT'S WRONG?

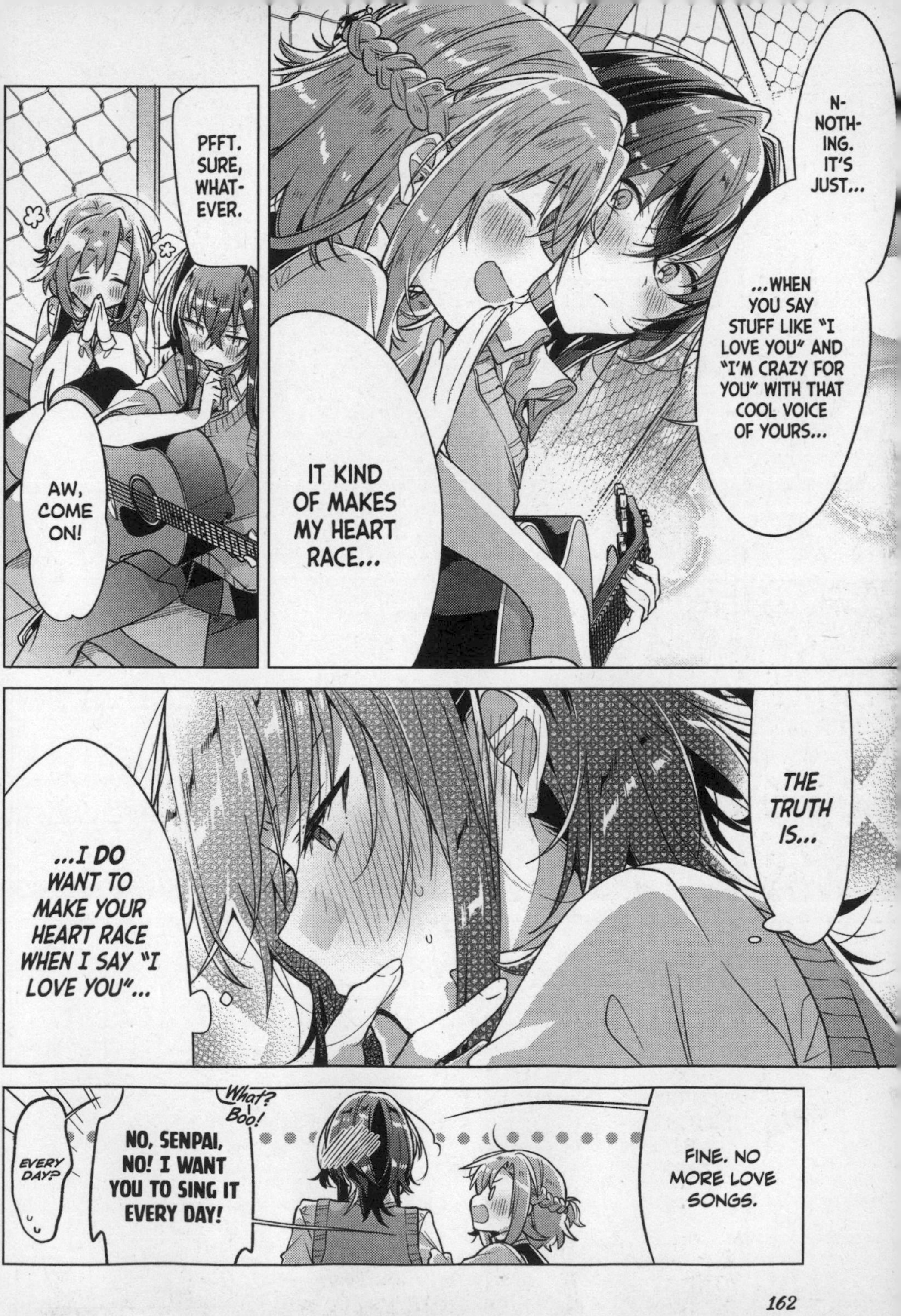
N-NOTHING. IT'S JUST...
...WHEN YOU SAY STUFF LIKE "I LOVE YOU" AND "I'M CRAZY FOR YOU" WITH THAT COOL VOICE OF YOURS...
IT KIND OF MAKES MY HEART RACE...
PFFT. SURE, WHATEVER.
AW, COME ON!
THE TRUTH IS...
...I DO WANT TO MAKE YOUR HEART RACE WHEN I SAY "I LOVE YOU"...
FINE. NO MORE LOVE SONGS.
What? Boo!
NO, SENPAI, NO! I WANT YOU TO SING IT EVERY DAY!
EVERY DAY?

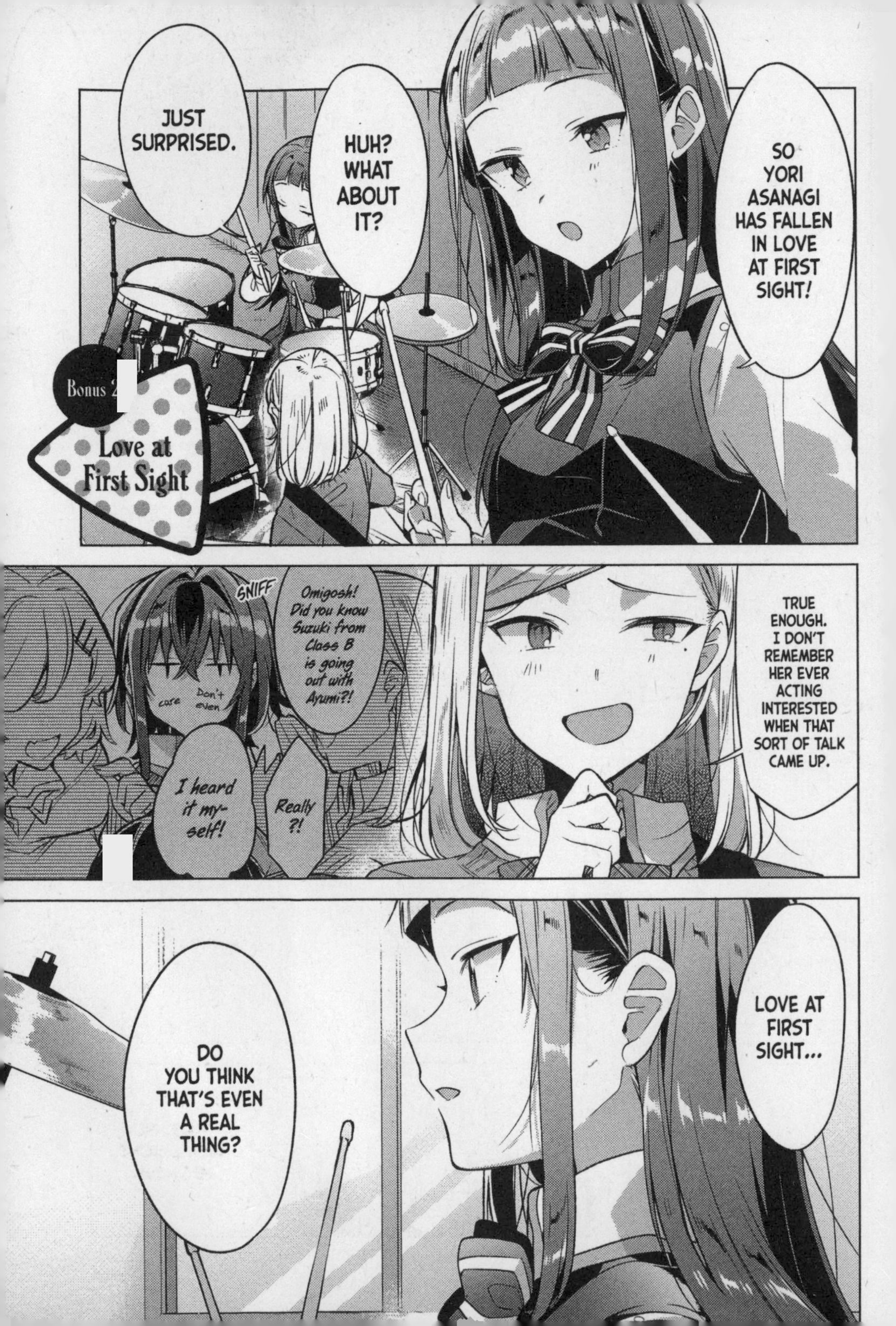
SO YORI ASANAGI HAS FALLEN IN LOVE AT FIRST SIGHT!
HUH? WHAT ABOUT IT?
JUST SURPRISED.
Bonus 2
Love at First Sight
TRUE ENOUGH. I DON'T REMEMBER HER EVER ACTING INTERESTED WHEN THAT SORT OF TALK CAME UP.
SNIFF
Omigosh! Did you know Suzuki from Class B is going out with Ayumi?!
Don't even care
Really?!
I heard it my-self!
LOVE AT FIRST SIGHT...
DO YOU THINK THAT'S EVEN A REAL THING?

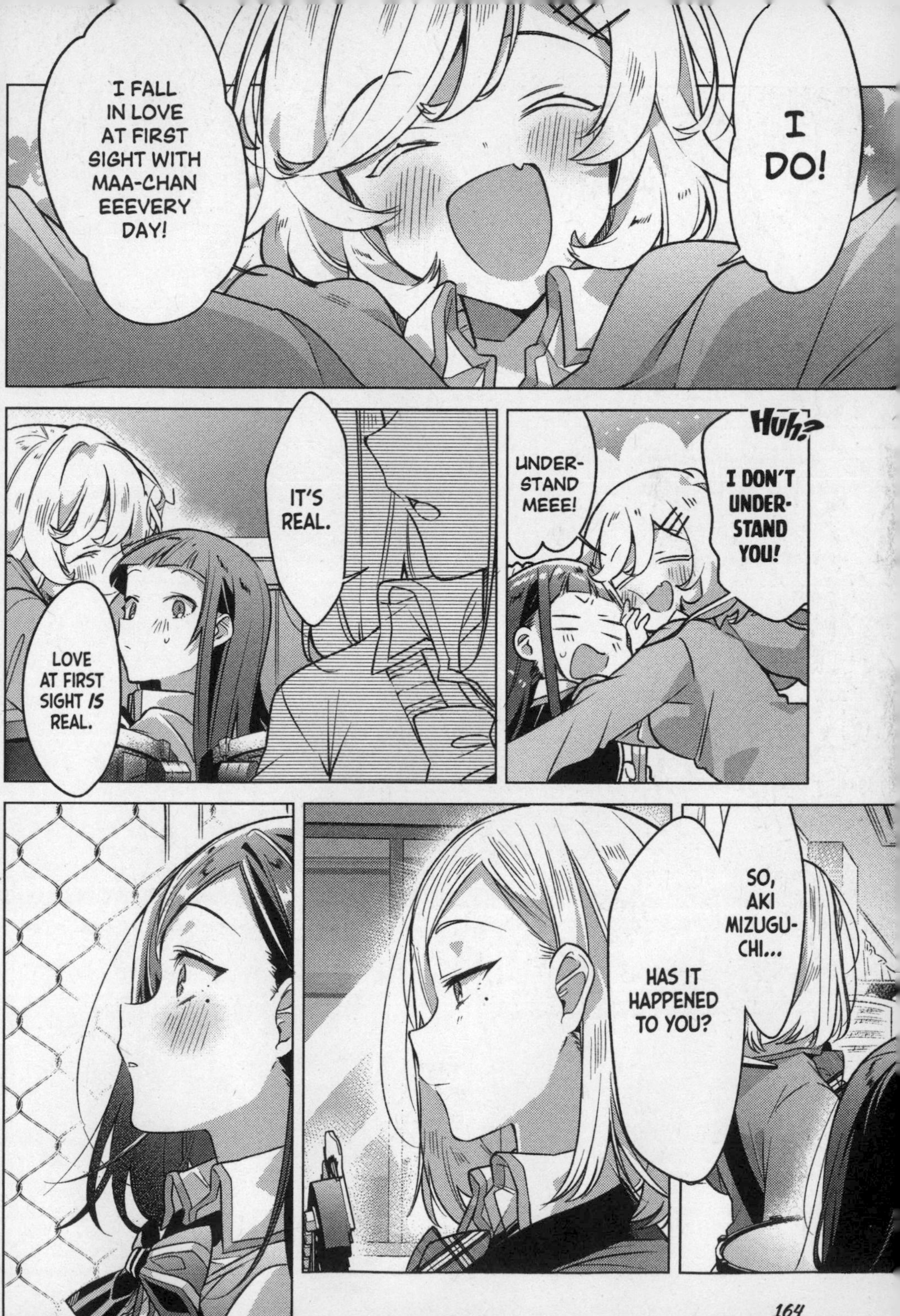
I DO!
I FALL IN LOVE AT FIRST SIGHT WITH MAA-CHAN EEEVERY DAY!
HUH?
I DON'T UNDER-STAND YOU!
UNDER-STAND MEEE!
IT'S REAL.
LOVE AT FIRST SIGHT *IS* REAL.
SO, AKI MIZUGU-CHI...
HAS IT HAPPENED TO YOU?

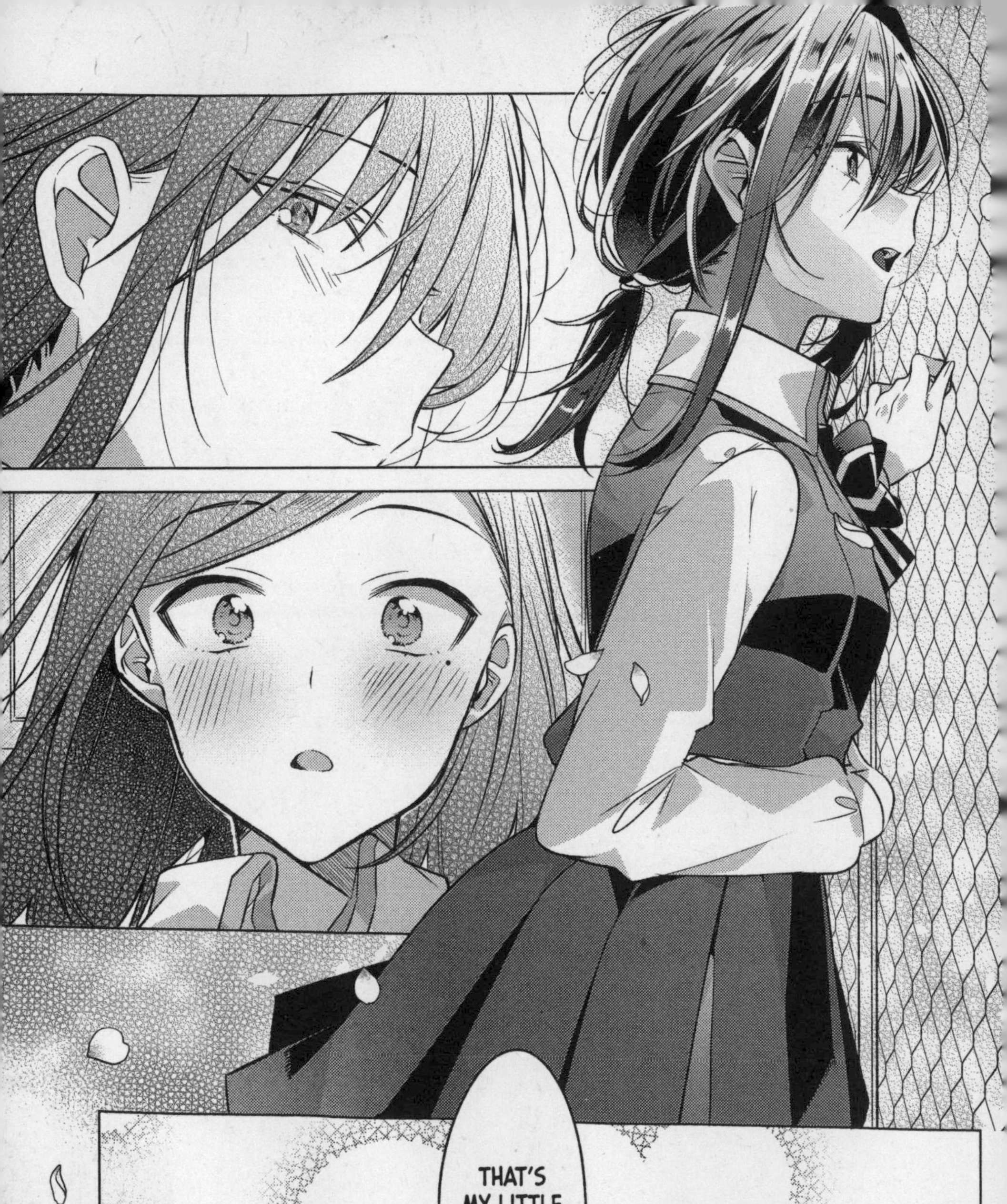
THAT'S MY LITTLE SECRET.

Afterword

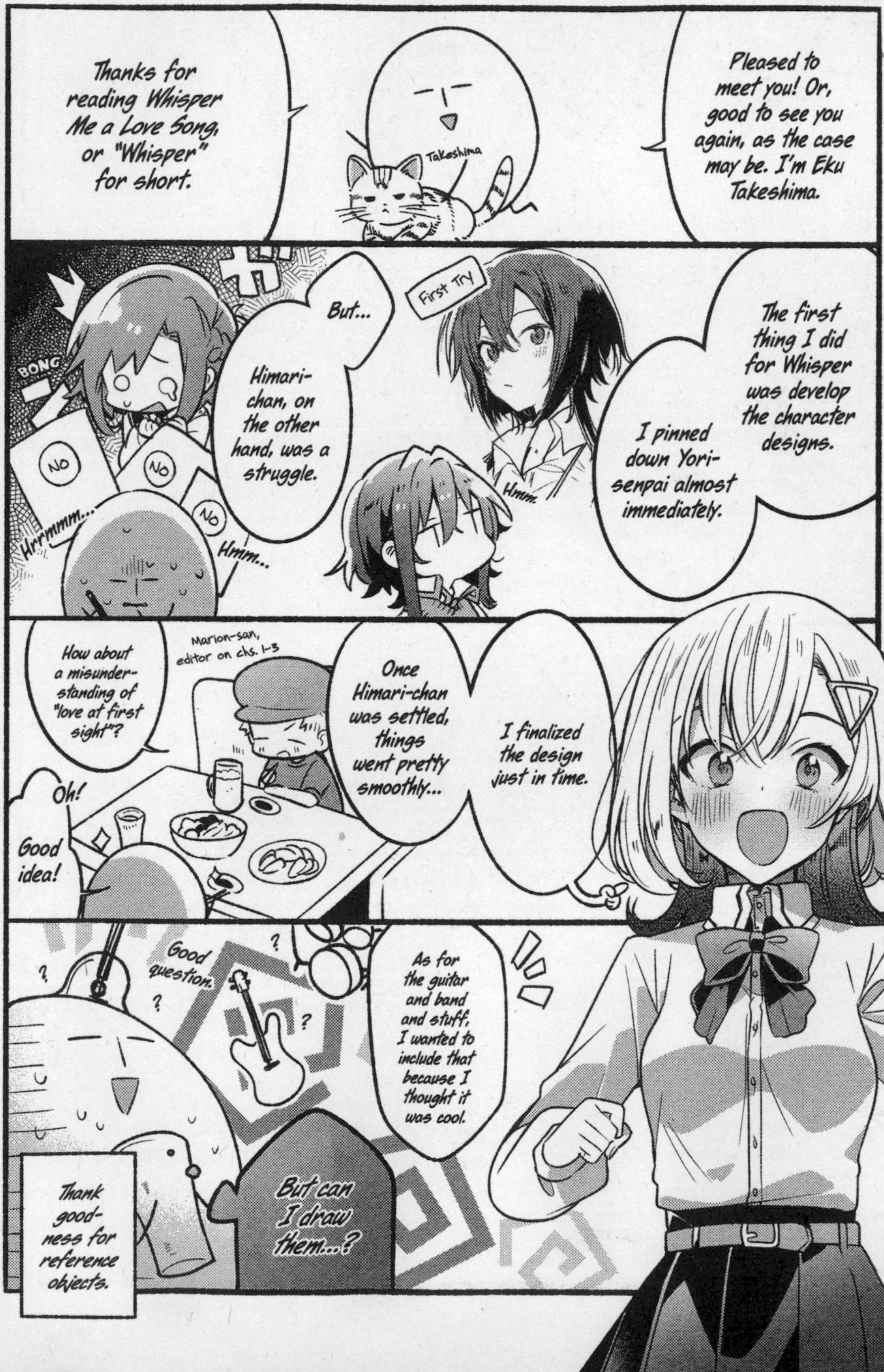

Pleased to meet you! Or, good to see you again, as the case may be. I'm Eku Takeshima.
Takeshima
Thanks for reading Whisper Me a Love Song, or "Whisper" for short.
The first thing I did for Whisper was develop the character designs.
I pinned down Yori-senpai almost immediately.
First Try
Hmm
But...
Himari-chan, on the other hand, was a struggle.
BONG
NO
NO
NO
Hrrmmm...
Hmm...
Once Himari-chan was settled, things went pretty smoothly...
I finalized the design just in time.
Marion-san, editor on chs. 1-3
How about a misunderstanding of "love at first sight"?
Oh!
Good idea!
As for the guitar and band and stuff, I wanted to include that because I thought it was cool.
Good question.
But can I draw them...?
Thank goodness for reference objects.

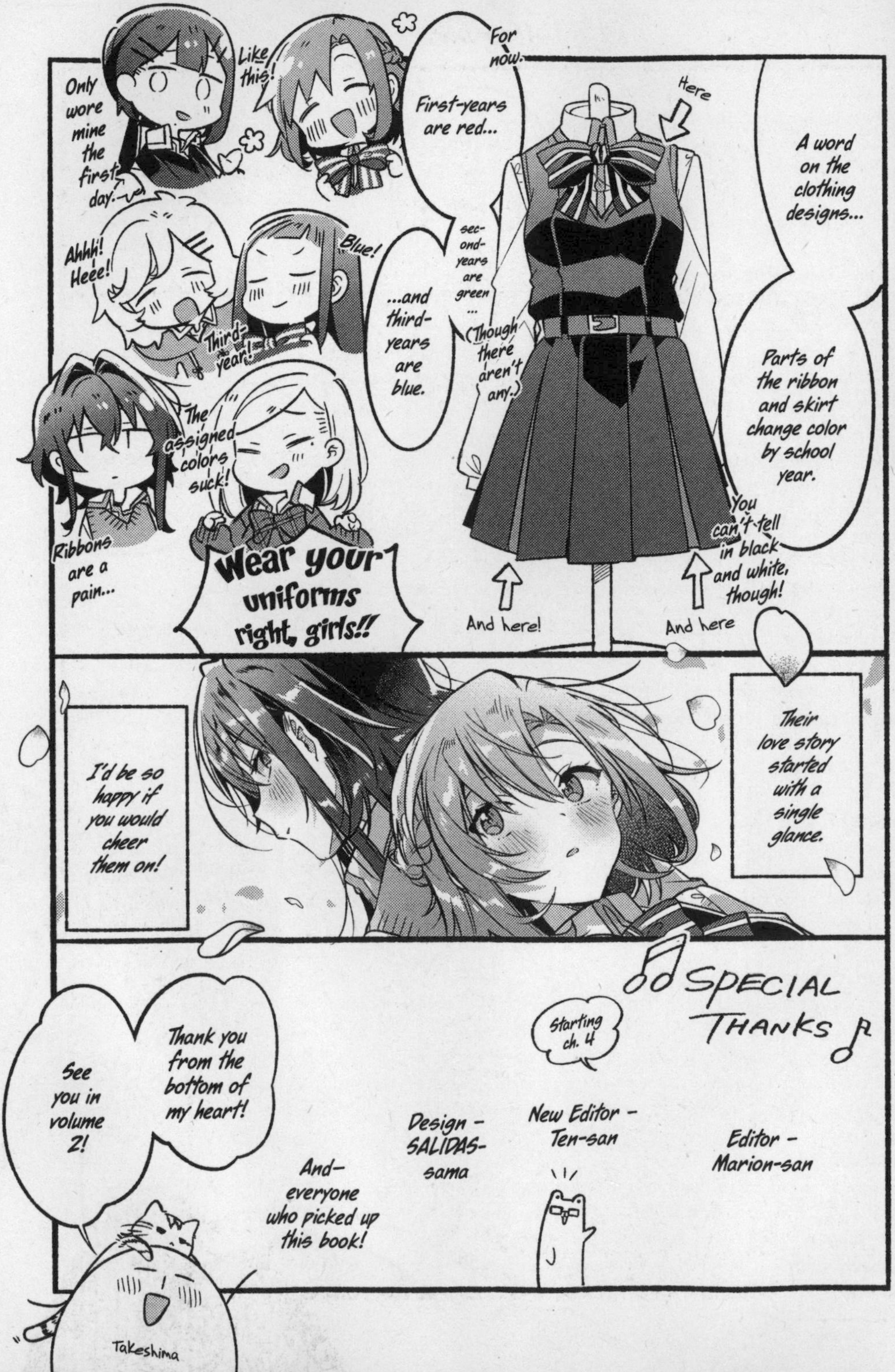
A word on the clothing designs...
Here
Parts of the ribbon and skirt change color by school year.
You can't tell in black and white, though!
And here
And here!
For now.
First-years are red...
sec-ond-years are green ...
(Though there aren't any.)
...and third-years are blue.
Like this!
Only wore mine the first day.
Blue!
Third-year!
Ahhh! Heee!
The assigned colors suck!
Ribbons are a pain...
Wear your uniforms right, girls!!
Their love story started with a single glance.
I'd be so happy if you would cheer them on!
SPECIAL THANKS
Starting ch. 4
Editor - Marion-san
New Editor - Ten-san
Design - SALIDAS-sama
And-everyone who picked up this book!
Thank you from the bottom of my heart!
See you in volume 2!
Takeshima

TRANSLATION NOTES

Senpai, page 2

Senpai (sometimes romanized as *sempai;* literally "a fellow who has gone before") is a term of respect for someone who is ahead of you in a particular discipline or social group. In the context of school, it typically means an upperclassman. It can be used as a noun or form of address on its own, or attached to a person's name like any other honorific ("Yori-senpai"). The opposite of senpai is *kouhai* (literally "a fellow who comes after").

School Is Starting, page 5

The Japanese school year begins in April. The cherry blossom (*sakura*) trees around the country generally bloom in March or April, so the beginning of the new school year traditionally takes place among a blizzard of pink blossoms. (Japanese schools typically operate on a trimester system, with the first term running from April to July, the second from September to December, and then a final stretch from January to late March. The students have breaks in between each trimester.)

The Same School, page 6

High school is not part of the compulsory educational curriculum in Japan, and students who choose to attend it (rather than going to, say, a vocational school) may have to take entrance exams, much like one might for college. Therefore, like college, friends may pick different high schools or not get into the schools they pick, so Himari is understandably happy to be able to stay with Miki. In Japan, elementary school comprises six years, with middle and high school being comprised of three years each.

The Same Class, page 7

In Japanese schools, students are assigned to a homeroom where they spend most of the school day, and it's the teachers, not the students, who move from room to room between periods. These homerooms are usually designated with a combination of a number, representing the class year, and a letter. So 3-B, for example, would be third year, class B. (The individual classes are sometimes known in Japanese as *kumi*, or "groups.") This can be seen on the sign on page 81, panel 1.

Lockers, page 15

It's considered inappropriate to wear outdoor footwear into a school (as it is in homes, temples, and dojo, among other places). Instead, each student has a pair of sandals reserved exclusively for indoor use. (On page 114, you can see Himari wearing a pair of sandals with her name on them.) The sandals are kept in these lockers, where they're taken out at the beginning of each day and put back at the end.

Club Affiliation: None, page 22

Most Japanese high schoolers belong to some kind of club where they spend their after-school hours. You can see the list of clubs available at Himari and Miki's school on the flyer on page 9; it suggests the wide variety of activities that are typically available to students. Kids who don't belong to any club are the exception to the rule, so much so that they're sometimes referred to as belonging to the *kitaku-bu* or "go-home [after school] club," which is the expression Miki uses here.

Blood Type, page 22

There's a longstanding folk belief in Japan that blood type influences personality. People with type-A blood are believed to be methodical, careful, and maybe a bit uptight, while people with type-B blood are thought to be relaxed and tackle life at their own pace. (AB people are considered to share characteristics of both, but by the same token, to be a bit Janus-faced.) Type O is seen as a little more flexible, being more open to definition by the person in question.

Tachibana-san, page 83
Kaori frequently refers to herself in the third person, which isn't that unusual for young Japanese women. The use of -*san* with one's own name is less common, but can sometimes be done in a facetious manner.

Bag, page 101
Himari seems to be eating a convenience-store snack food, a bread pouch with filling. (In this case, apparently strawberry.)

LIME, page 108
A nod to the messaging app LINE, which is very popular in Japan. The app did include the ability to trade friend information by shaking two phones at each other, but that functionality was discontinued in May 2020.

Marota, page 116
Maro is presumably from *maroyaka,* meaning "round" or "circular"; -*ta* is a typical name ending but is also the kanji for "fat" (*futoi*). (In fact, that's why it was traditionally included in children's names, as an auspicious character ensuring good health.) So Marota has a a sweet, but rather plump-sounding, moniker, similar to "Chubsie", if rendered in English.

Aeon, page 118
Aeon is a real chain of malls in Japan.

Himari's Bookshelf, page 124
Several of the books on the shelf near Himari in this panel are recognizable. From left, they include *Hare no Kuni no Appare-dan* and *Kimi ni Suki tte Iwasetai,* both by Eku Takeshima.

Fork, page 136
In Japan, putting your lips to something that has already touched someone else's lips is sometimes referred to as a *kansetsu kisu,* or "indirect kiss," and can be seen as having romantic implications. (Feeding someone food is also an especially loaded act in Japan, and indeed much of Asia.)

Monday-Night TV Drama, page 160
In Japanese, *Getsuku,* or *Gekku,* is short for "*Getsuyou kuji*" or "Monday at 9 pm." This is the time slot in which Fuji Television airs its most popular serial drama series, a practice it has maintained for at least thirty years. Although the exact show that fills the timeslot changes from season to season, the timeslot itself has become an institution, and its success led many other Japanese TV stations to run their dramas on Monday evenings as well.

Whisper, page 166
The Japanese title of the series is *Sasayaku You ni Koi wo Utau,* or "Sing Love Like a Whisper," abbreviated here as *Sasakoi.*

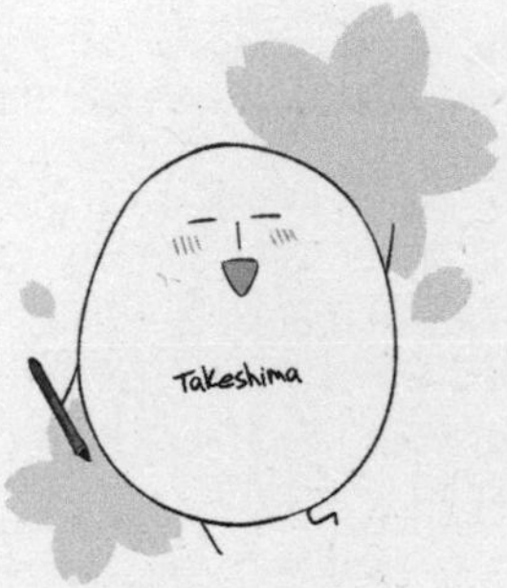
Takeshima

I hope you enjoy this story
of what happens when
two people fall in love at first sight.
Thanks for reading!

—Eku Takeshima

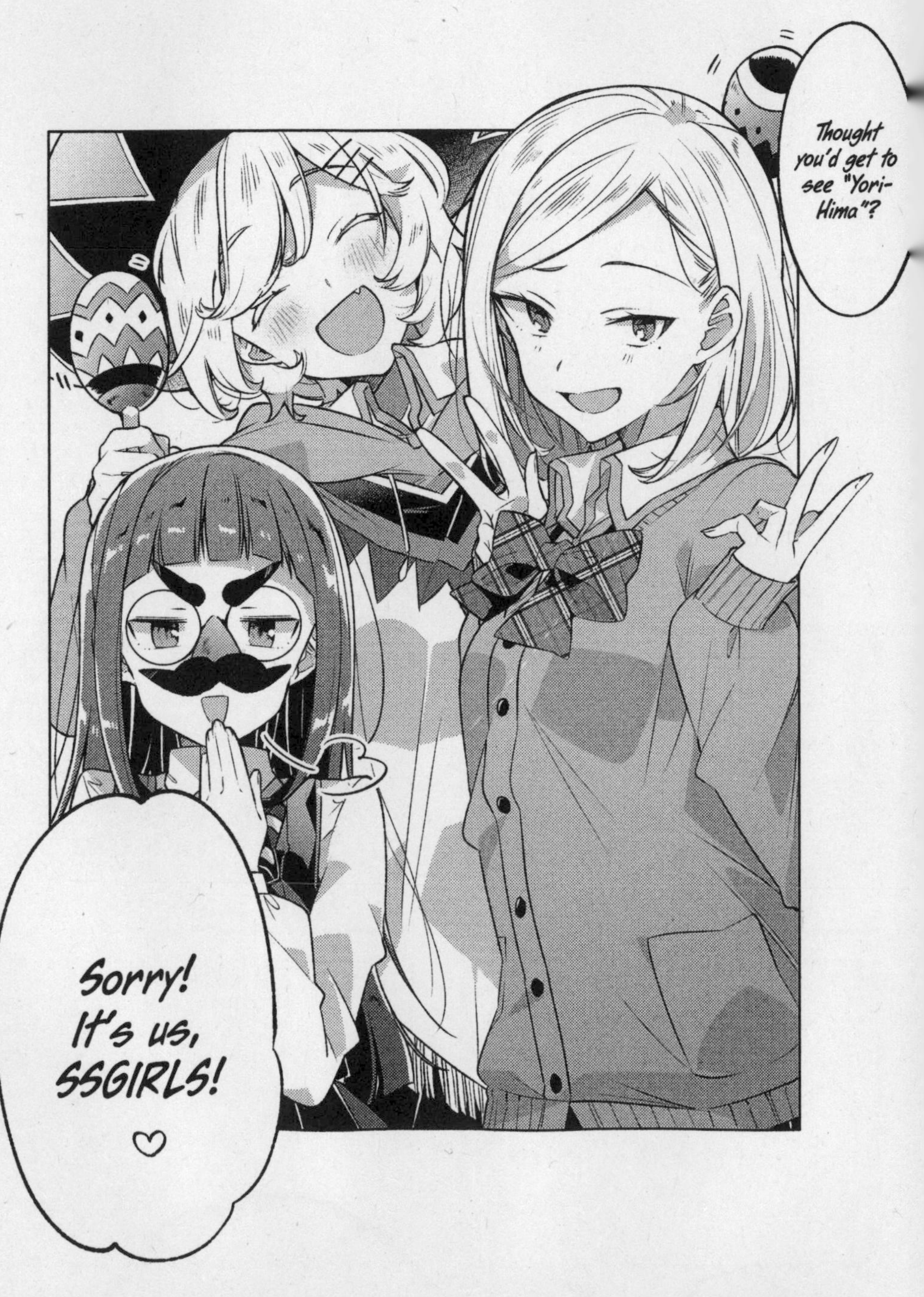
Thought you'd get to see "Yori-Hima"?
Sorry! It's us, SSGIRLS! ♡

One Day at Practice

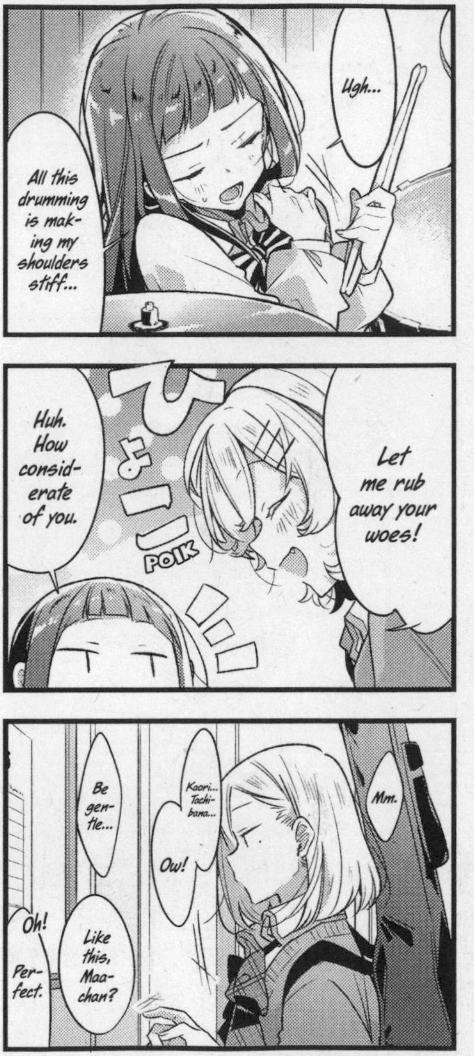
Ugh...
All this drumming is making my shoulders stiff...
Let me rub away your woes!
POIK
Huh. How considerate of you.
Mm.
Kaori... Tachibana...
Be gentle...
Ow!
Like this, Maa-chan?
Oh! Perfect.
Jeez, girls! Get a room! Just not this room!
Buh?
RUB もみ
RUB もみ

Meet the New Girl

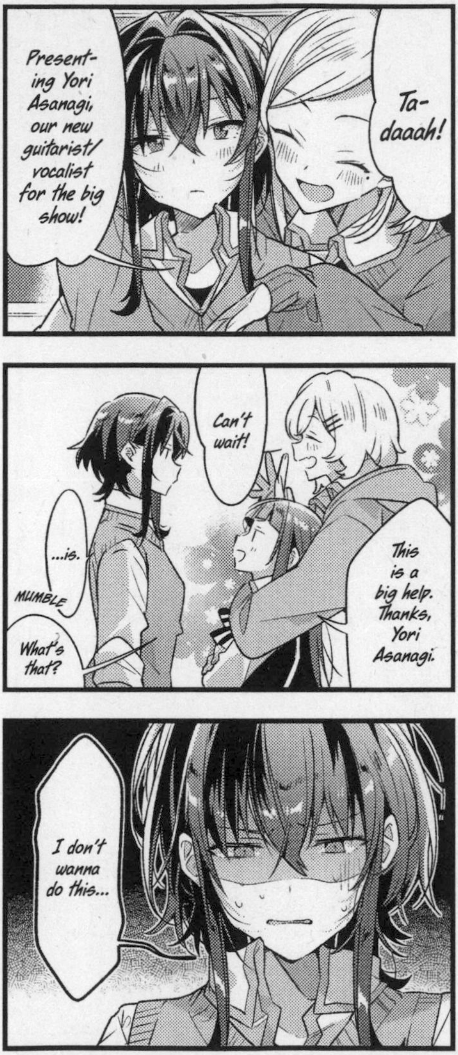
Ta-daaah!
Presenting Yori Asanagi, our new guitarist/vocalist for the big show!
Can't wait!
This is a big help. Thanks, Yori Asanagi.
...is.
MUMBLE
What's that?
I don't wanna do this...
She doesn't?

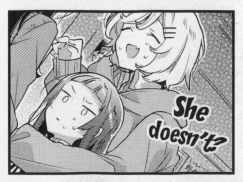

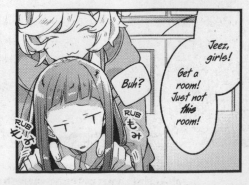

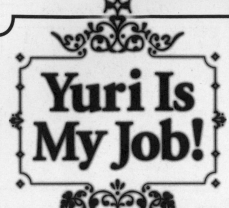

miman

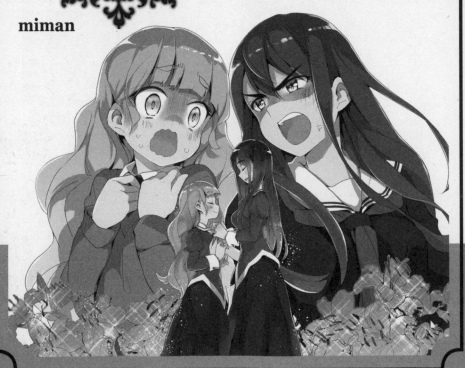

Hime is a picture-perfect high school princess, so when she accidentally injures a café manager named Mai, she's willing to cover some shifts to keep her façade intact. To Hime's surprise, the café is themed after a private school where the all-female staff always puts on their best act for their loyal customers. However, under the guidance of the most graceful girl there, Hime can't help but blush and blunder! Beneath all the frills and laughter, Hime feels tension brewing as she finds out more about her new job and her budding feelings...

"A quirky, fun comedy series... If you're a yuri fan, or perhaps interested in getting into it but not sure where to start, this book is worth picking up."
— Anime UK News

A SMART, NEW ROMANTIC COMEDY FOR FANS OF *SHORTCAKE CAKE* AND *TERRACE HOUSE*!

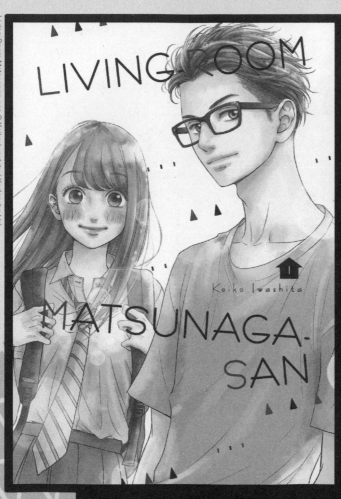

A romance manga starring high school girl Meeko, who learns to live on her own in a boarding house whose living room is home to the odd (but handsome) Matsunaga-san. She begins to adjust to her new life away from her parents, but Meeko soon learns that no matter how far away from home she is, she's still a young girl at heart — especially when she finds herself falling for Matsunaga-san.

PERFECT WORLD

Rie Aruga

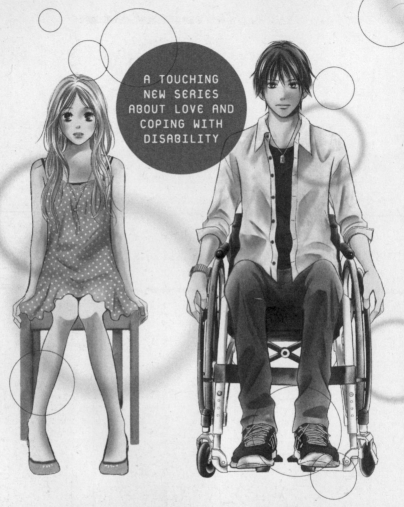

A TOUCHING NEW SERIES ABOUT LOVE AND COPING WITH DISABILITY

An office party reunites Tsugumi with her high school crush Itsuki. He's realized his dream of becoming an architect, but along the way, he experienced a spinal injury that put him in a wheelchair. Now Tsugumi's rekindled feelings will butt up against prejudices she never considered — and Itsuki will have to decide if he's ready to let someone into his heart...

"Depicts with great delicacy and courage the difficulties some with disabilities experience getting involved in romantic relationships... Rie Aruga refuses to romanticize, pushing her heroine to face the reality of disability. She invites her readers to the same tasks of empathy, knowledge and recognition."
—Slate.fr

"An important entry [in manga romance]... The emotional core of both plot and characters indicates thoughtfulness... [Aruga's] research is readily apparent in the text and artwork, making this feel like a real story."
—Anime News Network

Perfect World © Rie Aruga/Kodansha Ltd

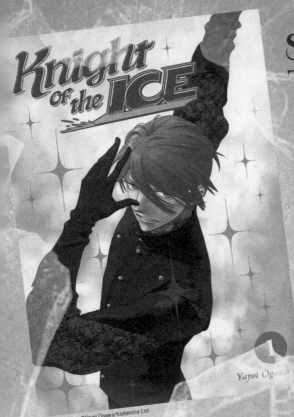

Knight of the Ice ©Yayoi Ogawa/Kodansha Ltd.

Yayoi Ogawa

SKATING THRILLS AND ICY CHILLS WITH THIS NEW TINGLY ROMANCE SERIES!

A rom-com on ice, perfect for fans of *Princess Jellyfish* and *Wotakoi*. Kokoro is the talk of the figure-skating world, winning trophies and hearts. But little do they know... he's actually a huge nerd! From the beloved creator of *You're My Pet* (*Tramps Like Us*).

Chitose is a serious young woman, working for the health magazine *SASSO*. Or at least, she would be, if she wasn't constantly getting distracted by her childhood friend, international figure skating star Kokoro Kijinami! In the public eye and on the ice, Kokoro is a gallant, flawless knight, but behind his glittery costumes and breathtaking spins lies a secret: He's actually a hopelessly romantic otaku, who can only land his quad jumps when Chitose is on hand to recite a spell from his favorite magical girl anime!

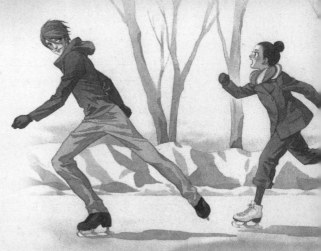

KC
KODANSHA
COMICS

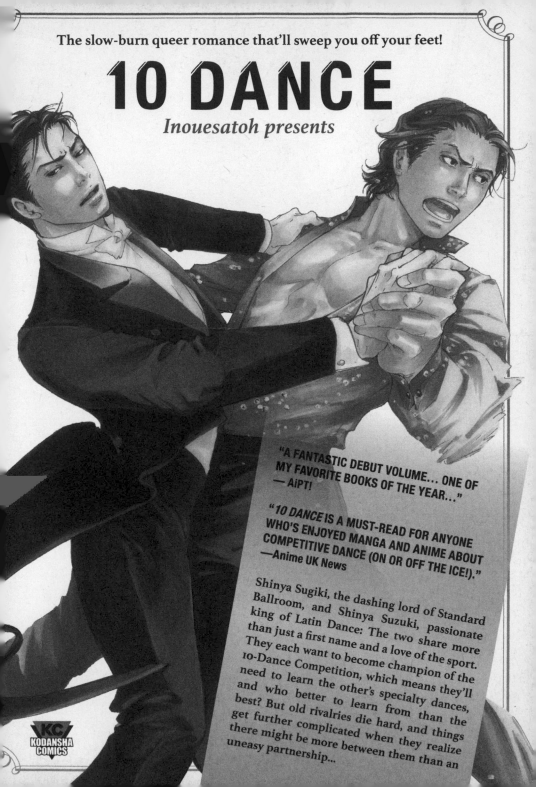

The slow-burn queer romance that'll sweep you off your feet!

10 DANCE

Inouesatoh presents

"A FANTASTIC DEBUT VOLUME... ONE OF MY FAVORITE BOOKS OF THE YEAR..."
—AiPT!

"10 DANCE IS A MUST-READ FOR ANYONE WHO'S ENJOYED MANGA AND ANIME ABOUT COMPETITIVE DANCE (ON OR OFF THE ICE!)."
—Anime UK News

Shinya Sugiki, the dashing lord of Standard Ballroom, and Shinya Suzuki, passionate king of Latin Dance: The two share more than just a first name and a love of the sport. They each want to become champion of the 10-Dance Competition, which means they'll need to learn the other's specialty dances, and who better to learn from than the best? But old rivalries die hard, and things get further complicated when they realize there might be more between them than an uneasy partnership...

KC
KODANSHA
COMICS

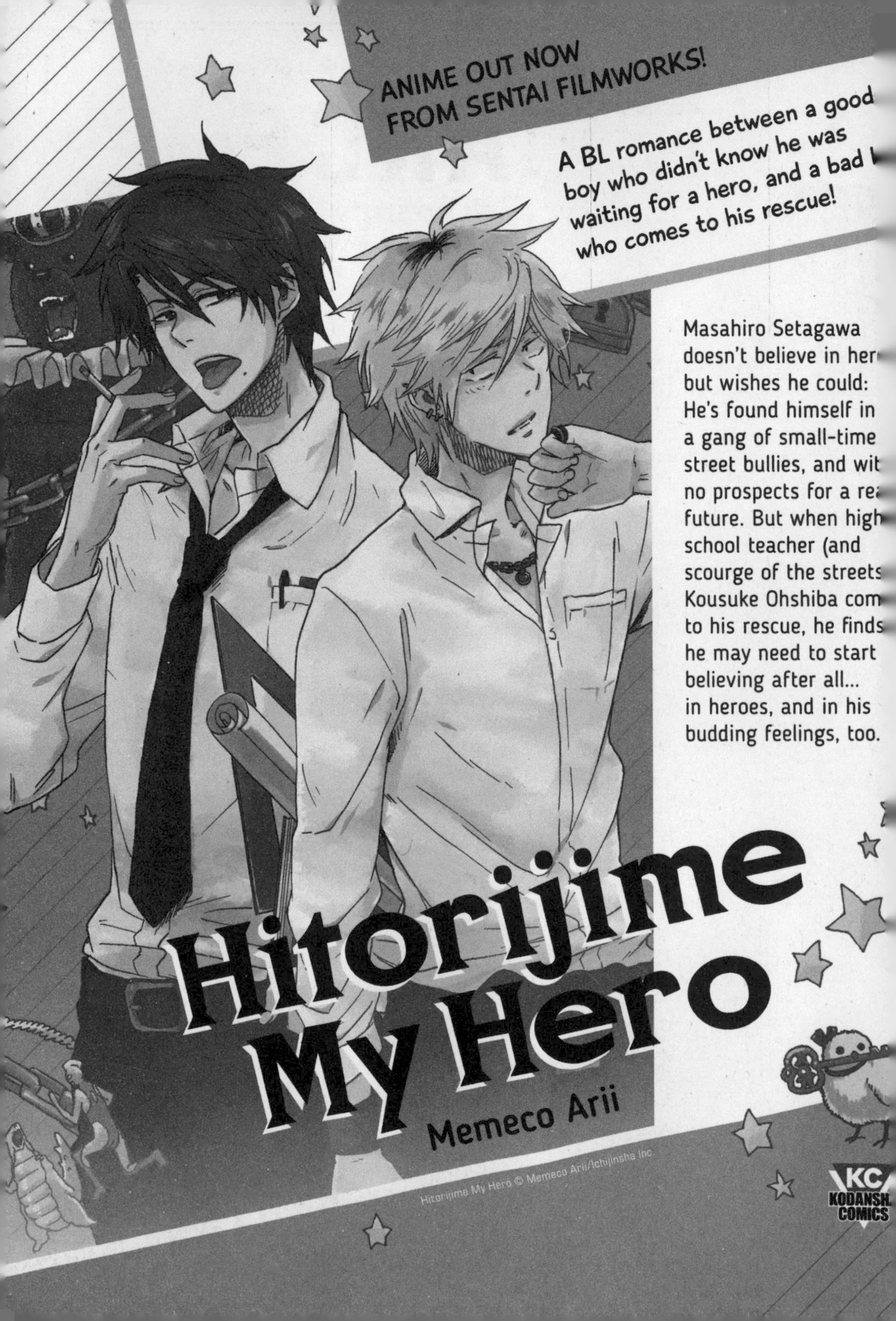
ANIME OUT NOW
FROM SENTAI FILMWORKS!
A BL romance between a good
boy who didn't know he was
waiting for a hero, and a bad
who comes to his rescue!
Masahiro Setagawa
doesn't believe in her
but wishes he could:
He's found himself in
a gang of small-time
street bullies, and wit
no prospects for a re
future. But when high
school teacher (and
scourge of the streets
Kousuke Ohshiba com
to his rescue, he finds
he may need to start
believing after all...
in heroes, and in his
budding feelings, too.
Hitorijime
My Hero
Memeco Arii
Hitorijime My Hero © Memeco Arii/Ichijinsha Inc.
KC
KODANSH
COMICS

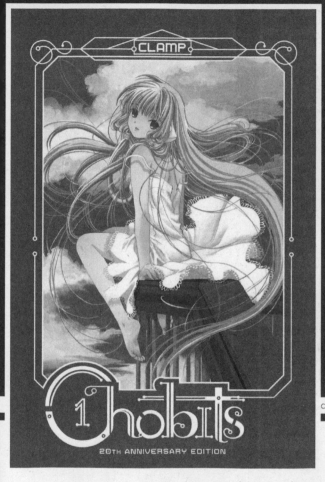

THE SWEET SCENT OF LOVE IS IN THE AIR! FOR FANS OF OFFBEAT ROMANCES LIKE *WOTAKOI*

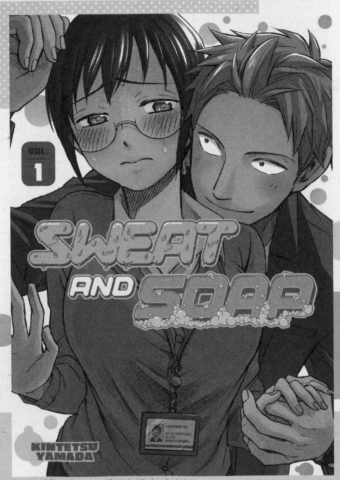

Sweat and Soap © Kintetsu Yamada / Kodansha Ltd.

In an office romance, there's a fine line between sexy and awkward... and that line is where Asako — a woman who sweats copiously — meets Koutarou — a perfume developer who can't get enough of Asako's, er, scent. Don't miss a romcom manga like no other!

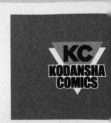

KC
KODANSHA
COMICS

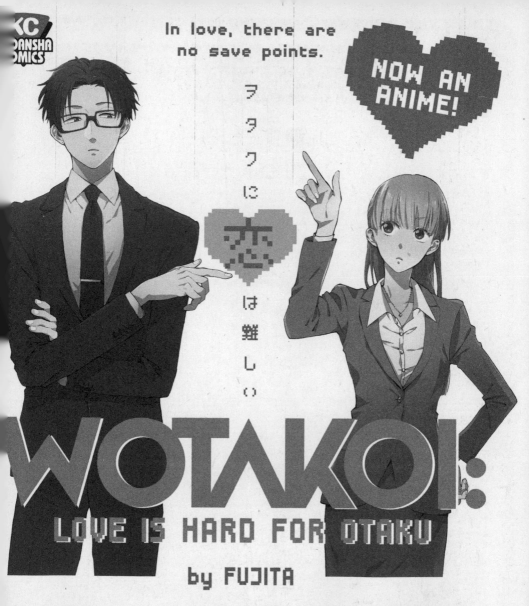

Narumi has had it rough: Every boyfriend she's had dumped her once they found out she was an otaku, so she's gone to great lengths to hide it. At her new job, she bumps into Hirotaka, her childhood friend and fellow otaku. When Hirotaka almost gets her secret outed at work, she comes up with a plan to keep him quiet. But he comes up with a counter-proposal: Why doesn't she just date him instead?

THE MAGICAL GIRL CLASSIC THAT BROUGHT A
GENERATION OF READERS TO MANGA, NOW BACK IN A
DEFINITIVE, HARDCOVER COLLECTOR'S EDITION!

CARDCAPTOR SAKURA
COLLECTOR'S EDITION
C L A M P

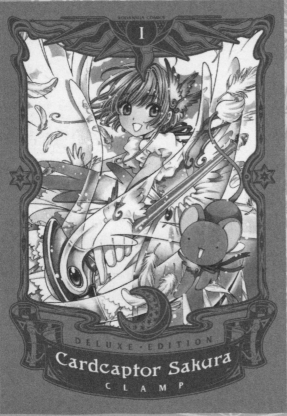

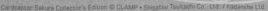

Ten-year-old Sakura Kinomoto
lives a pretty normal life with
her older brother, Tōya, and
widowed father, Fujitaka—
until the day she discovers a
strange book in her father's
library, and her life takes a
magical turn...

- A deluxe large-format
  hardcover edition
  of CLAMP's shojo
  manga classic
- All-new foil-stamped cover
  art on each volume
- Comes with exclusive
  collectible art card

KC
KODANSHA
COMICS

Whisper Me a Love Song 1 is a work of fiction. Names, characters, places, and incidents are the products of the author's imagination or are used fictitiously. Any resemblance to actual events, locales, or persons, living or dead, is entirely coincidental.

A Kodansha Comics Trade Paperback Original
Whisper Me a Love Song 1 copyright © 2019 Eku Takeshima
English translation copyright © 2020 Eku Takeshima

Published in the United States by Kodansha Comics, an imprint of Kodansha USA Publishing, LLC, New York.

Publication rights for this English edition arranged through Kodansha Ltd., Tokyo.

First published in Japan in 2019 by Ichijinsha Inc., Tokyo as *Sayasaku you ni koi wo utau*, volume 1.

ISBN 978-1-64651-115-0

Original cover design by SALIDAS

Printed in the United States of America.

www.kodanshacomics.com

9 8 7 6 5 4 3 2 1
Translation: Kevin Steinbach
Lettering: Jennifer Skarupa
Editing: Tiff Ferentini
Kodansha Comics edition cover design: Matt Akuginow

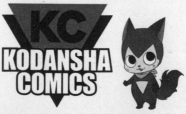

Publisher: Kiichiro Sugawara

Director of publishing services: Ben Applegate
Associate director of operations: Stephen Pakula
Publishing services managing editor: Noelle Webster
Assistant production manager: Emi Lotto, Angela Zurlo
Logo and character art ©Kodansha USA Publishing, LLC